# SACRIFICE AND MODERN THOUGHT

# Sacrifice and Modern Thought

EDITED BY
JULIA MESZAROS
AND
JOHANNES ZACHHUBER

OXFORD
UNIVERSITY PRESS

# OXFORD

UNIVERSITY PRESS

Great Clarendon Street, Oxford, OX2 6DP,
United Kingdom

Oxford University Press is a department of the University of Oxford.
It furthers the University's objective of excellence in research, scholarship,
and education by publishing worldwide. Oxford is a registered trade mark of
Oxford University Press in the UK and in certain other countries

© Oxford University Press 2013

The moral rights of the authors have been asserted

First Edition published in 2013

Impression: 2

Published in the United States of America by Oxford University Press
198 Madison Avenue, New York, NY 10016, United States of America

British Library Cataloguing in Publication Data

Data available

Library of Congress Control Number: 2013940151

ISBN 978–0–19–965928–9

Printed and bound in Great Britain by
CPI Group (UK) Ltd, Croydon, CR0 4YY

# Preface

Recent scholarship has increasingly brought to mind the extent of the impact religious and theological ideas have had on all aspects of modern European culture. The very diversity of this influence, which touches on philosophical and scientific theories as much as on literature, music, art, and architecture means that its interpretation and appreciation today needs interdisciplinary collaboration. The present collection of essays is the product of one such attempt. The contributors seek to explore together ways in which the perception of, and ideas about, sacrifice have developed since the beginning of early modernity and how they have in their turn shaped various cultural practices. Few other religious ideas would invite such study in quite the same way. Sacrifice has always arrested the European mind partly because of its controversial assessment in Christian theology, partly because of its central importance for Greek tragedy, partly because of its evident centrality to so many different historical religions.

While our collaboration, which stretches back to an initial series of events in 2008/9, has helped us widen our individual disciplinary scope, it has also repeatedly exposed the difficulties any such attempt encounters: the disciplinary context within which each of us work determines not only the selection of reality that we study, but often also imposes normative or quasi-normative assumptions about this reality and consequently about the methodologies most suitable to understanding it.

The resulting volume therefore does not present a single narrative of sacrifice in modernity. Rather, we respect the variety and polyphony of contemporary approaches to religion and to its presence in human culture but at the same time seek to engage them in conversation. In this process we were able to discover many areas of commonality, often surprising overlaps and mutual interferences between individual areas of specialization. While then the book does not claim to present a single story let alone a single theory of sacrifice and modern thought, it aims at more than a display of the different forms of contemporary scholarly engagement with sacrifice. Without imposing on them a unity they do not possess, the book hopes to show them as interlocking and mutually illustrative endeavours to come to an understanding of the complex phenomenon that is European modernity.

The editors could not have produced this book without the help of many individuals and institutions. The original research for this book was funded by the British Academy. A crucial editorial meeting of all contributors was only made possible by the generous support of Oxford's John Fell Fund. Trinity College proved a splendid host to all events that took place in preparation of the final publication. Most important, however, was the constant willingness of so many colleagues to devote their valuable time and intellectual energy to this project. This book is far more than the sum of its parts, and we are very conscious at this point how much we owe to the advice, criticism, feedback, and stimulation we received from all individual contributors.

From a publisher's point of view, an edited volume inevitably causes some concern, so we are all the more grateful for the helpful and supportive way Oxford University Press has dealt with our proposal right from the beginning. The critical response from their anonymous readers has been instrumental in improving the internal coherence of the collection. Lizzie Robottom in particular has proved a constant source of advice and encouragement during the final stages of producing the manuscript.

Oxford,
Julia Meszaros
Johannes Zachhuber

# Contents

# List of Contributors

**Nick Allen** was formerly Reader in Social Anthropology of South Asia at the University of Oxford.

**Pamela Sue Anderson** is Reader in Philosophy of Religion at the University of Oxford, and Fellow in Philosophy at Regent's Park College.

**David Brown** is Professor of Theology, Aesthetics, and Culture in the Institute for Theology, Imagination, and the Arts, and Wardlaw Professor at St Mary's College, University of St Andrews.

**Paul S. Fiddes** is Professor of Systematic Theology at the University of Oxford, and a Fellow (and former Principal) of Regent's Park College.

**Gavin Flood** is Professor of Hindu Studies and Comparative Religion at the University of Oxford, and Academic Director of the Oxford Centre for Hindu Studies.

**Jessica Frazier** is Lecturer in Religious Studies at the University of Kent, and a Fellow of the Oxford Centre for Hindu Studies.

**Derek Hughes** is Professor Emeritus of English and former Director of the Centre for Early Modern Studies at the University of Aberdeen.

**Philip McCosker** is Research Associate to the Norris-Hulse Professor of Divinity at the University of Cambridge.

**Julia Meszaros** is Postdoctoral Researcher in Theological Anthropology at the Katholieke Universiteit, Leuven.

**Jon Pahl** is Professor in the History of Christianity at The Lutheran Theological Seminary, Philadelphia.

**Wolfgang Palaver** is Professor of Systematic Theology, and Chair of the Institute of Systematic Theology at the University of Innsbruck.

**Laura Rival** is University Lecturer in Anthropology and Development at the University of Oxford, and Fellow of Linacre College, Oxford.

**Bettina E. Schmidt** is Senior Lecturer in the Study of Religions at the University of Wales Trinity Saint David.

**Johannes Zachhuber** is Reader in Theology at the University of Oxford, and a Fellow and Tutor at Trinity College, Oxford.

# 1

# Introduction

## Johannes Zachhuber and Julia Meszaros

1. Sacrifice without a doubt has been an obsession of modernity. There is
no other period in Western history, with the possible exception of late antiquity, that has seen a comparably sustained, critical engagement with this religious ritual, its theoretical underpinnings, and the problem of its theological,
ethical, and social justification. Theological as well as non-theological study
of religion has tended to identify it as the paradigmatic religious practice.
Attempts to decipher its meaning and offer a definition of its nature never
abated since they were first attempted in the sixteenth century. Its exploration
in drama, novel, opera, and film has provided lasting inspiration to some of
the greatest writers, composers, and directors during these centuries.

The present collection, while unable to explore every single facet of this
story, will shed light on many of its aspects and thus give an impression of the
breadth and variety of the field, its central ideas as well as major historical trajectories. In doing so, it hopes to break new ground. For, in spite of its prominence, modern fascination with sacrifice has remained a largely unrecognized
and neglected phenomenon. In fact, even to call it by this name may appear
counter-intuitive to many. After all, one major narrative of European modernity involves the notion of its systematic and increasing repudiation of sacrifice. And indeed, the idea that sacrifice as such should be rejected has been
popular in the West since the Reformation, albeit in different guises and with
different justifications: while early Protestants argued that the death of Christ
was the last sacrifice and that Christianity, therefore, had to be a non-sacrificial religion, eighteenth-century intellectuals rejected it as cruel and barbaric,
as well as incompatible with the true nature of religion. The latter view, to be
sure, contradicted the orthodox positions of both Catholics and Protestants
who, whatever their differences, affirmed in unison the principal legitimacy of
the Old Testament sacrificial cult as divinely ordained and 'fulfilled' in Christ's
death on Calvary. Increasingly, however, this assumption too was called into
question, most recently in the influential theory of René Girard for whom the

ultimate purpose of biblical revelation is the uncovering of sacrificial practices
as vicious and inhumane.

To cite this critical trajectory of rejections of sacrifice does not, however,
belie the powerful sway the topic has held over the modern mind. On the
contrary, the seemingly ongoing need to identify and combat persisting forms
of sacrifice and the concurrent intellectual obligation to explain, or narrate,
why they had to be resisted, have guaranteed for it a considerable degree of
public, academic, and popular attention. And not everybody, of course, agreed
that sacrifice had to be rejected. In response to the theological critique of sacrifice in early Protestantism, pivotal thinkers of the Catholic Reform stressed,
and dwelled on, the centrality of ritual and spiritual sacrifice for the Christian
Church. Their strongly affirmative interest in sacrifice continued to loom large
in subsequent centuries well beyond the confines of Catholic theology in the
technical sense of this term. Quite generally, where religion appeared as closely
related to community cohesion, sacrifice has been considered as the means of
mediating the tension between the 'selfish' individual and its role as part of the
social whole. Given the centrality of this particular dichotomy to modernity
with its permanent oscillation between the twin fears of collectivism and individualism, the ubiquity of sacrificial rhetoric in debates about themes ranging
from motherhood to civic commitment in general and to warfare in particular
is hardly surprising—but equally unsurprising is its controversial nature: some
are concerned that the rejection of sacrifice puts at risk human interpersonal
orientation, others perceive in its perseverance primarily an impediment to
the emancipation and the autonomy of the individual (see Chapters 5 and 3,
by Julia Meszaros and Pamela Anderson, respectively).

2. Modern fascination for sacrifice, then, is deeply ambiguous. In this, it is
emblematic for modernity's general attitude to its traditional past from which
it seeks to break free while being fearful, at the same time, about the consequences of its potential loss. This symbolic significance of sacrifice as a marker
of religion as we no longer know it, is arguably increased by the tenuous role it
has always played in Christianity. While it remains a moot point of theological
debate whether, or in what sense, the Eucharist is a sacrifice, it is a historical
fact that the Christianization of the West prompted the official discontinuation
of most forms of ritual sacrifice, even though many of those practices survived the introduction of Christianity for many centuries. Christian theologians have never found it altogether easy to define their assessment of sacrifice.
From early on, they perceived a rapprochement between the biblical critique
of cultic sacrifice, for example in the Psalms (Ps. 51:16–17), and its philosophical rejection by major Platonists such as Porphyry of Tyre.[1] The Church
Fathers had no hesitation exploiting this convergence in their apologetic writings to discredit Pagan religion whose gods could by definition not be gods as

[1] Porphyry, *de abstinentia* II.

they required human gifts for their own sustenance.[2] Yet the Christian Bible contained an elaborate sacrificial code in the Pentateuch, and evidence for animal sacrifice almost from the beginning of creation (Gen. 4:3–4). To explain this discrepancy, some early Christian authors resorted to the accommodation theory later made famous by the medieval Jewish thinker Moses ben Maimon.[3] According to this view, God permitted animal sacrifice to the Jewish people for a time while they were still under the influence of their traditional idolatry.[4] More influential, however, was Augustine's theory, which perceived in external sacrifices symbols of an internal act that attunes the agent to God. Sacrifice, in his celebrated definition, is 'every work which is done that we may be united to God in holy fellowship, and which has a reference to that supreme good and end in which alone we can be truly blessed.'[5]

Augustine's view soon became classical and in some way has remained the lowest common denominator of a variety of theological positions. In particular, his thought on the subject, as is evident in Chapter 9 by Philip McCosker, has been a major source of inspiration for the creative transformation of Catholic reflection on sacrifice in the twentieth century. Yet while Augustine can legitimately be cited to justify the broad reception of sacrificial language and conceptions within Christian theology and worship, his spiritualist interpretation could also be read as confirming the abolition of ritual sacrifice and its substitution by a wide variety of religious acts performed by laity and clergy alike and expressing individual and communal devotion to God. In this sense, Protestant moderates from Philipp Melanchthon to Martin Chemnitz in the sixteenth century to Daniel Waterland in the eighteenth claimed his lineage.[6] In response, the leading lights of the Catholic Reform argued that proper sacrifice had to be a ritual, performed by a priest and involving the destruction (immolation) of the offering.[7] As an attempted compromise in this hardened confrontation, the Cambridge Platonist Ralph Cudworth first suggested the theory that all sacrifices were meals in which God and men participated together: they were thus 'federal rites', and in this sense the Eucharist could perfectly well be a 'memorial meal' as the Protestants insisted and still be called a sacrifice.[8]

Whatever the theological merits of these positions, they served to direct attention to the question what sacrifice was: could it be any form of human offering that effected communion with God? Was it principally a common

[2] Eusebius of Caesarea, *de preparatione evangelica* IV 8–10; *de demonstratione evangelica* I 10.
[3] Moses Maimonides, *Guide of the Perplexed* III 32.
[4] Tertullian, *adv. Marcionem* II 18.
[5] Augustine, *de civitate dei* X 6, ET: Dods, 183.
[6] Melanchthon, *Apolog. conf. Aug.* XXIV (Bekenntnisschriften, p. 252); Chemnitz, *Examen conc. Trid.* loc. VI, art. 1 (p. 479); Waterland, *The Christian Sacrifice*, 124–126.
[7] Bellarmine, *de Missa* I 2, (vol. 3, p. 471); John de Lugo, *Disputationes* XIX 1 (pp. 520–523).
[8] Cudworth, *Discourse Concerning the True Notion of the Lord's Supper.*

meal in the process of which divine and human were joined in a mutually bind-
ing covenant? Or was it a ritual establishing divine–human communication
through the consecration of a medium? And if it was the latter, how important,
precisely, was the immolation of the victim? There is a clear trajectory flowing
from the sixteenth-century debates that emphasizes this particular aspect: its
argumentative purpose was originally to single out Christ's sacrifice on the
cross and its unbloody continuation in the Eucharist with its transubstantiation of bread and wine into the body and blood of the saviour. But members
of the French School of Spirituality applied this idea to sacrifice more broadly[9]
and thus gave rise to the question, unsettling ever since, of the relationship
between sacrifice and violence: Why is the annihilation of some being required
to establish communion between God and human beings? Does the spilling of
blood propitiate his wrath as Lutheran theologians averred?[10] Is ritual killing
a means of substitutionary expiation of sinful or guilty behaviour?[11] Or is the
violent character of sacrifice quite simply an indication that sacrifice is an element of culture that humanity is meant to overcome? The latter premise made it
possible for the abolition of sacrifices, intimated in the Christian scriptures and
affirmed, to various degrees, in Christian traditions, to become part of modernity's narrative of evolutionary progress from wild and violent savagery to the
civilization of eternal peace and brotherly love. As humanity grew towards a
better understanding of its own nature and that of the world, belief in the need
to destroy a victim in order to facilitate contact with the transcendent realm
was bound to recede and eventually disappear.

Given this close alignment between the critique of sacrifice and the world-
view of the Enlightenment, it is hardly surprising that sacrificial ideas were
endemic in its various anti-narratives as well. While the need to sacrifice *could*
appear as indicative of humanity's alienation from the divine, and the gradual
decline of this ritual, therefore, of their renewed reconciliation, to those more
sceptical about the same historical process, the disappearance of sacrifice would
be symptomatic for the more general disenchantment and secularization of
the modern world, which left behind material reality as an empty shell devoid
of meaning and significance. This idea could again take several shapes: in
thinkers like Juan Donoso Cortés, Joseph de Maistre, and Carl Schmitt it
underwrites a conservative political philosophy emphatically affirming sacrifice for the good of the community, as discussed in Wolfgang Palaver's essay
(Chapter 6); in those following Nietzsche's *The Birth of Tragedy*, on the other
hand, as the contribution by Derek Hughes illustrates (Chapter 15), sacrificial
motifs have been associated with the ecstatic, 'Dionysiac' element of classical

---

[9]  de Condren, *L'idée du sacerdoce*. Cf. Despland, *Recul*, 80–82.
[10]  Hollaz, *Examen theologiae acroamaticae*, 737.
[11]  Calvin, *Institutes* II 16, 6.

culture missing in modernity's one-sided focus on the rational, 'Apollonian' disposition.

Yet however much their assessment of sacrifice diverges, eighteenth- and nineteenth-century thinkers largely agreed in their focus on the *victima*, the object that is offered or sacrificed. This turn to the victim in the analysis of sacrifice can, as Johannes Zachhuber argues in Chapter 2, be seen as one of the most pivotal influences Christianity has had on Western discourse about sacrifice: it ultimately derives from the inscription of the death of Christ on the cross into the logic of the sacrifice on the Day of Atonement in the Letter to the Hebrews (Heb. 9:11–14). Yet this perspective as such does not prescribe a specific understanding of sacrifice. The Enlightenment and post-Enlightenment critics of sacrifice emphasize primarily violence and destruction in the sacrificial act—they see the *victima* as a victim—whereas its defenders perceive the same event as a transformation: the thing that is sacrificed, whether an external object or the self, is thereby changed from a profane into a sacred item, and this transformation signifies symbolically the need and the potential of the world as a whole to be remade in likeness of the divine. Sacrifice is here understood, as the Latin etymology suggests, as the act that makes something sacred or holy. Augustine had already argued that it was in this sense that the life of the Christian and, indeed, the life of the Church could be seen as sacrificial: Christians offer themselves not merely by 'making a sacrifice' but they 'are' the sacrifice, the *victima* or host, that is offered to God insofar as they permit themselves to be changed into beings who live in communion with God.[12]

This divergent reading of sacrifice under a shared victim-oriented perspective lingers on in contemporary theological debate about sacrifice and is fully in evidence in the present collection as well. In different ways, the chapters by Paul Fiddes, David Brown, Philip McCosker, Jessica Frazier, and Julia Meszaros are indebted to the argument that such an emphasis on renewal, sanctification, or even enchantment can counter the charge that sacrifice is fundamentally violent, whereas Wolfgang Palaver, Pamela S. Anderson, Jon Pahl, and Johannes Zachhuber—again in various ways and to different extents—remain more guarded in that regard. At the same time, the confessional differences established since the Reformation continue to inform contemporary approaches in theory and practice. And this not merely with regard to traditional points of theological disagreement: as Bettina Schmidt demonstrates in Chapter 13, religious and social toleration of sacrificial practices in non-Christian religions, which has been considerable in Catholic Latin America, erodes under the influence of Protestantism both at home (in Brazil) and abroad (Cuban immigrants in the US).

---

[12] Augustine, *de civitate dei* X 6.

3. Apart from the ongoing theological and quasi-theological debate about the nature and legitimacy of sacrifice, modern engagement with this topic has been fed by two further sources. One is the literary representation of mostly human sacrifice in Greek tragedy; the other is the increasing awareness of the variety of forms sacrifice has taken in different cultures over different historical periods and the resulting urge to find a scheme of classification that allows understanding them in their unity as well as in their individual difference. These three impulses—Judaeo-Christian ambiguity towards religious sacrifice, literary sacrifice in ancient tragedy, the challenging variety of sacrificial rituals in different religions—have never been entirely dissociated, which would be surprising given that they operated in the same cultural milieu and originate from the same period of time, the sixteenth century. Yet they owe their existence to different events taking place at roughly the same point in history: the Reformation, the rediscovery of ancient tragedies, and the intercultural encounters during the Age of Discovery. While sacrifice in sixteenth-century French tragedy was not unaffected by the religious controversies of the time,[13] it is evident that literary interest in the topic was only raised by the example of classical tragedy. As Derek Hughes points out in Chapter 15, such interest was largely absent throughout the Middle Ages even in an author like Dante. Similarly, the need to define the nature of sacrifice first emerges in theological debates in the wake of the Reformation controversies, but the challenge of a comparative theory of sacrifice is crucially shaped by European encounters with more overtly sacrificial cultures in other parts of the world.

Human sacrifice in Greek literature symbolizes the collapse, the perversion, and the disintegration of social order. As such, it was, implicitly or explicitly, juxtaposed to the regular, mandatory sacrifices that helped preserve and stabilize the social cosmos. This message chimed well with the general tendency in modernity to align sacrifice to the necessity of regulating the relationship between individual and community: 'good' sacrifice, accordingly, serves to integrate the individual into society whereas 'bad' sacrifice unsettles that balance. Overall therefore, the phases identified by Derek Hughes in the reception of themes from ancient tragedy correlate with the history of ideas trajectory described above: eighteenth-century Enlightenment writers and their descendants are attracted by the story of Iphigenia, which is understood as exposing the cruel consequences of the subjection of an individual life to the collective needs of polity, country, or class, whereas the nineteenth century brings to the fore the much more ambiguous images of Euripides' *Bacchae* with its grim depiction of the dramatic results of the failure to sacrifice.

Yet sacrificial themes were not simply carried over from their original ancient context into a modern one. Rather, their treatment became embedded

---

[13] Despland, *Recul*, 53–58.

into a cultural milieu from which traditional forms of sacrifice had largely, albeit not entirely, disappeared in practice, while theological, anthropological, historical, or scientific *theories* of sacrifice impressed themselves on the public imagination. This interaction has inflected modern adaptations of ancient themes and stories whose experiential backdrop no longer is the unquestioned reality of quotidian, ritual sacrifice but the much more precarious modern queries regarding its principal legitimacy or indispensability. To the extent that sacrifice is represented in modern literature, opera, or film as something negative, then, that criticism is often inspired by the fundamental rejection of sacrifice flowing from Protestant and Enlightenment ideas. Where it is endorsed, as Jon Pahl shows in Chapter 14, the frame is usually a more socio-political than religious propagation of the subjection of individual wishes and desires to the interests and needs of the community, *in extremis* the death of the soldier for his country. The purpose of such secularized affirmation of sacrifice in what has been called 'civil religion' is unashamedly the advancement of the ambitions of the modern nation state.

4. A third significant strand of modern engagement with sacrifice is constituted by anthropological and sociological attempts to understand, define, or classify it. Such attempts are not, as such, new to modernity, but the encounter with an increasing plurality of cultures, the recognition of the utter diversity and heterogeneity of sacrificial rites existing in them as well as the growing inclination to aim at comparative theories that did not privilege any one particular religious perspective and abstained from theological assumptions led to a proliferation of theories of sacrifice since the mid-nineteenth century which have dominated scholarship ever since.

Their novel approach and methodology notwithstanding, these theories have not broken radically with earlier ideas about sacrifice. Central concepts that have been proposed as characteristic of sacrifice include gift exchange, communion meal, propitiation, immolation, and divine–human communication all of which have featured in previous discussions about sacrifice as well. Equally, in continuity with earlier modern controversies is the disagreement between those who see sacrifice as a fundamental, time-invariant property of human culture and those who inscribe it into an evolutionary trajectory of religious history that may well have included periods before the introduction of sacrifice and may see its eventual abolition.

Perhaps the single most influential theory in anthropology and sociology of religion has been the one developed by Marcel Mauss and Henri Hubert. Nick Allen, in Chapter 10, offers a detailed analysis of their complex argument. Mauss and Hubert largely avoid philosophical generalizations and focus instead on the sacrificial ritual which they understand, in line with the principles of Durkheimian theory, as communication between the sacred and the profane. This communication is made possible by the consecration of a previously profane object in a ritual act facilitated by a priest, the 'sacrificer', who acts on behalf of the person or group of persons bringing the sacrifice (the 'sacrifier') for their individual or communal benefit. One characteristic of this theory is its largely formal and structural approach to sacrifice, which it captures primarily in its ritualistic elements with comparably little emphasis on underlying ideas, mythological or theological principles. This must appeal to anthropologists confronted with a huge variety of cultural sign-systems defying easy unification. It may then be typical that the one element in their theory for which Hubert and Mauss have been heavily criticized by later anthropologists, such as E. E. Evans-Pritchard and Luc de Heusch, is their affirmation of the Durkheimian binary of profane and sacred—even though, as Nick Allen suggests, Mauss may have tried to move beyond this limitation in his later career.

The same characteristic, however, that made this theory attractive to empirically working anthropologists and historians of religion, may have reduced its appeal for those seeking to connect sacrifice to major hypotheses about human nature or human society. Precisely among the latter constituency the very different theory advanced over the last couple of decades by René Girard has gained enormous currency. While the empirical foundations of his theory have frequently been called into question, his ideas have proved hugely inspirational for a wide variety of scholars working in areas ranging from theology to film study, and from literary criticism to political theory. Girard's theories are critically discussed in various chapters of the present collection. For him, sacrifice is the violent expulsion of a scapegoat in the interest of community cohesion. Underlying this theory, as Jessica Frazier explains in Chapter 7, is a specific understanding of human desire and agency; human beings, according to Girard, desire by imitating the desires of others. This mimetic structure of human desire provides for the communal bond between individuals but undermines it at the same time. Human beings need the other for the orientation of their desires but by the same token they become each others' rivals. Mimetic desire thus leads to hatred and violence which can, and does, become endemic, ultimately threatening the existence of the community as a whole. Sacrifice, Girard holds, is the cultural mechanism intended to stave off the potentially mortal danger for society that arises from the negative consequences of mimetic desire. It functions by targeting an individual 'scapegoat' onto whom the antisocial emotions are projected and whose removal leads to the expiation of dysfunctional elements from the life of the community.

Several questions can be directed at this account: Jessica Frazier asks, most fundamentally, whether Girard's identification of human desire with irrational mimesis is tenable. She objects that Girard's theory begs the question by suggesting a solution to problems that may not even arise without his own, problematic hypotheses: as soon as mimesis ceases to be an uncontrolled impulse and is at least partly directed by rationally informed wishes and preferences, Girard's gloomy view of human culture and with it the need to 'sacrifice' scapegoats loses much of its plausibility. Paul Fiddes and Wolfgang Palaver, on the other hand, accept Girard's analysis at least to an extent but ask what follows from the recognition that such forces operate in human culture (see Chapters 4 and 6). Palaver discusses the political consequences: while initially a radical and pacifist response rejecting any violence in human society as illegitimate may seem most appropriate, such an approach may fail in the face of the very real persistence of violence and evil in the world. Drawing on the thought of Aby Warburg as well as Girard's own later transformations of his original theory, Palaver defends a moderately realist approach that steers a middle course between the sacrifice-affirming theories of Joseph de Maistre and Carl Schmitt on the one hand and an idealist refusal to recognize the existence and abiding significance of evil and violence in the world. From a theological perspective, Fiddes asks what, if Girard is right about mimetic violence, follows for the Christian understanding of the atoning death of Christ. Girard, at least in his original theory, rejected its sacrificial interpretation: for him, the cross merely exposes the truth about the scapegoating mechanism endemic in all culture. Drawing on Hans Urs von Balthasar and Julia Kristeva, Fiddes urges that such a view remains incomplete as it fails to explain how Christ's death on the cross enables individual and communal renewal.

Different from both Girard's and Mauss' theories is the view that sacrifice is essentially renunciation. This idea was championed by the nineteenth-century anthropologist E. B. Tylor who saw in it the evolutionary end product of the idea of sacrifice as gift:[14] once purged of the connotation of transactional reciprocity, the offering symbolizes an attitude of the individual willing to abnegate or renounce something that is his or her own. In the present collection, this view is expounded and defended by Gavin Flood in Chapter 8. It has, for him, the advantage of avoiding the economic, transactional logic inherent in any explanation of sacrifice that relies on the principle of gift exchange while steering clear as well of the more problematic assumptions in Girard's and similar theories that see sacrifice as cathartic. Instead, it permits relating sacrifice to fundamental properties of human nature, such as temporality or mortality. The ability, and the willingness, to sacrifice are an expression of humanity's separation from the realm of nature and, consequently, the existential possibility, and indeed the need, of human beings to relate to, and shape, their own being. In locating sacrifice thus at the roots of the human condition, this theory agrees with Girard's view. Yet whereas for the latter this human tendency to sacrifice evokes our dark side, the destructive aspect of our willing and desire, and our failure successfully to negotiate the relationship between individual and collective identities, seeing sacrifice as renunciation associates it much more with the positive opportunities that come with the special

---

[14] Tylor, *Primitive Culture*, 375–410.

position humanity holds in the world and which allow us to be no mere slaves to our biological instincts, impulses, attractions and repulsions.

Modern anthropological theories of sacrifice have come with the promise to replace older theological theories with more scientific, empirical, and methodologically controlled approaches. Yet it has remained controversial whether and to what extent this attempt has been successful. Over the years, critics such as Marcel Detienne and Jean-Pierre Vernant have averred that the very concept of sacrifice is a brainchild of a Christian or post-Christian culture and cannot hope to serve as a concept explaining religious practice in other parts of the world.[15] Without entering this debate directly, Laura Rival comes to a similar conclusion in Chapter 11. Her attempt to analyse the structure and meaning of the various human 'sacrifices' conducted by the Aztecs does not lead her to an endorsement of any one particular theory of sacrifice but rather to the question how far they are helpful in understanding such cultural and ritual practices. This may well indicate that our concepts of sacrifice are in fact interconnected, more closely than we sometimes realize, with the complex processes that have, over the centuries, shaped modern thought.

5. The various contributions to the present collection do not aim to give a single, systematic, and coherent narrative of sacrifice and its relation to modern thought. They represent various disciplinary approaches and traditions, and contributors do not always take the same side in the controversies that have shaped modern ideas about sacrifice. Yet as authors and editors noted in the process of their collaboration, their essays do interrelate: sometimes at points one would anticipate but often in unexpected and surprising ways. It is hoped that this proves the broader point the present book seeks to make, that, while there is no single impulse, no individual idea that underlies and explains modern fascination with sacrifice in its entirety, the different stories that can, and must, be told about it intersect, mutually influence and illustrate each other. Secular, anthropological, and sociological interest in sacrifice has never become entirely detached from theological concerns; inner-Christian controversies have continued to shape perceptions and evaluations of sacrifice even where their theological principles were no longer shared and their origin was scarcely remembered. At the same time, cultural and political concerns about sacrifice, acquaintance with other cultures, and the images of sacrifice created by artistic representation have left their mark on theological debates however much they were intended to be determined by their own principles. Again, artistic uses of the image of sacrifice have been embedded in theoretical discussions about its meaning and evaluation in anthropology, history of religion, or in theology.

What, arguably, connects all these different influences and concerns is the fact that Western modernity's fascination with sacrifice is predicated on

---

[15] Detienne/Vernant, *The Cuisine of Sacrifice*, 20.

the latter's precarious status as a ritual within this culture. Debating sacrifice usually is tantamount to an attempt to analyse and understand *other* cultures: Greco-Roman antiquity, ancient Judaism, Vedic religion, the Aztecs, or contemporary 'primitive' cultures. This is not to say that sacrifice has not been detected within modern societies themselves. Some see it wherever there is victimization, others perceive it expressed, more positively, in acts of self-giving and the renunciation of individual desires. Yet the relation of these 'sacrifices' to ritual sacrifice as it would have been practised in most cultures at some point, is rather complex. What critics object to are practices and mechanisms of victimization in our own day and in cultures we live in or hear about through the media, and these practices are understood or read as sacrifice. It is fair to say that to most people who would have known 'normal' sacrificial practice as part of their religious lives, this identification would appear anything but obvious. It may not be mistaken, but it rests on a rather elaborate, albeit mostly implicit, interpretation of sacrifice without which the underlying identification of sacrifice with almost any form of victimization could not be imagined or formulated.

The affirmation of sacrifice as the willingness to give something up for the sake of others likewise presupposes an abstraction from a ritual that has ceased to be unquestionably self-evident. It is, arguably, inspired by the notion that our humanity is so fundamentally constituted by our relationships that its preservation at times warrants nothing less than the sacrifice of one's self to another. The point of this defence of sacrifice, of course, is not to reintroduce 'sacrifice' as it has been practised in traditional religion; what is demanded is an ethicized version of sacrifice as a moral act that the individual feels called to.

Has sacrifice, then, become a mere metaphor, a symbolic term denoting certain desirable or despicable individual or collective attitudes and actions? This may be true for some instances, but it cannot explain the pervasiveness of sacrificial ideas throughout modernity. It is arguable, and the present book intends to argue this point, that this ongoing intellectual and rhetorical fascination with sacrifice is, much rather, indicative of the peculiar relationship modern 'secular' societies have to their religious heritage which, in a sometimes uncanny way, seems to be both absent *and* present, both a thing of the past *and* surprisingly alive and formative.

# 2

# Modern Discourse on Sacrifice and its Theological Background

Johannes Zachhuber

Most contemporary discussions about sacrifice are not theological in character. Yet the absence of overtly theological arguments from these debates does not mean that the specific concerns of Christian theology are equally absent from them. It is my aim in this chapter to illustrate how modern, secular discourse about sacrifice still draws on theological ideas and, in fact, needs this background to be properly understood. It is, perhaps, needless to say that by arguing this case I do not intend to deny the presence of various other sources of influence on contemporary ideas of sacrifice; nor does my argument per se serve to disown the legitimacy of modern, secular concern for this cultural practice. Historical lineage, after all, cannot easily tell us whether what we think or do is right or wrong; it does, however, help us better understand it: in this sense, my argument in this chapter is meant to be hermeneutical.

My second caveat must be that by focusing on the trajectory from theological to non-theological thought about sacrifice, I do not wish to imply that meaningful reflection about sacrifice within Christian theology has come to an end. This would obviously be false, and several contributions to the present book demonstrate the vitality of this discourse and its ongoing significance. My interest in this chapter, however, is not in self-consciously theological reflection about sacrifice; it is in those contemporary references to 'sacrifice' we might wish to call a 'survival' (to use Tylor's celebrated phrase) of religious language in contexts that today are no longer governed by theological principles. While some of those may have become entirely devoid of deeper meaning, I would contend that this is not universally the case: the rhetorical urgency that is usually attached to the mention of sacrifice at least suggests otherwise.

How can we describe this secular or quasi-secular usage? Following Ivan Strenski,[1] I would suggest that two somewhat conflicting ideas are central: on

---

[1] Strenski, *Theology*, 1–2.

the one hand, there is a *critical* view for which sacrifice is associated with violence and, therefore, cruelty. Sacrifice is the wasteful loss of human life for a
supposed gain in some public good. This negative evaluation of sacrifice may
refer to the willingness of a political or military leader to 'sacrifice' others in
the interest of a larger project. It may, however, also denote self-sacrifice especially where the latter appears as a misguided subjection of the individual to
the demands of social or cultural norms; as we have become more familiar
with the potential of self-harm inflicted to itself by an individual under the
influence of collectively shared ideologies, our suspicion towards altruistic,
sacrificial acts has increased.

The other strand in contemporary references to sacrifice is focused more
on the potential loss of communal cohesion that is indicated by the receding
willingness of individuals to give up something precious to them for the good
of the group. Sacrifice is encouraged or even demanded as a symbol of people's
commitment to their class or nation, as a token for the person's awareness
of the value they gain from their integration into a functioning social whole.
Such affirmation of sacrifice is predicated on the perception that modernity
has brought about a slackening of social cohesion often expressed through the
term 'individualism' gesturing at the spectre of a society consisting of intrinsically selfish individuals held together only by the fragile bond of their calculated self-interest.

Both views are not detached from theoretical and academic debates: the
link between sacrifice and violence has been emphasized in pivotal contributions by René Girard and Walter Burkert. In different ways, both connect the
historical origins of the ritual with the need for early human society to cope
with aggression and the spilling of blood. For Burkert, sacrifice arose specifically as a response to the regular killing of animals by palaeolithic hunter cultures[2] whereas Girard, as several other contributors to this volume explain in
more detail, perceives it as the ritual re-enactment of an original expulsion of
a scapegoat by means of which community cohesion was only established.[3]
More important, however, than their problematic constructions of historical
or pre-historical origins is that their perception of the sacrificial act is firmly
victim-oriented; what is done to the *victima*, its immolation, determines the
interpretation of sacrifice as such.

By contrast, the alternative, popular view, according to which willingness
to sacrifice correlates with the integration of the individual into a larger social
whole, considers sacrifice from the point of view of the person bringing the
sacrifice, the sacrifier as Hubert and Mauss call them.[4] What are the reasons
that motivate or indeed demotivate an individual to give up something for a

---

[2] Burkert, *Homo Necans.*
[3] Girard, *Violence.*
[4] Hubert/Mauss, *Sacrifice*, 10.

'transcendent' good? Here the influence of Émile Durkheim and his school
has loomed large: from his early work on suicide, the French sociologist
saw anomy as the great threat to a society whose members were no longer
properly integrated. His later theory of religion was inscribed into that same
diagnosis: religion *is* community cohesion and secularization, consequently,
a lessening of those cohesive forces, which can potentially have detrimental
consequences for the very existence of modern societies.

The two ways in which contemporary discourse mostly refers to sacrifice,
then, correspond to specific conceptions, if not theories, of sacrifice. This is
not trivial; sacrifice as has often been noted is a polyvalent term and the ritual
it originally denoted, a complex sequence of acts with various participants.
How one thinks or speaks about it therefore at least partly depends on one's
perception, on what one sees when envisioning a sacrifice. The views that were
briefly sketched differ in that one emphasized the passive suffering of the offering, whereas the other fastens on the psychology and the moral attitude of the
'sacrifier'.

Both, however, are the result of specific transformations of the concept of
sacrifice in Christian theology. They derive, or so I shall argue, from the deeply
ambiguous, even precarious position sacrifice has held in the theory and practice of Christianity from the very beginning: sacrifice was part of a dispensa-
tion that had come to its end but at the same time continued to hold sway over
theological and spiritual reflection with unique intensity due to the way the
'end of the law' (Rom. 10:4) was identified with the Christ event. I shall proceed, therefore, from a brief historical sketch of the origins of Christian reflections about sacrifice to move on directly to their substantial transformation in
early modernity. The latter results, as I shall show, in the imperative of dutiful
sacrifice as service for the common good on the one hand, its critical rejection
as senseless violence against innocents on the other.

## 1. THE ORIGINS OF CHRISTIANITY AND THE 'END OF SACRIFICE'

*The End of Sacrifice* is the title Guy Stroumsa has given to his landmark study
into the transformation of religion in late antiquity.[5] The term of course, as
Stroumsa himself recognizes, is hyperbolic: sacrifice did not end in late antiquity; in fact, the religions originating during this period, rabbinic Judaism,
Christianity, and Islam all develop their own complex, but ambivalent attitude
to sacrifice which combines critique with reinterpretation and transformation.

---

[5] Stroumsa, *End of Sacrifice.*

Yet Stroumsa is surely right to see the decline of ritual sacrifice along with the emergence of monotheism, a stronger emphasis on the self, the codification of religious norms in revealed books, and the detachment of religion from any particular political entity as symptoms of a fundamental paradigm shift in religion occurring during the first millennium.

It is this world into which Christianity evolves, and within the broader parameters of its culture, the Christian religion unmistakably is aligned with the forces of modernization. Emperor Julian the 'Apostate', a romantic conservative who in the mid-fourth century made a last-ditch attempt to restore the old order, lays this charge at the feet of the 'Galileans':[6]

> Why do you not sacrifice [...]? [...] The Jews agree with the Gentiles, except that they believe in only one God. That is indeed peculiar to them and strange to us; since all the rest we have in a manner in common with them—temples, sanctuaries, altars, purifications, and certain precepts. For as to these we differ from one another either not at all or in trivial matters.[7]

Elsewhere in his treatise, the emperor permits the Christians to reply with the argument that 'on our behalf Christ was sacrificed once and for all.'[8] This is indeed perhaps the most intuitive answer a theologian may be inclined to give to the question why Christians from the very beginning did not practice traditional forms of sacrifice: for them, the death of Christ was the perfect and therefore last sacrifice. Yet while this argument is occasionally adduced by early Christian authors,[9] it does not, on the whole, dominate Christian attitudes to sacrifice in late antiquity.

Throughout the New Testament, evidence for a critical rejection of Jewish sacrifice is scarce. Paul calls Jesus Christ 'our paschal lamb' (1 Cor. 5:7); he does not say that the slaughtering of lambs at Passover is wrong. Jewish ritual sacrifice, however, was confined to the temple in Jerusalem and thus no longer part of everyday worship for the vast majority of Jews living around the Mediterranean. It was altogether discontinued after the temple's destruction in 70AD even though its principal significance continued to be affirmed by the Rabbis. One of Emperor Julian's more fanciful projects therefore was the rebuilding of the temple: in his calculation, Jewish sacrifice would then resume and Christians would be exposed as the one religious group without a proper sacrifice.[10] The plan never came to fruition but points to the partly contingent character of the abolition of ritual blood sacrifice in Judaism.

An analogous plan, obviously, could not have been offered to the Christians, but historical evidence suggests that nevertheless early Christian responses

---

[6] For Julian's attitude to sacrifice cf. Belayche, 'Sacrifice during the "Pagan Reaction"'.
[7] Julian, *contra Galilaeos*, 306.
[8] Julian, *contra Galilaeos*, 354 A.
[9] Eusebius, *de demonstratione evangelii* I 10.
[10] Belayche, 'Sacrifice during the "Pagan Reaction"', 117.

to sacrifice mirrored closely the pragmatic strategies adopted in Hellenistic Judaism to cope with the absence of ritual sacrifice: its reinterpretation as primarily an internal act of devotion to God and the endowment of originally non-sacrificial rituals, such as prayers and meals, with a quasi-sacrificial character. Thus, beginning from the late first or the early second century, the Lord's Supper is referred to as 'sacrifice' (*thusia*). Its supersession of the Jewish sacrifice is justified with Mal. 1:11: 'In every place incense is offered in my name, and a pure offering'.[11] The verse had already been popular in Hellenistic Judaism, as we know from Justin Martyr (*c.*150):[12] it was applied to 'the prayers of the individuals' in the diaspora as being superior to the temple cult in Jerusalem. While the apologist insists that the prophetic word is fulfilled only in the Christian Eucharist, he explicitly agrees with his Jewish interlocutor that 'prayers and giving of thanks, when offered by worthy men, are the only perfect and well-pleasing sacrifices to God'.[13] Both strategies, then, are seen here in combination: sacrifice is fundamentally redefined as an internal and ethical disposition of the believer. The Eucharist, as its very name suggests, was considered in this sense a 'sacrifice of prayer and thanksgiving', while as a ritual it has direct parallels with Jewish morning prayers that were developed in the diaspora as substitutes for the temple cult.[14]

This approach reaches its apogee in Augustine's discussion of sacrifice in book ten of *The City of God*, the most extensive Patristic treatment of sacrifice, which in many ways was to become the classical point of reference for later theologians.[15] According to the Bishop of Hippo, sacrifice is every work that establishes community between human beings and God. It can, but does not have to, be ritual: Old Testament sacrifices, therefore, were justified as symbols of the interior act of orienting the person towards their creator. They had to be abolished at some point so that no one would confuse the outward activities with their real, spiritual meaning, which for Augustine comprises attitudes such as contrition (cf. Ps. 51:16–17), glorification (Ps. 50:14–15), as well as moral behaviour ('do justly, love mercy, walk humbly with God', cf. Mic. 6:8). In sum: 'all the divine ordinances [ ... ], which we read concerning the sacrifices in the service of the tabernacle or the temple, we are to refer to the love of God and our neighbour'.[16]

[11] *Didache* 14, 1–3.

[12] Justin, *Dialogus* 117.

[13] Justin, *Dialogus* 117, Ed: Robertson/Donaldson, 257. The traditional attitude is summed up well in Sallustius' *de diis et mundo* 16, 1: 'Prayers without sacrifices are only words'.

[14] Cf. Mazza, 'The Eucharist in the First Four Centuries', 35–40. Mazza helpfully argues that these parallels illustrate the precise sense in which the early Eucharist was considered a sacrifice, but fails to point out that they also imply a radical discontinuity with traditional ritual sacrifice.

[15] Augustine, *de civitate dei* X 4–6.

[16] Augustine, *de civitate dei* X 5.

Augustine's argument distinctly betrays its late ancient context. Christians were faced with the lingering reality of pagan sacrifices, which they rejected, but also with the literary heritage of the sacrificial cult ordained in the Mosaic law, which they defended as a divine institution while at the same time justifying its discontinuation in Christianity. The most promising response to this challenge seemed to consist in a symbolic theory which relocated the essence of sacrifice from a sequence of acts to their underlying intellectual and volitional motivation: 'That which in common speech is called sacrifice is only the symbol of the true sacrifice' (*illud, quod ab omnibus appellatur sacrificium, signum est ueri sacrificii*).[17] This strategy, however, was not without ambivalence: as Augustine's own argument shows, it could be used to justify ritual sacrifices, such as those of the Jewish cult prior to the coming of Christ and now of the Eucharist, but it could also be cited in support of their discontinuation, 'in order that men might not suppose that the sacrifices themselves, rather than the things symbolized by them, were pleasing to God or acceptable in us'.[18]

At no point, then, in the New Testament or throughout late antiquity were Christians opposed to sacrifice as such. They inherited a world in which traditional forms of sacrifice, as they had been prescribed in the Pentateuch and were similarly practised across the Mediterranean, were declining, and Christianity's ascent to the official religion of the Roman Empire doubtlessly precipitated this decline. Their theological response, prepared in the prophetic books of the Old Testament and in Hellenistic Judaism, was a theory affirming sacrifice at a psychological, volitional, and motivational level, as an attitude of devotion to God, which could but did not have to find expression in ritual form.


## 2. FROM POST-REFORMATION CONTROVERSIES TO THE MODERN AFFIRMATION OF SELF-SACRIFICE

Augustine's theory of sacrifice remained unchallenged for the next twelve hundred years. From the sixteenth century, however, the problem of sacrifice became once again burning, and the ambiguities of the Patristic theory permitted starkly divergent responses to the question of its lasting significance in Christianity. More importantly for the present purpose, however, the alternative between the Protestant claim that the death of Jesus was the last and perfect sacrifice and the Catholic affirmation of the truly sacrificial character of the Mass redirected attention to the question of what sacrifice was. In search

---

[17] Augustine, *de civitate dei* X 5.
[18] Augustine, *de civitate dei* X 5.

for an answer, both Catholic and Protestant authors turned to the death of Christ: for the first time, the crucifixion of Jesus truly became the paradigm for sacrificial theory. The Augustinian view therefore, in which this was evidently not the case, satisfied neither side: Protestants sought to affirm that there was a categorical difference between the earlier sacrifices that were required to propitiate God's wrath until the Christ event and everything that happened since. Christian acts of prayer and worship therefore, including the Eucharist, could be called sacrifices in the Augustinian sense as long as it was clear that their affirmation did not mitigate the unique importance of the Christ event.[19] Catholics, on the other hand, were insistent that in continuity with the Christ event, the Eucharist constituted the Church's only proper sacrifice and was not to be confused with the many acts of mercy, worship, and even martyrdom that could, more broadly, be designated by that term.[20]

The problem with making the crucifixion the paradigmatic sacrifice was that, prima facie, it was not at all evident *that* the events surrounding the death of Jesus could be understood as a sacrifice. The saviour may well be the *victima*, but who is the sacrificer: the Roman procurator? The mob? The Jewish authorities? None of these seem to qualify; as Thomas Aquinas put it: 'whoever offers sacrifice performs some sacred rite, as the very word "sacrifice" shows. But those men who slew Christ did not perform any sacred act, but rather wrought a great wrong.'[21]

The most influential attempt to cope with this difficulty is given in the biblical Book of Hebrews already: in his sacrificial death, Christ was both victim and priest. In fact the text refers to Christ as the high priest who once a year entered the Holy of Holies to make a sacrifice to atone for the 'sins committed unintentionally by his people' (Heb. 9:7). Jesus of course did not have to atone for his own sins (as the author of Hebrews doesn't fail to point out)— and clearly the point (elsewhere in the New Testament) of comparing him to the victim (for example, the paschal lamb) was to emphasize his purity and innocence. Thus the idea emerges that he acts here in a dual role—as sacrificer and as victim. While outwardly he is subject to an act of violence, he is also, perhaps primarily, actively bringing this event about as the mediator between humanity and God.

Early Protestantism, both Lutheran and Calvinist, developed this idea into the theory of Christ's 'priestly office' (*munus sacerdotale*) which is, together with his offices as prophet and king, one of the three works he accomplished during and through his Incarnation. Christ as the God-man reconciles the world to God through his obedience in accepting, on behalf of all

---

[19] Hollaz, *Examen theologicum acroamaticum*, 1139.
[20] Bellarmine, *de Missa* I 2 (p. 477).
[21] Thomas Aquinas, *Summa Theologiae* III, q. 48, art. 3, obi. 3 (vol. 4, p. 290). The same problem is discussed in Bellarmine, *de missa* I 3 (p. 478–479).

humanity, the punishment the latter would have incurred by trespassing God's commandment:[22]

> Christ through his passive obedience took upon himself the sins of the whole world and atoned voluntarily for the punishments human beings owed by spilling his most precious blood and suffering the most ignoble death on behalf of all sinners so that sins will not be imputed to those who believe in Christ as their saviour for eternal punishment. [23]

Christ's sacrifice is interpreted then in terms of *obedience*. He willingly suffers the consequences of God's wrath that otherwise would have been directed against humanity in general. He is sacrificed, but the notion of 'obedience' suggests that his role is not like that of other victims. Rather, he accepts this role for himself; indeed he offers himself up to propitiate the wrath of God for the sake of his fellow humans.

We can easily see why this particular concept seemed attractive to the early Protestants. It aligned the death of Christ with atoning sacrifices of the old covenant. By insisting on the propitiatory character of his Passion, they could set this sacrifice apart from the offerings of thanksgiving Christians were still asked to bring in a variety of ways.[24] Yet the theory of Christ's priestly office also transformed and modified the idea of sacrifice as ritual. While in the ideal and perfect sacrifice the *victima* is killed to restore communion with God, he is not merely slaughtered. In fact the historical details of his killing are in an important sense irrelevant for its interpretation. Whether his death was ultimately due to a fanatical mob or to the political machinations of his enemies, their part in this event could not have made Christ's death sacrificial. Rather, it is his own acceptance of this outcome that gives the event its significance. *He* is the priest bringing the sacrifice; *he* offers something, his own life, to God. He is both offering and being offered—this is the tantalizing thought we are asked to accept. As required by the logic of the crucifixion, this theory collapses the sacrificial ritual into a single event and reduces the number of persons involved effectively to one, even though this one individual, admittedly, is the God-man.

It must not be ignored that the overt purpose of the Protestant theory, in contrast to its contemporary Catholic rival, was to make sacrifice practically irrelevant for contemporary believers. Its conceptualization was designed

---

[22] Lutheran theology at some point distinguished further between active and passive obedience, but this never became generally accepted as it seemed to suggest that Christians themselves had no obligation to follow the divine commandments. Cf. Schmid, *Dogmatik*, 259–261.

[23] Oboedientia passiva Christus totius mundi peccata in se transtulit et poenas iis debitas ultro luit, sanguinem suum pretiotissimum fundendo et mortem ignominiosissimam pro omnibus peccatoribus obuendo, ut credendibus in redemtorem Christum peccata ad aeternam poenam non impunetur (Hollaz, *Examen theologicum acroamaticum*, 737).

[24] Melanchthon, *Apologia* XXIV (p. 253); Hollaz, *Examen theologicum acroamaticum*, 1139.

to make plausible its absence from true Christianity. There is no doubt that to some extent this was successful: during the first two centuries after the Reformation, sacrificial language is largely absent from Lutheran and Calvinist devotional texts. Two doctrinal transformations happening during the eighteenth century, however, changed this and turned the idea of Christ's obedient self-sacrifice into a popular, universally applicable concept.

The first of those changes concerned the notion of God's wrath; this was increasingly criticized and ultimately rejected by many. By the mid-nineteenth century, the Protestant mainstream had been swayed by the argument that a God who is said to be 'love' cannot at the same time be wrathful.[25] Yet the traditional idea of Christ's atoning sacrifice was completely bound up with the notion of God's wrath. His death was meant to be a propitiating sacrifice. Once such propitiation became unnecessary or problematic all that remained of Christ's obedience was the notion that he lovingly and humbly fulfilled his earthly ministry patiently accepting his own suffering and death as its culmination. This indeed is the transformed version of Protestant soteriology one finds in nineteenth-century theologians, such as the German Lutheran, Albrecht Ritschl,[26] and the American Congregationalist, Horace Bushnell.

Ritschl believed that the death of Jesus was necessary for himself and for his followers because only by accepting it he could offer final proof for the principles he had represented in his life.[27] Ritschl still framed his interpretation in traditional sacrificial language and appealed to the priestly office and to Christ's obedience, which for him, characteristically, became an obedience of vocation.[28] Christ did not have to propitiate God's wrath (a notion Ritschl strongly rejected), but reintroduced human beings into community with God through the ethical and spiritual practice of the Kingdom of God. Such a practice is, according to him, tantamount to a triumph of spirit over nature, and it is for this reason that it needs submission to death as its seal of confirmation. James Richmond explains this as follows:

> The positive meaning of the death of Christ is that it is the glorious outcome of his life-long dedication to his vocation—he willingly accepts as the dispensation of God his death at the hands of violent adversaries 'as the highest proof of faithfulness to his vocation.[29]

---

[25] Cf. Schwager, 'The Theology of the Wrath of God'; Volkmann, *Der Zorn Gottes*.

[26] On Ritschl, see: Richmond, *Ritschl*. On the work of Christ esp. ch. 5. For Ritschl's influence on the emergent science of religion cf. Jones, *The Secret of the Totem*, ch. 2, and the critical assessment of this reading by Strenski, 'Durkheim's Bourgeois Theory of Sacrifice'.

[27] Ritschl, *Rechtfertigung und Versöhnung*, vol. 2, 41–88, esp. 41–42. Cf. Marsh, *Albrecht Ritschl*.

[28] Cf. e.g. Ritschl, *Unterricht in der christlichen Religion* §§ 50–51 (pp. 67–69).

[29] Richmond, *Ritschl*, 184. The reference is to Ritschl, *Justification and Reconciliation*, 477.

Bushnell, on the other hand, sought to replace the notion of propitiation by expiation. Out of his love for us, Christ: '[...] in what is called his vicarious sacrifice, simply engages, at the expense of great suffering and even of death itself, to bring us out of our sins and so out of their penalties.'[30] Bushnell's preferred analogies for this vicarious sacrifice are motherhood and patriotism:

> The patriot or citizen who truly loves his country, [...] how does it wrench his feeling [...] when that country, so dear to him, is torn by faction, and the fate of its laws and liberties is thrown upon the chance of an armed rebellion [Bushnell writes this in 1866!]. Then you will see how many thousands of citizens, who never knew before what sacrifices it was in their power to make for their country's welfare, rushing to the field and throwing their bodies and dear lives on the battle's edge to save it.[31]

Christ's sacrifice here is the outpouring of God's perfect love for his creature whose suffering and agony calls him forth to action on their behalf. All love, according to Bushnell, is sacrificial because it entwines the lover with those he loves, and God's love is supremely so.

While Bushnell's idea of sacrificial obedience is much more active than Ritschl's, both agree on an understanding of sacrifice as *self*-sacrifice. The identity of priest and victim in Christ has here been fully merged into the notion that his willingness to give something up for the sake of others *in itself* becomes emblematic of sacrifice. Insofar as Christ's death expresses such an attitude, it can be called sacrificial.

The full impact of this transformation of the notion of sacrifice, however, only becomes evident once it is seen in conjunction with a second development. A fundamental pillar of Protestant orthodoxy was the tenet that the death of Christ was the final sacrifice. What did this finality mean for the religious practice of his followers? In one sense, certainly, they were expected to emulate him, but were they allowed to interpret their own actions in sacrificial terms? The Reformers and subsequent orthodoxy tended to argue that the death of Christ was something Christians looked back to and recognized as the token of their salvation. It did not have exemplary significance for their own lives;[32] they should not think of *sacrificing themselves* the way Jesus had done.

A major transformation in this regard, however, took place in the late seventeenth and the early eighteenth century. This change can be well observed, for example, in Bach's Passion Oratorios. Where he uses traditional texts from the sixteenth and seventeenth centuries, in the chorals, their reflection on the passion strongly emphasizes the difference between the situation of the

---

[30] Bushnell, *The Vicarious Sacrifice*, 41.
[31] Bushnell, *The Vicarious Sacrifice*, 46–47.
[32] Cf. Lage, *Martin Luther's Christology and Ethics*, 98–102.

believer and that of the saviour. *He* suffers for *their* salvation; it is this asymmetry believers are asked to appreciate:

> I am the one, I should atone:
> bound, hand and foot,
> in hell.
> The scourges and the bonds
> and what you have endured—
> my soul has merited that.[33]

Yet the contemporary, eighteenth-century texts underlying the arias reflect on the passion narrative on the basis of sympathy and identification. The believers find in the passion narrative a paradigm for their own Christian existence:

> My Jesus remains silent at
> false lies,
> in order thereby to show us
> that his merciful will
> is inclined to suffer for us,
> and that we in similar pain
> should be like him,
> and remain silent in persecution.[34]

This way of seeing the suffering of Christ in parallel with the afflictions encountered by the believers during their lives is taken for granted in Ritschl's interpretation of the death of Christ. To quote again from Richmond's study: 'When we are struck or slandered [...] Christ's call to us is to *share in his patience* so that we may lift ourselves above our misfortunes and the world which administers them.'[35]

Bushnell, likewise, draws a direct parallel between the sacrifice of Christ and the 'universal' practice of vicarious sacrifice associated with love:

> [The vicarious sacrifice of Christ] only does and suffers, and comes into substitution for, just what any and all love will, according to its degree. [...] Nothing is wanting to resolve the vicarious sacrifice of Jesus, but the commonly known, always familiar principle of love, accepted as the fundamental law of duty, even by mankind. Given the universality of love, the universality of sacrifice is given also. Here is the deepest spot of good, or goodness, conceivable.[36]

---

[33] Marissen, *Bach's Oratorios*, 35: 'Ich bin's ich sollte büßen, / an Händen und an Füßen / gebunden in der Höll. / Die Geißeln und die Banden, / und was du ausgestanden, / das hat verdienet meine Seel.'

[34] Marissen, *Bach's Oratorios*, 50: 'Mein Jesus schweigt zu falschen Lügen stille. Um uns damit zu zeigen, dass sein Erbarmens voller Wille vor uns zum Leiden sei geneigt, und dass wir in dergleichen Pein ihm sollen ähnlich sein und in Verfolgung stille schweigen.'

[35] Richmond, *Ritschl*, 183.

[36] Bushnell, *The Vicarious Sacrifice*, 48.

It is fascinating to note at this point the extraordinary rapprochement in the nineteenth century between these Protestant and contemporary Catholic views on self-sacrifice. Sixteenth-century theologians, such as Robert Bellarmine, had sought to protect the unique nature of the Eucharist as the Church's only proper sacrifice, in continuation of Christ's atoning death, by means of a strongly ritualistic definition:

> Sacrifice is an external oblation made only to God in which, for the strengthening of human infirmity and the proclamation of God's majesty, a material and durable object is consecrated by a legitimate minister in a religious rite and transformed so that it is fully destroyed.[37]

Already in the late seventeenth century, however, this strong ritualism gave way to a more ethical and spiritual interpretation of sacrifice.[38] The French School of Spirituality (Bérulle, Condren) integrated Bellarmine's theory into an overall Augustinian framework: sacrifice for these writers was primarily internal and spiritual but at the same time aimed at the destruction of the victim:

> Sacrifice [...] requires the consumption and total destruction of the object [sc. the victim], and if sacrifices are not consummated through the destruction of hosts and victims, this is because of the imperfection of the human cult and the impotence of the human person who is not capable of more. Thus [the victim's] death is merely a representation of that total destruction of the object which ought to have happened in the sacrifice.[39]

Charles de Condren's work, from which this quotation is taken, unequivocally applies Christ's sacrifice to the spiritual 'annihilation' of the individual Christian and thus contributes to the proliferation of the ideal of self-sacrifice. By the nineteenth century, this line of thought had produced ideas almost indistinguishable from those advanced by the time's liberal Protestants: Christians are asked to emulate Christ's 'infinite obedience',[40] and while this obedience is still called 'self-annihilation',[41] this self-abnegation is now couched in terms of altruism and duty towards the common good:

> From the spirit of sacrifice and from it alone true society is born: it makes subjects as much as it makes kings. To be obedient is not difficult for those who have heard and appreciated this word: 'If any want to become my followers, let them deny themselves and take up their cross daily and follow me' (Luke 9:23). Renouncing oneself in this way, one henceforth lives only and entirely a life of dedication, following the example of Jesus Christ.[42]

[37] Bellarmine, *De missa* I 2 (p. 477).
[38] Despland, *Le recul du sacrifice*, 80–85.
[39] Condren, *L'idée du sacerdoce*, 48.
[40] de Lamennais, *Essay de l'Indifference* IV 15 (vol. 4, pp. 77, 80–81).
[41] de Lamennais, *Essay de l'Indifference* IV 15 (vol. 4, p. 79).
[42] de Lamennais, *Essay de l'Indifference* IV 15 (vol. 4, p. 83).

It is at this point that we can perceive in one, important strand of contemporary, secular discourse about sacrifice the result of theological developments, a convergence of streams that had parted in early modernity but continued to be fed by the same biblical and Patristic tributaries. Sacrifice as an expression of selfless commitment to the good of the community is the end-result of a trajectory that previously saw the transformation of the idea that the death of Jesus was a propitiating sacrifice offered by himself into the notion of Christ's sacrificing his own life through active love, self-demotion, and patient suffering on behalf of his friends. This self-sacrifice is, further, understood ethically to express the example and the ideal of Christian existence.

This could be applied to more extraordinary situations—we have seen Bushnell refer to war and analogous uses were extremely popular during the First World War. Yet overall more typical is its appropriation to the ideal of civic vocation in what Charles Taylor has called the 'affirmation of ordinary life'.[43] This willingness to 'sacrifice' by giving up for the benefit of others and in the interest of one's community continues to loom large in contemporary discourse on sacrifice.

## 3.  SACRIFICE AND THE PERSPECTIVE OF THE VICTIM

The identification of sacrifice as self-sacrifice, while becoming dominant only in the eighteenth century, goes back to Augustine. By contrast, the association of sacrifice with an act of violence committed to an innocent victim seems a genuine product of European modernity. While recent discussions of sacrifice invite the implication that this link was perceived for a long time, historical evidence suggests otherwise: in modern European languages, the emergence of a generic use of 'victim' and its derivatives for objects of acts of violence, injustice, or abuse is a secondary phenomenon clearly derived from Christological discussions. It is not aligned to debates about sacrifice until the eighteenth century.[44]

This is not to deny that the particular cruelty and the human suffering at the heart of the Christian atonement were noted much earlier. Yet it seems to have been, originally, the external more than the internal perception of Christianity which focused on this aspect. From the Platonic philosopher Celsus in the second century onwards, the charge that Christianity glorifies suffering and generally under-achievement has accompanied its history. In

---

[43] Taylor, *Sources of the Self*, 211–302.
[44] Despland, *Le recul du sacrifice*, 139–147.

the late nineteenth century, Friedrich Nietzsche emphatically reiterated this claim.[45] It would be simplifying things unduly to attribute this perception of Christianity entirely to the notion of Christ as *victima*, but clearly the founder's death on the cross must have played its role.[46] By contrast, theological reflections on the death of Christ initially did not emphasize his pain or physical suffering. Nor did other forms of representation: the first crucifix depicting a visibly suffering Christ only dates from the early Middle Ages.[47] It is part of the devotional revolution during the high Middle Ages that Christ's physical pain, symbolized through the spilling of his blood, becomes a dominant feature of Christian perceptions of the cross and its often drastic rendering, a favourite motive of religious art.[48]

Early modern theological developments could not but exacerbate this trend. In the debates about the nature of sacrifice that followed the Reformation, both sides insisted, albeit for different reasons, on the centrality of the immolation of the victim.[49] For Protestants this underlined the plausibility of their claim that the death of Jesus was the perfect—and final—proper sacrifice. Catholics, on the other hand, sought to prove that only the destruction of the material of the host through transubstantiation guaranteed the validity and efficaciousness of the Eucharist as the genuine continuation of the Christ event. Both lines of argument did not in any obvious way advance cruelty to victims— Protestants held that since the death of Christ sacrifice had become redundant while for Catholics the true sacrifice merely involved the offering of bread and wine. Yet in these discussions the view gained currency that the essential property of sacrifice was the violent destruction of a sentient being, paradigmatically the crucifixion of Jesus Christ.

It was, therefore, in opposition to this particular view that, beginning from the eighteenth century, sacrifice was rejected as the wilful annihilation of life. As Derek Hughes shows in his contribution to the present collection (Chapter 15), antisacrificial attitudes dominated eighteenth-century adaptations of *Iphigenia*. In Fénelon's *Aventures de Télémaque*, the idealized inhabitants of Salento are characterized by their refusal to immolate the sacrificial victim: the animals are 'presented' at the altar but not killed.[50] The same era sees the emergence of the view that the paradigmatic

---

[45] Cf. for Celsus his scathing comments on Christ's death and his later remarks on the attractiveness of Christianity for those who are contemptible: *Alethes Logos*, fr. II 16–26 and III 44–63 with clear echoes of 1 Cor 1:21ff. For Nietzsche see: *Zur Genealogie der Moral* I 7 (p. 267).

[46] Nietzsche's 'transvaluation of values' is clearly present in the preaching of Jesus himself, e.g. in his Beatitudes (Mt 5:3–10).

[47] Beutler, *Der älteste Kruzifixus*.

[48] Cf. Walker Bynum, *Wonderful Blood*.

[49] Carraud, 'De la destruction'.

[50] Despland, *Le recul du sacrifice*, 141–142.

sacrificial victim is a human being.[51] This implication reinforces Voltaire's critique of religion as inherently cruel: no religion without sacrifice, no sacrifice without the immolation of a victim and thus, ultimately, without the killing of human beings.[52] It is not difficult to recognize behind these three notions theological principles emphatically affirmed by Counter-Reformation thinkers; the critical twist *against* the continuation of sacrifice, meanwhile, was furnished by arguments culled from their Protestant opponents.

Eighteenth-century rejection of sacrifice, then, was in many ways inspired by opposition to the Christocentric construction of sacrifice as the immolation of a (human) victim in post-Reformation debates. A proper theological 'turn to the victim', on the other hand, did not happen until much later. Finding in Jesus Christ's sacrifice the model for all human suffering in the world really was a theological idea of the twentieth century. After the First World War, Christological and soteriological argument increasingly moved away from the view according to which Christ's sacrificial dying represented a model of heroic acceptance of the consequences of his mission and towards an emphasis on the relevance of suffering in the world as expressed through the centrality of this event.[53] God reveals himself precisely through his abasement—this was already the fundamental idea in Luther's theology of the cross,[54] and this conviction stands behind many modern interpretations which stress the innocent suffering of the victim.

It is this development that has finally led to the identification of sacrifice with the suffering of innocent victims as it is encountered most famously in René Girard's theory, but which is, in less articulate forms, widely held in contemporary societies. Girard himself has sought to support his view through a wide-ranging theory of culture in which a particular interpretation of Christianity and the biblical *writings* play a major role. As the present chapter should have demonstrated, history at best offers partial confirmation of Girard's narrative. He is hardly right in identifying every sacrifice with an act of victimization; even within Christianity his theory relies largely on specific developments since the Reformation which emphasized the immolation of the victim and subsequently provoked radical opposition to the very notion of sacrifice. It is, however, arguable that the post-Reformation theories are the

---

[51] It is interesting that in Thomas Aquinas the fact that in the crucifixion a human being is killed is still cited as an argument against the sacrificial interpretation of Christ's death: 'But human flesh was never offered up in the sacrifices of the Old Law, which were figures of Christ: nay, such sacrifices were reputed as impious' (ST III, q. 48, art. 3, obi. 1 [p. 290]).

[52] Despland, *Le recul du sacrifice*, 144–145.

[53] Fiddes, *The Creative Suffering of God*, and his contribution to this volume.

[54] Cf. his *Heidelberg Disputation* Theses 19–21: 'Non ille digne Theologus dicitur, quit "invisibilia" Dei "per ea, quae facta sunt, intellecta conspicit", sed qui visibilia et posteriora Dei per passiones et crucem conspecta intelligit. Theologus gloriae dicit malum bonum et bonum malum. Theologus crucis dicit id quod res est (*Werke in Auswahl*, vol. 5, p. 379).

result specifically of an attempt to understand sacrifice from the vantage point of the Christ event and thus far Girard's intuition to see in the ensuing critical trajectory a result of the biblical narrative is not far-fetched.

## 4. CONCLUSION

What has Christianity done to the concept of sacrifice? How has it influenced the ways in which people today, whether or not they are theologians, speak about sacrifice? I started from the observation that Christianity emerged in a historical situation that saw the end of most traditional sacrifices. The Christian response to this, as exemplified by Augustine, was pragmatic and followed largely the example set by Hellenistic Judaism: sacrifice was in principle affirmed but reinterpreted as an internal attitude of religious devotion to God and its manifestation in moral behaviour. Sacrifice thus became self-sacrifice, a sacral transformation of the person which could, but did not have to be, symbolized by an external offering. The case for this re-imagination of sacrifice as self-sacrifice was largely made on the basis of Old Testament texts contrasting empty rituals with true spirituality and morality. In the sixteenth century, by contrast, the debates about sacrifice triggered by the Reformation turned to the death of Christ as the paradigmatic sacrifice and therefore emphasized the violent destruction of the victim as a central component of the sacrificial act. Self-sacrifice now became associated with annihilation, with patient endurance in hardship, and with obedient suffering. While Catholic and Protestant interpretations went radically different ways initially, the two sides eventually settled on similar views endorsing altruistic acts of self-submission for the benefit of the greater good in a spirit that could be, and has been, adapted eagerly by nation states and civic societies ever since.

At the same time, the Christocentric turn in sacrificial theory during the Reformation period also gave rise to the critical argument that sacrifice was essentially cruel and brutal, the senseless taking of human life. It is from this trajectory that, since the eighteenth century, the usage of *victima* for any kind of 'victim' became popular in European languages: instances of unjust and cruel human suffering were thus inscribed into a sacrificial logic, they became types of the suffering *victima* on the cross. There lies some irony, then, in the fact that this universalization of the sacrificial logic went hand in glove with a fundamental rejection of that very logic. As the contribution by Wolfgang Palaver to this volume evidences (Chapter 6), the argument cuts both ways even today: it appears that *if* sacrificial mechanisms are recognized in all human violence, these mechanisms must be denounced, and sacrifice must be rejected. Yet if it is also true that only their identification *as* instances of victimization transformed acts of violence from unexceptionable parts of human culture into something truly reprehensible, this would indicate that the category of sacrifice is inadmissible for the peaceful future of human society.

In the final instance, it is this paradox that Christianity has bequeathed to the modern world. While it was predicated on 'the end of sacrifice' as it had been known and practised by most cultures for thousands of years, this religion has given to discourse and reflection about sacrifice the most central place imaginable. With only little exaggeration we can say that this is our own situation today still.

It is characteristic that this situation offers the semantic possibility of classifying various practices *as* sacrifice. This happened in Hellenistic Judaism, then throughout Christian history and continues in secular modernity. While one can hardly decree such interpretations illegitimate or wrong, it seems important to recognize that these debates would not exist if it were not also true that in a rather obvious way sacrifice is absent from society as we know it. There is a sense in which we are unwilling to believe that anything that has existed in human culture would ever totally and utterly leave us. In the case of sacrifice this certainly seems to be the case; whether this is cause for worry or comfort is very much an open question today.

# 3

## Sacrifice as Self-destructive 'Love'
### *Why Autonomy Should Still Matter to Feminists*

#### Pamela Sue Anderson

Love on bended knee is no love at all as far as I am concerned, even if love sometimes arouses passion in us that makes us yield to the loved one.[1]

## 1. INTRODUCTION: SACRIFICE AND GENDER OPPRESSION

In this chapter, my aim is to assess a gender-specific difficulty with 'sacrifice' and, in response, to propose that a certain 'principled autonomy' should matter to feminists when it comes to love and self-sacrifice. As will be seen, I appropriate Onora O'Neill's Kantian, modal conception of principled autonomy as 'the *capacity* to adopt principles that *could* be adopted by all' for my hermeneutics of autonomy.[2] Autonomous reasoning makes all the difference for what I will propose is an ethics of non-sacrificial love. As 'non-sacrificial', this love would not require self-sacrifice as a necessary condition for ethical and ritual practices in (Christian) societies today, even though there could still be autonomy of sacrifice in social relations.[3] My overall argument concerning 'gender' intends neither to oppose paternal to maternal identities nor to sever sacrificial acts of love from male and female autonomy.[4]

---

[1] Badiou, *In Praise of Love*, 67.
[2] O'Neill, *Bounds of Justice*, 44.
[3] The role of sacrifice in social or interpersonal relations is very well-defended by Meszaros, 'Sacrifice and the Self', Chapter 5, in this volume.
[4] This chapter will maintain that 'gender' is always located at the intersection of other social and material structures, including religion, race, class, ethnicity, and sexual orientation. The implication is that a woman's (or a man's) gender does not make all women (or all men) the same as each other. See Crenshaw, *On Intersectionality*.

As I will seek to demonstrate, for those of us who think that their non-heteronomous selves and gender equality matter in love relations, the decisive problem in fixing ethical roles is that compulsory norms of self-sacrificial love, especially those maintained by patriarchal religions, have intensified perverse forms of gender oppression. It is my contention that those religions dominated by an ethics of self-sacrificial practice undermine the 'appropriate' confidence of women and of men in their capacity to reason for themselves about personal and social relations. Inappropriate control of a person's reasoning is a persistent feature of gender oppression; such control destroys the 'ethical' confidence necessary for mutual self-respect and self-knowledge in loving relations. Previously I have contended that re-visioning gender in philosophy of religion is both possible and necessary.[5] Now I contend that such re-visioning would include a new vision for social-religious practices; and this vision would inspire ethical confidence, ensuring neither over-confident nor under-confident subjects in love.

According to recent moral psychologists, 'sacrifice' has been implicit in both the virtuous, or 'caring,' role of women as determined by their maternal relations and the earliest stage of the infant's ethical development when she must 'break' from the mother's body. In *Sacrificial Logics: Feminist Theory and the Critique of Identity*, Alison Weir engages with Julia Kristeva's account of the infant's 'founding separation' from the maternal body.[6] Weir encourages a feminist re-interpretation of this break with the mother which occurs when an infant begins to develop social relations in a patriarchal culture. This feminist re-visioning is necessary, if we are to build upon both Kristeva and Weir, to 'replace the sacrificial basis of contemporary social relations and social institutions.'[7] This sacrificial basis would include the ritual practice of sacrifice by religious institutions, but also the religious principle of ethical altruism; these have shaped—and often unwittingly damaged—social relations in patriarchal cultures. So, the present chapter finds support from Weir and Kristeva to urge a re-visioning of the social identities and the spiritual practices which have determined gender oppression under patriarchy.

Weir is helpful in articulating the possibility of a non-sacrificial identity for women and men within a social order no longer based on the sacrifice of

---

[5] Anderson, *Re-visioning Gender*, ix, 1–3, 15, 18, 26–27, 29–30, 97, 138–139, 153–154, 164–170, 178–180.

[6] Kristeva, 'Women's Time', 188–213; and Weir, *Sacrificial Logics*, 146–184.

[7] This separation is a break from, in Kristeva's terms, 'the archaic mother' who is, arguably, a 'patriarchal fantasy' of complete gratification, see Kristeva, 'Women's Time', 204–205, 210–211. Concerning the patriarchal order which (i) characterizes 'religions dominated by men', (ii) appears in a variety of manifestations, (iii) tends toward monotheism and a transcendent god, see Sered, *Priestess Mother Sacred Sister*, 67n, 104–115, 170–173, 205.

women, or of any social group or individual by another.[8] Weir's own argument for a non-sacrificial model of identity builds upon Kristeva as follows:

> I want to argue that Kristeva is, in effect, calling for a differentiation between the violence of separation, which is unavoidable, and the violence of domination, which can perhaps be overcome. The interiorization of the founding separation means that separation must be accepted as a subjective experience.
>
> ...this development in the subjective experience of identity corresponds to a development in other forms of identity: gender identities and the identities of social collectivities need to be reconceptualized through a reflexive and affective acceptance of internal differentiation, of the existence of the other within...
>
> [T]his process can only be achieved through...a development in our understanding of the sacrificial logic, and of the need to replace it with a logic of inclusion.[9]

Recent studies in the anthropology of religion are also helpful in telling a story about the gender-specific role which has been given to the blood of animal sacrifice in 'the great religious' rituals.[10] In *Priestess Mother Sacred Sister: Religions Dominated by Women,* Susan Starr Sered finds the fact that the vast majority of religions in the world are male-dominated, while 'religions dominated by women' are scattered across the world.[11] But Sered tells a revealing story about the difference between bloodless sacrifice and the ritual symbolism of blood. Basing her ideas on W. Robertson Smith's suggestions that 'kinfolk, God, and the sacrificial victim were believed to share the same blood' and that animal sacrifice was the earliest way 'to converse with the gods', Sered concludes that men have needed to postulate 'common blood', since their kinship ties have always had an element of uncertainty: 'By ritually killing an animal and sharing its consumption, groups of men ingest common blood.'[12] In contrast, it is rare that the ritual 'sacrifices' in women's religions involve the blood of animal life. Again, according to Sered's findings, 'women's religions' will share alimentary (e.g. vegetable) gifts in sacrificial ritual and ethical acts. As will be further discussed, these are bloodless sacrifices in which women's practices of sacrifice involve reciprocal giving as in a shared meal.

---

[8] For a highly relevant theological account of the transformation of individuals (and of society) into the mutual giving of women and men, which can respond specifically to the violence of sacrifice as understood by Kristevan psychoanalytic theory, see Fiddes, 'Sacrifice, Atonement, and Renewal', Chapter 4, in this volume.

[9] Weir, *Sacrificial Logics*, 150.

[10] Sered, *Priestess Mother Sacred Sister*, 136–138; cf. Jay, *Throughout Your Generation Forever*, 1–29.

[11] Sered, *Priestess Mother Sacred Sister*, 11, 39.

[12] Sered, *Priestess Mother Sacred Sister*, 136–137; cf. Smith [1889].

## 2. THE SACRIFICIAL RELATIONS IN RELIGIONS DOMINATED BY WOMEN RATHER THAN MEN

In this second section I take a closer look at the role which gender plays in those (few) 'religions' scattered around the world which are 'dominated by women' today and at women's sacrificial roles in religions more generally.[13] As already noted, when it comes to religions in the world, male dominance is near universal. Yet patriarchy itself takes on different forms depending on social and cultural institutions (such as the Church, the Temple, the Mosque, or the Synagogue). Feminist anthropologists have tended to treat 'religion as the ideological foundation and justification for patriarchy', arguing that 'through religious doctrine and ritual women and men are persuaded of the "rightness" of male dominance.'[14]

However, Sered also admits that perhaps 'because religion frequently emphasizes such internal experiences as belief, faith, and mysticism (all of which are difficult to legislate or supervise), in many cultural situations women have found room to manoeuvre within the religious sphere.'[15] The evidence which Sered gathers about gender and religion supports the view that women's identities, for instance as mothers, and the religious practices which arise from these identities are socially—rather than strictly physiologically—constructed. This explains the large variety of religious rituals in the world performed by women, at the same time as the strong similarities when it comes to gender and issues of health and childcare in the social constructions of religious institutions. Ritual roles of women in different religions are often related to maternity, to physical changes in a woman's body, to care of family, especially of children, and healing. [16]

It follows that certain distinctive characteristics of sacrificial relations in religions derive from the difference gender makes to social roles and to physical make-up, especially in birthing and familial relations. As already explained, animal sacrifice in religions dominated by men is often thought necessary for the blood which strengthens, proves, or dramatizes the bonds between men. In contrast, in religions dominated by women the bonds between family members are already known empirically to be 'in the blood' and so, blood rituals to establish kinship are not necessary for religious sacrifice by women. Instead, because in most cultures women prepare food, alimentary rituals and the

---

[13] Sered, *Priestess Mother Sacred Sister*, especially 4, 12–16, 136–138, 173, 198f, 286. Sered claims that in 'religions dominated by women,' or 'female-dominated religions,' 'women are the majority of participants and leaders, there is no higher level male authority that ultimately directs these religions, and that these religions focus on women as ritual actors'. This does not imply any 'physical dominance or institutionalized power inequality between men and women' (11–12).

[14] Sered, *Priestess Mother Sacred Sister*, 4.

[15] Sered, *Priestess Mother Sacred Sister*, 4.

[16] Sered, *Priestess Mother Sacred Sister*, 16.

sharing of a meal sacralize women's everyday activities; that is, food rituals in women's religions are public, communal, and in some sense at least, sacred. Such religious rituals involve both natural and supernatural food: both the humans and the gods eat. So, the sacrificial meal in women's religions tends to be an act of social sharing, a public communion, a confirmation of fellowship and a bridge created between this world and other worlds, between life and afterlife.

Building upon the above, three gender-specific interpretations can be offered concerning the sacrificial basis of religious institutions and the part played by gender in their religious practices of sacrifice. First of all, women's religions have flourished in societies where women have a relatively high level of personal and material freedom. Women's religions in these societies are 'the official, mainstream, and/or state-supported religion within its specific cultural context'[17] and in religions dominated by women their rituals do not worship a superior female saviour. Instead, the social context of women's religions is 'characterized by relatively egalitarian relationships between the sexes, and relatively equal valuation of men's and women's economic and ritual status.'[18]

Second, if the task is to understand why certain gender traits characterize almost all women's religions cross-culturally, then it is most helpful to look at motherhood as 'the human experience that most clearly impacts on women differently than on men'; according to Sered, the 'matrifocality' of female-dominated religions define a kinship system in which 'the structurally, culturally, and affectively central role of the mother is seen as legitimate.'[19] This focus on motherhood, including the mother's concern for childcare, is in sharp contrast to the gender focus on women in male-dominated religions: when adult men are in charge, then women are dealt with and defined by their identities as wives.[20]

Third, the role of blood in ritual acts of sacrifice practiced in a male-dominated religion such as (orthodox) Christianity can make sense anthropologically (and not only theologically) of God the Father's sacrifice of his only Son. The Eucharistic ritual includes the sharing of wine as literally or symbolically the blood which binds together those persons who drink 'the blood' of the innocent, divine victim; repetition of this ritual gratefully recalls the death of the God-man for human redemption. Moreover, this interpretation of the male-dominated ritual of human sacrifice at the heart of the Christian religion represents and unites divine-human suffering as a self-sacrificial act of love. The blood which is shed in one specific sacrifice is understood as redeeming human beings from their own sin and lack of love. In this context,

---

[17] Sered, *Priestess Mother Sacred Sister*, 283; also see, 43, 277.
[18] Sered, *Priestess Mother Sacred Sister*, 46–47.
[19] Sered, *Priestess Mother Sacred Sister*, 283–284; also see 71–87.
[20] Sered, *Priestess Mother Sacred Sister*, 71.

self-sacrifice is equally a ritual act of communion and an ethical act of an individual—for which both men and woman show gratitude to the Father—often
in submission.[21]

In the end, whether we approach sacrifice via male-dominated religions
or female-dominated religions, the crucial concern in the present chapter is
the different roles given to differently gendered subjects in ritual and ethical
acts of sacrifice. Although a problem for men, it is even more often a problem for women in religious institutions that a destructive form of love has
been enforced by practices of self-sacrifice without 'principled autonomy'. This
Kantian conception of autonomy is, as stated at the outset, 'the *capacity* to
adopt principles that *could* be adopted by all.'[22]


## 3. SACRIFICE AND A LOSS OF CONFIDENCE IN THE SELF'S CAPACITY TO REASON

In my third section I shall propose a hermeneutics of principled autonomy as a
necessary tool for uncovering, by way of an internal critique of Christian ritual
practices of sacrifice, the self-undermining harms of gender oppression, notably in patriarchal forms of religion. In this sort of critique, autonomy is recognized in its loss by a subject who finds she lacks her own capacity to reason. In
particular, it should be possible to pinpoint the lack, or loss, of confidence in
a subject's own reasoning precisely where it leaves her action heteronomous;
that is, a woman, or an oppressed man, can become dangerously over-bur-
dened by passive submission to other-directed religious norms of self-sacrifice
as 'love' under domination.

Female autonomy tends to be obscured and/or destroyed by the compulsory
norms of sensitivity and attentiveness to the suffering of others under conditions of oppression, precisely when the sensitive and attentive woman herself
is already suffering her own religious forms of gender oppression.[23] Generally,
for such subjects within a patriarchal religion, this excessive burdening carries
an intrinsically painful weight of extreme sensitivity to the suffering of others;
the longer these unjust conditions persist, the more the emotional overload in
that individual life will only increase the hopelessness of this self-destructively
'loving' subject; these are subjects who practice sacrifice without adequate
regard for their own self.[24]

---

[21] Coakley, 'Kenosis and Subversion,' 3–39.

[22] O'Neill, *Bounds of Justice*, 44.

[23] As stipulated in note 4 (above), 'gender' is understood in intersectional terms; oppressive
constructions of gender always intersect with other social and material mechanisms of oppression, including religion, race, ethnicity, class, and sexual orientation.

[24] See Tessman, *Burdened Virtues*, 93, 96.

In her 2012 Gifford Lectures, Sarah Coakley sketches a novel conception of 'sacrifice regained' as an ascetical form of Christian altruism.[25] She appropriates, on the one hand, a contemporary evolutionary understanding of sacrificial behaviours and, on the other hand, a medievally inspired ascetic practice of sacrificial love.[26] In particular, Coakley claims to be able to 'untangle the demonically perverse from the divinely transformative in sacrifice.'[27] In her fourth Gifford lecture, Coakley takes a leap back to a practice of 'ascetical sacrifice' and to an idea of 'gender fluidity' which she finds in the Cappadocian Fathers.[28] In fact, over many years, Coakley has been trying to re-instate this medieval fluidity of gender into the contemporary personal, social, political, and material relations which make up our constructions of gender today.[29]

However, I would insist that it is necessary to be cautious here before making a leap and simply assuming this medieval fluidity. The gendering[30] of ritual acts of submission and sacrificial love in which feminine and masculine subjects have been given religiously specific and often unequal roles creates the very serious danger of merely re-enforcing historical forms of gender oppression. In particular, despite Coakley's image of gender's fluidity, which might be attractive, the danger of privileging submission would be inculcating, perhaps unwittingly, the compulsory heterosexual norms of self-surrendering love; it is just not clear that treating gender as fluid can overcome specific forms of injustice which are already embedded in the social and material conditions of both the recent and the past history of Christianity. That ritual and social practices of submission in self-sacrificial love have been ethically self-destructive becomes most apparent in the psycho-sexual and anthropological roles played by women in religions traditionally dominated by men. As already argued, patriarchal conceptions of sacrificial love in Christianity have been premised upon heteronomy and gender inequality. The decisive difficulty for the argument of this chapter is that heteronomy and inequality undermine the principled autonomy in ethical practices of love.

---

[25] Coakley, 'Sacrificed Regained'. It is not possible here to do justice to Coakley's highly provocative, theological vision of 'sacrificed regained'. However, her more extensive development of a distinctive Christian conception of submission before God, which links up to her current ascetical form of self-surrender in sacrifice (e.g. to 'trials and sufferings'), raises a critical concern (at least for feminists). Her distinctive conception of submission, depending as it does on medieval ascetics, still seems difficult to dissociate from an intensely patriarchal form of self-sacrificing love. Even if Coakley finds 'power' in submission, how can the one who submits be certain to avoid a perversion of this power in self-deception, violence, and/or injustice?

[26] Coakley, 'Sacrificed Regained', Lecture 4, 16–21.

[27] Coakley, 'Stories of Evolution', Lecture 1, also, 9; 'Sacrificed Regained', Lecture 4, 18–19.

[28] Coakley, 'Sacrificed Regained', Lecture 4, 17.

[29] Coakley, 'Visions of the Self', 72–88.

[30] For a fuller discussion of gendering, see Anderson, 'The Lived Body, Gender and Confidence', 163–180; *Re-visioning Gender*, 49–52, 59–62, 89–92.

Nevertheless, Coakley argues for a Christian ethics of ascetical sacrifice which would be divinely transformative. She contends that 'the ascetic sacrificial role is one that no society or evolutionary group can do without' in one way or another; and if a society 'refuses this goal and unthinkingly demands such sacrifice of those who have not themselves made the choice (the poor, the old, the neglected), then this is bad "sacrifice" and only ultimately leads to violence'.[31] So, Coakley seems to admit that some sense of free choice is also necessary. At least she cautions against a society which 'unthinkingly demands such [bad] sacrifice', urging the preservation of a choice in taking up a sacrificial role in society, or within a group, or between interrelated groups.[32] Perhaps, Coakley herself has experienced freedom in the choices she had made in her life. But it can still be argued that within the context of patriarchal religions there simply is no such thing as 'a free choice' for all women in their sacrificial role; and this is precisely the problem with gender oppression under patriarchy.

In *Sacrifice Imagined: Violence, Atonement and the Sacred*, Douglas Hedley (who appears consistent with Coakley's views of Christian sacrifice) finds Christ representing the paradigmatically human in 'willing self-sacrifice', or sacrifice as 'self-renunciation'.[33] By contrast, Hedley portrays Kantian 'autonomy' in a caricature of the secular individual, while claiming that this autonomous individual is so unlike Kant's own later portrait of 'the suffering' of Christ as paradigmatic of the crucifixion of human inclinations by the sublimity of duty.[34] I would urge Hedley to rethink his reading of Kant's writings on autonomy. But it would not be too far from the truth, if we concluded that both Coakley and Hedley would find the 'virtuous' agent (including Christ's virtuous suffering as represented in Kant's *Religion within the Boundaries of Mere Reason*[35]) to be the subject who willingly makes self-sacrifices. And yet, Hedley's Platonic reading of Kant's account of the 'fallenness' of human inclinations in the *Religion* will not support the feminist case being advocated in

---

[31] Coakley, 'Stories of Evolution', 8–9.

[32] Coakley, 'Stories of Evolution', 10–11. Compare Blum, Homiak, Housman and Scheman, 'Altruism and Women's Oppression', 222–247. I contend that Christian conceptions of altruism which treat ethical sacrifice as completely the opposite of rational autonomy, as if sacrifice alone is altruistic and autonomy is selfish, have done a great damage to Kantian autonomy but also to liberation from gender oppression.

[33] Hedley, *Sacrifice Imagined*, 109–110 and 128–130. For a bold and highly articulate defence of sacrifice as act of refusal or renunciation with global, human significance for communal life (rather than for individuals), see Flood, 'Sacrifice as Refusal', Chapter 8, in this volume. The feminist problematic which I am addressing focuses on a very specific problem of gender injustice which may or may not cut across the phenomenon of sacrifice as a communal activity; this will depend on the nature of the community and on the principles which underlie practices of ritual sacrifice.

[34] Hedley, *Sacrifice Imagined*, 130.

[35] Kant, *Religion within the Boundaries of Mere Reason*, 39–215.

the present chapter, that Kantian autonomy is *not* about rejection of our sensuous nature as fallen.[36]

In *Burdened Virtues: Virtue Ethics for Liberatory Struggles*, Lisa Tessman engages questions central to feminist theory and practice, querying the nature and role of ethical virtues—for, example, 'servility'—in the struggle for liberation from oppression. Tessman focuses on the ways in which devastating conditions confronted by selves both limit and burden their ethical goodness.

To give my own example, think of familial conditions where sexual abuse is common place and a young woman struggles against self-harm only to give into 'killing' sexual relations with men in her family: the possibility of autonomous reasoning concerning these self-sacrificial relations is not there. Similar sorts of examples could be given of communities where racial abuse is the norm and the impact this has on young men whose violent acts cannot be understood in terms of 'the *capacity* to adopt principles that *could* be adopted by all'; that is, 'the capacity for autonomy'.[37] Gender oppression exists for young black men, as much as women, in situations where racial oppression intersects with gender. The intersection of variable social structures of oppression such as race and religion shapes and differentiates gender relations across our global world.

Tessman herself argues that the very conditions of gender oppression require the oppressed to develop a set of virtues that carry an ethical cost to those who practice them: she calls these 'burdened virtues'.[38] In this way, she uncovers ethical issues which have been missed by other feminist philosophers and by theologians such as Coakley. But Tessman also helps us to make sense of an experience which requires, as I am arguing, a hermeneutics of principled autonomy. She uncovers how it is that the ethically autonomous subject may lose confidence in her capacity to love, and in knowing which principles enable her or him to flourish in this life.

In particular, Tessman raises the question of the confidence of women who are living as a subordinated group. Women as a subordinated group appear to be like any other human being who lacks the virtue of, what Kant would call, 'self-respect'.[39] This lack undermines confidence in our capacity for ethical goodness, suggesting that virtue could be equally described in terms of 'servility to structures of oppression', or even, 'internalized self-hate', which violates the Kantian duty to oneself.[40] We find this in the masochist or sadomasochist. Put simply, this lack of ethical self-confidence reveals a situation

---

[36] Hedley, *Sacrifice Imagined*, 128–130. cf. Kant, *Religion within the Boundaries of Mere Reason,* 121 (6:83).

[37] For background to this contemporary conception of Kantian autonomy, see O'Neill, *Bounds of Justice*, 42–44.

[38] Tessman, *Burdened Virtues*, 96–106, 108–109, 164–168.

[39] Kant, *The Metaphysics of Morals*, 159, 162, 164 (6:399, 402–404).

[40] Hill, 'Servility and Self–Respect', 87–104; and Tessman, *Burdened Virtues*, 65–67.

of heteronomy—of exclusively other-regarding traits—without principled autonomy as a reciprocal, equally self-regarding and other-regarding virtue. In Tessman's words:

> the lack of opportunity to develop the character trait of (appropriate) confi-
> dence—a typical problem of gender oppression—may stand in the way of a wom-
> an's pursuing challenging and meaningful lines of work or other projects...The
> same trait may also be necessary for becoming a strong resister of injustice....It is
> helpful for understanding how oppression operates to recognize how members of
> structurally subordinated groups are harmed by enduring conditions that make
> the development of certain virtues particularly difficult.[41]

## 4. KANT AND THE HERMENEUTICS OF PRINCIPLED AUTONOMY

Returning to Onora O'Neill's contemporary Kantian conception of autonomy, let us consider how this can provide the crucial element for my hermeneutics. Mention has been made (in the previous sections) of this Kantian, principled autonomy which means acting on principles that *could* be adopted by all.[42] But I am also suggesting that this Kantian autonomy enables us to interpret what is latent in religious practices and in ethical actions. O'Neill defends this Kantian autonomy as putting 'a modal, reflexive constraint' on the principles which could be adopted as ethical.[43] So, when principled autonomy is applied to an individual's reasoning—say, about love and sacrifice—autonomy would essentially allow no one to think in her place or to act in place of her; and yet, she could be related to all of those others who could adopt principles any ethical agent ought to (and so, could) adopt. Such autonomous reasoning can help us to distinguish between pernicious and non-pernicious acts of altruism and love. Kantian autonomy also helps to bring out the decisive significance in understanding political and religious necessity of human autonomy for a social life in a 'kingdom of ends'. Taking seriously Kant's virtue of self-respect would also mean aiming at virtuous action practiced in a community of non-heteronomous individuals. Contemporary Kantians may extend this aim to each and every human subject of every class, race, ethnicity, sexual orienta-tion, and gender flourishing in a world where human beings—no matter their gender conditions—can hope for a good life.

---

[41] Tessman, *Burdened Virtues*, 56–57; also see 66, 108–109.
[42] O'Neill, *Bounds of Justice*, 43. Cf. Kant, *Groundwork of the Metaphysics of Morals*, 30–31, 46, 53, 63–65 (4:420, 4:440, 4:447, 4:459, 4:461).
[43] O'Neill, *Bounds of Justice*, 43–44. For her own application of principled autonomy, see O'Neill, *Autonomy and Trust*, 73–95.

Interestingly, when it comes to the paradigmatic role given to sacrifice in Christian moral theology, Kant himself thinks that 'through reason we cannot form any concept of how a self-sufficient being [Jesus Christ] could sacrifice something that belongs to his blessedness, thus robbing himself of a perfection.'[44] Here Kant's decisive difficulty with the sacrifice of Christ is at once epistemological and ethical: how could He, the God-man, who is, was, and always will be without imperfection submit to punishment and death on the cross, even though perfectly innocent? As one interpretation of the Christian story goes, God would enact a vicarious act of suffering in sending his only begotten Son to suffer and die in the place of human beings who are not innocent. But it is this which remains for Kant quite simply incomprehensible! This sacrificial act also appears to be heteronomous, and so, non-moral, if not immoral. Why would this sacrificial death be necessary for God who possesses perfect goodness, omnipotence, and complete self-sufficiency?

All too roughly, if we recognize—not solve—this twofold Kantian difficulty we can find the necessary ground in Kant's 'moral religion' for questioning when the sacrificial rituals at the heart of Christian life, which are ritually repeated by Christian believers globally, take the form of a self-destructive act (of love).[45] For Kant, when a ritual practice is heteronomous, then the agent is not free. In other words, her or his unfree action is not premised on human autonomy as thinking, reasoning, and hoping for herself. Christ's sacrifice is incomprehensible to us as mere human beings, precisely because He is perfect both as human and as divine. No heteronomous act, or mere human practice of self-sacrificial love, could be fully rational or perfectly moral for Kant.

Nevertheless, Christ's self-sacrificial love is believed to both destroy and restore ethical ties. Kant himself could say that the epistemological part of the difficulty is that the human knower cannot comprehend the divine. For a non-divine man or woman, *what* would be *destroyed* in being forced to sacrifice their life for another, or in suffering passively and self-destructively for another, would seem to be autonomy, not as independence but as *self-activating and immanent love*.[46] So, in contrast to this human autonomy (of love), what sense can we make of Christ's sacrifice as both human and divine?[47] Can it be both immanent and transcendent? If Christ's transcendent love of humankind can only be recognized when women and men act autonomously (as they ought to do), then the present hermeneutics of principled autonomy should uncover, in order to transform, that human subject who exhibits a loss of confidence

---

[44] Kant, *Religion within the Boundaries of Mere Reason*, 107n (6:65).

[45] Anderson and Bell, *Kant and Theology*, 36, 85–87.

[46] Badiou, *In Praise of Love*, 64–67. I boldly appropriate Badiou's conception of self-activating and immanent love as compatible to O'Neill's principled autonomy insofar as this 'love' becomes a principle of autonomy, that all could follow.

[47] For an answer to this question, consider Fiddes, 'Sacrifice, Atonement, and Renewal', Chapter 4, in this volume.

in her own capacity to reason, in order to cultivate equally self- and other-regarding virtues. A Kantian moral agent does not seek to be transcendent, but to be autonomous, for instance, in what I support as self-activating and immanent love; and here 'love' is a significant principle that could be adopted and shared by all.[48] Each of us as only human does not have the power of a divine love; so, when we 'try to be divine' or 'remain in human sorrow', we run the danger of self-deception and of failure to recognize divinely shared love; and this point of misrecognition is the real (Kantian) danger of inappropriate confidence. Either under-confidence or over-confidence would both return women and men to the unjust relations of gender oppression and leave us in hopeless incomprehension of our religious and ethical selves. Even if we do not comprehend the divine, we have hope in enabling human autonomy and so, transforming self-destructive practices. Autonomous thinking as human thinking can still leave a place for divine initiative, in this case, for Christ's act of love.

Arguably, when taken too literally by human subjects, both the ritual act of sacrifice and the communal meal recalled in Christian Eucharistic practices could become a self-destructive love rather than a constructive love of self inasmuch as another. It would be 'self-destructive' in claiming either too much about ourselves, as if we were divine, or too little about ourselves, as if human love was heteronomous. Yet a Kantian hermeneutics of principled autonomy has helped us to question whether self-sacrificial love, especially if it is imposed onto one gendered grouping as determined by another more privileged gendered group is ethical and just. Injustice in sacrificing oneself is an especially acute problem for those (female/gay/lesbian/transgender) subjects who already live in conditions of gender oppression and given to self-destructive practices. In lacking self-respect, their vulnerability is intrinsically painful and personally damaging on an epistemic level. Can we ever know as human agents whether sacrifice is an autonomous act of love? Perhaps not, nonetheless, we can recognize heteronomy, while seeking autonomy.

Alain Badiou, for one, has no trouble answering 'no' to love 'on bended knees', that is, in submission to another; so, he rejects heteronomy. For Badiou, there can only be non-transcendent love, insisting that immanent love is what we have in this life.[49] This love—or, image of love not on bended knees—becomes the basis of non-passive, non-submissive, joyous, and just love. Is Badiou's conception of non-sacrificial love consistent with any other French philosopher's account of the self in the twentieth century? In *Oneself as Another*, Paul Ricoeur's hermeneutic of Kantian autonomy gives the ground for answering this question in the affirmative. The self and the other need not

---

[48] O'Neill, *Autonomy and Trust*, 85.
[49] Badiou, *In Praise of Love*, 66–67.

be in an asymmetrical relation, in which the self submits to another; nor need the self be split into two so that the sensuous self submits to the rational self.

Thus, unlike Hedley, Ricoeur rejects a Platonic reading of Kant's distinction between inclinations and duty, or sensible and intelligible.[50] Instead Ricoeur reads Kant as demonstrating that the malice of the human heart is more 'devious' than any sensuous nature; so, there is no point in sacrificing one's sensuous nature or the self's inclinations. Instead it is the devious disposition of the human heart which requires transformation in ethical acts of self- and other-regarding love.[51] I would maintain that neither Ricoeur nor any other Kantian (in contrast to a Platonist) philosopher advocates the sacrifice of one's sensible self, or sensuous nature; corruption is not in the blood, or in the human body, but in how a disposition is ethically cultivated and maintained.

## 5. THE SACRIFICIAL BASIS OF CHRISTIANITY: RELIGION DOMINATED BY THE FATHER?

In *The Virgin Mary, Monotheism and Sacrifice*, Cleo McNelly Kearns presents a magisterial account of the gendering of orthodox Christianity, focusing on the gender of monotheism and of sacrificial discourse in the bible and, especially, in Roman Catholicism. Kearns boldly asserts that the Father 'both instigates and often performs the act of sacrifice' in monotheism.[52] But she equally focuses on the role of blood in Christian forms of sacrifice: 'In all of its vulnerability and vitality, blood marks and symbolizes matters of humanity and divinity, gender, kinship, procreation, life, and death.'[53] So, blood is at the heart of sacrifice in monotheism, as much as it is at the heart of gender in the history of Christian theology. But as Kearns also asserts, 'the discourse of sacrifice... [is] widespread in human cultures,... with a particular bearing on constructions of gender, motherhood, and fatherhood in religious and social life.'[54]

Kearns takes much of her insight into the constructions of motherhood and fatherhood in religious life from her psycholinguistic understanding of (similar to Weir) Julia Kristeva, but also, from her own study of sacrifice, from Abraham's willingness to sacrifice his son Isaac to God's sacrifice of his Son.

---

[50] Ricoeur, *Oneself as Another*, 215n25 and 216n28; cf. Hedley, *Sacrifice Imagined*, 128–130.

[51] For more discussion of this interior, yet relational change to the human subject, see Fiddes, 'Sacrifice, Atonement, and Renewal', and Meszaros, 'Sacrifice and the Self', Chapters 4 and 5, respectively, in this volume.

[52] Kearns, *The Virgin Mary*, 36.

[53] Kearns, *The Virgin Mary*, 36.

[54] Kearns, *The Virgin Mary*, 23.

Motherhood in Kristeva's writings helps Kearns to tease out the gendering of fatherhood and the role of fathers in Old Testament and New Testament practices of ritual sacrifice. The ethical question concerning gender and the damaging side of sacrifice for female identity is raised in Kearn's study of the Virgin Mary as a paradigmatic figure of maternal self-giving.

The damage done to women by the ethical formation of traditional Roman Catholicism in emulation of Marian sacrifice focuses upon Mary's purity, but also Mary's suffering in complete acceptance of her passive role as the Virgin Mother in her son's conception, his birth, earthly life, suffering in death, and resurrection to eternal life. If Kant had a difficulty in comprehending Christ's innocent self-sacrifice as non-autonomous, feminists have an even more difficult problem in trying to comprehend the story of a heteronomous virgin-mother whose purity renders impossible any sense of freedom or responsibility: her life is one of submission to her predetermined role in life and in relation to God the Father.

Kearns offers some constructive background here, while Kristeva directs her (and us) to the damaging psycho-sexual problems suffered by those women who have been taught to be 'virtuous' like the Virgin Mary and to seek solace from Marian suffering, when they fail—necessarily!—to be virgin-mothers. But indirectly Marian sacrifice re-enforces the dominant roles of the Father and of the blood of the victim (the Son) in religious sacrifice. As Kearns argues:

> Mary is very much the exception that proves the rule. For when and where she is most present, she is so primarily if not solely the basis of an emphasis on her provision of the material body of the victim, her virgin motherhood, her maternal connection with the divine, and her freedom from the contaminations of the blood of fertility and childbirth in its regard.
>
> Thus, at the high church end of the spectrum of Eucharistic sacrifice Mary's is the body in which the victim of sacrifice was formed and through whom its effects may be distributed to the community. Hers is the presence that recalls the death of Christ in its full material reality, and hers is the image most often found close to what comes to be understood as the altar of sacrifice, the altar on which the elements of bread and wine blessed by Jesus become—though in what sense is widely debated in Christian theology—his body and his blood shed for many in remission of sins during the crucifixion. In this process, the miraculous conception of Mary's child and her witness to his life, death, and resurrection come to make her for many Christians—though not all—the pillar of orthodoxy and the patroness par excellence of a new ecclesiastical order extending through time.[55]

Kearns is not only a respected Christian theologian but, as implied already, an author of essays on French feminist theory.[56] A dominant focus in the latter

---

[55] Kearns, *The Virgin Mary*, 267.
[56] Kearns, 'Kristeva and Feminist Theory', 49–79; Kearns, *The Virgin Mary*, 42–45. Cf. Reineke, *Sacrificed Lives*.

is the suffering of women to whom the myths concerning the Virgin Mary—as the figure who is 'alone of all her sex'[57]—have given consolation; these are women unwittingly or not suffering gender oppression under patriarchy. Kristeva herself makes feminists readily aware that the orthodox Christian conception of Marian sacrifice does not tackle the problems of patriarchy, even if providing help to live within patriarchal constraints concerning gender, love, and sacrifice.

Consider Kristeva's female analysand who apparently has overcome anorexia. As Kristeva explains, this woman continues to struggle:

> ...she has replaced the old alimentary suicide with passionately erotic and 'killing' relations with men...[and she admits] 'When I say God, I think of an absolute suffering...an ineluctable sorrow, to the point that, in the end, you become persuaded that it's normal, and even that it's sweet.'[58]

Kristeva concludes that 'It is the jouissance of sacrifice, desired, and submitted to, that she [who is speaking above] calls "God".'[59] Needless to say, those particular sacrificial acts of 'love' in jouissance can hardly be distinguished from masochism or sadomasochism under the gender oppression of patriarchal relations.

## 6. TWENTY-FIRST-CENTURY ENLIGHTENMENT: NON-SACRIFICIAL LOVE AND AUTONOMY

In this penultimate section, I would like to propose a new Enlightenment story—or 'fable'—about the ethical development of a young person. This fable derives from Michèle Le Doeuff's own account of the ethical formation of autonomous and attentive reasoning in a young girl named Dawn.[60] This fable is offered as an alternative to the myth and cult of the Virgin Mary who accepts her sacrificial role, suffers, and consoles without any apparent reasoning of her own.

In her 2006 Weidenfeld Lectures, 'The Spirit of Secularism: On Fables, Gender and Ethics', Le Doeuff demonstrates the ethical significance of a highly distinctive fable of non-sacrificial love for twenty-first-century men and women.[61] Essentially, the ethical lesson of this fable is: in order to gain

---

[57] Kristeva, 'Stabat Mater', 160–186; cf. Warner, *Alone of All of her Sex*.
[58] Kristeva and Clément, *The Feminine and the Sacred*, 23. For additional discussions of love, suffering, and psychoanalysis, see Kristeva, 'Freud and Love' and 'Exterrestrials Suffering', 40–48, 53 and 372–383, respectively. Cf. Anderson, 'Liberating Love's Capabilities', 201–226.
[59] Kristeva and Clément, *The Feminine and the Sacred*, 24.
[60] For my early discussion of this, see Anderson, 'Liberating Love's Capabilities', 201–226.
[61] Le Doeuff, 'The Spirit of Secularism'.

wisdom reciprocally we need to take care not to force 'a girl' to grow up to be a goddess of maternal love with sacrificial and tragic relations to men, to other women, to gods, and goddesses.[62] In reinvigorating a fabulous narrative about ethical and intellectual development, Le Doeuff lends herself to the recreation of an enlightening message about a young girl whose vulnerability needs to be protected, in order for her heart, which is reason, to enlighten (autonomous loving relations), and not to be darkened by oppressive relations. Cultivation of reason in her relations to others is meant to protect Dawn from self-abuse and other-abuse. It is crucial that Dawn's open, rational nature is also allowed to provoke qualities, or virtuous dispositions, of tenderness, attentiveness, and wise generosity in those who love her.[63]

Le Doeuff herself discovers the main characteristics of this female figure from her reading of another woman writer: Maria Zambrano.[64] Zambrano creates a style of poetic reasoning in which the symbolic—as in the figure of Dawn—has a philosophically significant role to play in human understanding. Le Doeuff picks up crucial elements of this poetic style for the philosophical imaginary,[65] challenging traditional imagery about young girls, love, reason, mature women, motherhood, and divinity. In retelling Dawn's story, Le Doeuff appropriates Zambrano's poetic reasoning about a girl whose heart is reason, in order to create an ethical fable of hope for non-patriarchal men and women today. The heart becomes a symbol for a fresh understanding of a human soul and of human love. If we extrapolate a bit more, then this philosophical imaginary about a young girl's heart begins to personify a liberated love, and not the bonded love of a deified female, whether a goddess of suffering love or of motherhood in submission. Le Doeuff insists that Dawn should not be forced to become divine.

My own contention is that Le Doeuff's retelling of the narrative about Dawn offers us the elements for enacting a new Enlightenment which would be free of gender oppression and of self-destructive forms of sacrifice, at least, for ethics and secular life. Of course, other fables about ethical and intellectual

---

[62] Le Doeuff, 'The Spirit of Secularism', Lecture 4, 'Not a goddess, she!'
[63] This reference to 'the heart' is different from either mind or body, male or female, encompassing aspects of both sides; it is not exactly the soul either; yet it is clearly significant in creating the distinctive identity of the young girl prior to her adolescence at which time her self-identity becomes challenged by her changing body, her sexuality, her female beauty, her sexually specific pleasure; the goal is a joy which will be more than sexual: perhaps, something like the intellectual joy found in Spinoza's intellectual love of God. In this light, the heart is a fundamental and encompassing term for what needs to be protected, and not sacrificed to a patriarachal stereotype, in the young girl as she grows up, generating the wisdom of love. For a crucial backdrop to Le Doeuff's thinking on *le coeur*, see Zambrano, *Les clairières du bois*, 65–80.
[64] Le Doeuff discovers a story about Dawn who remains human, unlike the goddess 'Dawn' of classical literature, in Zambrano, *De l'aurore*.
[65] Le Doeuff, *The Philosophical Imaginary*, 2–7, 124–128.

development could be discovered and, equally, could help to ameliorate the pernicious practices of gender oppression in religious ethics.

Perhaps an obvious alternative would be Luce Irigaray's appropriation of both Greek mythology and the Christian myth of the Virgin Mary, in order to portray how women and men can become divine and so fulfil their gender ideal.[66] However, in the context of my hermeneutics of autonomy, an internal critique of patriarchal religions of sacrificial love would reveal the possibility of reinventing gender relations and so love, in ways similar to Dawn's ethical formation, but not to the Virgin Mary's cult of submission and self-sacrifice.

Imagine Dawn as a fabulous figure for an ethics of non-sacrificial love. Each dawn begins anew, offering hope for each woman and each man to be attentive and tender to one another. To learn to love a young girl would involve those persons closely related to her, practicing tenderness and firm thinking, not unthinking force. So, it is not only Dawn who develops ethically, but those others who are near to her equally learn to love insofar as they allow her to flourish; they become more tender and loving in mutually constructive relations. A revised ethics is implicit in this new Enlightenment fable whereby a young girl holds out a promise for practical wisdom, while women and men create ethical dispositions (e.g. being tender yet firm in thinking and acting) in being drawn to the vulnerability of Dawn.

Le Doeuff's figure of Dawn is unlike other well-known philosophical figures of wisdom; for instance, the owl of Minerva takes flight at night creating a story about dusk. Instead, the dawning of a new day is the starting point for the alternative fable, which arguably comes after 'the dark': whether the still dominant nocturnal imagery refers to the era of medieval or of post-modern darkness, Dawn in contrast brings light to certain unfathomable difficulties, especially to the sexual violence and living death which have enslaved women through the era of darkness.

If additional, provocative imagery was needed, the title of the fourth of Le Doeuff's Weidenfeld Lectures is 'Not a goddess, she!' Or, we might rephrase this, and say, 'not a Virgin Mary, she!' If Dawn grows up without having imposed on her humanly impossible, patriarchal gender roles of self-destructive sacrifice which enshrine a goddess in bonded love and stereotypical beauty (ethereal beauty can also be sexist) then her own reasoning will enable non-oppressive practices of love and goodness; the fable suggests that these will shine upon humanity and its relations of autonomy and attentiveness. This fable—similar to what we have found in Weir's *Sacrificial Logics*—implies that a woman's oppression is shaped by an ethical development whereby the myths of patriarchy gradually enslave the relations of men and women to certain gender norms. Yet liberation can be achieved if the young girl retains and deepens an

---

[66] Irigaray, 'Divine Women', 57–72; cf. Anderson, 'Transcendence', 27–54.

adolescent heart which has been treated tenderly; reason is allowed to develop freely. Rather than sacrificial love the fable portrays an open, inclusive love. In turn, this love is wisely protected by the heart which, as Le Doeuff tells us, *is* reason.

## 7. CONCLUSION

In the present chapter I have endeavoured to expose some of the psychological, ethical, and political dangers for women in religious rituals and acts of sacrifice. The fundamental problem is that gender oppression can re-enforce painful burdens of attending to the suffering of others, when the woman who attends to the pain of others is already suffering under domination. Under oppressive conditions, religious practices requiring asymmetrical acts of sacrificing/non-sacrificing love (especially for women and other sacrificing subjects who are socially constructed as an inferior gender) merely make a bad situation worse. I have argued for enabling subjects to discover their own capacity to reason about love in relations to one another. Yet this requires enlightenment concerning how we can transform one another in an ethics of non-sacrificial love.

This chapter has questioned how it is that sacrifice in contemporary moral theology remains a self-destructive form of love, at least for patriarchal gender constructions. I have explicitly employed a hermeneutics of autonomy, and implicitly a hermeneutics of suspicion in an immanent critique of heteronomous practices of sacrifice, in order to re-vision forms of gendered confidence. If ethical, this confidence would not conceal either an overly self-confident subject or a subject completely lacking in appropriate self-confidence. Instead, addressing sacrificial practices from a standpoint of gendered confidence is necessary in order to transform the masochism and the sadomasochism damaging religious practices: the new vision is to equalize relations between human subjects, exposing how it is that God as male (i.e. Father) has meant male is divine and so, superior to female and other non-Fathers who face ineluctable sorrow.

To recall the words of Kristeva's analysand, we again capture the self-destructive nature of patriarchal forms of sacrificial love and human–divine relations: 'When I say God, I think of an absolute suffering...an ineluctable sorrow, to the point that, in the end, you become persuaded that it's normal, and even that it's sweet.'[67] The problem with this distortion of human–divine love relations to the point where 'ineluctable sorrow' becomes 'normal' and

---

[67]  Kristeva/Clément, *The Feminine and the Sacred*, 23.

'sweet' is the loss of confidence in one's own capacity to distinguish between a good, flourishing life and the bad, destructive forms of self-harm. This self-harming indicates an acceptance of violent forms of self-sacrificial 'love'. This so-called love exhibits a complete failure of the loving subject to reason auton-omously; and this is the reason (some) feminists still think that autonomy matters!

# 4

## Sacrifice, Atonement, and Renewal

### *Intersections between Girard, Kristeva, and Balthasar*

#### Paul S. Fiddes

### 1. INTRODUCTION

Is the image of sacrifice of any use in our late-modern world? I mean, is it use-ful for understanding the dynamics of society, the growth of the person at a psychological level, and the redemptive work of God in the world? Even more to the point of this chapter, is it of use in opening the way to a *renewal* of life in individual and society? Can the image of sacrifice be of any help in the making of peace in a divided society and a broken personality? Doubt has been cast on whether sacrifice has any power of renewal from two directions. First, those who follow René Girard in finding sacrifice at the very foundation of human society think that the concept of violent sacrifice certainly helps us to *under-stand* the nature of social life, but that it offers no clues to the *transformation* of that life. Sacrificial mechanisms in society need to be exposed, deconstructed, and then rejected if we are to become disciples of a non-violent Christ. Second, feminist thinkers suspect that talk of sacrifice, and especially the virtue of self-sacrifice, is 'one of the most resistant forces in the west to the alleviation of...oppression.'[1] Women are always being asked to sacrifice themselves, and such an appeal only results in the powerful taking over the powerless.

In this chapter, I intend, then, to bring together two thinkers who have deep problems with the concept of sacrifice from these two angles, René Girard him-self and Julia Kristeva. With these two I want to connect a Christian theologian, Hans Urs von Balthasar, who finds a sacrificial death of Christ to be essential for God's renewal of human life. These three persons—an anthropologist, a psycho-analytical philosopher, and a theologian—have not just been arbitrarily thrown together. Balthasar enters into deliberate debate with Girard. Although Kristeva's

---

[1] Anderson, 'Weakness', 112. See further her chapter in this volume ('Sacrifice as Self-destructive "Love"').

direct references to Girard are occasional, she shares her basic argument with him: that the symbols of language and culture are shaped by sacrifice.[2] Further, at one highly significant point Kristeva finds Balthasar's theology of atonement illuminating for her analysis of the human psyche, despite the fact that feminist theologians are usually strongly opposed to the sexual stereotyping they find in Balthasar and are likely to set Kristeva up against him.[3]

By exploring some intersections between these three thinkers on the theme of sacrifice, and through a particular focus on the work of Kristeva, I hope to develop a certain idea of sacrifice that might have the power not only of explanation but renewal.

## 2. THE FOUNDATIONAL SACRIFICE

Beginning our exploration with Girard and Kristeva, we find them agreeing that sacrifice is foundational to society, though they differ on the nature of the sacrifice. For Girard, the basic drive in human affairs is desire. This desire is mimetic; in our desiring we imitate others as followers of their model. We learn from each other what to desire, and we desire what others desire.[4] Because there are never enough goods to possess, this mimetic desire leads to social instability and conflict, and we cope with the ensuing crisis by identifying a scapegoat. An individual or group is made the focus of guilt, deemed to be at fault for disorder or damage in society, and killing the victim releases tension and restores harmony. The persecution of Jews in the Middle Ages and the Witch Trials of Puritan America are manifestations of an underlying scapegoat pattern which is expressed in archaic myths such as that of Oedipus. As Girard stresses, society is thereby stabilized and restored, but it is not renewed or transformed. The community is enabled to survive only for a time until the tendency towards conflict reasserts itself and the need for sacrificing a victim re-emerges. There is an important implication here too for the symbolic system of culture. In the process of mimesis social differentiation is lost since people conform to a sameness of desire and are plunged into chaos, all distinctions gone; the sacrifice restores otherness between people and establishes culture. Meaning and language itself is thus dependent on violence done to a victim.

Now, Kristeva is in agreement with the basic dynamics of this social analysis, but with one huge difference. With other feminists such as Luce Irigaray,

---

[2] Both Girard and Kristeva are dependent here on Freud's study *Totem and Taboo* for the links between language, violence, and the sacred. This is well demonstrated by Reinecke, 'Mother in Mimesis', 67–82.

[3] E.g. Beattie, *Catholic Feminism*, 208–229.

[4] Girard, *Violence*, 81–108; Girard, *Things Hidden*, 326–351.

she insists that the founding sacrifice is matricidal.[5] The primordial victim is the mother, and all women with her. Women can be victims without being literally killed: they have often been the goods that men desire, and they have been disposed of within a patriarchal contract so that they 'live the sacrifice'.[6] Kristeva thus criticizes Girard for refusing to see any sexual differentiation in the act of sacrifice.[7] Tina Beattie further suggests that it is hardly an accident that women have generally refused to collaborate with the victimization of scapegoats throughout history, since they themselves are pushed to the margins of society and their oppression is built into a social contract which favours men.[8]

Kristeva identifies two dimensions of the sacrifice inflicted on women, social and psychological. In social life, the bodies of women have been subjected to a symbolic system which is male-dominated. Women have been seen as the biological life-givers, men as the meaning-givers. The system of moral law has been inscribed, or 'cut into' the human body, and especially into the female body.

> The prohibition 'cuts': *bereshit* is the first word of the Bible. All religions, using the trenchant effects of language...celebrate the sacred as a sacrifice...this sacrifice is the one that inscribes language in the body, meaning in life. And it does so through a prohibition that does not need to kill to cut, but confines itself to setting out a moral system.[9]

Women are particularly subject to this sacrifice, writes Kristeva. The *jouissance*, the extreme pleasure of a woman's reproductive body is imprisoned within a word, an image, a statue, in a cultural system that reflects the 'law of the father'. This imposed sacrifice is evident in the abhorrence shown to the maternal body and the physical processes associated with it; the mother is, in Kristeva's terms, 'abjected', excluded as impure.[10]

This social exclusion and separation reflects, however, an even more foundational sacrifice of the mother, which Kristeva explores within the psyche. In the development of human subjectivity the child must break from the mother: to attain a child's own sense of self-identity the mother must be abjected, sacrificed, violently rejected. Moreover, this point of separation is also the boundary which the growing subject has to pass over to reach the realm of language and meaning, where subject is separated from object.[11] According to Kristeva, a person moves from deep, precognitive immersion in the life of the body to a

---

[5] For this critique of Girard, see: Irigaray, *Ethics of Sexual Difference*, 75ff. Cf. Kristeva, *Powers of Horror*, 56–75.

[6] Kristeva, 'Women's Time', 199.

[7] See Kristeva's critique in her *Revolution in Poetic Language*, 250, n. 100.

[8] Beattie, *New Catholic Feminism*, 210–211.

[9] Kristeva/Clément, *Feminine and the Sacred*, 15.

[10] Kristeva, *Powers of Horror*, 1–15, 99–103.

[11] E.g. Kristeva, *Powers of Horror*, 5–6; Kristeva, *Black Sun*, 9–30.

social life which is shaped by the symbols of language, and these—as we have already seen—privilege the male and patriarchy.

There is no time here to explore Kristeva's debt here to Freud and his version of the Oedipal triangle, nor to clarify her *differences* from Freud in her focus on the abjection of the mother rather than patricide. Nor can we do more than register in passing Kristeva's debt to Jacques Lacan and his idea of the symbolic realm as 'the law of the father'. Our concern here is simply to make clear that for Kristeva the sacrifice of women in society echoes the primal sacrifice of the mother in the development of human subjectivity. These are violent acts, though they need not involve literal murder. As Kristeva makes clear in her study of the laws of impurity in the Book of Leviticus, ritual killing has been replaced in the Hebrew-Christian tradition by an act of *separation* which is nevertheless the doing of violence to the body.[12]

## 3. TYPES OF SACRIFICE

I have sketched—all too briefly—the basic thought of Girard and Kristeva on the foundational sacrifice in order to underline the way they are using the term 'sacrifice'. In this modern debate, sacrifice is violence done to a victim in order to establish order in society and meaning in the realm of language. In other words, it is the syndrome of the scapegoat (although, as we shall see, Kristeva also re-imagines sacrifice in order to *overcome* the human propensity for scapegoating).

Here we must register an oddity, as we consider the way that the New Testament employs the language of sacrifice for God's atoning act in Christ, a usage which itself reflects the portrayal of sacrifice in the Hebrew Bible. The Book of Leviticus contains instructions for the ritual of the scapegoat, literally a goat on which the sins of the people are ritually laid and which is then driven out into the wilderness to die of thirst and starvation (Lev. 16:8–10). This might well be seen as symbolizing the way that human beings are 'scapegoated' by society. But the scapegoat ritual in Hebrew religion is not classified as a sacrifice, since it is not offered to God. It is offered, says the text, 'for Azazel', which either means a 'precipice' in the desert over which the goat may finally fall, or a desert demon which will destroy it.[13] In accordance with this distinction between scapegoat and sacrifice, the death of Christ in the New Testament is understood with the help of the image of sacrifice in the ancient Hebrew temple, but there is no reference to the image of the scapegoat. The first time that this typology is used appears to be in the later Epistle of Barnabas.[14]

---

[12] Kristeva, *Powers of Horror*, 90–112.
[13] Vaux, *Ancient Israel*, 509.
[14] *Epistle of Barnabas*, 7:6–11. Cf. Justin Martyr, *Dialogue with Trypho*, 40.

In making this point I am not making a historical quibble. There is no reason why the term 'sacrifice' should *not* be applied by an anthropologist to the scapegoat ritual, whether it involves human or surrogate animal killing. The scapegoat syndrome may also, for a Christian theologian, be illuminating for understanding the death of Christ, as Frances Young has shown.[15] I am simply observing that we should not confuse one meaning of sacrifice with another, and that the meaning of sacrifice cannot be exhausted by the modern popularity of the scapegoat concept. There may be richer resources in the image of sacrifice than this, and more possibility of linking sacrifice with renewal if we explore other dimensions. This, we shall see later, is exactly what Kristeva does herself in her account of a healthy growth of the human personality.

It would be well to remind ourselves, then, of three types (or dimensions) of sacrifice we find in the Hebrew Bible.[16] First, there is the gift-offering, in which something precious is offered to God as a sign of thanksgiving. Second, there is a communion-offering in which sacrificers and their God share in a common fellowship meal. Third, there is the 'sin-offering' (making atonement) which is intended to deal with the problem of the sin that lies upon the community because of lack of obedient love to God and because of the presence of injustice in society. Sin is making the community unclean or impure, and it has to be removed or 'expiated', that is 'wiped out'.[17] In Hebrew ritual the 'sin-offering' is not understood as propitiating or appeasing God, but as something that God *does*, using the act of sacrifice to expiate the sins of individuals and the community.[18] This is why the predominant metaphor in the New Testament Book of Hebrews, which envisages the death of Christ as a sacrifice, is that of cleansing (e.g. Heb. 10:19–22). The Hebrew law codes of the Torah offer no rational explanation as to how the sin-offering works, but there may well be a clue in the declaration attributed to God by priestly theologians in Leviticus 17:11: 'the life of the flesh is in the blood; and I have given it for you ... to make atonement for your souls.' This may mean that the life which is in the blood is poured out to disinfect a contaminated community, and to renew old life with new energy. The scapegoat ritual fits into this world-view, not as a sacrifice, but as another way of dealing with sin. Instead of being cleansed away by God through the sacrifice, it was expelled from the community on the back of the goat.

[15]  Young, *Sacrifice and the Death of Christ*, 106–111, 125–130.
[16]  This classification was popularized by Gray, *Sacrifice*, 14–21. Gerhard von Rad rightly cautions that the three dimensions interweave: Rad, *Old Testament Theology*, I, 255.
[17]  The Hebrew word for atone, *kipper*, translated *hilaskesthai* in the Septuagint perhaps means something like to 'cover over', but its meaning has to be deduced from its use.
[18]  So Rad, *Old Testament Theology*, I, 262–272.

The image of the atoning sacrifice was attractive to the early Christian community as a metaphor for the death of Christ, while at the very same time claiming that this was the 'final sacrifice'.[19] All three meanings of sacrifice from the Hebrew scriptures—gift, communion, and sin-offering—were used to interpret the crucifixion of Christ which at first seemed disastrous and baffling to his followers.[20] Expiation especially seemed an apt image for the experience of having life cleansed and sin wiped away in some mysterious way by this death. As the tradition of the church developed, cultural factors made the idea of propitiation, or appeasing the righteous anger of God, more attractive as a tool of communication of the gospel, but I agree with those who find the theory unworthy of the character of God as love, and an infringement of the freedom of God in subjecting divine mercy to some eternal principle such as law; even more to our present concerns, it is largely useless for understanding the possibilities of human renewal.

We should note in this connection that when Girard identifies a God-ward side to the primitive scapegoat ritual, which may not be overt, it is that of propitiation, which (as we have seen) does not actually belong to the rite in the Hebrew scriptures. Girard claims that God is understood to sanction the murder of the scapegoat, being even more offended by the supposed crime of the victim than society. In this world-view, a violent God is appeased by an act of violence,[21] and it is not surprising that Girard protests that the mechanism of sacrifice needs to be exposed for the lie that it is.


## 4. THE CRITIQUE OF SACRIFICE

In Girard's account of sacrifice, while the scapegoat is innocent, it is misrepresented by the persecutors as being guilty. Social memory perpetuates the lie that the scapegoat was unclean and responsible for the disorder of society. Mythology is thus created from the viewpoint of the powerful.[22] In a second stage of Girard's thought, he becomes convinced that it is possible to break free from this cycle of violence, *if* the story of the scapegoat is told from the viewpoint of the victims. The myth of redemptive violence is exposed when the innocence of the victim is disclosed, and this is what Girard finds happening in the Bible, first gradually in the Old Testament through such stories as

---

[19] E.g. Hebrews 10:11–14. See Zachhuber, 'Modern Discourse on Sacrifice and its Theological Background', Chapter 2, in this volume, for the ambiguity about sacrifice this situation created.

[20] The three dimensions are intertwined: see Matt. 26:27–28; Mark 10:45; Luke 22:19–20; John 1:29; Rom. 3:25; 1 Cor. 11:25; 1 Cor. 15:3; Heb. 2:17; Heb. 10:5–10; 1 John 4:10; 1 Pet. 1:18–19, cf. Rom. 12:1, Heb. 13:15. Further, see Fiddes, *Past Event and Present Salvation*, 61–82.

[21] Girard, *Violence*, 274–275, 279–280.

[22] Girard, *Scapegoat*, 76–99.

Abraham and Isaac and the Servant of Isaiah 53, and then fully in the Gospel story of the Passion of Jesus.[23] The Gospels are not myths because they do not function as a myth, to reinforce the guilt of the scapegoat or suppress collective murder. As we read the story we see ourselves as the persecutors and are liberated from the power of the myth of sacred violence. Human life can be transformed by the disclosure of the truth, and then the vicious circle of mimesis, sacrifice, and violence can be overcome by the making of a counter-culture which is revealed in the story of Jesus. The mimesis of desire can be replaced by a mimesis of Jesus and his way, which is the kingdom of God. Girard writes, 'A non-violent deity can only signal his existence to mankind by having himself driven out by violence—by demonstrating that he cannot establish himself in the Kingdom of Violence.'[24]

In Christ's example of suffering love, meeting violence with forgiveness, Girard sees the invitation to a new kind of discipleship, based on the mimesis of Christ who has no acquisitive desire. In his thought up to 1994, Girard thus maintains that the earliest Christian reflection on Jesus was devoid of ideas of sacrifice; in the Book of Hebrews, he thinks, we have a relapse back into sacrificial culture and the establishing of institutions through violence. The death of Jesus is not a sacrifice, he insists, in two senses. First, God does not require or want it for either propitiation or expiation. Second, the result of the death of Christ is not the restoration of society by means of the victim's death, as in the usual cycle of sacrifice. Instead, the whole system of symbols in human culture is threatened, and there will be a crisis of apocalyptic proportions and total chaos unless society turns to another model for imitation, that of the non-violent kingdom of God. There is the promise of renewal, but not of a mere restoring of balance, and renewal will not come through sacrifice.

Here, there enters on the scene our third conversation-partner, Hans Urs von Balthasar, who registers the strongest objection to Girard, while recognizing the ambitious 'dramatic nature' of his project. He writes:

> What takes place on the Cross, according to this theory, if…the power-less Father-God demands nothing in the nature of an 'atoning sacrifice'? To put it more concretely: the Church regards the Eucharistic celebration as a representation of the 'sacrifice of the cross' in which Christ has effectively offered himself for mankind: how then can she present and offer Christ's self-surrender to the divine Father if the latter…has 'no pleasure' in it, since he did not *want* the Cross, and even less *commanded* his Son to accept it?[25]

---

[23] Girard, *Things Hidden*, esp. 180–187; cf. Girard, *Scapegoat*, 100–124; Girard, 'Mimesis and Violence', 18–19.

[24] Girard, *Things Hidden*, 219; cf. 182, 430.

[25] Balthasar, *Theo-Drama*, IV, 309–310.

Critics of Balthasar have been suspicious of his apparent solicitude for the 'power' of God, and suspect him of wanting precisely the kind of violent God whom Girard is exposing. Balthasar is, however, wanting to situate the cross in the eternal drama of self-giving within the Trinity, rather than seeing it as a totally contingent and even accidental event of human activity in which God the Father has no involvement. Here, as we shall see, he has an unexpected ally in Kristeva; she thinks that the story of the Passion of Christ will lack its psychological effect on the human personality if there is no notion of the cross as a gift of God's love. But more of that later.

Presenting his own understanding of the sacrifice of Christ, Balthasar highlights the element of exchange in atonement. Christ changes places with sinners, and this is both an identification and a substitution. He carries the sins of the world which are loaded on to him not just in a psychological transfer by human beings, as in Girard's portrayal,[26] but also by God; and God is satisfied by venting his wrath or his righteous anger upon these sins. 'God's anger strikes him instead of the countless sinners, shattering him as by lightning', reflects Balthasar.[27] It is vicarious suffering, in that Christ experiences the effects of human sin, including the response of God towards sin—that is, he experiences utter alienation and forsakenness, the very darkest point of human existence. Balthasar stresses that it is not strictly accurate to say that Christ is being 'punished' instead of others.[28] Since Christ identifies with human sin he experiences the judgement of God *on* human sin, but he is not himself being objectively punished. Here he stands with Karl Barth who understands Christ as bearing the impact of God's 'no' against sinful human life, a 'no' which follows as a simple consequence from the human 'no' against God.[29] Barth, however, stresses that the point of this plunging into the dark night of forsakenness from the Father is to *expiate* sin, to take sin into the darkness of death and nothingness and kill it there. Atonement is expiation. Balthasar, by contrast, wants to hold on to some notion of atonement as appeasing God's anger, and this makes it very difficult to distinguish his understanding of vicarious suffering from punishment. The problem of sin is dealt with, not by expiating it (wiping it out), but by 'separating the sinner from his sin' and then 'diverting' or 'deflecting' the anger of God away from sinners towards Christ who bears the sin. While Balthasar does not explicitly use the word 'appease', he does speak of Christ thus 'pacifying' the anger of God. Balthasar writes, 'God's anger at the rejection of divine love encounters a divine love (the Son's) that exposes itself to this anger, disarms it, and literally deprives it of its object.'[30]

---

[26] Balthasar, *Theo-Drama*, IV, 311–312, 317.
[27] Balthasar, *Theo-Drama*, IV, 348.
[28] Balthasar, *Theo-Drama*, IV, 297.
[29] Balthasar, *Theo-Drama*, IV, 346. See Barth, *Church Dogmatics*, IV, Part 1, 253.
[30] Balthasar, *Theo-Drama*, IV, 349.

In this complex account, there are elements that we shall need to retain if we are to conceive how the sacrifice of Christ might renew the world. With Kristeva, as we shall see, I suggest that there is an element of separation and forsakenness in the story that cannot be lost. But with Balthasar's implication of appeasement, we seem to be on the territory of the scapegoat and trapped in a world-view from which Girard wants to liberate us.

In Girard's later thought, expressed in an essay of 1995 and (it seems) as a result of conversation with Raymund Schwager, he modifies his view on whether and how the death of Christ is a sacrifice. He had already admitted that the death of Christ could be called a sacrifice in the general sense of a self-surrender which was of benefit to others,[31] and now he suggests that there is actually a continuity between this and earlier views of sacrifice. Christianity has a positive view of self-sacrifice which transforms the pagan idea of sacrifice (scapegoating). Moreover, Jesus' self-giving in the cross is a divine recapitulation of the scapegoat ritual, in order to subvert it: God recapitulates the ritual, to expose it for what it is.[32] God is thus involved in the deconstruction of pagan sacrifice through the cross: God is involved purposefully in exposing it, rather than the exposure being a matter of sheer human contingency. Though Balthasar's account of Girard is too early to comment on this movement in his thought, we may notice that Girard still says nothing of the involvement of God in terms of a mutual self-giving between Father and Son, or a separation in God such as we find in Balthasar himself. There is a continuity of sacrifice, but it is continuity with an unsatisfactory view of sacrifice.

Turning now to Kristeva, we find that she too has a critique of the sacrificial mechanism in society and psyche. Her psychoanalytical account means that she has to retain *some* idea of sacrifice in human development: unless the mother is abjected there can be no entry for the child into the realm of language. However, she works hard to make the separation from the mother less violent, and more a matter of mutual love. She has three basic strategies for doing this, one to do with the image of the mother, one to do with the image of the father, and a third which reformulates sacrifice.

First she develops a maternal discourse which she sees as capable of disturbing the patriarchal realm of symbols, so reducing the violence done by language on the body. Woman's body is resistant to the cutting into it of the word. 'The vaginal body, that dwelling place of the species, imposes on woman an experience of...interior reality that does not allow itself to be easily sacrificed by the prohibition.'[33] A primary maternal body cannot be entirely suppressed,

[31]  Girard/Adams, 'Violence, Difference, Sacrifice', 29–30.

[32]  Girard, 'Mimetische Theorie und Theologie', 20–28. There is only a hint of this idea, however, in Girard's later book, *I See Satan Fall Like Lightning*: 'God voluntarily assumes the role of the single victim and makes possible...the full disclosure of the single victim mechanism (p. 130)', cf. 151.

[33]  Kristeva/Clément, *Feminine and the Sacred*, 16.

and this is the source of an aspect of the linguistic realm that Kristeva calls the 'semiotic'. As distinct from the symbolic the semiotic is prediscursive, expressing an original libidinal multiplicity over against the monolithic tendencies of culture; it has the capacity to irritate and subvert the symbolic. There are sanctioned forms of disturbance within patriarchal society in which the semiotic finds expression and in which the maternal body is recovered: these are the experience of childbirth, and the use of poetry. Poetic language relies upon multiple meanings and so challenges the law of unity. For Kristeva there is something 'in play' beyond or outside rational discourse, something which goes 'beyond the theatre of linguistic representations.'[34] Where the semiotic breaks into the symbolic there is a resurgence of infantile drives arising from the *jouissance* of the subconscious. This moment of extreme, disruptive pleasure includes sexual pleasure, but can also be experienced through art and literature.

Kristeva suggests that the language of poetry recovers the maternal body, a field of impulse full of diversity unlike the monolithic realm of patriarchal culture. Poetic speech is characterized by rhythm, sound play, and repetition, movements which reflect primal movements of love and energy. Here Kristeva envisages the semiotic as flowing from a realm that she denotes as the 'chora', taking the concept from Plato's *Timaeus* where it refers to an unnameable space which exists between Being and Becoming. She develops the concept of *chora* as a womb-like, nurturing space of origin, as the pre-linguistic receptacle of subconscious drives and archetypal relations with the mother *and* the father. The *chora*, she writes, 'precedes and underlies figuration and...is analogous only to vocal or kinetic rhythm.' Poetry, in its rhythms of sound and idea, reflects the *chora* which is a place 'constituted by movements.'[35]

There is something else also to which the maternal body alerts us. Kristeva points out that in the experience of motherhood there is a splitting and dividing of the subject which need not involve conflict and repression. In pregnancy and birth there is a separation of one person from another which leads to love.[36] Changes in relationship between mother and child show subjectivity as a relational process in which violence is not inevitable, though it involves the mother in pain at every stage. This in turn, beyond motherhood, makes us aware that there can be many other differences within a person and between persons (including sexual difference) which need not be a matter of external conflict.[37]

However, for all this, the question persists as to whether, in her psychoanalytic account, culture and its symbolism is always going to dominate over the rather shadowy 'maternal body'. In this perspective, in order for the subject

---

[34] Kristeva, *In the Beginning was Love*, 5.
[35] Kristeva, *Revolution in Poetic Language*, 25–26.
[36] Kristeva, 'Women's Time', 206.
[37] Kristeva, 'Women's Time', 210.

to grow up and become aware of its own identity it *has* to enter the realm of the law of the Father. The journey of the self into subjectivity is thus marked by determinism. Childbirth and poetry can offer moments of subversion, but must they be only temporary and finally futile disruptions? Other feminists, like Judith Butler, have thus levelled the accusation against Kristeva that her account can never escape violence and can never renew society.[38] She needs to have some means for subverting the symbolic from within or she will end in sheer despair.

So we move to a second strategy, which concerns the area of dawning consciousness that she calls 'the imaginary'. On the very boundary between the body and language, on the verge of separating from the mother, the self imagines an image of a *father*, a father who belongs to the earliest, pre-linguistic life of the individual.[39] Yes, this is indeed the pre-oedipal 'father of pre-history' in Freud's theorizing, and so supposedly not yet a gendered figure, but the key move that Kristeva makes is to privilege *this* kind of 'father' over the definitely male father who appears subsequently in Freud's famous oedipal triangle. According to Freud, at the oedipal stage the child desires what the father desires sexually, the mother. The result is conflict, in which the growing child wants to kill the father and have an incestuous relation with the mother. Girard takes a similar line, but stresses more than Freud that the image of the father is a 'model of mimetic desire'; the child wants to model himself on the father, to *copy* the desire of the father, and so inevitably comes up against a prohibition— 'thou shalt not'. Mimesis or imitation thus leads to rivalry and violence. Girard identifies this mimetic desire first of all in the psyche, and then sees it playing itself out externally in society, as we have seen. He writes that in this growth of consciousness 'the link between desire and violence has been forged and in all likelihood will never be broken'.[40] Imitation leads to conflicts over what people desire, and comes to a climax socially in the killing of the scapegoat.

Kristeva takes a different direction in her psychoanalytic analysis. In her later writing she finds that the desire of the imaginary father is not the root of violence; this father is not a figure of conflict but of relational love.[41] The father is a third person, an external figure, an Other in this intimate relation between the child and the mother. The imaginary father awakens the subject to the love that comes with difference. As the child faces the emptiness at the heart of desire that it envisages will come with separation from the mother, it discovers that it can welcome the other and the other opens itself with welcoming love. There is a love that points to the presence of another. As Martha Reineke puts it in her comparative study of Kristeva and Girard: 'In this love story, at

38  Butler, *Gender Trouble*, 93.
39  Kristeva, *Black Sun*, 134–135, 207; Kristeva, *Tales of Love*, 26–31.
40  Girard, 'Freud', 233.
41  Kristeva, *Tales of Love*, 23–30, 42–50.

the very splitting that establishes the psyche, the subject uncovers an open space and is supported in being between the One and Another. Because love promises that for the One there is Another, love promises being in difference.'[42]

Reineke goes on to say: 'In theological terms [love] promises God', but we must not get to this point too quickly in our own exploration. The point is that at the very moment of rupture, the violence of abjection and separation is lessened by a promise of communion. The story of the making of subjectivity is a tale of love. Every difference experienced by the subject originates here, in this imaginative area of the psyche, including sexual difference. Differences do not begin in the symbolic sphere, and so they need not be associated with the oppression of the body.

From here we move on to a third strategy of Kristeva, which is her re-imagining of sacrifice.

## 5. RE-IMAGINING SACRIFICE

So far, by linking the term 'sacrifice' with the oppression of the body and abjection of the mother, Kristeva has been using it in essentially the same way as Girard does in his anthropological account: violence is inflicted against another to establish order in society and meaning in language. Kristeva differs from Girard in finding this sacrifice imposed on women in particular, though not exclusively. The self-sacrifice to which they are often summoned is to surrender to this imposition. In his earlier work Girard looks for a non-violent way of life that will entirely overturn the sacrificial mechanism of society and offer an alternative; in his later account he looks for a Christian idea of self-sacrifice to have a similar transforming effect. From her own perspective, and in dialogue with the earlier work of Girard, Kristeva looks for ways of keeping the image of sacrifice but reducing the element of violence.

In an essay which reflects on Holbein's picture of the dead Christ in the tomb, Kristeva suggests that Christianity has in fact brought about a 'change in the conception of sacrifice'.[43] We can detect three elements of that change which she identifies and welcomes. First, examining the word 'expiate' and its Greek and Hebrew equivalents, she comes to the view that expiation implies 'more of a reconciliation than the fact of "undergoing punishment"'. She concludes:

> This leads one to see in the Christian expiatory 'sacrifice' the offering of an acceptable and accepted gift rather than the violence of shed blood. The generous change

---

[42] Reineke, 'The Mother in Mimesis', 74.
[43] Kristeva, *Black Sun*, 130. In this context she offers an approbation of Girard's view of the exposure of sacrificial mechanisms by the Christian Gospel: see 131, and also Kristeva, *Tales of Love*, 142, 395, n.16.

of the 'victim' into a saving, mediating 'offering' under the sway of a loving God is without doubt...specifically Christian. It represents something new for the Greek and Judaic worlds, something of which they were unaware, or else they viewed it...as scandalous.[44]

However, far from being new to Judaism, the gift-offering was a well established type of sacrifice, as I have already mentioned. Though Kristeva is quite right to associate 'expiation' with reconciliation rather than punishment, she still misses its essential Hebrew meaning of a cleansing or renewal of life which *results* in reconciliation; she now simply identifies the concept with gift. Stressing a loving gift rather than scapegoating enables her to see the whole child–mother–father relational triangle through the lens of sacrifice. In what Kristeva calls 'the dynamics of primary identification', the image of the father that arises in the growth of subjectivity is not the demanding Freudian super-ego, but a self-giving father. The subject, says Kristeva, enters the realm of 'trinitary logic'.[45] As the subject has to face separation from the mother it shares in an exchange of gifts of love; in later life, identifying with the suffering Christ in the story of the Passion, it can share imaginatively in an exchange between the Father and the Son. Now we can see why Kristeva, like Balthasar, would resist Girard's earlier exclusion of God the Father from the event of the cross.

In another essay, 'God is Love', Kristeva stresses that the Christian idea of *agape* is that God takes the initiative in loving; the gift of the father, the sacrifice of the son, comes to us without our having to deserve it. This gift-love has an implication for the subject which is learning to speak and use language, she affirms: the subject is set into motion by an Other, by an initiative of love who 'turns his suffering into an offer and a welcome'.[46] Referring to the scapegoating kind of sacrifice, she defines it as an offering that, by *obliterating* some substance or person, creates meaning for the community. But love is a gift that accepts total suffering and loss to allow a meaning 'which is always there to manifest itself to the members of the community'.[47]

At any stage of life a person can recapitulate the experience of 'primary identification' with the self-giving father. It often happens when we are thrown back unwillingly into the situation of being 'on the boundary' between body and language in a state of depression or melancholia. Once again we approach the void of separation and draw back from crossing it. But at many points, a person can identify with the story of Christ and enter into the self-sacrifice which is an exchange of gifts of love. This brings us to a second element that Kristeva identifies in her new meaning of sacrifice. Rethinking the abjection of the mother

---

[44] Kristeva, 'Women's Time', 206, 210, 131.
[45] Kristeva, *Black Sun*, 135.
[46] Kristeva, *Tales of Love*, 140.
[47] Kristeva, *Tales of Love*, 142.

as separation, she observes that there are *many* moments of separation in the growth of the personality, a series of 'splittings' and 'traumatic partings'[48] which enable a subject to gain its identity and autonomy. This, she observes, is what Hegel called 'the work of the negative'. Now, the story of the Passion of Christ has a separation or rupture at its heart, a break in the bond linking Christ to his Father. Here Kristeva appeals to the idea of a 'hiatus' or gap[49] that is central to the theology of the cross in Balthasar, and so our theologian reappears on the scene. While she only footnotes a reference to him at this point,[50] his portrayal of the cross is pervasive in the text. Indeed, his whole understanding of the Trinity as a drama of giving and receiving in love is very close to her idea of the exchange of love-gifts in a 'trinitary logic'.[51]

For Balthasar, the separation in communion at the cross, marked by the cry of forsakenness, is only possible because there is already, eternally, a 'self-destitution' of love which constitutes the Father, Son, and Spirit in their self-gifting to each other, a 'gulf' between them which is 'founded on the infinite distinction between the hypostases'.[52] There is already an infinite distance between the Son and the Father through the pouring forth of the Son from the being of the Father. What greater distance could there be than a giving away of Godness by the Father in begetting the Son? While the Father does not cease to be God, such an infinite self-gift amounts to a gulf of 'Godlessness'. This distance has room for all the distances between persons that there are within the world of finitude, including those of sin.[53] Here Balthasar is able to deal with the issue of human sin in a way that is much less violent than his scenario of the pacifying of the anger of God.

Our rejection of God, he affirms, causes something like suffering in God. Since 'there is nothing outside God',[54] there is only one place where our 'no' *can* be spoken, and that is—ironically—within the glad response of the Son to the Father. Just as our 'yes' to God leans upon the movement of thanksgiving and obedience that is already there in God, like the relation of a Son to a Father, so we speak our pain-giving 'no' in the same space. Our 'no' is a kind of 'twisted knot' within the current of love of the Son's response.[55] So Balthasar says, 'The creature's No, its wanting to be autonomous without acknowledging its origin, must be located within the Son's all-embracing Yes to the Father, in the Spirit.'[56]

---

[48] Kristeva, *Black Sun*, 132–133.

[49] Kristeva, *Black Sun*, 132.

[50] Kristeva, *Black Sun*, 272, n.28. Kristeva references Balthasar's *La Gloire et la Croix* (1975) 3:2. Kristeva mentions no pages, but relevant sections in the English text (*The Glory of the Lord*, Vol. VII) are on 'Self-abandonment' (142–161), 'The time of discipleship' (pp. 188–201: see 'hiatus', 190), and 'Trinitarian self-giving' (pp. 391–398).

[51] See Balthasar, *The Glory of the Lord*, VII, 391–398.

[52] Balthasar, *Mysterium Paschale*, ix; Balthasar, *Theo-Drama*, IV, 323–325.

[53] Balthasar, *Theo-Drama*, IV, 323–324

[54] Balthasar, *Theo-Drama*, IV, 333.

[55] Balthasar, *Theo-Drama*, IV, 330.

[56] Balthasar, *Theo-Drama*, IV, 329.

The drama of human life can only take place within the greater drama of the divine life.

Kristeva has little to say about sin and human rejection of God in relation to the story of the cross.[57] As a psychoanalyst she finds that the 'rupture' or break in the experience of Christ on the cross provides an image and a narrative for the many separations that build up the psychic life of individuals. It brings to consciousness the essential dramas that are internal to the becoming of every subject. The narrative has cathartic power, and offers support to those who are in the unbearable anguish of separation and loss of meaning, especially in a state of depression. She observes that healing comes when the identification with the forsakenness of Christ is combined with the primary identification with the father in the exchange of gifts of love. Where this primary identification is missing, we are left only with the aspect of separation, and this she finds depicted in the awful minimalism of Holbein's portrait of the dead Christ. Here we are confronted only with a 'metaphor of severance', stripped of what she calls 'the antidepressive carrier wave' of Christianity.[58]

The aspects of sacrifice as separation and mutual gift lead to a third element in Kristeva's thought. Self-sacrifice follows the pattern of the cross as a dying to self in hope of new life, or resurrection. Following Hegel, she affirms that death is infinite love, the renunciation of self for the sake of another: 'This negative movement which belongs to Spirit', she quotes, 'is inner conversion and change.'[59] She regrets that this insight has taken the dualistic form in Christianity of a suppression of the body in favour of the 'spirit', which is only an interior version of the oppression of bodily life by the 'prohibitions' of the moral law in society, a 'cutting' into the body by symbols which belong to the 'law of the father'. True self-sacrifice for the sake of the other moves towards resurrection, reconciliation, restoration and so the establishing of the self in communion with others. It follows the baptismal track of dying and rising with Christ. To those feminists who are suspicious of any mention of self-sacrifice, as playing into the patriarchal game, she suggests that it is in fact part of the healthy growth of the subject in its own identity.

## 6. SACRIFICE AS EXPIATION

It should be clear by now that I prefer Kristeva's re-imagining of the image of sacrifice to Girard's earlier abandonment of it, or even to his later qualified

---

[57] But she does speak of love as the reversal of sin in *Tales of Love*, 141.
[58] Kristeva, *Black Sun*, 135.
[59] Kristeva, *Black Sun*, 135. The quotation is from Hegel, *Lectures on the Philosophy of Religion*, 3:63.

account in which the willingness to die in order to expose the primitive mechanisms of sacrifice can be called a kind of sacrifice. Kristeva is able to use the rich resources of the story of the Passion as being a drama in God, involving 'separation' and an exchange of self-giving in a way strikingly similar to Balthasar. Girard's concept of self-sacrifice lacks this 'trinitary logic' of the gifts of love.

However, we return to my opening question about the renewal of life in the individual and society. How can a social life which is marked and broken by the violence of sacrifice be transformed? Kristeva's answer is that of the psychoanalyst. If an individual can bring to consciousness his or her inner struggles and divisions, using the image of sacrifice in a more healthy way, then this will work out into a society where we cease to oppress and sacrifice each other. In a letter to a friend she writes, hopefully, 'What if the ancestral division between "those who give life" (women) and "those who give meaning" (men) were in the process of disappearing? What do you think? It would be a radical upheaval, never before seen. Sufficient to herald a new era of the sacred...'[60]

While she highly values the resource of images in the Judaic-Christian tradition, in the end these are subordinate to psychoanalysis. Unlike Hegel's sublation of the image into the concept, *both* religion and psychology offer only images or 'illusions' in the realm of the imagination, but one set of images— the growth of the psyche—is decisive. God the Father and the Father of Desire are both images in the consciousness, but we may have to do without God as religious images cease to grip the modern mind. There will be a loss of an opportunity for clients to make an empathetic identification with the Passion of Christ, which Kristeva regrets, but she can continue a therapeutic regime without it.

For Girard, on the other hand, renewal comes through the creating of a community which is committed to the exposing of the myth of redemptive violence, and so is devoted to the way of Christ, to forgiveness, and non-violence. This is not an optional extra for renewal, since the deconstruction of the scapegoat myth will result in chaos in a society unless it is replaced by discipleship in the kingdom of God. We are, he believes, facing such an apocalyptic catastrophe in western culture today. Nor does imitation of Christ mean an end to violence since his disciples will find violence inflicted upon them. Violence cannot be escaped; it has to be transformed. Girard is placing his hopes in a cognitive shift in the way society sees itself, and in the power of discourse to form a *community* in its habits as well as an individual. But the question is whether his particular account of the Passion of Christ will have the power to produce this transformation. Will Girard's story have the capacity

[60] Kristeva/Clément, *The Feminine and the Sacred*, 18.

to shape and renew a community of forgiveness? Even in Girard's later version, where the cross is a divinely subversive recapitulation of the scapegoat sacrifice, the story is still simply about the exposure of scapegoating.

There is an interpretation of the Passion in sacrificial terms which retains the aspect of separation which both Balthasar and Kristeva find essential for the power of the story, which avoids the implications of divine violence to which Girard rightly objects, and yet which still incorporates the idea of Christ as 'bearing' human sin. I mean sacrifice as *expiation*, in the full sense of 'cleansing' from sin, where God is the actor in the drama rather than the one acted upon. Christ enters into the human situation of alienation and estrangement, a death-like state which is the inevitable consequence of turning away from the divine purpose for creation. This brings a breach right into the heart of the triune life of God. The point of this identification is not to appease God, but to overcome—i.e. expiate—sin and raise to new life those who die to themselves in Christ. While this drama echoes the Old Testament sacrificial rite of the sin-offering, we can no longer think of sin as some kind of entity, some patch of uncleanness which exists in its own right and which can—in Balthasar's words—be 'detached' from the sinner. Sin is an attitude of the creature towards the Creator, a lack of trust and a stance of rejection. It cannot float free of created beings, whether human or otherwise. This means that we can only think of the 'expiation' of sin as the transforming of the sinner, or the changing of persons.[61] The objective power of the cross of Jesus is to transform personalities, to enable them to recognize their relatedness to God and neighbour, and to renew that relation which already exists within the space God makes for creation within a triune life.

As a psychoanalyst Kristeva understands the power of identification, and suggests that we should understand 'substitution between the Saviour and the faithful' precisely as identification.[62] She fears that is 'too anthropological and psychological from the point of view of a strict theology',[63] but her lack of theology is not in the idea of identification itself. It is in her applying it only to *our* empathy with Christ, in dying and rising with him. She fails to follow through her insight into the exchange of gifts by speaking of the identification of God with humanity in the cross of Jesus. A fuller understanding of expiation is to be found in exceeding Kristeva's story of empathy with the dead Christ by adding the empathy of *God* with us.

Such a theology can give to the church a discourse of the cross which has symbolic power to overturn a culture based on a scapegoating kind of sacrifice.

---

[61] Similarly Gavin Flood understands sacrifice as a metaphor for 'an inner transformation, an *anabasis*, which we might see in terms of an enacted metaphor for fundamental human motivations towards meaning...' ('Sacrifice as Refusal', Chapter 8, in this volume).

[62] Kristeva, *Black Sun*, 133.

[63] Kristeva, *Black Sun*, 134.

This narrative can thus be effective not only in the interior life of the individual as described by Kristeva, but in its social effect of building a community of disciples as described by Girard. A creative text can construct a context;[64] a shared story can form the stories by which communal beings live. Thus the expiating sacrifice of Christ transforms human life, giving human beings the motivation to make their lives a gift-offering to God and to others.

[64] See Derrida, 'Signature, Event, Context', 320.

# 5

## Sacrifice and the Self

### Julia Meszaros

Modernity rightly regards sacrifice and self-sacrifice as ambiguous and some-times even dangerous concepts. However, as other contributions to this vol-ume illustrate, it is more difficult to do away with or dismiss these concepts than its modern critics have tended to suggest. As I argue below, the notion of self-sacrifice in particular not only retains a tenacious place within a Christian and theological context but remains relevant also to more secular attempts to come to grips with the *humanum*, or with that which defines us in our human-ity. In this essay I thus explore the connection between sacrifice and human selfhood. Is there a—seemingly paradoxical—link between self-sacrifice and the fullness of being? What would such sacrifice look like and what is it con-ditioned on? In giving thought to these questions, I do not wish to champion an uncritical endorsement of self-sacrifice. As Pamela Sue Anderson rightly emphasizes, in this volume, the notion of self-sacrifice is easily exploited for all manner of oppressive purposes that trample on the needs and potential of the individual human person. I do, however, wish to propose that the peren-nial allure of the concept derives from an, oftentimes vague, awareness that we cannot do full justice to our human potential without some recourse to the notion of self-sacrifice.

I begin the following discussion by briefly highlighting some of the modern criticisms of self-sacrifice. I then go on to offer some reasons as to why, in spite of these legitimate concerns, a mere dismissal of self-sacrifice as destructive of the human being may nonetheless be considered unsatisfactory. I finally draw out three conditions, on the basis of which self-sacrifice can be considered to build up and fulfil, rather than stifle the self.

## 1. SELF-SACRIFICE CONTESTED

The notion that self-sacrifice constitutes a precondition for the discernment of truth about oneself is, so Michel Foucault observes, one of the earliest and most pivotal Christian experiences.[1] According to Foucault, the earliest monastic practices of 'ascetic maceration exercised on the body' and 'continuous verbalization of the thoughts' to a spiritual superior are paradigmatic instances of a kind of self-sacrifice that entails not only 'a radical change in the way of life' but something more total and, it appears, violently destructive.[2] As Foucault sees it, these practices are expressions of a fundamental Christian sense that 'you will become the subject of the manifestation of truth when and only when you disappear or you destroy yourself as a real body or as a real existence.'[3] The view that self-sacrifice stands counter to the human subject's real existence and contrasts with a more positive understanding of the emergence of the self is, in a more unambiguously critical way, shared also by Friedrich Nietzsche. On Nietzsche's view, Christian endorsements of selflessness and self-sacrifice betray an unnatural glorification of self-victimization that instils undue self-denial or even self-hatred. More recently, the notion of self-sacrifice has been criticized from a feminist perspective. As Barbara H. Andolsen observes, the notion of sacrifice is here perceived as 'something destructive to the self.'[4] Brita Gill-Austern argues that the Christian tendency to understand love in terms of self-sacrifice or self-denial may lead women to lose sight of their own personal needs and desires and, instead, to revel in their suffering.[5] Daphne Hampson suggests that, with respect to women, the commendation of self-sacrifice is complicit with covert forms of socially sanctioned injustice, and Pamela Sue Anderson finds 'that self-sacrifice treated as a "moral virtue" exhibits perhaps the greatest danger for western women who suffer under the dominance of systems of male-privileged gender hierarchies.'[6] Anderson's important concerns about the hazardous effects of a self-sacrificial morality find expression also in this volume.

Whether implicitly or explicitly, these voices direct us to the dangers that endorsements of self-sacrifice may encounter. Foucault's discussion suggests that where self-sacrifice is seen as foundational to the self, our 'real body' and 'existence' cannot be valued, protected, and nurtured.[7] Nietzsche suggests that the attempt to make a moral norm of self-sacrifice reflects the power-hungry ressentiment of the weak, whereas feminist thinkers have, by contrast, tended to see in self-sacrifice a manifestation of patriarchy that further disenfranchises particularly those who already lack physical and emotional strength and power.[8] All these perspectives serve as a warning of the many hidden ways in which the concept can propagate violence towards the self and thus drain

---

[1] Foucault, 'Hermeneutics of the Self', 221.
[2] Foucault, 'Hermeneutics of the Self', 221.
[3] Foucault, 'Hermeneutics of the Self', 221.
[4] Andolsen, 'Agape', 77.
[5] See Gill-Austern, 'Love Understood as Self–Denial'.
[6] Hampson, *Theology and Feminism*, 123–126 (Mary Daly has rejected the notion of self-sacrifice on similar terms. See, e.g., Daly, *Beyond God the Father*); Anderson, 'Weakness', 111.
[7] Foucault, 'Hermeneutics of the Self', 222.
[8] One frequent suggestion of such feminist arguments is that women are more prone to self-giving than men—indeed, that their sin tends to be a neglect or even suppression rather than an

the life, or the very will to live, out of a human being. Where self-sacrifice is understood in terms which allow such harm it is indeed an invalid moral norm. But does the need to counter any kind of oppressive morality necessitate or warrant an outright condemnation of self-sacrifice as self-destructive? Several points of consideration suggest otherwise.

The Christian theologian, of course, is confronted with the summons to lay down his life for his friend or with the promise that it is through losing his life that he gains it—that is, with notions which have traditionally been understood in terms of self-sacrifice and which may be difficult to account for without recourse to sacrificial language.[9] Yet it is not only from a Christian, or dogmatic, point of view that the notion of (self-)sacrifice seems harder to leave behind than some modern critiques of the concept suggest. As Wolfgang Palaver points out in Chapter 6, simply condemning self-sacrifice (or its proponents) as being responsible for various social ills bears the danger of, once again, falling into the simplistic and problematic logic of scapegoating, or of seeking to restore innocence through putting the blame for one's flaws on another.[10] Furthermore, where critics of self-sacrifice seek to replace the concept with more evidently balanced and reciprocal notions such as friendship, mutual relationship, or 'mutually cultivated care,' it often remains unclear how such mutuality is first achieved and sustained.[11] As Erin Lothes Biviano for instance suggests in a recent study on self-sacrifice, 'ironically, until conditions of greater equality and justice are more fully realized, sacrifice under harsh circumstances is often needed to bring about such community.'[12] In our finite world, love and justice at times require us to clench our teeth and offer up certain personal desires precisely in order to help others to become free and strong subjects capable of genuine love and mutual care. One-sided celebrations of mutuality *over against* self-sacrifice have also been perceived to brush over the question of how we can make positive sense of human suffering. Linda Woodhead has warned that 'feminist theology is at risk of idealizing a life free of suffering.'[13] It would seem to be in the same vein, that Sarah Coakley calls for the need to distinguish 'between abusive suffering on the one hand and a productive or empowering form of "pain" on the other.'[14]

---

elevation of self—such that the normativity of self-sacrifice will lead to destructive self-effacement especially among women (see, e.g., Goldstein, 'The human situation: a feminine view'; Hampson, *Theology and Feminism*, 123–126; Daly, *Beyond God the Father*, e.g. 53–54).

[9] John 15:13; Luke 17:33. Linda Woodhead points this out in 'Spiritualising the Sacred'.

[10] As Angela West points out, feminists themselves have a tendency to scapegoat other women where these defend anything contrary to feminist ideology (see West, *Deadly Innocence*, 53–54).

[11] See John MacMurray (address to the Student Christian Movement Quadrennial Conference), Margaret Farley ('New Patterns of Relationship'), and Pamela Anderson ('Weakness'), respectively.

[12] Biviano, *Paradox of Christian Sacrifice*, 225.

[13] See Ramsay, 'Losing One's Life', 129.

[14] Ramsay, 'Losing One's Life', 129.

These warnings against a straightforward dismissal of self-sacrifice are all rooted in attempts to acknowledge, and make sense of, some of the most central features of human life and experience. The overwhelming generosity of a person who gives up his life for another, the need to take responsibility for oneself and others in spite of compromising external conditions, the willingness to undergo hardships for the sake of justice, or the human ability to find meaning in suffering, are only some aspects of human life that have been expressed with the help of the concept of self-sacrifice. They all share a particular connection with the human being's distinctive ability to look beyond himself and, as Gavin Flood argues in Chapter 8, to renounce some of his own immediate interests and desires for the sake of a good that transcends these. While self-sacrifice is undoubtedly an ambiguous concept susceptible to abuse, a simple repudiation of it may thus put at risk also this significant aspect of our humanity. It seems complicit with a problematic neglect of the relational nature of the human self and the costs this sometimes implies. A total departure from self-sacrifice would thus seem to be founded in a problematic understanding of the self as a one-dimensional, private, even autarkic reality, or in a utopian denial of the extent to which our status as relational subjects confronts us with conflicts of goods. This may explain why, as Foucault implies, modernity's attempts to conceptualize the self as self-constituting have had little success. Where we seek to find out the truth about ourselves, or to 'founding' what Foucault calls 'the hermeneutics of the self', the notion of self-sacrifice thus continues to haunt us even in post-Christian modernity.[15]

Resisting Foucault's somewhat hesitant suggestion that we may have to leave behind the hermeneutics of the self altogether, and accept that the self simply is 'nothing else than the historical correlation of the technology built in our history', I now wish to discern in which sense self-sacrifice may be considered not only compatible with the flourishing of the human self but, at times, crucial for it.[16] I will approach this question in recourse to the thought of a philosopher at once profoundly modern and highly critical of aspects of modernity—the Christian existentialist Gabriel Marcel (1889–1973). I will propose three conditions for the fruitfulness of self-sacrifice. Firstly, the validity of self-sacrifice is tied to a recognition of the human self as an intrinsically relational reality, whose good—and flourishing—is intertwined with that of others. Secondly, self-sacrifice has to be based on, and emerge out of, love. Thirdly, self-sacrifice in the ultimate sense of giving one's life for another can properly take place only in the context of a firm conviction that the good of the human being extends beyond this life and world. These criteria are, I will finally suggest, not only met in Christ's own self-sacrifice on the Cross but *intrinsic to* His self-sacrifice. As such, they must be seen as paradigmatic not only for secular but

---

[15] Foucault, 'Hermeneutics of the Self', 222.
[16] Foucault, 'Hermeneutics of the Self', 222.

also for Christian understandings of self-sacrifice, and help counter some of the theological interpretations of self-sacrifice that feminist and other modern critics have rightly taken issue with.

## 2. INTERSUBJECTIVE RELATIONALITY

In the twentieth century, modern or post-Cartesian assertions of the autonomous individual are increasingly met with philosophies portraying the human self as a reality emerging in and through personal relationships that culminate in a form of mutuality or reciprocity. In various ways, this is true of representatives of the personalist movement such as Martin Buber, but also of Paul Ricoeur's philosophy in *Oneself as Another*.[17] Buber famously argued that where the human being meets another not as an 'It' but as a 'Thou', he creates a space between himself and the other, from which God speaks and within which self and other are revealed to one another. Buber suggests that it is only in the context of the (conscious or unconscious) mutuality of such so-called 'I–Thou relations' that the human self emerges in its true, personal fullness.[18] As Biviano has shown, Ricoeur's explorations of 'the constituent role of the other in one's selfhood' lead him to develop an 'ontology of mutuality' that he portrays as a foundation for self-sacrifice.[19] In the following, I will focus on the thought of another modern thinker broadly in this tradition, the Christian existentialist Gabriel Marcel. Marcel's thought is of interest to an examination of sacrifice in modern thought in that he both takes a thoroughly modern and for the most part secular perspective—that of existentialism—while also remaining profoundly critical of certain modern tendencies such as the preference for 'technique' over mystery, and for individual autonomy over communion. Similarly to Buber and Ricoeur, Marcel denies that human persons are self-constituting or self-contained realities. According to Marcel, the human self must rather be seen as essentially and inevitably related to, even permeated by and bound to the other. This becomes evident for instance in the fact that, as Merold Westphal puts it, human beings find themselves 'obliged' by the other, as experienced in the call of duty.[20] According to Marcel, human beings have the freedom to deny this bond, yet doing so comes at the price of true selfhood.[21] This can only be attained where the individual acknowledges and

---

[17] Buber, *I and Thou*; Buber, *Between Man and Man*; Ricoeur, *Oneself as Another*; Farley, *Just Love*.

[18] Buber, *I and Thou*, 62.

[19] Biviano, *Paradox of Christian Sacrifice*, 121, 128. See especially Ricoeur, *Oneself as Another*, 317–319.

[20] Marcel, *Creative Fidelity*, xii.

[21] Marcel, *Mystery of Being*, vol. 2, 107.

acts out its relatedness to what lies outside of itself: the self or 'ego is the more itself the more it is *with* the other and not directed at itself.'[22] The human being is, Marcel finds, fully itself only where it is 'orientate[d] ... towards something other than itself.'[23]

Marcel pictures this active recognition and embrace of one's ontological dependency as 'a mak[ing] room for' and a 'receiving' of the other in one's self.[24] He describes this relationality, which he considers to lie at the very root of being, as one of 'intersubjectivity.'[25] Intersubjectivity signifies the human self's relation to others: the true human self is neither an isolated unit standing over against others nor simply an instance of its species, one among many. Instead, it is a *particular* reality whose individuality derives from a participatory and interpersonal *relation* with other subjects. This relational ground and destiny of human selfhood is what distinguishes the human being from objects.[26] Marcel further proposes that the human self is *intrinsically* intersubjective. 'Every man', he argues, 'finds within him another self...' which is inclined to give up on his being, yet which he must win over and unite with in order to survive in the face of existential struggles.[27]

Marcel explicitly states that such intersubjectivity, which corresponds with what he refers to as an 'anti-Cartesian' 'metaphysic of "we are" rather than "I think"', constitutes the precondition and foundation not only for prayer but, significantly for our present discussion, also for sacrifice.[28] 'There can', he states, 'be no justification for sacrifice, it cannot even be thought of, except *from the point of view of an ontology which is rooted in intersubjectivity.*'[29] Marcel applies this statement primarily to self-sacrifice in the total sense of giving one's life for another. I will turn to this particular case of self-sacrifice further below. First, however, I want to suggest that even the validity of self-sacrifice in the more general sense of 'giving up one's own interests or wishes in order to help others or to advance a cause' rests on the kind of relational ontology Marcel conceptualizes in terms of intersubjectivity.[30]

It would seem that self-sacrifice can only be understood in this general sense of giving up certain interests or desires if the self is a reality whose being consists not only in sheer existence but comprises also certain 'loves', 'pursuits, activities, and relationships.'[31] Only on this basis can we reasonably identify, say, a parent's sacrifice of a certain personal interest or pursuit for his child as a

---

[22] Marcel, *Mystery of Being*, vol. 1, xiii.
[23] Marcel, *Mystery of Being*, vol. 1, 201.
[24] Marcel, *Creative Fidelity*, 88f.
[25] Marcel, *Mystery of Being*, vol. 2, 150.
[26] Marcel, *Mystery of Being*, vol. 1, 221.
[27] Marcel, *Mystery of Being*, vol. 2, 161.
[28] Marcel, *Mystery of Being*, vol. 2, 9, 106.
[29] Marcel, *Mystery of Being*, vol. 2, 150.
[30] *New Oxford American Dictionary*.
[31] Rosati, 'Self-Interest and Self-Sacrifice', 319.

sacrifice of *self*. If one wants to avoid the dubious view that the good of others warrants a diminishment of one's self because it is *generally* more important than one's own good, then such an association of one's interests with one's self raises the following question: how can a sacrifice of something which defines the self nonetheless be compatible with the self's good, or even build up the self? Self-sacrifice cannot, it for instance seems, be compatible with the good of the self where this good is reduced to the autonomous pursuit and satisfaction of merely individual loves and interests. Instead, it appears that self-sacrifice and the good of the self are compatible only where this good, and indeed the identity, of the self in fact exceeds those loves and interests of a person, which do not directly connect him with others.

This brings us back to Marcel's notion that self-sacrifice can be justified only on the basis of an ontology rooted in intersubjectivity. The view that the being and good of the self is *more closely* tied to the being and good of the other than to a pursuit of certain personal or individual interests corresponds with Marcel's notion of intersubjectivity, and, as I would argue, specifies the sense in which self-sacrifice for the other can be considered to build up the self. If the human self is an intersubjective reality, or a reality whose being is ontologically, and mysteriously, tied up with that of other selves, then one's self-sacrifice to another will positively affect, express, and promote also the self's own being and, with this, its good. This is because the ontologically demanded intersubjectivity of the self entails commitments to persons and causes other than ourselves. These will at times clash with the realization of the interests of our ego, or of that part of ourselves which is concerned with interests which are independent of others. Even from the perspective of its own selfhood and good, the intersubjective human being will want to subordinate and at times sacrifice certain immediate personal goods to those commitments which more explicitly bind him to other subjects. Such commitments may, at times, be more genuine an expression of his selfhood, and indeed more important to preserving and affirming his self, than the pursuit of desires and interests not directly benefiting or even affecting the other.

Insofar as certain individual interests are given up *for the sake of* another's good with which they clash, self-sacrifice can, on the basis of Marcel's notion of intersubjectivity, be conceptualized as constructive of human selfhood therefore (as well as destructive of certain personal desires). This must not be understood to mean that the pursuit of one's personal preferences and interests is a principally secondary matter. The above leaves open when what should be sacrificed: it highlights merely the ultimate interdependence of the good of self and other, and the possibility that the sacrifice of what Rosati calls 'self-affecting commitment' may be more genuine an expression of and conducive to one's selfhood than the sacrifice of 'other-affecting commitment'.[32] It

---

[32]  Rosati, 'Self-Interest and Self-Sacrifice', 324.

does however mean that preferences which are *intrinsically* self-enclosed or self-isolating are incapable of promoting the good of self or other and thus deserve to be countered independently of any further considerations.[33]

At the same time, the present account of self-sacrifice implies the illegitimacy of sacrificing the true subjectivity of the self—or a person's individual gifts, needs, and vocation—for that of another. The interdependence of self and other means also their equal importance. Marcel's ontology of intersubjectivity thus only legitimizes self-sacrifice for the good of another where this sacrifice does not destroy the self's true subjectivity, which leaves room for and receives the other and which is necessary to the other's flourishing as much as to that of the self. The proper rootedness of self-sacrifice in intersubjectivity means that self-sacrifice must necessarily take place between *subjects*. Self-sacrifice must issue from the *subject* and be directed towards a *subject* and its well-being qua true subject. Although self-sacrifice may entail bearing a certain act of violence towards oneself out of love for the other and in order to avoid yet greater violence, it will never legitimately seek out or condone violence to the human subject.[34] Biviano is indeed right to conclude that sacrifice 'that accepts violence or evades growth is sinful.'[35] Likewise, self-sacrifice cannot be enforced: geared towards building up human subjects, sacrifice must be both freely given and freely received. As noted, the human being has the freedom to deny or to affirm, and creatively shape his intersubjective relations with others, and, thus, his own selfhood, identity, and good. The authenticity and, with this, the merit of self-sacrifice rides on whether it issues from and expresses a *free* affirmation of intersubjectivity. Where intersubjectivity is thus recognized and affirmed freely, it is also nurtured and developed. This leads us to my second point, the interdependency of self-sacrifice on love.

## 3. SELF-SACRIFICE AND LOVE

As a free giving and receiving between subjects, self-sacrifice properly manifests and builds a bond or relationship between these subjects that lies at the root of the very subjectivity and, thus, the individual being of the partners in relation. In a sense, then, self-sacrifice is the occasional cost of those commitments to others that are definitive also for one's own self. As such, it is an act of fidelity both to oneself and to the other. This does not, however, mean

---

[33] It is this kind of a false, self-enclosed self which, I would contend, spiritual traditions advocating a 'dying to self' seek to counter.

[34] It may be legitimate, though admittedly risky, to speak of violence against the supposedly self-enclosed or self-sufficient, false 'self'.

[35] Biviano, *Paradox of Christian Sacrifice*, 118.

that self-sacrifice is adequately described as the result of rational *calculation* about what best serves one's own good. If we follow Marcel's identification of intersubjectivity and love,[36] self-sacrifice much rather emerges out of and promotes love.

The rootedness of self-sacrifice in love runs counter to the kind of abstract *ethic* or 'doctrine' of self-sacrifice that would seem to promote oppressive self-victimization. Love, or what I would describe as the deeply felt concern and will for the good that unites self and other, is no abstraction but always concerns a particular and concrete relationship between subjects with individual capacities and needs. It is only where this living reality calls for and inspires self-sacrifice that sacrifice will bear fruit. This means, firstly, that the adequacy of self-sacrifice is tied to the particular needs of a specific love-relation. Though true love may go hand in hand with a general willingness to self-sacrifice, it will not always call for self-sacrifice. Secondly, the rootedness of self-sacrifice in love means that self-sacrifice, like love, can only ever be given freely and from a position of inner resourcefulness, freedom, and plenitude. Grounded in love, self-sacrifice can never be imposed or issue from a position of oppression or deprivation. Rather, genuine self-sacrifice emanates from within a person's inner core, and constitutes a response to the mysteriously compelling impetus of love of another. Love properly engages the whole person. Consequently, true self-sacrifice can be said to emerge out of nothing less than a person's deepest, irresistible and overflowing *desire* to affirm another in a free, gratuitous, and in some sense impassioned manner.

Self-sacrifice is thus tied to, or correlative with, the resources and capacities of the particular agent as well as the demands of a particular situation: we can only give according to what we have received.[37] Traumas such as experiences of war or paedophilia, but even simple forms of deprivation such as neglect, may therefore tragically weaken a person's capacity for self-sacrifice and, with this, his ability to fully affirm and existentially realize his intersubjectivity. Nonetheless, since human intersubjectivity, as Marcel understands it, is an ontological reality implicitly undergirding every human life, the foundations for its existential realization remain even in the most wounded subject. Especially where such a view is coupled with a notion of divine grace, it becomes clear that an a priori determination of the worldly conditions for the subject's affirmation of intersubjectivity and, thus, of self-sacrifice is impossible.

Meanwhile, I would add that the interdependency of self-sacrifice with the capacities of the subject concerns also the human being's *capacity of judgment*. The self-sacrificing subject must be able to discern both whether he can shoulder a certain sacrifice and 'when sacrifice is important'.[38] A defence of the

---

[36] Marcel, *Mystery of Being*, vol. 2, 55, 170, 156.
[37] Biviano, *Paradox of Christian Sacrifice*, 100; see Andolsen, 'Agape', 75.
[38] Biviano, *Paradox of Christian Sacrifice*, 100.

worth of sacrifice must necessarily value and foster (rather than undermine) the subject's potential capabilities therefore, and his capacity of judgment in particular. Further, and although self-sacrifice is geared towards fulfilling another's need, I would suggest that the interdependency of self-sacrifice and love means that a subject's self-sacrifice *to* another can never properly occur simply *for* or 'on behalf of' the other but is grounded in, reflective of, and aimed at the bond *between* self and other.[39]

The merit, or even the reality, of self-sacrifice indeed depends on its arising out of, and seeking to affirm and foster, a loving union between subjects that founds both their being. This underlines the extent to which self-sacrifice in no way contradicts a desire for self-fulfilment. Since love never involves and fulfils only one but at least two persons, true self-sacrifice must be distinguished from a 'pathology of giving', which ends in a 'moral suicide where one person abdicates and annuls himself completely for the benefit of another.'[40] Marcel thus rightly insists that one can only sacrifice oneself on the basis of certainty that, given the circumstances, such sacrifice is the most truthful expression of one's own being, and thus leads also to one's own fulfilment.[41] Self-sacrifice is warranted only where a person recognizes a loving bond with another to be more fundamental to his being than the pursuit of his individual flourishing— a recognition which is, to be sure, a moral as well as a cognitive achievement. In continuity with Andolsen's view that the 'full expression of the Christian ideal is mutuality', the inter-dependency of self-sacrifice and love means that self-sacrifice is properly rooted in the recognition, and geared towards the affirmation and existential realization, of a deep-seated mutuality of being.[42]

The interdependency of self-sacrifice and love further underlines that true self-sacrifice is at odds with the attempt to play self and other off against each other. Self-sacrifice thus understood rests on a recognition of the equal importance of self and other, precisely *for* one another, and thus respects and seeks to promote the freedom and agency, creativity and well-being of each. The very relevance of the notion of 'self-sacrifice' over against concepts like 'self-denial' or 'self-discipline' lies in the fact that where the latter suggest a more private act of mere privation or divestment, 'self-sacrifice' brings out this interpersonal meaning and purpose of certain acts of renunciation.[43] Again, self-sacrifice is distinct from an act of altruism, a term which seems to imply a dichotomy between self and other as much as its opposite counterpart, egoism. It is with regard to *our* being that certain personal interests can be weighed up against another's more fundamental needs and deemed worth sacrificing. In this light, true self-sacrifice does not

[39] Anderson, 'Weakness', 124.
[40] Marcel, *Mystery of Being*, vol. 2, 100.
[41] Emphasis added. Marcel, *Mystery of Being*, vol. 1, 205.
[42] Andolsen, 'Agape', 79.
[43] This particular significance of self-sacrifice does not make notions of self-denial or self-discipline redundant or misguided.

appear to be so far removed from the 'mutually cultivated care' that Anderson has offered as an alternative to sacrifice, although the notion of self-sacrifice does arguably make more explicit the extent to which love for another at times implies a high, though freely chosen, cost.[44] The notion that it is self-sacrifice rooted in love that furthers the being of self and other corresponds also with the insight, which theologians and others have recently taken up from sociobiologists, that being develops not so much through competition as through cooperation.[45] Rooted in an understanding of human beings as distinct but relational creatures whose good is inseparable from that of the other, self-sacrifice undermines attempts to dichotomize individual advantage and cooperation.

This cooperative feature of self-sacrifice manifests itself also in another respect. Similarly to Buber's notion that the mutuality of I–Thou relations will not tend to be immediate, visible, or even conscious, Marcel considers self-sacrifice to be prompted by a '*call*', which emerges from a person's inner 'depths', yet which the person is not 'articulately aware of' and which he would find impossible to adequately put into words.[46] A person finds himself compelled to sacrifice himself not only by the external and visible needs of the other but also, and importantly, by a mysterious but deeply felt summons. It is in a twofold sense, then, that his self-sacrifice, though freely made, has the character not of an arbitrary and autonomous decision but of a *response*. This not only gives further meaning to the proposed interrelation of self-sacrifice and mutual relation but also points to a mysterious ground of self-sacrifice—a ground which, Marcel suggests, transcends this life.[47] With this, the interdependency of self-sacrifice and love leads us to the third criterion which I suggest is relevant at least to self-sacrifice in the ultimate sense of giving one's life.

## 4. THE TRANSCENDENCE OF THE GOOD OR LIFE AFTER DEATH

It has become clear that, rooted in intersubjectivity and love, self-sacrifice is the manifestation of, and properly geared towards the preservation and development of, a bond between subjects—a bond which lies at the foundation of the human person's very being. This means that self-sacrifice can only legitimately go as far as the death of the self where the respective partners in relation

---

[44] Anderson, 'Weakness', 124. At the same time, the more rooted self-sacrifice is in a person's freedom and love, the less uncomfortable and the more joyful it will be.

[45] See, e.g., Lynn Margulis and Michael Nowak in biology, and Sarah Coakley, James Alison and Erin Loathes Biviano to name only a few theologians who have recently taken up these themes.

[46] Marcel, *Mystery of Being*, vol. 1, 206.

[47] For an account of how sacrifice functions 'as a site for mediating the human encounter with mystery', see Gavin Flood, 'Sacrifice as Refusal', Chapter 8.

are seen to be *bound* to one another and to participate in one shared good even after death. Marcel's example of a person sacrificing his life for his child is instructive here. Such a sacrifice is driven 'by a faith whose content he [the man sacrificing himself] cannot in the first place make clear' but which 'turns on a certain supra-personal unity between his child and himself.'[48] A person can only sacrifice himself on account of 'feel[ing] sure [...] that there will not be an end of him, but rather that he will survive, [in this case], in his child.'[49] Indeed, even in the case of this ultimate self-sacrifice, it must, according to Marcel, still hold true that the sacrificer 'has, without any doubt at all, the feeling that through self-sacrifice he is reaching self-fulfilment', that is, that '[g]iven his own situation and that of everything dear to him, he realizes his own nature most completely, he most completely *is*, in the act of giving his life away.'[50]

Marcel recognizes that this implies the assumption that self-fulfilment is not a this-worldly matter but 'takes place at another, an invisible level.'[51] Similarly to the mentioned call, which emerges from a person's inner depths and which prompts the ultimate sacrifice, the sacrificer may—or, rather, will—not be able to conceptualize this mystery surrounding his fulfilment. It exceeds what can be grasped. Despite this, he must, however, be utterly sure that his sacrifice does indeed constitute also his own fulfilment. Only then can he legitimately make the ultimate sacrifice, because only then can his self-sacrifice legitimately be said not only to issue from love but also to foster love, which always takes place between two or more subjects. According to Marcel, then, the ultimate self-sacrifice is intrinsically and necessarily intertwined with an acceptance of the view that human flourishing transcends the biological and this-worldly dimension, and, with this, an acceptance of immortality.

Prima facie, this immortality can be conceptualized in different ways. Marcel's example seems to permit the interpretation that the parent's conviction that they will live on in their progeny sufficiently motivates their self-sacrifice for their child. If it is true, however, that self-sacrifice depends on the intersubjective relationship between two persons and if it is also true, as I have argued, that true sacrifice precludes the elimination of the subjects involved, it would appear that more specifically a continuity of personal existence beyond death is required. In either case, Marcel rightly insists that the immortality underpinning the sacrifice of one's life refers not to the destiny of 'an entity which is isolated and closed in on itself' but to 'the destiny of that living link', 'the intersubjective unity formed by beings who love one another and who live in and by one another.'[52] A person's total self-sacrifice must be tied to a sense of certainty that the reality of the intersubjective bond

---

[48] Marcel, *Mystery of Being*, vol. 2, 150.
[49] Marcel, *Mystery of Being*, vol. 2, 150.
[50] Marcel, *Mystery of Being*, vol. 1, 205.
[51] Marcel, *Mystery of Being*, vol. 1, 205.
[52] Marcel, *Mystery of Being*, vol. 2, 155, 150.

or love, which he affirms in his sacrifice and which founds both the other's and his own being, is not destroyed by physical death.[53] Sacrifice can only be said to rest on love in the sense I have outlined if both (or all) partners in relation—and thus also the person sacrificing himself—are in some sense able to share in the fruits of that sacrifice, even after death. True self-sacrifice ultimately enables an increase and not a decrease in being, including that of the sacrificer. Without some kind of a personal immortality, the sacrificer's participation in the fruits of his sacrifice of his life would be lacking. According to Marcel, it is indeed where it rests on belief in immortality that the gift of one's life differs from mere suicide. While the latter rests on a denial of intersubjectivity and consequent despair, the former rests on this 'metaphysical' hope and on an affirmation of a love or a 'mutual pledge' which entails 'the promise of eternity', Marcel argues.[54]

The above references to a mysterious call, to the eternal, and to a metaphysical hope for a fulfilment which exceeds this life, manifest the manner in which Marcel's account of the reality and validity of self-sacrifice insistently pushes towards what he calls the *mystery of being* and, with this, to God. In the final instance, Marcel indeed writes, 'it is of the very essence of self-sacrifice that it is not able to give a rational account of itself.'[55] The ultimate root and justification of self-sacrifice lies beyond the confines of human reason and points to a mysterious fount of being— in the same way as 'my life infinitely transcends my possible conscious *grasp* of my life at any given moment; fundamentally and essentially it refuses to tally with itself.'[56] Just as I do not, ultimately, 'know what I live by nor why I live', so that which sustains love and, with this, self-sacrifice ultimately remains mysterious, Marcel's account implies.[57] The very fact that the human being perceives his life as bound to 'act[s] of self-dedication' means that 'human living [...] seems also essentially the living of something other than itself', Marcel suggests.[58] Though ultimately remaining mysterious, this 'other' gives a foundation to the deeply felt call that prompts human self-sacrifice, and the intrinsically responsive nature of such sacrifice.


## 5. SELF-SACRIFICE FROM A CHRISTIAN PERSPECTIVE

With the above, I have followed Marcel in basing the legitimacy of self-sacrifice on an ontology which ultimately issues in, or points to, a transcendent origin of being. A more explicitly Christian perspective on self-sacrifice lends

---

[53] See Marcel, *Mystery of Being*, vol. 2, 150–151.
[54] Marcel, *Mystery of Being*, vol. 2, 155; Marcel, *The Philosophy of Existentialism*.
[55] Marcel, *Mystery of Being*, vol. 1, 203–204.
[56] Emphasis added. Marcel, *Mystery of Being*, vol. 1, 206.
[57] Marcel, *Mystery of Being*, vol. 1, 206.
[58] Marcel, *Mystery of Being*, vol. 1, 210.

further weight to the above proposals. As divine self-offerings and self-sacrifices, the Incarnation and the Crucifixion both constitute affirmations of the
loving bond par excellence: God's covenant with humanity. The Incarnation
and the Crucifixion also correspond with and illuminate the *mysterious* origin and nature of self-sacrifice. The Incarnation is God coming to share His
life, the Crucifixion God sacrificing Himself to us. In both cases that which
is given—God-self—is the ultimate mystery. The divine self-sacrifice furthermore not only explains why human self-sacrifice is of a responsive nature or
based, as Marcel has suggested, on a 'call' but also entails an element of mutuality itself. Thus, Christian self-sacrifice is, as Edward Kilmartin observes, 'in
the *first* place, the self-offering of the Father in the gift of the Son, and, in the
*second* place, the unique response of the Son in his humanity to the Father,
and, [only] in the *third* place, the self-offering of believers in union with Christ
by which they share in his covenant relation with the Father.'[59]

These features point to significant overlaps between the criteria for self-
sacrifice proposed by Marcel and God's self-sacrifice in Christ. As the latter
quotation indicates, this becomes yet more evident if self-sacrifice is, as Robert
Daly has demanded, contextualized within the perfect love relations between
the three persons of the Trinity.[60] The Trinitarian love relations underline 'that
true sacrifice is a profoundly interpersonal event', that the fullness of being
entails a mutual giving and receiving of love, and that it is such loving relationality rather than any glorification of violence that Christ's own self-sacrifice
rests on.[61] Considering self-sacrifice in relation to the Trinity also gives further
weight to the notion that the loving relationship which founds being transcends
the material dimension and, thus, physical death. Where the Crucifixion is
seen as a result of the Trinitarian love relations—that is, as an outward manifestation of the Son's 'interior self-giving to the Father'—it becomes somewhat
clearer that the violence surrounding it is not intrinsic but accidental to the
divine self-sacrifice.[62] Jesus' suffering and death were not ends in themselves
but hardships he accepted 'as the consequence of his unswerving commitment
to mutual love.'[63] Jesus did not 'desire death on the Cross as a manifestation
of total self-surrender' and we should therefore not seek Jesus' suffering itself,
but his 'absolute dedication to love which highlights human dignity.'[64] Under
the structures of finitude and sin, love will at times call for self-sacrifice and
will, with this, entail some (usually negligible) degree of suffering. Similarly,
daily human challenges and losses can be offered up as sacrifices of love. While

---

[59] Kilmartin as quoted by O'Collins, *Jesus Our Redeemer*, 165 (cf. Kilmartin, *Eucharist in the West*, 381–382).
[60] Robert Daly, *Sacrifice Unveiled*, 173–175.
[61] Robert Daly, *Sacrifice Unveiled*, 173.
[62] O'Collins, *Jesus Our Redeemer*, 165.
[63] See Andolsen, referring to Beverly Wildung Harrison, in 'Agape', 78.
[64] Andolsen, 'Agape', 78.

Jesus' regard for his own needs (rest, prayer, retreat, drink) indicates that the willingness to undergo suffering out of love does not mean suffering should be sought out, the rootedness of self-sacrifice in love thus helps to clarify how suffering can be meaningful or serve a higher purpose.[65]


## 6. CONCLUSION

I have argued that it is on account of our relationality that we must hold on to the notion of self-sacrifice, and that the nature of our relationality must inform our understanding of legitimate self-sacrifice. In doing so, I have offered only one reason for the relevance of self-sacrifice. The conflicts of goods that our finite world presents us with, as well as the need to combat evil constitute other such reasons, which I here assumed without explicit consideration.[66] Yet, a relational anthropology is critical to endorsing some form of self-sacrifice: it is only if and insofar as the human self is constituted by its relations with others such that its being, and well-being, cannot be separated from that of the other that self-sacrifice can potentially build up and fulfil rather than undermine the human self.

Such an anthropology, which I have not here been able to argue for in any depth, undoubtedly goes against modern views according to which the self is ultimately founded in its own, individual subjectivity. It also runs counter to more recent proposals that the self is a mere historical construct. Yet its correspondence with significant, quintessentially human experiences and behaviours suggests that it merits reconsideration. As Gabriel Marcel and, more recently, Paul Ricoeur have argued, such an account of our humanity need not deny individual subjectivity but rather suggests that this status corresponds with—and is indeed founded in—our relationality and interdependency with others. According to this view, the human being becomes who he truly is qua individual the more he acts out his ontological relation with others by actively entering into committal relations with them and by participating in their good.

I have sought to show that if the human self must be understood not only as a finite and fallen but also as such a relational reality, then the good of both self and other will at times be tied to self-sacrifice. Human relations are then so determinative of a person's identity that the commitment to them warrants the sacrifice of other, lesser goods conflicting with this commitment. That is,

---

[65] In the Christian tradition, corporal and spiritual works of mercy not typically described as suffering have been termed sacrificial (see e.g. Rom. 12:1; 1 Pet. 2:5).

[66] For an insightful account of how sacrifice is not only prompted by the limitations resulting from human finitude but also an attempt to transcend finitude, see Gavin Flood, 'Sacrifice as Refusal', Chapter 8.

even from the perspective of the self's own welfare, fidelity to the relational bond with the other may be more important than the pursuit of other, perhaps more immediately felt interests and desires. Based on such an anthropology of intersubjectivity, true sacrifice involves a gain as well as a cost for the sacrificer and must be coupled with a concrete and active concern for the self. If self-sacrifice undermines the very core or integrity of the self then it ultimately undermines its own cause: without the self the other, too, is unable to flourish. Thus, as Biviano has pointed out in reference to Ricoeur, 'the cost of sacrifice defeats the purpose of confirming discipleship if it threatens to undermine *ipse*-identity, that is, the conscious *will* to keep promises as an expression of one's core identity.'[67] Self-sacrifice is tied to a concern for, or is dependent on, the freedom, agency and resourcefulness of the human self in a way that should, to some extent at least, appease feminist critics.

The importance of these features for the reality and efficacy of self-sacrifice finds further recognition in my affirmation that self-sacrifice can only be defended if it is embedded in, motivated by and geared towards a relationship of love: such a relationship naturally involves, founds, and builds up the being both of the beloved and of the lover who sacrifices something of himself. The rootedness of self-sacrifice in love also means, however, that although the sacrificer will by no means be disinterested in the gain attained through his self-sacrifice, the legitimacy of his self-sacrifice depends on its freedom from calculations of this personal gain. Such calculations would assume a false opposition between self and other, and would undermine the freedom and gratuity of love. Instead, the only legitimate motivation and, indeed, the gain of self-sacrifice consists in a loving bond that is its own end. Self-sacrifice as here proposed thus steers clear of the polarizations of self-interest and disinterestedness that so often bedevil discussions of the concept.[68]

I have, finally, argued that self-sacrifice gains further legitimacy and importance when one accepts that the flourishing of the human self extends beyond this world. This is because it is only then that even the sacrifice of one's life can be said to build love relations. As I would suggest with Marcel, an anthropology of intersubjectivity indeed points to and ultimately corresponds with a participatory metaphysics. By this I mean the view that the human being is embedded in a universe ontologically characterized by, and destined for, mutual relationship and communion between distinct realities, the source of whose being is itself of a relational nature and stands in mutual relations with the distinct realities of the world. Alongside the desire to assert human autonomy, this affinity between an anthropology of intersubjectivity and a participatory metaphysics arguably contributes to modern rejections of self-sacrifice.

---

[67] Biviano, *Paradox of Christian Sacrifice*, 144.
[68] See e.g. the debate between Brandt, Overvold, and others (Brandt, 'Rationality, Egoism and Morality'; Overvold, 'Self-interest and the Concept of Self-Sacrifice').

If the welfare of the human person is, as many modern thinkers will assume, confined to this world then many instances of self-sacrifice must be rejected as lying beyond the boundaries of rational self-concern, appearing instead merely as acts of violence to the self. Yet insofar as belief in a transcendent ground of being and in immortality remains an option even in modernity, such a conclusion is not, I have tried to suggest, a necessary one.

The modern sensitivity to the potential violence of self-sacrifice has, in any case, drawn sorely needed attention to the dangers implied in unqualified endorsements of the concept, and has shown the need to discern the criteria or governing principles that self-sacrifice is subject to. These, I have followed Marcel in arguing, entail an anthropology of intersubjectivity, the rootedness of self-sacrifice in love, and, ultimately, an affirmation of the immortality of the human being—and thus a metaphysic that is far from normative in modern thought.

# 6

## Sacrificial Cults as 'the Mysterious Centre of Every Religion'

### *A Girardian Assessment of Aby Warburg's Theory of Religion*

Wolfgang Palaver

In his book *The God Delusion*, Richard Dawkins draws our attention to John Lennon's song 'Imagine' (1971), in which Lennon calls us to 'give peace a chance'.[1] Dawkins, an atheist, endorses Lennon's song because of its hope for a world without 'religion'. Lennon dreams of a world without heaven and hell, 'above just sky'. While I think Lennon is wrong to think that peace demands the abolishment of religion, this is not my present concern. Instead, I wish to discuss Lennon's suggestion that peace demands the abolishment of sacrifice, which is often connected with nationalism and militarism. The following passage is central in this regard: 'Imagine there's no countries / It isn't hard to do / Nothing to kill or die for / And no religion too / Imagine all the people / Living life in peace'. The hope that there may be 'nothing to kill or die for' reflects the modern anti-sacrificial attitude. Thirty years ago when I became a pacifist and a conscientious objector I roughly believed in the kind of world intimated by these lines of 'Imagine'. I rejected sacrifice without being aware that in order to avoid sacrificing others I might be forced to sacrifice myself, to give up my own claims, even to risk my own life. The following reflections will recurringly come back to this problem so elegantly overlooked by Lennon and many of his pacifist followers—including myself.

---

[1] Dawkins, *God Delusion*, 1.

## 1. BETWEEN THE SACRIFICIAL THINKING OF POLITICAL CATHOLICISM AND THE MODERN ABOLISHMENT OF SACRIFICE

The question of sacrifice raises one of the most difficult problems of every theory of religion. There are at least two pitfalls we have to be aware of and which we easily fall into. Let me first address the pitfall into which many traditional Catholic thinkers have fallen. Without distinguishing between archaic and Christian concepts, they strongly emphasize the necessity and inevitability of sacrifice and don't hesitate to draw political consequences from this point of view. A telling example is the tradition which developed from the Catholic reactionaries Joseph de Maistre and Juan Donoso Cortés to the German law scholar Carl Schmitt. All three represent sacrificial thinking as an offspring of the scapegoat mechanism that René Girard discovered as the origin of human culture. Again and again, they affirm the age-old sacrificial logic that a few drops of blood may prevent streams of blood. According to Donoso Cortés the three following things have to be believed: 'That the effusion of blood is necessary, that there is a manner of shedding blood which is purificatory, and another mode which is condemnatory.'[2] Everything depends on the spilling of blood: 'We can say that blood is the manure of the plant we call *genius*.'[3] According to Maistre, the world is nothing but a huge sacrificial altar and war is divine:

> The earth cries out and asks for blood... Thus is carried out without cease, from maggot to man, the great law of violent destruction of living things. The entire world, continuously saturated with blood, is nothing but an immense altar where all that lives must be slaughtered without end, without measure, without slackening, until the devouring of all things, until the extinction of evil, until the death of death... War is therefore divine, in and of itself because it is a law of the world... War is divine in the mysterious glory which surrounds it, and in the no less inexplicable attraction which draws us to it.[4]

Similar thoughts about war were also expressed by Juan Donoso Cortés. The Spaniard, too, believed that the abolishment of war would result in the destruction of the world. Like Maistre, he strongly supported capital punishment, which is another offspring of the foundational murder. Both consider the death penalty necessary because, like war, it reduces violence inside a society such that any abolishment of it risks 'a more bloody future': 'Blood will then gush forth from the rocks, and the earth will become a hell.'[5] De

---

[2] Donoso Cortés, *Catholicism, Liberalism and Socialism*, 284; cf. Palaver, 'Reading,' 62–64.
[3] Maistre, *Considerations*, 29.
[4] Quoted by Bell, *The First Total War*, 310–311; cf. Girard, *Battling*, 84.
[5] Donoso Cortés, *Catholicism, Liberalism and Socialism*, 292.

Maistre shows his position on capital punishment in his celebration of the executioner, whom he views as the central figure of political order: 'All greatness, all power, all subordination rest on the executioner. He is the terror and the bond of human association. Remove this mysterious agent from the world, and in an instant order yields to chaos: thrones fall, society disappears.'[6] The writings of Maistre and Donoso Cortés give a central role to those passages in the Bible—such as Hebrews 9:22 ('Without the shedding of blood there is no forgiveness of sins')—whose ambivalence tends to obliterate the difference between the biblical perspective and archaic religiosity.[7] But although our repugnance concerning the main theses of these two writers is understandable we should be aware that these thinkers are not supporting war and capital punishment for completely immoral reasons. Rather, like traditional religions, they seek to foster cultural and political peace through the controlled and well-aimed use of violence.

In the twentieth century, the German law scholar Carl Schmitt developed a political theology, which followed in the footsteps of the Catholic reactionaries Maistre and Donoso Cortés. Like them, he justifies sacrifices demanded by war. He sharply criticized pacifistic liberalism as attempting to create a 'a world without the distinction of friend and enemy and hence a world without politics' that thereby loses also the strength to demand sacrifices.[8] Such a 'pacified globe' does not recognize an antithesis 'whereby men could be required to sacrifice life, authorized to shed blood, and kill other human beings.'[9]

Whoever is aware of this tradition of political Catholicism might shy away from those Catholic hymns sung in praise of sacrifice that today are connected with a critique of the liturgical reform undertaken by the Second Vatican Council. The German writer Martin Mosebach rightly calls himself a 'Stone Age Man' in his book *The Heresy of Formlessness* where he emphasizes the importance of sacrifice, while claiming at the same time that it does not matter what is sacrificed by the priest on the altar.[10] Without any hesitation does he view his participation in the sacrifice of the mass as a continuation of a long human tradition comprising human sacrifices as well as animal and bloodless sacrifices.

Against such versions of Catholic understandings of sacrifice, the Reformation and the Enlightenment led to the modern abolishment of sacrifice that characterizes our world of today. Especially liberalism is deeply influenced by its break with the sacrificial thinking that has its origin in the archaic world. One can recognize a line of anti-sacrificial thinking going from Thomas Hobbes to John Rawls and Jürgen Habermas in our age.[11] According

---

[6] Quoted by Berlin, *The Crooked Timber of Humanity*, 117.
[7] Maistre, *Opfer*, 36; Donoso Cortés, *Catholicism, Liberalism and Socialism*, 288.
[8] Schmitt, *Concept of the Political*, 35.
[9] Schmitt, *Concept of the Political*, 35; cf. Palaver, 'Critique'.
[10] Mosebach, *Häresie der Formlosigkeit*, 12, 16.
[11] Palaver, 'Critique,' 43–47.

to Hobbes' definition of the law of nature, it 'is forbidden to do, that, which is destructive of his [a man's] life, or taketh away the means of preserving the same.'[12] The unilateral option of the Sermon on the Mount, which calls the individual to risk his own life in tragic situations where there is no alternative between killing and being killed, is against Hobbes' understanding of natural law. The individual is not allowed to risk his own life, but has to look after his own self-preservation, the highest obligation of this early version of liberalism. Modern versions of liberalism emphasize this anti-sacrificial stance even more. John Rawls, the most prominent representative of contemporary liberalism, deals with the problem of sacrifice in his criticism of utilitarianism. Against utilitarian justifications of individual sacrifices for the sake of an increase of the overall utility, Rawls emphasizes the inviolability of the individual:

> Each person possesses an inviolability founded on justice that even the welfare of society as a whole cannot override. For this reason justice denies that the loss of freedom for some is made right by a greater good shared by others. It does not allow that the sacrifices imposed on a few are outweighed by the larger sum of advantages enjoyed by many.[13]

Not unlike Hobbes, John Rawls also rejects the idea of a unilateral self-sacrifice. Jürgen Habermas, similarly, explains in several of his books that modern 'rational morality puts its seal on the abolition of sacrifice.'[14] Taking military duty, capital punishment, the duty to pay taxes and the duty to education as his examples he claims that the 'normative core' of 'enlightenment culture' consists 'in the abolition of a publicly demanded *sacrificium* as an element of morality.'[15] In the context of the German discussion about a monument memorizing the Holocaust, Habermas again makes clear that it is especially the connection of sacrifice and cults of war that explains his critical view of sacrifice. He especially criticizes the traditional 'cult of sacrifice' which, 'still during my own youth, was devoted to the image of the heroic dead, of the supposedly voluntary sacrifice for the "higher" good of the collective. The Enlightenment had good reasons for wanting to abolish sacrifice.'[16]

## 2. RENÉ GIRARD'S THEORY OF SACRIFICE

Girard's mimetic theory is especially helpful for a critique of the types of sacrificial thinking summarized above. According to Girard, archaic religion and

---

[12] Hobbes, *Leviathan*, 91 [chap. 14].
[13] Rawls, *Theory of Justice*, 3–4.
[14] Habermas, *Justification*, 34 [translation corrected].
[15] Habermas, *Constellation*, 101; cf. Habermas, *Time*, 166.
[16] Habermas, *Time*, 46.

culture originate from a foundational murder—the so-called scapegoat mechanism. Many different myths from a broad variety of cultures show traces of a primordial crisis of a war of all against all that was succeeded by a stage of peace and order brought about through the expulsion or killing of one member of these early tribal groups. These scapegoats became the gods of these archaic tribes because they were not only seen as the troublemakers that caused the crises but also as those beings that enabled the community to live in peace. The scapegoat mechanism—Girard uses also the term 'victimage mechanism'[17]—is the origin of the archaic sacrifice.

Sacrificial rites are, according to Girard, an imitation or repetition of the scapegoat mechanism. In order to strengthen the peace that followed the foundational murder, the groups repeat consciously and in a controlled way what they seem to have experienced during the crises that led to the foundational murder. Wherever cultural order is based on the sacrifice of single victims by the collective we are facing a sacrificial culture stemming from the scapegoat mechanism. As Christians we legitimately criticize such types of order. Girard refers to reactionary Christian thinkers like Joseph de Maistre or Carl Schmitt in order to emphasize how their way of divinizing the social order is much closer to the sacrificial patterns of archaic religion than to genuine Christianity.[18] These thinkers represent a distortion or mutilation of Christianity.

Contrary to thinkers like Maistre, Donoso Cortés, or Schmitt, Girard emphasizes a fundamental difference between archaic religions rooted in the scapegoat mechanism on the one hand and religions that stem from biblical revelation on the other. Archaic religions side with the persecuting mob justifying the victimization of scapegoats. By contrast, the biblical tradition is characterized by its rehabilitation of the persecuted victims. The Passion of Christ is the narrative that shows most convincingly how strongly Christianity sides with the innocent victims of persecution. In order to distance himself from the field of religious studies and its tendency to identify myth and Bible, the early Girard vehemently rejected the use of the term sacrifice to describe Jesus' laying down of his life on the cross, reserving the term sacrifice only for archaic religious practices.[19] At that time, Girard understood the traditional Christian use of the term sacrifice as a relapse behind the non-sacrificial position of the Gospels. He detected such a distortion already in the New Testament, especially in the Letter to the Hebrews in which the death of Jesus is interpreted from the point of view of sacrifices in the Old Testament.[20] Although Hebrews avoids a total relapse into an archaic understanding of sacrifice in so far as

---

[17] Girard, *Things Hidden*, 95.
[18] Girard, *Reader*, 203.
[19] Girard, *Things Hidden*, 240–243.
[20] Girard, *Things Hidden*, 227–231. Girard referred especially to Heb. 9:22–26 and Heb. 10:11–14.

it sees Jesus' death as the perfect and definitive sacrifice, the singular non-sacrificial position of the Passion narratives was, according to Girard, lost in this part of the New Testament.

Girard, however, did not maintain his initial, radical repudiation of the term sacrifice. Seeking to avoid extremes, he not only criticized the Catholic reactionaries but also rejected the opposite political attitude, the divinization of social disorder and revolution. His long-time collaboration with Raymund Schwager, a Jesuit who was teaching dogmatic theology in Innsbruck, made him aware that an emphasis on the difference between archaic sacrifice and Christian self-giving love did not in itself prevent him from falling prey to humanistic and progressive illusions in his understanding of sacrifice. First signs of a changing attitude are already visible in his book *The Scapegoat* from 1982. Here Girard offers a more nuanced treatment of the Letter to the Hebrews.[21] Later on, he fully moves beyond his initial position. In an interview with Rebecca Adams, conducted in 1992, he very openly criticizes his earlier position. He admits that he was scapegoating Hebrews and also scapegoating the word 'sacrifice', really 'trying to get rid of it'.[22] Regarding his interpretation of Hebrews, he even goes so far as to say that he was 'completely wrong'.[23]

The most extensive treatment of his new approach to sacrifice can be found in his contribution to the Festschrift that was published on the occasion of Raymund Schwager's sixtieth birthday in 1995.[24] Since the publication of this article, Girard has repeatedly explained his changed attitude to sacrifice.[25] Most important in this respect is the French single volume republication of his first four books from 2007. In a long footnote Girard distances himself from his earlier position and even deletes a passage from *Things Hidden since the Foundation of the World* that by then had become most questionable to him.[26] How can we summarize Girard's new position on sacrifice?

First of all, Girard maintains that the difference between 'archaic sacrifices' and the 'sacrifice of Christ' is so great that hardly anything greater can be conceived.[27] In a later interview he emphasizes this difference despite the fact that he now uses the term sacrifice for both these acts:

> No greater difference can be found: on the one hand, sacrifice as murder; on the other hand, sacrifice as the readiness to die in order not to participate in sacrifice as murder.[28]

---

[21] Girard, *Scapegoat*, 200.
[22] Girard/Adams, 'Violence, Difference, Sacrifice', 29.
[23] Girard/Adams, 'Violence, Difference, Sacrifice', 28.
[24] Girard, 'Mimetische Theorie'; Girard, *Celui*, 63–82.
[25] Anspach, *René Girard*, 125–142; Girard, *Quand*, 15, 171; Girard, *De la violence*, 28, 1001; Girard, *Evolution*, 216–217; Vattimo/Girard, *Christianity, Truth, and Weakening Faith*, 92–93.
[26] Girard, *De la violence*, 28, 998, 1001; cf. Girard, *Things Hidden*, 243.
[27] Girard, *Celui*, 76.
[28] Girard, *Evolution*, 215.

In these words we find a clear criterion to distinguish between archaic sacrifices and the Christian sacrifice. Whereas the archaic type does not exclude murderous violence, Christian sacrifice is identified with a self-giving that is ready to suffer violence in order not to hurt or kill innocent people.

Girard holds to his view developed in his earlier work that there is a fundamental difference between myth and the Bible. But this important distinction does not have to be understood as a radical separation negating any connection between archaic religions and Judaeo-Christian revelation. According to Girard, if we take the whole of human history into account, there exists a 'paradoxical unity of all that is religious'—an expression by way of which Girard refers indirectly to an ontology of peace that is rooted in creation and that has a forming influence on the archaic religions, too.[29] Whoever rejects this unity—and we modern people are tempted to deny it—easily turns towards scapegoating: by holding a seemingly innocent and pure position one thinks oneself justified in condemning all archaic attempts to make peace.

The Canadian philosopher Charles Taylor clearly understands this temptation that haunts the Abrahamic religions from their very beginning as well as our modern world in general, when he indirectly refers to Girard's mimetic theory. According to Taylor, the 'recreation of scapegoating violence both in Christendom...and in the modern secular world' results from attempts at reform that try to break with the past entirely: 'It is precisely these claims fully to supersede the problematic past which blinds us to the ways in which we are repeating some of its horrors in our own way'.[30] Modern massacres—the slaughter of indigenous people in Latin America legitimated by the rejection of human sacrifice is one telling example—are the result of this moralistic attitude of a *corruptio optimi pessima*, a corruption of the best always leading to the worst.[31]

Through Raymund Schwager's influence, Girard was able to avoid these pitfalls by understanding Christian redemption in a way that maintains its fundamental difference from, as well as its connection with, archaic sacrifice. According to Girard, Jesus' substitutionary self-giving of his life has to be understood as a 'divine re-employment of the scapegoat mechanism': 'God himself re-employs the scheme of the scapegoat at his own expense in order to subvert it.'[32] It is Christ's sacrifice on the cross that overcomes archaic sacrifice.

Girard's emphasis on the paradoxical unity of all that is religious opens his theory towards an inter-religious perspective because it no longer relies on an unbridgeable ditch between Christianity and all other religions. It is also important to understand, with Girard, that we cannot easily put aside

[29] Girard, *Celui*, 79.
[30] Taylor, *A Secular Age*, 772.
[31] Palaver, *Theory*, 234–236.
[32] Girard, *Celui*, 80.

all violence that necessitates sacrifice. Violence—as long as it remains part of human relations—is either transferred to someone else (scapegoat mechanism) or overcome by someone ready to endure it (Christian self-giving). Girard does not rely on an ontology of violence that inescapably governs all human relations. But he is aware of how often violence plays an important part in human relations. His anthropology is a profound and sound unfolding of what is best in the tradition of original sin without succumbing to its weaknesses.

In his understanding of violence, Girard comes close to the French philosopher and mystic Simone Weil, whose work significantly influenced his mimetic theory. Weil, on the one hand, emphatically maintained that to 'imitate divine Love, no force must ever be exercised' but, on the other hand, distanced herself clearly from those people who ignored the significance of force.[33] Weil sharply criticized those who disregard the influence violence can have on our lives: 'They lie to themselves, if need be, in order not to learn about it.'[34] In a reflection on the class struggle, she showed how important it is to recognize the violence that accompanies those who are in command over others.[35] Whoever would condemn the struggle of the oppressed against this form of violence, justifies the privileges of the ruling class. Weil sharply rejected those 'spell-binders' whose 'advocacy of social peace presupposes the safeguarding of privilege, or at least the right of the privileged to veto any change they dislike.'[36] It is deeply misleading to ignore the role of violence in human relationships. But it would also be wrong to think that we cannot escape the spiral of violence. It is wrong to believe that there is only the possibility of returning violence with violence. Both Weil and Girard recognize violence as a common phenomenon without, however, giving in to fetishizing it as is typical of all ontologies of violence.[37] Like Girard, Weil understood that voluntary suffering provides a way out of the dominance of violence. A righteous person must imitate God who has freely consented to suffer: 'By love he must imitate Love, who never suffers anything without having consented to suffer it.'[38]

Girard has frequently referred to the biblical story about the Judgment of Solomon (1 Kgs 3:16–28) to explain his understanding of sacrifice—a biblical text Girard always held in high esteem.[39] Two women are quarreling about who is the true mother of a living child. After Solomon decides to divide the child in two, the bad mother accepts his judgment and demands the death of the child. She represents the sacrificial spirit of the scapegoat mechanism.

---

[33] Weil, *Intimations*, 120.
[34] Weil, *Intimations*, 116.
[35] Weil, *Selected Essays*, 162.
[36] Weil, *Selected Essays*, 170.
[37] Weil, *Intimations*, 116; Girard, *Things Hidden*, 330–331.
[38] Weil, *Intimations*, 120.
[39] Girard, *Things Hidden*, 237–245; Girard, *Celui*, 77–80; Girard, *Evolution*, 214–217.

The good mother, on the other hand, sacrifices her rights to the child when she asks the king to spare the life of the child and give it to the other woman. She even risks her own life since her behaviour could let her appear as a liar. In his earlier interpretations of this text, Girard suggested that one should not use the term 'sacrifice' with respect to either of these mothers. He wanted to strengthen the difference between archaic sacrifice and Christian sacrifice. In his later work, however, he talks about the danger that goes along with this view. He criticizes it for its illusionary assumption that there exists some 'neutral ground that is completely foreign to violence'.[40] Archaic sacrifice and Christ's sacrifice 'are radically opposed to one another, and yet they are inseparable. There is no non-sacrificial space in between, from which everything could be described from a neutral viewpoint.'[41] To claim that kind of neutral ground implies the attempt to avoid even the smallest costs that may have to be paid to overcome violence. Because violence is rooted in mimetic rivalries between human beings, it will not simply disappear without anyone being ready to sacrifice his own desires or a willingness to prefer suffering to violating someone else. Sacrifices in this sense are the only means to overcoming archaic sacrifice.

We can refer to contemporary examples in the realm of military ethics to show how the attempt to avoid sacrificing others can cause soldiers to risk their own lives. Moshe Halbertal who, as a philosopher, contributed to the Israel Defence Forces' ethics code claims—from my point of view rightly—that soldiers have to risk their own lives in order to protect the lives of the opponent's civilians. He refers to a telling example from the year 2002:

> In Operation Defensive Shield…Israeli army units faced a tough battle in the Jenin refugee camp. The army refused to opt for the easy military solution—aerial bombardment of the camp—because it would have resulted in many civilian deaths, and it elected instead to engage in house-to-house combat, losing 23 soldiers in the battle. [42]

Similarly, Avishai Margalit and Michael Walzer criticize claims that the safety of Israeli soldiers should take precedence over the safety of the Palestinian civilians.[43] Against such ethical arguments they claim that soldiers have to take an extra risk in order to protect the lives of others.

Simone Weil was able to express the difference between archaic sacrifices and Christian self-giving without relying on any illusionary neutral ground in regard to violence: 'The false God changes suffering into violence. The true God changes violence into suffering.'[44] The exodus from the world of archaic sacrifices is therefore not a complete break with the archaic world but its

---

[40] Girard, *Celui*, 80.
[41] Girard, *Evolution*, 216.
[42] Halbertal, 'The Goldstone Illusion', 24.
[43] Margalit/Walzer, 'Israel: Civilians and Combatants'.
[44] Weil, *Gravity*, 72.

transformation. The existing amount of violence has to be transformed. From this perspective, sacrificial Catholicism is not completely false but a starting point that has to be taken seriously while needing, of course, further clarifications and precise descriptions of different types of sacrifice. Girard adopted such a view in his most recent book *Battling to the End*, in which he discusses Madame de Staël's Catholic understanding of sacrifice and its parallels with Joseph de Maistre. Regarding Maistre's understanding of sacrifice Girard insists that:

> the anthropology that was being sketched in this case was still in its infancy. It cannot grasp the revealing reversal of *Things Hidden Since the Foundation of the World*. De Maistre's work contains an aborted meditation on sacrificing the other and sacrificing oneself: the victims are innocent, but at the same time the sacrifices have to have an expiatory function. Nonetheless, it was on this romantic loam that anthropology took root, and a science of religion beyond theological speculation became possible.[45]

The importance of transformation was underlined in this book with reference to Hölderlin, in whom Girard recognizes an important attempt at relating archaic and Christian sacrifices to each other.[46] Girard's turn towards a deeper understanding of the meaning of transformation once again brings him close to Raymund Schwager's dramatic theology with its emphasis on the transformation of sacrifice.[47]

## 3. ABY WARBURG'S THEORY OF RELIGION: THE NEED FOR TRANSFORMATION

The work of the art historian Aby Warburg (1866–1929) in many respects precedes the mimetic theory of René Girard. Warburg is especially enlightening with regard to Girard's later reflections on sacrifice. One can immediately recognize some obvious parallels. Both these thinkers came to the field of religious studies from the outside, from other disciplinary approaches, and both are also interdisciplinary thinkers going far beyond the narrow boundaries of usual disciplinary perspectives. Again and again, Warburg as well as Girard focused on important existential questions. A neat separation between personal life and theoretical work is foreign to their way of thinking.

This may be the reason for their common interest in the work of Nietzsche— an interest which does not prevent them from recognizing the enormous

---

[45]  Girard, *Battling*, 170–171.
[46]  Girard, *Battling*, 120–130, 217.
[47]  Schwager, *Jesus in the Drama of Salvation*; Niewiadomski, 'Transzendenz und Menschwerdung'; Siebenrock/Palaver/Sandler, 'Wandlung'.

danger that comes along with Nietzsche's celebration of Dionysus. According to Warburg, Nietzsche tried to 'make common cause with...the uncanny breath of the demon of destruction' but could finally not live up to the 'orgiastic states of the ancient world'.[48] Girard similarly claims that Nietzsche's mental breakdown follows his siding with Dionysus.[49] Connected with their interest in Nietzsche is a special attention to the passionate dimensions of human life and its violent potentials.

In the centre of Girard's theory, we find mimetic or imitative desire that easily but not necessarily turns into rivalry and violence between human beings. Warburg connects mimesis with the passions, and his theory differs in this regard from many other concepts of mimetic aesthetics.[50] One of Warburg's notes is especially revealing in this respect:

> The principle of identification reveals itself in social life in the following ways; / Comparison with the dynamic movement of another: following, obeying. / Comparison with reflex actions through reflex repetition of the other both in movement and at rest: imitation (mimicry). / Comparison with the scope of the other: property.[51]

Both these two thinkers focus especially on the question of violence in regard to religion. According to Girard, violence is the 'heart and secret soul of the sacred'.[52] Similarly, Warburg is aware of the bloody roots of religion and culture. In his lecture on the serpent ritual of the Hopi given in Kreuzlingen in 1923, he mentions the 'blood-soaked cultic roots' from which we cannot break away completely.[53] Two years later, he claims in another lecture that 'human sacrifices' belong to the 'horrific primordial elements' which build the 'basis of nearly all religions'.[54] Finally, we also have to mention the introduction to Warburg's picture atlas *Mnemosyne* in which he mentions a 'murderous cannibalism' and a 'primordial drive to sacrifice human beings'.[55]

But neither Warburg nor Girard adopt a static understanding of the meaning of violence in regard to religion. Both are evolutionary thinkers discussing religion in an evolutionary framework. At the centre of Girard's mimetic theory we find the idea that the biblical narrative undermines the scapegoat

---

[48] Quoted by Gombrich, *Aby Warburg*, 257.

[49] Girard, *Quand*, 154, 199; Girard/Goodhart, 'Mimesis, Sacrifice, and the Bible', 51.

[50] Empathy is an important concept in the writings of Warburg. In one of his unpublished notes he uses the term 'mimische Einfühlung' translated by Gombrich with 'bodily empathy' (Gombrich, *Aby Warburg*, 157; cf. Rampley, 'Symbol'). Gombrich's reference to the meaning the 'act of grasping' has for Warburg, who understands it 'as the most primitive of the contacts between man and the external world' comes close to Girard's concept of acquisitive mimesis (Gombrich, *Aby Warburg*, 252).

[51] Quoted by Rampley, *Remembrance*, 115.

[52] Girard, *Violence*, 31.

[53] Warburg, *Images*, 34.

[54] Warburg, *Sternglaube*, 98.

[55] Warburg, *Bilderatlas*, 3–4.

mechanism. The Passion and Resurrection of Jesus Christ bring about the final exposure of the foundational murder that governs archaic religion. Warburg recognizes a similar move away from the world of archaic sacrifices. His lecture in Kreuzlingen from 1923 includes many references to this theme, while underlining at the same time that this exodus went along with many relapses back into archaic religion: 'The deliverance from blood sacrifice as the innermost ideal of purification pervades the history of religious evolution from east to west.'[56] Warburg for instance detects 'a remnant of idolatry' in the story of the 'brazen serpent idol' erected by Moses to cure the poisonous bites of the snakes (Num. 21:4–9).[57] But in the same breath he also explains how much the prophetic tradition fought against this temptation referring to the fact that under King Hezekiah, who was influenced by the prophet Isaiah, the serpent idol was destroyed (2 Kgs 18:4):

> The prophets fought most bitterly against idolatrous cults that engaged in human sacrifice and worshipped animals, and this struggle forms the crux of Oriental and of Christian reform movements down to the most recent times.[58]

Early Christianity in particular was, according to Warburg, characterized by such a fight against idolatry. He refers to the example of Paul throwing a viper into the fire without being exceptionally impressed—contrary to many pagans (Acts 28:1–6):

> In the battle against pagan idolatry, early Christianity was more uncompromising in its view of the serpent cult. In the eyes of the pagans, Paul was an impervious emissary when he hurled the viper that had bitten him into the fire without dying of the bite.[59]

But such a rejection of archaic religion could again relapse into superstitious magic. Warburg refers to feasts in Malta that developed in connection with this story of Paul. Later on, on the basis of John 3:14–15 ('Just as Moses lifted up the serpent in the wilderness, so must the Son of Man be lifted up, that whoever believes in him may have eternal life.'), medieval theology often made uncritical connections between the serpent idol in the Old Testament and Jesus' crucifixion:

> Nothing attests to the indestructibility of the animal cult as does the survival of the miracle of the brazen serpent into the medieval Christian world view. So lasting in medieval theological memory was the serpent cult and the need to overcome it that, on the basis of a completely isolated passage inconsistent with the spirit and the theology of the Old Testament, the image of serpent devotion became paradigmatic in typological representations for the Crucifixion itself.[60]

---

[56] Warburg, *Images*, 38.
[57] Warburg, *Images*, 45.
[58] Warburg, *Images*, 45.
[59] Warburg, *Images*, 45.
[60] Warburg, *Images*, 46–47.

Warburg's reference to the typological alignment of the crucifixion to the pre-vented sacrifice of Isaac points in the same direction.[61] But even when Warburg refers to relapses into archaic religion, his analyses remain very careful; thus he does not fail to point out that in medieval theology the comparison of the rais-ing of the serpent with the crucifixion was 'expressly considered as an evolu-tionary stage that has been surpassed.'[62] Referring to Botticelli's 'Madonna and Child with an Angel' from 1470 and to Raphael's 'The Sacrifice at Lystra' from 1515 (a painting based on Acts 14:8–18), Warburg's lecture from 1925 also explicates how the detachment from human sacrifice was visually expressed in the Christian tradition.[63] With the help of Raphael's 'Mass of Bolsena' (1512) and other paintings, Warburg's picture atlas, too, expresses the 'rejection of sacrifice' that he valued in Christianity above all.[64] I will discuss Raphael's 'Mass of Bolsena' more closely below.

In a letter to his niece Gisela from May 1929, Warburg summarizes his view of the exodus of the biblical religions from the world of archaic sacrifice. Especially interesting in this regard, taking into account his own Jewish ori-gins, is the distinction he draws between Judaism and Christianity:

> Regarding the evolution of sacrificial cults (which for every religion is the mys-terious centre), Judaism has taken a heroic mediating position of enlightenment insofar as Elijah inflicted an incurable moral defeat on the child-slaughter-ing priests of Moloch; but animal sacrifice remained. In this respect, the Jews remained pagans in the Mediterranean Basin. Only the revolutionary heirs of Judaism, the Christians, tried to purify the house of God from the smoke of the sacrificial altar through an imaginary but complete detachment from the bloody sacrifice.[65]

The most interesting parallel with Girard, however, can be found where Warburg deals with the theological debates about the Eucharist at the end of his life. He was especially interested in the relationship between the Eucharist and primitive sacrificial cults. Warburg perceives a difference between Christianity and archaic religion, but also claims that the latter can be tamed but never completely overcome.

In the picture atlas it is especially the last plate (No. 79) that focuses on the Eucharist. Among the pictures Warburg arranged on this plate is Raphael's 'Mass

[61] Warburg, *Images*, 48.
[62] Warburg, *Images*, 49.
[63] Warburg, *Sternglaube*, 43, 106–108.
[64] Gombrich, *Aby Warburg*, 278.
[65] Quoted in Raulff, *Wilde Energien*, 70. Stroumsa recently underlined that not only Christianity but that, after the destruction of the Second Temple, rabbinic Judaism, too, sig-nificantly transformed its understanding of sacrifice: 'To a certain extent rabbinic Judaism and Christianity would both remain sacrificial religions, but very special sacrificial religions because they functioned without blood sacrifice.' (Stroumsa, *End of Sacrifice*, 63–64). Cf. Halbertal, *Sacrifice*, 7.

of Bolsena' which depicts the miracle that led to the installation of Corpus
Christi, the feast that celebrates the Catholic understanding of the Eucharist.
Despite the fact that this painting refers to a crude legend about a bleeding
wafer, it expresses, according to Ernst Gombrich, in Raphael's interpretation a
'deep spiritual experience: The priest sunk in deep contemplation, the groups
of the faithful moved to gestures of profound devotion and upward striving.'[66]
Warburg's own, notable interpretation of this painting is expressed specifically
in a long note in his *Diary of the Warburg Library*:

> Yesterday with Vreeken gripping discussion;...told him that I am neither anti-
> Catholic nor Protestant but could imagine (and wish for) a Christian religion of
> the future which is aware of the function of the metaphorical 'as' as a problem
> to struggle with. With all its activist 'hoc meum corpus est' the North fails to
> notice how the Catholic Church since the time of the Mass of Bolsena has rid
> itself of primitive magic....He [the Dutch visitor] looked optimistically into the
> future hoping that the work rhythm of grand enterprises and the new architecture
> will result in something like the avoidance of passion experiences....The Dutch
> nation simply was not, as I told him, in war.[67]

The Dutchman Vreeken represents in the eyes of Warburg the modern world
of the North that is closer to the Reformation and the Enlightenment and thus
more easily tempted to shut out reality by naively overlooking violence as it is
present and partly tamed in archaic religion and in Catholic symbols. With the
expression *hoc meum corpus est* Warburg refers to the modern cult of the body, a
pictorial representation of which is also present on the last plate, and its unconscious juxtaposition to the symbol of the Eucharist: *hoc est corpus meum*:[68]

> I ask myself: does this swimmer know what a monstrance is? Does this brawniest—
> I do not refer to his person but to the type—need to know the meaning of that
> symbolism which is rooted in paganism and which provoked such strong resist-
> ance in the North that Europe was split in half?...the brutal juxtaposition shows
> that the cheerful *hoc meum corpus est* can be set beside the tragic *hoc est corpus
> meum* without this discrepancy leading to an outcry against such barbarous breach
> of decorum.[69]

This juxtaposition of the monstrance with the modern cult of the body is connected to Warburg's critical remarks against modern technology in his lecture
in Kreuzlingen. Warburg thought that human beings will never be able to free
themselves completely from their archaic roots, and attributed certain dangers
to a type of Enlightenment that relies primarily on 'mathematical signs' and
technology. According to Warburg, the:

---

[66] Gombrich, *Aby Warburg*, 278–279.
[67] Warburg, *Tagebuch*, 498 [4.8.1929].
[68] Gombrich, *Aby Warburg*, 280–281.
[69] Quoted by Gombrich, *Aby Warburg*, 280–281.

culture of the machine age destroys what the natural sciences, born of myth, so arduously achieved: the space for devotion, which evolved in turn into the space required for reflection.... Telegram and telephone destroy the cosmos. Mythical and symbolic thinking strive to form spiritual bonds between humanity and the surrounding world, shaping distance into the space required for devotion and reflection: the distance undone by the instantaneous electric connection.[70]

In these reflections on technology, Warburg indirectly criticizes also the dangerous 'avoidance of passion experiences'.

In light of Warburg's sceptical attitude towards certain elements of modernity it is obvious that he considered a complete break with our archaic past as dangerous as the continuation of, or the return to, the archaic way of life. It is not surprising therefore that he came so close to a Catholic position that rumour had it that he had converted to Catholicism. Warburg understood Catholicism as an important bridge between an archaic past and an enlightened future. Concerning the struggle about the metaphorical 'as' in the theological debates on the Eucharist, he was interested in the 'space for reflection' one must find between the magic world-view of archaic religion and a mathematical abstraction which thinks it can completely break with the past and its archaic roots. Warburg claimed the need of a 'receiving station that registers the give and take between the past and the present' in order to contain the 'chaos of unreason by means of a filter system of retrospective reflection'.[71] Similar to Girard's insight that the archaic sacrifice needs to be transformed, Warburg underlines the need for a transformation, converting but not ignoring all the energies that are more openly visible in archaic religion. In June 1928 he wrote about himself: 'I am not a revolutionary reformer but an energetic transformer'.[72]

Warburg's emphasis on transformation, a term that is characterized by an interesting tension with the term 'reformation', comes close to Girard's later theory of sacrifice, which is catholic albeit not in a narrowly confessional sense of the term. As is expressed in the final sentence of the mentioned diary note ('The Dutch nation simply was not... in war'), it is important to understand how dangerous it is to overlook the reality of violence that often forces us to choose between sacrificing others and freely accepting self-sacrifice. The judgement of Solomon and the Passion of Christ are important biblical examples in this regard. If we look at the last plate of Warburg's picture atlas we are alerted to many different contexts for violence, in the personal as well as in the political sphere: Church power, a ritual suicide in hara-kiri style,

---

[70] Warburg, *Images*, 54.
[71] Gombrich, *Aby Warburg*, 281.
[72] Warburg, *Tagebuch*, 285; Raulff, *Wilde Energien*, 126–127. Warburg's emphasis on transformation comes close to Habermas's more recent post-secular approach: 'Secularization functions less as a filter separating out the contents of traditions than as a transformer which redirects the flow of tradition.' Habermas, *Awareness*, 18.

punishment and executions, a military parade and the Papal Swiss Guard, an ammunition wagon, the stabbing of the Host and the persecution of the Jews, the treaty of Locarno (1925), the last communion of Saint Jerome, and a train accident with one person dying. Gombrich summarizes the last two plates of the picture atlas thus: 'News photographs...of the signing of the Concordat with Mussolini were juxtaposed with renderings of the Mass and of the Eucharist...to remind viewers of the seriousness of the issues involved.'[73] Whoever shuts out such tragic dilemmas is easily tempted to justify the sacrifice of others in a disguised form.

This problem is illustrated in the anti-sacrificial concepts of liberalism mentioned in the beginning of this essay. Hobbes is a good example of the sacrificial consequences of an anti-sacrificial liberalism. He is not only an early representative of liberal individualism but also a mentor of the absolutist state. What starts as an anti-sacrificial individualism ends as a sacrificial ideology of an absolutist state emasculating individuality. Moshe Halbertal rightly emphasizes the sacrificial nature of the modern state referring also to its indirect connection with Hobbes' philosophy:

> Humans never created a greater altar to Molech than the centralized state. The modern state's hunger for human sacrifice is insatiable....The history of the modern state is in some ways a return of the repressed. In its demand for self-sacrifice, the centralized state manifests the vengeful eruption of the sacrificial desire that Hobbes everywhere attempted to marginalize.[74]

Similarly, Jean-Pierre Dupuy has convincingly shown that John Rawls was finally not able to overcome sacrifice entirely.[75] Rawls' theory remains consistent only insofar as it excludes all those situations necessitating sacrifice. Contrary to Rawls, Habermas does not exclude tragic situations entirely and expresses his admiration for those people who follow the biblical command to love and who are willing to sacrifice for their neighbours in ways that cannot be demanded morally. 'Supererogatory acts can be understood as attempts to counteract the effects of unjust suffering in cases of tragic complication or under barbarous living conditions that inspire our moral indignation.'[76] Similarly, in his 2004 discussion with Cardinal Ratzinger, who later became Pope Benedict XVI, Habermas maintains that every democracy relies on sacrifices of its citizens, although these cannot be enforced by law but may only be suggested to them. A democracy relies on voluntary acts of sacrifice:

> In a democratic constitutional state, a legal obligation to vote would be just as alien as a legal requirement to display solidarity. All one can do is suggest to the

---

[73] Gombrich, *Aby Warburg*, 301.
[74] Halbertal, *Sacrifice*, 105–107.
[75] Dupuy, *Self-Deconstruction of the Liberal Order*, 12–13.
[76] Habermas, *Justification*, 35.

citizens of a liberal society that they should be willing to get involved on behalf of fellow citizens whom they do not know and who remain anonymous to them and that they should accept sacrifices that promote common interests. This is why political virtues, even if they are only 'levied' in small coins, so to speak, are essential if a democracy is to exist.[77]

Beginning with John Lennon's song, I have attempted to show that the demand that there should be nothing 'to kill or die for' is an oversimplification: it cuts out all the difficult and tragic situations we may face in our life. For a long time, Simone Weil, too, was a pacifist. In one of her late reflections on this issue she emphasized in what way pacifism may turn into a danger, and thereby addressed the second pitfall we may face regarding sacrifice. This is not the pitfall into which thinkers like Maistre or Schmitt fall. Yet it too is a dangerous one:

> Pacifism is only capable of causing harm when a confusion arises between two sorts of aversion: the aversion to kill, and the aversion to be killed. The former is honourable, but very weak; the latter, almost impossible to acknowledge, but very strong.[78]

As a negative example Weil refers to French pacifists 'who had an aversion to being killed, but none to killing' and who therefore rushed hastily to collaborate with Germany in the July of 1940.[79]

---

[77] Habermas/Ratzinger, *Dialectics of Secularization*, 30.
[78] Weil, *Need*, 159; cf. Palaver, 'Frage.'
[79] Weil, *Need*, 159.

# 7

## From Slaughtered Lambs to Dedicated Lives
### *Sacrifice as Value-Bestowal*

Jessica Frazier

Does the endemic rule of mimesis mean that we can never desire that which is genuinely of value? Many of the modern theories that explain sacrifice as a mechanism for moderating our brute tendency toward violence or conflict, are historically rooted in experiences that suggested a diminishment in humanity's ability to pursue the values it holds most high. During the twentieth century extravagant levels of violence recurred repeatedly despite the fact that the world was, for the first time, able to see, condemn, and follow its perpetration through modern media, from print to radio, film, and the internet. This has introduced traumas of its own, casting doubt on the very rationality of the human person and our ability to master our destructive instincts. Anthropological narratives of the 'struggle with the self' have flourished.

In order to recover a picture of a 'whole' self, which desires what it judges to be most desirable, a notion of *rational* rather than merely biological or mimetic passions is required. Girard's tragic sacrificial narrative of borrowed values and consequent violence is driven by Schopenhauer's 'hydraulic' model of desire—a model that takes it to be a brute, unceasing, indiscriminate force which 'must be vented...*hurled* upon some object'.[1] On this model, desire incapacitates the discriminatory abilities of the individual and compels humans to do things that conflict with their other concerns—for survival, understanding, or justice, for instance. Immersed in his cultural heritage, Girard does not pause to question the provenance of this conception, or consider the other models of desire and sacrifice that are embedded in the history of religions, many of which are explored in the discussions in the present volume.

But Girard's model is philosophically incomplete; *chosen desire*, understood as the product of our own value-bestowing discriminative reasoning, must

---

[1] Skerrett, 'Desire and Anathema', 795.

lie at the causal root of Girard's chain of mimetic desires—for the original model must choose its desire, and the model itself must be chosen by the imitator. Thus, one can supplement Girard's causal narrative with a very different notion of desire as a process in which evaluative reasoning about projected outcomes helps us to bestow value on carefully chosen models. In restoring chosen desire alongside mimetic desire, we restore the possibility of a unified subject in which passion arises as a development of evaluative reasoning, rather than an opposing force in the psyche. This enables us to value, desire, and act in a coherent way.

In light of this primary form of desire, we can seek to expand the ethnology of sacrifice by noting ways in which original, chosen desire is expressed in sacrifices of quite different kinds from those rituals patterned on the Ancient Near Eastern model familiar to Girard, Burkert, and others. Girard's account imitates the methodological flaws of his own models (Frazer, Malinowski, Freud, and others), leading him to dismiss meanings attested by many insiders. His interpretations are bolstered by a hermeneutic of suspicion that methodologically rejects all competing readings of religious rituals by judging them to be part of the self-delusory nature of scapegoating. As such, it stands in particularly bad faith with the contemporary phenomenology of religion.

A wider view uncovers alternative traditions of sacrifice that reflect the form of desire that underlies discriminative evaluation. This is expressed in affirmative sacrifices such as we see in *animistic offerings* that express care of the family-spirits, in ritualized *sacred servant* dedications of a life to the service of a higher value, and in *ascetic self-sacrifices*. In this restoration of value-bestowal in Girard's narrative, what lies in the balance is the self. Is the sacrificing human a strong agent who desires as an expression of its reasoned values, or an essentially needy and mindless mimetic device caught in a positive feedback over which it has no control? There have been numerous attempts to recuperate Girard's model by emphasizing that our natural flaws can be counteracted by reference to the unique mimetic model provided by Christ, and affirming the inter-relational character that the mimetic principle lends to human life. Indeed, in the current volume Wolfgang Palaver offers a creative development of this aspect of Girard's theory (see Chapter 6). But we will see that even Girard's own model assumes the possibility of a strong, decision-making human self that is impassioned by a discriminative form of desire.

## 1. SACRIFICIAL DESIRE AS BRUTE DESIRE

Girard's model of mimetic desire as automatic, unreasoning, self-deluding, and incessant—in short as a form of brute will that desires without regard to the value of either the object or model of desire, has led to a contemporary situation in which '...all truths are treated as equal, since there is said to be no objective Truth, you are forced to be banal and superficial. You cannot be truly committed to anything, to be "for" something—even if only for the time being.'[2] Girard uses this specific account of desire to construct a neat cage around the human subject. His model plays out the implications of Schopenhauer's picture of the human psyche as a hydraulic device: we are subject to automatic internal forces that must be channelled and accommodated unless they are stopped by a complete cessation of all will. They are determinative of our actions rather than determined by them and so they are essentially non-negotiable: even his solution through the imitation of Christ remains subject to the notion of mimetic desire. Although Girard seeks to divorce himself from Freud's libidinal model of desire, his trap is based on Schopenhauerian principles, and follows a Freudian design. He seems to accept the notion that humans are, as Schopenhauer puts it, 'a compound of needs, which are difficult to satisfy...a continual striving.'[3] Schopenhauer hints at an endemic nature to our striving, and represents this drive through the metaphor of a natural force, such that '...we resemble such phenomena as smoke, fire, or a jet of water...we shall see everywhere a constant fighting and mighty struggling for life and existence...life has no true and genuine value in itself, but is kept in motion merely through the medium of needs and illusions.'[4] In seeking to outline the function of the psyche pragmatically, as if it were an 'apparatus', Freud adds to this natural-law-based model the descriptive idiom of engineering physics, and speaks of the 'innate needs' of the human psyche in terms of 'forces' that are the 'ultimate cause of all activity'.[5] The psyche's energies can be stored, expended, redirected, and displaced, but they are not made, destroyed, or changed in quantity in any normal psychic processes; and they are as free from the influence of the reasoning mind as any other physical forces. As Freud puts it, humanity quickly finds to its discontent that 'arguments are of no avail against their passions.'[6]

Girard grounds the passions in metaphysical need rather than biological need, but the former is also 'libidinal' in character because it is automatic in its origination, arising from a 'domain in which human uncertainty is most extreme', generating in man 'intense desires, though he may not know precisely for what', and operating as a necessary, insatiable and on-going process in the human psyche.[7] As with biological needs, humanity has little awareness and no control of these forces within the psyche, and like biological needs for limited resources such as food or family-members (as opposed to purely psychological

---

[2] Girard, *Ratzinger* (online source, no pagination).
[3] Schopenhauer, *Aphorisms*.
[4] Schopenhauer, *Aphorisms*, 52.
[5] Freud, *Outline*, 18–19.
[6] Freud, *Future*, 8–9.
[7] Girard, *Violence*, 155.

needs for unlimited resources such as guidance, comfort, or confidence), metaphysical need creates competition over a limited resource: identity. Girard argues strongly against Freud's notion of desire because it is cathectic, locating value in the desired object rather than in the imitative model.[8] But once Girard's desire is generated it follows the 'energic' model established by Freud and Schopenhauer before him in that it must be satisfied and cannot be mastered but only redirected to alternative objects, or transformed into other forms of psychic energy such as violence. 'Violence', Girard writes, 'is not to be denied, but it can be diverted to another object, something it can sink its teeth into.'[9] It can be deflected 'upon a relatively indifferent victim' thus 'absorbing all the internal tensions, feuds, and rivalries pent up by the community,[10] in a process of 'displacement' represented through images of flow, of a 'rising tide' and a redirection into proper channels.[11] He even ascribes a biological compulsion to aggression:

> ...the physiology of violence varies little from one individual to another...Once aroused, the urge to violence triggers certain physical changes that prepare men's bodies for battle. This set toward violence lingers on; it should not be regarded as a simple reflex that ceases with the removal of the initial stimulus...Violence is frequently called irrational. It has its reasons, however, and can marshal some rather convincing ones when the need arises. Yet these reasons cannot be taken seriously, no matter how valid they may appear.[12]

Girard's unmasking of desire's real reasons reveals a chain of causation that starts with a Platonic model of attraction: the lack of 'being' leads us to imitate another, and our imitative action fills that lack by borrowing 'being' from the model. The very act of imitation is thus not the expression, but the *satisfaction* of a desire, although this process generates the unwanted side-effect of mimetic desires that then are unleashed to follow their own 'physiological' momentum toward competition and a physiologically self-perpetuating urge to violence. Girard's focus throughout is on the physiologically self-perpetuating aggression that results from the mimetic desires. We might ask about the origins of the initial *metaphysical* desire, and the effects of its fulfilment—as Wolfgang Palaver points out in Chapter 6, this theory appears to be telling us about universal existential factors in human reflection. But Girard is more concerned with the end than the beginning of the causal chain.

The model of desire as unreasoning brute force predominates in Girard's earlier 1972 narrative of sacrifice in *La violence et le sacré*. Girard's later paper 'Mimesis and Violence' is more careful to work through the logic of the

---

[8] Girard, 'Freud'.
[9] Girard, 'Sacrifice as Sacral Violence', 74.
[10] Girard, 'Sacrifice as Sacral Violence', 77.
[11] Girard, 'Sacrifice as Sacral Violence', 79.
[12] Girard, *Violence*, 2–4.

mimetic impulse in a systematic way. Here the violence toward the scapegoat is not directly linked to the aggression that has been created and needs catharsis. Rather, it is seen as providing an implicit logical solution to the impasse, such that it replaces the old desire of the group with something new and shareable to desire together. Here the crux of the solution appears to lie in the way in which the scapegoat facilitates mimetic cooperative desires, rather than in catharsis.

But in this myth of origins mimetic desire maintains its determinative influence, and there is no escape from aggression for the form of cooperation that disrupts rivalry is still an aggressive one. Thus, on Girard's model we are bound by a chain of key psychological features that elude our discriminative influence: (a) the automatic character of metaphysical desire's generation, direction, and continuation such that it appears to operate without being directed by the discriminating choice of our own models, and is never satiated because it is not aimed at obtaining concrete goals but rather at a continual self-transformation; (b) the automatic character of mimetic desire's generation, its direction as an imitation of the model's desires, and its continuation as an instrumental rather than an intrinsic desire cannot be satiated by the object desired; and (c) the character of aggression as a determining force that must be expended.

What is lacking throughout this causal chain is any element of independent, reasoned generation of chosen desires. Imitation is all. Girard writes that mimesis is the 'birth of desire', and thus we should not fall into 'the lie of spontaneous desire', or the 'illusion of autonomy'.[13] He speaks of 'spontaneity' as something generally lost to humans; Emma Bovary's cheap fiction has stolen it from her, and Don Quixote's chivalrous heroes from him, as all of our mediators—good and bad—have stolen it from us.[14] Girard ridicules anyone who deliberately follows his own desires because he believes them to be the reflection of their object's intrinsic value. Such a person is a '...romantic vaniteux [who] always wants to convince himself that his desire is written into the nature of things, or which amounts to the same thing, that it is the emanation of a serene subjectivity, the creation ex nihilo of a quasi-divine ego.'[15]

It would seem impossible for a 'serene subjectivity' to rationally direct desire towards independently valued goals on this model. The automatic functioning of metaphysical and mimetic desire and the energy of aggression together form a system that operates automatically, trapping the rational subject within its over-mastering physics. Mimesis is necessary because there is no reasoning with the brute desires (metaphysical, mimetic, and aggressive) within; they *must* be fed.

---

[13] Girard, *Triangular Desire*, 43.
[14] Girard, *Triangular Desire*, 36.
[15] Girard, *Triangular Desire*, 43.

## 2. MIMETIC DESIRE AS COOPERATIVE DESIRE AND PURE ENJOYMENT

In the years after Girard's initial articulation of his theory of mimetic desire as the 'fall' from which human violence proceeds he and others have come to recognize some of the difficulties with his view. While his Christian apologetic agenda has become more explicit, a number of Christian theologians have felt concerned with the centrality of humanity's fallen-ness, such that sin becomes 'the controlling factor'[16] to which Christ's soteriological actions defer, springing from an initial 'need, offense, or deficit'[17] in the essentially negative economy of human nature. This sits ill with many contemporary theological tastes, and more problematically it also suggests a determinism that conflicts with Girard's proposed means of escape from the trap of violence. In his later work, Girard has sought to highlight the positive forms of mimesis as offering means of escape from the trap created by desire. He invites such positive readings by reminding us that mimetic power can also create a great capacity for intelligence and learning. 'Positive Girardians' have agreed with his construction of desire, and gone on to suggest non-violent forms that mimetic desire might take. Two popular approaches consist either of altering the object of desire so that it no longer generates competition but rather a beneficial outcome, or of altering the nature of desire itself so that it no longer generates acquisitiveness and competition.

An example of the former approach is the suggestion that the main *acquisitive* desires to which humans are subject are not for limited commodities that necessitate competition, but rather for states of being that necessitate cooperation. Girard's biological model of need for food and water is premised on the image of isolated cavemen competing for the same apple, goat, mate, or patch of fertile land. As Mary Midgley points out, this picture of man the aggressive competitor has been reinforced over the last centuries by post-Darwinian notions of evolutionary competition, Malthusian economics, Herbert Spencer's defence of capitalism, and Nietzsche's apology for the will. But the reality of survival, she argues, requires that mimetic social cooperation outweigh individual competition, resulting in the social contract which ensures our survival far more effectively than could any isolated combat in the proverbial forest.[18]

Similarly Girardians such as Rebecca Adams[19] and Jean-Michel Oughourlian[20] have suggested the possibility of mimetic desires that turn us away from the egoistic index of our own pleasure. Girard implies that desiring

---

[16] James Alison, *Joy*, 7.
[17] Lowe, *Salvation*, 237.
[18] Midgley, *Evolution*, 140.
[19] Adams, 'Loving Mimesis'.
[20] Oughourlian, *Genesis*.

what another desires automatically puts us in competition for the object of desire. But mimetically mirroring the other's desire for something need not cause us to desire it for oneself, particularly if we already possess an abundance of the desired thing (I have a large number of apples and have eaten my fill, but I now see someone else hungrily craving a taste of one), or do not ourselves enjoy it (I do not actually enjoy eating apples, but I see that others do). In such cases I experience desire vicariously without personal acquisitiveness, and thus without any cause for competition. Such an experience could give rise to empathy, possibly sympathy, and perhaps even generosity. Sherwood Belangia attributes a Platonic precedent to this strategy by suggesting that the mimesis of desire for abstract objects such as the ideal 'forms', love of which underlies the successful community in *The Republic* and constitutes the essence of all love in *The Symposium* can (a) avoid the competitive implications of imitating another's desire, and (b) transform the desire itself into a transformative urge to *become* rather than to *have*.[21]

Thus, desire need not militate toward acquisition. It can even be transformed into *enjoyment*, a non-acquisitive and non-competitive, mature form of pleasure. On this model the subject foregoes acquisition, not as a sacrifice made in grudging deference to the ethical imperative of non-violence, but rather as a sophisticated way of increasing pleasure by prolonging desire into a state that is itself satisfying. Many 'erotic' forms of religious devotion—such as Islamic and Hindu ecstatic devotion—apply this model to the divine object, choosing to enjoy passion rather than to sate and thus quench it.[22] James Hans suggests that enjoyment offers a fundamentally secular counterpoint to Girard's model of desire, arguing that theism compounds the problem of competitive desire by training us into an over-arching attitude of dissatisfaction with what we have (this world) and desire for what is otherworldly and essentially different from what we possess. If, as Hans suggests, this is a culturally-trained habit of thought, then it is contingent and can be changed. Thus, secularism, by contrast, can teach us a disposition of enjoyment of the world in which we live, thereby turning us from the acquisitive-competitive impulse that leads to violence.[23] Indeed, Feuerbach is a secular precursor of this approach, agreeing that sacrifice is 'the most essential act of natural religion', but suggesting that the sense of debt that he believed to be implied in sacrificial offerings should be counteracted by learning to appreciate our unproblematic, guilt-free access to 'a *named, finite earthly* happiness, a determined enjoyment, such as the enjoyment of love, or of beautiful music, or of moral liberty, or of thinking.'[24] Here we are offered a notion of desire that does not have to be denied by

---

[21] Sherwood Belangia, 'Metaphysical Desire', 197–209.
[22] Frazier, *Reality*.
[23] Hans, *Fate*.
[24] Feuerbach, *Essence*, 71.

the will because it has no competitive or violent outcome; rather the will operates in tandem with the desire, transforming, intensifying, and fulfilling it, and mimesis only increases this effect without creating competition.

Each of these alternatives—non-competitive mimesis and non-acquisitive enjoyment—allows for desire as a mimetically generated state that retains earthly models (unlike Girard's vertical mimesis of Christ alone), without needing to be curtailed or diverted by the higher ethical reasoning of the individual. In each of these pictures we see a self that is an agent free from internal conflict, able to operate in accord with both its passions and its higher reasoning.

## 3. THE ROOTS OF ORIGINAL DESIRE: POSSIBILITY-ASSESSMENT AND VALUE-BESTOWAL

These all remain Girardian accounts in that they focus on desire as a product of metaphysical need and the mimetic habit that it creates in the psyche, charting its genesis from that point of origin. We cannot escape mimesis, we can only hope for a positive outcome, or try to transform our mimetic desire into something less problematic than mere competitive acquisitiveness. What we cannot do is 'own' our motivations as linked to our own evaluation, motivation, and considered choice. Thus we still live in a world where, as Girard puts it, 'all truths are treated as equal, since there is said to be no objective truth' and one 'cannot be truly committed to anything' or ' "for" something'. This is one of the problematic outcomes of a model of the self as bi-partite, in which reason keeps its own counsel and desire follows a separate trajectory, at best negotiating a wary compromise. However, rational choice must also have a place in the operation of human desire, intervening with freely chosen evaluations and bestowals of value at key points in Girard's account.

Firstly, while at times Girard seems to claim that all desire is mimetic, it is of course logically impossible for this to be the only form of desire. There must be an original desire that is not itself generated mimetically, but arises from an independent valuation, or *choice*, by the original desirer. Girard admits only one intrinsic desire—metaphysical desire which is essentially a general desire to acquire particular desires through others—but for anyone to desire anything in particular, there must be a possibility of desiring independently on the basis of actual assessments and bestowals of value. Value-bestowal and appropriate desire should exist in Girard's world, despite the fact that Girard is sceptical about such 'cathectic' desire, rejecting Freud's intrinsic valuing of the mother in the Oedipus complex for instance.[25] John Milbank observes this

---

[25] Girard, 'Freud', 230.

lacuna in Girard's argument, and makes the point that by failing to offer a central account of desire's initial origin, Girard does not allow for the possibility of appropriately desiring something of actual value. This has problematic ethical implications, not least for the notion of a Christian's ability to choose to imitate Christ. Just as Girard asks why Freud banished mimetic desire from his account, one might ask why Girard 'hides' from our capacity for *intrinsic discrimination* and cathectic desire in his own narrative, even though his own proposed course of action relies upon it.

Secondly, once metaphysical desire is conceived, we must still choose the one whom we imitate. Girard seems to want to suggest that this is automatic, using the 'familial' model of humans in natural proximity to a select handful of others, rather in the way that Freud does. He would have it that we imitate those who naturally come into our field of awareness most forcefully. Yet we will often be presented with more than one companion, and more than one desire, and many of the novelistic examples that prompted Girard's theory involve *literary* models such as the romantic heroines admired by Emma Bovary, or the knights emulated by Don Quixote, rather than immediate parental contacts. These models must have been chosen from among a wider range of cultural heroes; imitation cannot be *fully* automatic; Girard's own suggestion that we imitate Christ presupposes this ability to use this capacity for *preferential discrimination*.

Thirdly, once the model is chosen, and the mimetic desire is generated and—if it is acquisitive towards a limited resource—transformed into aggression, we can still use our discriminatory capacities to choose its direction. This happens in Girard's account when the true cause of violence is revealed and the sacrificer decides, although he cannot escape mimetic desire, to shift his mimesis toward a passive model (Christ). In acknowledging that we can choose the victim rather than the competitor as a model, Girard acknowledges the possibility of *directional discrimination*. One might find the vulnerability of the victim, or the fear of the onlooker to be more compelling than the aggression of the competitor/accomplice. One might be as moved to mimesis by the nurturing attitude of the parent, or the enjoyment of the aesthete, as by the desire of the hungry caveman or the jealous lover. Girard argues that the 'victory of the Cross' can overwhelm that of violence, and there may be other kinds of 'victory of love against the scapegoating cycle of violence.'[26]

Girard's argument presupposes these three processes of rational discrimination—*intrinsic discrimination* of the value of the object, *preferential discrimination* of certain models over others, and *directional discrimination* between different objects and forms of desire/aggression—as forms of value-bestowal that challenge the rule of brute desire. In the very presentation of plural cases of mimesis in novels such as *The Brothers Karamazov*, we are presented with the

---

[26] Girard, *Ratzinger.*

reality of evaluation and choice.[27] Why does Alyosha imitate Father Zossima's abstract non-competitive desires to positive effect, while Dmitri imitates Father Karamazov's acquisitive desires to competitive but not violence effect, and Smerdyakov imitates Ivan's desires, generating not violent competitive desire, but violent hatred nevertheless? Is not Alyosha's mimesis seen as a well-judged discipleship, or at least one in which the mature recognition and embracing of the religious values underlying the imitation of his youthful hero provides the main thrust of his narrative trajectory, particularly after Zossima's death? Girard discusses these texts, but he largely prefers to ignore proactive characters such as Alyosha and Raskolnikov who spontaneously choose new better desires. Instead he explores those in whom liberation from mimesis coincides with the ultimate relinquishing of the problem of desire: death. Because Girard cannot account for the independent value-bestowal entailed in original desire, he argues that only the non-desire of death can free characters such as Julien Sorel in *The Red and the Black*, Stefan Trofimovitch in *The Possessed,* and Don Quixote.[28]

Girard passes over these moments of evaluative 'owning' of our desires perhaps because he has no faith in any values formulated by mere human beings. He speaks of choice in terms of variously legitimated forms of violence and warns of a world in which our definition of legitimate and illegitimate 'becomes a matter of mere opinion', leaving us to make our way through 'a world with no absolute values'.[29] For Girard these concerns extend to all humanly-originated truths. Underlying our tendency to rivalry, it is really our inability to make definitive choices that lies at the root of desire's trap. For Girard we can only move away from the choices that lead to violence by reference to values given to us by God through 'the introduction of some transcendental quality'.[30] Thus the fault of Emma Bovary and Don Quixote is not that they choose badly; it is that they try to choose at all.

But although he does not intend it, Girard's own model of the imitation of Christ is also impacted by the lack of a strong account of valuing. We may imitate Christ but unless our choice of God as a model is supported by good reasons then it will be merely another mimesis, no better than any other. For, not having undergone the process of evaluation, the mimetic desirer will not understand the supporting rationale that makes a model desirable. Mimetic value is blindly independent of evaluative reasoning, leading to a desire that has no sense of the outcome in respect of which the object is desired. By contrast, in the original desirer all the features of human nature work in tandem: the projection to future states that underlies evaluation and anticipation,

---

[27] Girard, *Desire*, 48.
[28] Girard, *Triangular Desire*, 34.
[29] Girard, *Violence*, 25.
[30] Girard, *Violence*, 25.

and the attraction of the passions. The original desirer, as opposed to the mimetic desirer, is in harmony with himself, and in good faith with his future.

Girard's reading of Don Quixote is curious in that it is determined to ignore the suggestion that Quixote is a 'good' or 'original' reasoned desirer, who sees our life-models as driven by an objective appreciation of their values. He quotes a speech from the novel as revealing mimetic desires, yet the models that Quixote himself gives are not spurious but appear as a litany of 'good' models—that is, a guide to quality:

> ...when a painter wants to become famous for his art he tries to imitate the origi-
> nals of the best masters he knows; the same rule applies to most important jobs
> or exercises...the man who wishes to be known as careful and patient should and
> does imitate Ulysses...just as Virgil shows us in the person of Aeneas the valor of
> a pious son and the wisdom of a valiant captain...in the same way Amadis was
> the post, the star, the sun for brave and amorous knights, and we others who fight
> under the banner of love and chivalry should imitate him.[31]

Note that Cervantes reverses Girard's causality of desire: it is the qualities of care and patience that motivate our imitation of Ulysses, the banner of love and chivalry that spur Quixote to make Amadis his own model. This form of desire recalls Plato's account of Eros in the *Symposium* as the guiding spirit of attraction to that which will lead us toward the abstract values that we most approve.

## 4. SACRIFICE AS LIFE-DEDICATION, VALUE-BESTOWAL, AND SELF-SACRIFICE

If this is the form of desire that is lacking in, but necessary to, Girard's account, then one might ask how it impacts on the actual traditions of sacrifice that exist—practices that he sees as a hermeneutic key to the history of human-ity's negotiation of its own desires. We could expect to see forms of sacrifice that reflect the original discriminatory form of desire and its positive outcome for humanity, existing alongside the Ancient Near Eastern paradigm of poly-theistic altar-based blood-offerings on which Girard focuses. He refers to both Biblical texts and the Vedic texts of the early Aryan peoples of India as exem-plars of sacrifice.[32] But at least two other equally widespread styles of sacrifice existed concurrently with this tradition. The first is the practice of animist spirit offerings. The vast majority of sacrifices undertaken globally as a dedicated gift to a being with special religious status (i.e. a deity, spirit, ancestor, guru, saint or

---

[31] Cervantes, quoted in Girard, *Triangular Desire*, 34.
[32] Girard, *Sacrifice*.

other guide such as a Buddha) are non-violent gifts in which the criterion for the offering is that it is something that most people would *value and enjoy*. Thus in offerings to spirits throughout Asia (as also in other indigenous cultures) sacrificers give of their own possessions: food, drink, baubles, and ornaments, objects of enjoyment such as toys and clothing all find their place on the spirit altar. Incense and flowers are common precisely because they are things that the sacrificer enjoys and thinks the spirit will also enjoy—in Thai families people may go shopping for attractive outfits that a female spirit will enjoy, leaving them in the shrine where she lives. Ancestor-offerings that affirm continuing regard for a dead relative are gift-sacrifices of the same kind. The genesis of value in this context is clearly traceable to a projection about potential positive experiences, and such offerings are thus a gifting of one's own experiences of value, marked as sacred in making them possible for a valued other.

The animist offering also acts as a sacrifice (rather than merely a gift) in that something must be 'given up' in order to attest that one values the recipient. Whereas the scapegoat theory sees all sacrificial objects as essentially anonymous and interchangeable vehicles of catharsis, this form of sacrifice sees the sacrificial object as determined cathectically by its value as a source of positive experiences. Thus objects are not anonymous and interchangeable substitutes, nor purely symbolic totems—rather it is precisely their value to the sacrificer that determines their value as a sacrifice. In this case sacrificial status functions as something that calibrates the ratio of loss and gain, as Derek Hughes puts it in Chapter 15 of the present volume in the context of the military sacrifice of lives that are meant to be seen not as mere fodder, but as unique and irreplaceable. The most celebrated such sacrifice in the Judaeo-Christian tradition is Abraham's potential sacrifice of his son, in which the value of Isaac is not that he is a simple vehicle of violence, but rather that he is of immense value to his father, the sacrificer; a fact that the frame-narrative of Abraham's efforts to find an heir makes clear. The story could easily have had God ask Abraham to sacrifice a random boy; anyone would serve for the purpose of scapegoating. But this would have told quite a different story, with quite a different significance, testing Abraham's ethics rather than his personal valuing of his God. The point is picked up by Jesus himself when he observes that the pennies of a poor widow please God more than the money bags of a wealthy man. Our ability to discriminate values and choose between them is at the heart of this form.

This feature of offering-sacrifices as an exchange of one valued thing for another leads to the second form of non-violent sacrifice: *self-sacrifice*. Given that Isaac's value is determined by his importance to Abraham rather than as a generic life, Abraham's sacrifice can be seen as an instance of *self-sacrifice*. Girard portrays blood-sacrifice as the original form, with self-sacrifice as a stage on the way to Christ-like reform. But many contemporary scholars believe Vedic ritual and the Indian tradition of renunciation found in Yogic, Buddhist, and Jain traditions, to have developed concurrently, with brahminical Vedic sacrifice paralleling the meditative inner disciplines that existed at the Eastern end of the Gangetic Plain in the region of Magadha.[33] In ascetic cultures, it is not another that is sacrificed, but oneself, and not necessarily through death but rather through the giving up of certain kinds of experiences. Thus the sacrifice most explicitly takes the form of a ritualized instance of evaluation, choice, and enactment of one's values by 'sacrificing' them. This appears to reflect a fixed economy of exchange that governs our own discriminative evaluation: to get something, one must give up other possibilities.

Yet this form of sacrifice does not obtain to objects so much as to situations. In the *Yoga Sutras*, the yogi's possibility of a family life is sacrificed in favour of the possibilities afforded by the skill of mental and physical focus. The *Bhagavad Gita* explicitly defines the yogi as a discriminative self-directed reasoner who has made 'sacrifices' for clearly defined outcomes that arise from that very action: 'Some yogis perform the service of worship to celestial controllers, while others study scriptures for Self-knowledge... Some give charity and offer their wealth as a sacrifice... All these people are the knowers of sacrifice, and are purified by their sacrifice.'[34] Inversely in the later ecstatic tradition represented by the medieval devotional poetry of the *Gitagovinda* in which the devotee's desire for God is portrayed as a form of blissful suffering, the banal pleasures of comfort are sacrificed in favour of the heightened sensitivity to divine joy achieved through refined passion. In her evaluation of Aztec practices in Chapter 11 of the present volume, Rival suggests that shamanistic notions of inter-subjectivity meant that even their human sacrifices were partly sacrifices of the shared self, rather than a scapegoated Other. In some cases the victim chose to die for the community: martyrdom could also be seen as a form of self-sacrifice, and its model in Christ reminds us that Jesus is Girard's exemplar of the discriminative sacrificer as *self*-sacrificer. In these cases it is clear that the sacrifice is a way of expressing and committing to an underlying cathectic value (in Abraham's case a good relationship with God, in Jesus' case the good of the many rather than that of the few, in the Yogi the experience of perspicuous equanimity or in the devotee the enjoyment of the divine rather than that of mundane objects). In each case discriminatively chosen desire is highlighted, and violence is absent.

The two traditions—of gift-sacrifice and self-sacrifice—are united in a particularly illuminating form of offering that was interlaced with the blood-sacrifice tradition in the Ancient Near East, complicating Girard's violence-based genealogy. *Divine servant* traditions made the sacrifice of human life not through ritualized killing, but through dedicated living. A popular practice in Mediterranean, Ancient Near Eastern, and Indian theistic temple-based

---

[33] Bronkhorst, *Magadha*.
[34] *Bhagavad Gita*, 4.25–30.

traditions was the gift of a person sent to the house of God, to dedicate his or her life in the service of its divine resident. Such lives—often those of a daughter or son but sometimes the sacrificer him- or herself—as temple-servants, temple-dancers, oracles, possession-vehicles, or divine spouses, suggest that the essence of life-sacrifices was the ultimate gift of a lived life of experience and action. The fact that numerous violent temple-sacrifice traditions viewed death as the gateway to a post-mortem life lived in the divine realm, supports the idea that the significance of many animal and human sacrifices lay in their potential for life, not for death.

All these offerings express the human experience of 'valuing' something and acting upon that value by making a reasoned relinquishing of one thing of value in favour of something of higher value. As such they express the very union of reasoned value-bestowal and consequent attraction that lies at the root of chosen desire. They also reveal the root violence entailed by these value-bestowing sacrifices: the realization that we must lose certain possibilities, give up certain valued outcomes, in favour of others that we prefer. Such is the nature of value-bestowal itself.

This reading of sacrifice can be mapped onto violent instances of sacrifice in interesting ways. One prominent (if not actually common) form of self-sacrifice is the suicide-attack, a violent act that appears to combine aggression with self-sacrifice. Some have interpreted this as a continuation of the victim-displacement pattern, with the self as the new scapegoat sacrificed for the good of the community.[35] Alternatively it could be seen as the definitive gesture of staking one's desires on a non-instinctual, carefully reasoned bestowal of value on something that lies well beyond the sphere of personal gratification. Girard argues that where there is violence, 'reasons cannot be taken seriously, no matter how valid they appear. Violence itself will discard them.'[36] But much religious violence—against both the self and the other—asks to be taken seriously as a defence of some lives at the loss of others based on carefully calculated outcomes. This principle of the good of the few for that of the many pervades modern conceptions of society, from taxation to military defence. We must also take seriously the significance of death for those who see it as a transition to a new life of post-mortem experiences. One need not condone, but one must, as David Brown also emphasizes, in this volume, understand even violent practice in terms of its reasons and values—otherwise Girard's psychology of automatic desire becomes merely a form of reduction that, as the anthropologist Elizabeth Traube noted, is itself violent toward not the body, but the agency of the Other.[37]

---

[35] Juergensmeyer, *Cosmic War*.
[36] Girard, *Violence*, 2.
[37] Traube, *Incest*.

## 5. CONCLUSION

Girard's sacrificer is the epitome of the weak self: compulsively imitating others, incapable of value-bestowal and intrinsic desire. Such a subject has no evaluative reasoning or decision-making agency, and it is divided against itself: the desire for being, for the other's object, and eventually for aggression itself are all frustrated by the concurrent fear of destruction. Such a subject is caught between reason and passion, fear and desire. Girard's Christian is, by contrast, a stronger self with the discriminative power to assess potential models and redirect its mimesis to a transcendent model. Yet it is still a divided self: reason must negotiate with the forces of mimetic desire. A still stronger self would be one in which the original desires naturally coincided with one's values.

I have tried to show that Girard's suggestion that all desire is mimetic cannot work, and that any mimetic account must be anterior to the pre-existing operations of autonomous desire. The self must have desires which are 'owned' by its evaluative reasoning, and as such it is a 'strong' subject—aware of its options to feel and do a variety of things, and confident about its ability to evaluate options, and bestow value appropriately. This self does not struggle with itself, but rather possesses desires of a kind which do not cause it difficulties, partly because its desires spring from the ethical and practical projections of reason. They are the desires of a subject that sees whole situations, rather than just models and objects.

Alyosha Karamazov, that most strong and proactive of the characters cited by Girard as having moved beyond mimesis, discovers his own desire whilst kneeling before the corpse of his 'model' Father Zossima 'as if before a shrine', 'to offer thanks and to love.'[38] In his moment of arriving at desire Alyosha expresses himself by embracing the earth, 'drenching it with his tears, and passionately swearing to love it.'[39] If this is an expression of Girard's vertical transcendent mimesis, it is a curious one for it is shaped in a language not of renunciation and victimhood, but of commitment, offering, overwhelming passion, and non-vertical love. In a novel full of powerful potential models, Alyosha appears as the discriminative desirer in a world of imitators. He is a sacrificer of whom we may say, as Dostoevsky says of Alyosha, that his desires and offerings sprang from appropriate value-bestowal so that, at that moment, he 'was not ashamed of his passion.'[40]

[38] Dostoevsky, *Karamazov*, 456.
[39] Dostoevsky, *Karamazov*, 456.
[40] Dostoevsky, *Karamazov*, 456.

# 8

## Sacrifice as Refusal

### Gavin Flood

Sacrifice is a category central to our understanding of religion and, it could be argued, of human cultural life. In this chapter, I wish to argue that we need to understand sacrifice not only in terms of an economy of exchange or socio-psychological catharsis, as some major theorists have done, but that behind such exchange, behind catharsis, sacrifice confronts us with the naked *aporia* of human life. We need to understand sacrifice in starker, existential terms. While the function of sacrifice can be seen in the context of propitiation of divine powers, expiation of impurity, gift-exchange, communion, the bonding of groups, or even the violent release of pent up energy, a deeper meaning of sacrifice must be sought in terms of transcending death and of affirming life against nothingness. From this perspective, sacrifice is akin to asceticism or renunciation because it plays out a paradox of the affirmation of life through its destruction. Sacrifice challenges finitude and mortality through the affirmation of life by death and the fundamental revelation or insight that birth in some sense follows death. The power of this affirmation lies in the characteristic of sacrifice as refusal: the refusal of death (and time) and therefore the refusal of meaninglessness.

In light of Heesterman's work,[1] refusal indeed appears as one of the central elements of sacrifice. Refusal works at different cultural levels. It can refer to the renunciation of something of human benefit in order to achieve a higher good, and it can also refer to a rejection of finitude, or of death. If a central theme of religions is the transformation of the human condition, then sacrifice speaks to this theme in various ways. It particularly does so, however, when it is understood in terms of refusal, which is geared precisely towards an inner transformation. Religious traditions have clearly understood this renunciatory

[1] I am indebted to Heesterman for inspiring these thoughts about 'refusal' and for alerting me to some relevant scholarship. Heesterman, *The Broken World of Sacrifice*, 7–18. I would also like to thank Johannes Zachhuber for his comments and for encouraging these thoughts about refusal.

dimension and have developed concepts of sacrifice as metaphor for an internalization of outer practice and recognition of its centrality to human striving for transcendence. This link between sacrifice and renunciation was worked out, for example, in the long history of Indian religions where renunciation was understood as a response to sacrifice. Although the idea of a sacrificial logic in the Indic historical context cannot be developed here, the current chapter will sketch the idea of sacrifice as refusal, and conclude with a methodological claim that a hermeneutical understanding is more appropriate for penetrating this existential layer than a causal explanation.

Some recent scholarship has underplayed the importance of sacrifice: Marcel Detienne has understood ancient Greek sacrifice in political and economic terms involving food distribution,[2] and Jonathan Z. Smith has even said of sacrifice, as he said of religion, that it is the creation of the scholar's imagination.[3] These claims, as Heesterman has argued in the context of vedic material, are exaggerated and there is clearly a body of sacrificial texts and performances that are central to many religions. Less sceptical theorists than Detienne and Smith have understood sacrifice within an economy of exchange, although this emphasis tends to occlude the centrality of sacrifice in ordering religious life and understanding religious action. Sacrifice in the sense of the violent immolation of living beings has itself been understood as a metaphor for an inner transformation, an *anabasis*, which we might see in terms of an enacted metaphor for fundamental human motivations towards meaning, a meaning that is formed through refusal or renunciation. Sacrifice must indeed be understood not only in terms of social function, but in terms of the formation of religious meaning, in terms of the desire to transcend time and death, and in terms of a denial or refusal of death and nothingness. The origins of sacrifice might well be very ancient—perhaps in Palaeolithic hunting traditions, as Burkert argues,[4] or in Neolithic farming communities. Irrespective of its origins, however, sacrifice has, in certain traditions, become a way of ordering the world, of expressing hope, and of giving life meaning. This ordering of the world through sacrifice has often, although not only, occurred at times of crisis, at times of the disruption of normal events and the need to re-establish normality within a community. The reinterpretation of sacrifice in Christianity, Judaism, Hinduism, and Buddhism, and its transformation into an ethical category is a further articulation of the way sacrifice expresses meaning and orders human relationships to the world, to time, and to death.[5] As Hedley argues in a recent study, sacrifice is 'a universal component of the

---

[2] Detienne, 'Culinary Practice and the Spirit of Sacrifice', 3. Political power cannot be exercised without sacrificial practice.

[3] Smith, 'The Domestication of Sacrifice', 179.

[4] Burkert, *Homo Necans*, 12–22.

[5] On the Christian and Rabbinic rejection of literal sacrifice, see Stroumsa, *End of Sacrifice*.

human imaginary'.[6] In spite—or perhaps because—of this, it has proven an elusive reality hard to define and explain.

## 1. WHAT IS SACRIFICE?

The term 'sacrifice' covers a range of practices and cultural themes and we might speak of a 'family of sacrifice'.[7] Although it is useful to restrict the term to the ritual killing of an animal, there are widely acknowledged metaphorical extensions of sacrifice, which becomes appropriated by narrative: sacrifice is fundamental to the stories we tell about ourselves. The range of sacrificial practices involves ritual killing, usually of an animal and sometimes of a human, offerings of the victim or of parts of the victim to non-human powers, and the consumption of parts of the offered animal in the sacrificial meal. Heesterman identifies three major components: ritual killing, destruction, and feast, with destruction as one of the problematic dimensions that stand in the way of seeing sacrifice in the more simple terms of food distribution.[8] The principal meanings evoked by the English term are the violent immolation of a living being for appeasing a wrathful deity, expiation of sin or impurity, and giving up something precious or relinquishing some condition for the sake of another or a higher goal.

Sacrifice is still present in our attempts to avoid misfortune and there are still magical residues in modern cultures, such as in vowing to perform a certain task or a certain ascetic practice in return for a divine favour. But the energy release model does not sufficiently account for the ways in which communities face transcendence through sacrifice, nor for its narrative and metaphorical appropriations. Of these the most notable metaphorical extension is war. War in ancient India was understood in terms of sacrifice and this theme is commonplace today when we speak of soldiers sacrificing their lives for the greater good of the country or cause. Bataille perceives the link between sacrifice and war in his idea of the excess of energy that needs to be wasted to bring society back to a state of equilibrium; and in contemporary western society, it is war that best approximates to any residue of a sacrificial culture geared towards ordering or making sense of the world. But these 'horizontal' accounts of sacrifice need to be supplemented with 'vertical' accounts that take seriously sacrifice as a site for mediating the human encounter with mystery.

---

[6] Hedley, *Sacrifice Imagined*, 2.
[7] Burkert cited by Heesterman, *The Broken World of Sacrifice*, 9.
[8] Heesterman, *The Broken World of Sacrifice*, 14.

Over a hundred years ago, in 1898, Hubert and Mauss offered the following definition of sacrifice:

> Sacrifice is a religious act which, through the consecration of a victim, modifies the condition of the moral person who accomplishes it or that of certain objects with which he is concerned.[9]

This is still a relevant understanding and the introduction of the phrase concerning the condition of the moral person is key: literal sacrifice changes the community and metaphorical sacrifice, the relinquishing of personal desire for something or someone else, also brings about change. But Hubert's and Mauss' account is really a description of the essential features of sacrifice rather than an explanation in functionalist or other terms. *Explanations* of sacrifice have typically fallen into two general groups—sacrifice as an economy of exchange or consumption on the one hand, and sacrifice as catharsis on the other. Yet while both kinds of theory have much to offer as explanatory accounts, both approach sacrifice in terms of cultural function. To lay bare the bones of sacrifice, as both naked violence and as metaphor, we need to expose it to the light of a starker existential truth of human life: that we are consumed by death and wish to transcend it. Sacrifice, I here propose, says that death is not final and presents the refusal of death through its embrace. This embracing of death, which is paradoxically the embracing of life, is a refusal of death through renunciation. To develop this thesis we need to place it in the context of what we might call the cultural functionalist views.

## 2. CULTURAL FUNCTIONALISM

In the social sciences, cultural functionalist explanations of sacrifice have been predominant. These understand sacrifice in terms of conspicuous consumption or purification through catharsis, the expurgation of impurity or the release of pent up energy. Indeed, among theories of sacrifice, explanations of sacrifice as catharsis have been most significant in the last hundred years. Freud long ago offered a psychoanalytic account of sacrifice through an examination of Totemism. According to Freud, we find in Totemism two prohibitions, one being the rule against killing the totem except in an annual sacrifice and the other the rule that marriage must occur outside of the totemic group (an incest taboo). These prohibitions reflect the primal sacrificial act of the sons killing the father and marrying his wives (their mothers). This primal

---

[9] Hubert/Mauss, *Sacrifice*, 13.

murder is re-enacted in sacrifice.[10] There is, of course, no evidence for the primal murder or the kind of early hominid groups that Freud envisaged, nor is it clear that Totemism is a survival of the earliest kind of religion. But with the above Freud instigated an important way of thinking that has been significantly developed by Girard and Burkert who share Freud's view that the violence in a society becomes channelled into the sacrificial victim, which thereby achieves a return to society's equilibrium.[11] Bataille's theory of sacrifice, too, is inspired by Freud, and combines a cathartic theory of sacrifice with a theory of exchange. It is this latter thesis which is closer to the existential dimension of sacrifice that I wish to bring out.

Bataille presents a political economy of what he calls 'the superabundance of biochemical energy' (la surabondance de l'énergie biochimique) whose source is ultimately the sun, which is 'the principle of life's exuberant development' (le principe de son développement exubérant).[12] In *La part maudite*, which Bataille published in 1949 (revised in 1967 and translated into English as *The Accursed Share* in 1991), he presents the argument that any general economy in a society in time produces an excess and that this wealth finds expression in one of two ways. It is either consumed in luxury or destroyed in acts of violence that threaten the social order—in the modern context as war and in earlier times as sacrifice. The 'accursed share' (la part maudite) is the surplus energy expended by a system: if energy cannot be used for growth it is inevitably and necessarily wasted. Solar radiation that is the source of life is abundant and the sun gives without receiving. Living matter (la matière vivante) receives this solar energy and stores it within the boundaries of the space it inhabits. An organism uses this energy for its growth and once that growth has achieved its maximum extension, once it has reached its limit and filled the space allotted to it, then there is an excess produced that needs expression in some way other than growth.[13] An organism that has used all the energy it requires for growth produces excess that needs release. Bataille gives a somewhat prosaic example of this when he refers to the energy of growth in duckweed that fills the space of a pond: once the pond has reached saturation point, this energy needs to be dissipated. Such dissipation occurs in the form of heat. This biological model of energy build up and release, Bataille argues, also functions in human societies.

From a general discussion of solar energy that builds up in the biological organism and, indeed, in the total system of organic life, Bataille seamlessly moves into a discussion of human society where, he argues, the same

---

[10] Freud, *Totem and Taboo*, 43–224. For a critique, see Evans-Pritchard *Theories of Primitive Religion*, 41–43.

[11] See Hamerton-Kelly, *Violent Origins*.

[12] Bataille, *La part maudite*, 65

[13] Bataille, *La part maudite*, 67.

principles apply. Societies and people reach a limit to growth, and the supera-
bundant, unneeded energy finds release in luxury—particularly in art and in
non-reproductive sexual activity, but also in war. Thus labour and techniques
(le travail et les techniques) have allowed the growth of human societies and
the excess energy thereby produced from 'the pressure of life' (la pression de
la vie) is consumed (i.e. released) in 'conflagrations befitting the solar origins of its movement' (des embrasements conformes à l'origine solaire de son
mouvement').[14] If this excess is not consumed in luxury, then it erupts as war
and the twentieth century's two devastating wars bear witness to the release
of excess energy built up through the labour and economic growth of the
nineteenth century.

The excess or superabundance of energy in any system, whose origin is the
outpouring of solar energy, is destined for waste and Bataille sees sacrifice in
this context as the outpouring of excessive energy within a society. Excessive
consumption (as in a potlatch), war, and sacrifice are linked as expressions of
energy within a general economy. Indeed, the potlatch is central to Bataille's
argument and his discussion of it as the expression of surplus energy is more
extensive than his discussion of sacrifice itself. While Bataille's main concern
is contemporary society and how human beings can free themselves from this
organic inevitability of the release of energy in destructive ways, in order to
understand the present he presents historical analyses, especially of Aztec
society. Bataille's Aztecs are the very opposite of us morally (se situent morale-
ment à nos antipodes); whereas for us production is important for them consumption is important and they were more concerned with sacrificing than
with working.[15] My reading of his somewhat complex argument is as follows.

First of all Bataille posits a distinction between subjectivity associated with
intimacy and the order of things associated with work, production, and the
real world. The human sacrifice of Aztec society was the sacrifice of slaves,
namely warriors who had become slaves through conquest. As slaves the
victims were bound to labour as their captor's property; the slave becomes a
thing, a commodity, he becomes part of the order of things. Drawing on the
master-bondsman theme in Hegel, Bataille observes that the slave accepts his
situation, which is preferable to dying.[16] The slave prefers to become part of the
order of things, prefers to become objectified rather than to die. The owner of
the slave becomes the sacrificer of the sacrificial victim who represents the sacrificer. The victim (who is a slave) is degraded to the order of things, made into
an object, but at the same time he has the same nature as the subject, the sacrificer, whom he represents. Sacrifice heals the world and 'restores to the sacred
world that which servile use had degraded, made profane' (restitue au monde

14   Bataille, *La part maudite*, 76.
15   Bataille, *La part maudite*, 34.
16   Bataille, *La part maudite*, 94.

sacré ce que l'usage servile a dégradé, rendue profane).[17] In the distinction between subjectivity linked to intimacy versus objectivity linked to labour, the victim, who has been made an object through slavery, is partially returned to the realm of intimacy through becoming the *sacrificial* victim. Furthermore, the owner or subject comes to be identified with the victim and through the restoration of the victim with the sacred realm, is himself restored. Religion is centrally concerned with this restoration.

To achieve this restoration the sacrificial victim must be destroyed; the sacrifice destroys that which it consecrates. This destruction is the destruction of the link with labour and profitable activity and so is an excess, a superabundance. In the process of destruction the victim cannot, of course, be returned to the real order and this refusal of the real order, the world of work, is a principle that 'opens the way of arousal, it releases violence in itself, reserving a domain where it rules without equal' (ouvre la voie au déchaînement, il libère la violence en lui réservant le domaine où elle règne sans partage).[18] The world of subjectivity, the world of the night for Bataille associated with the dream of reason and with madness, is given violent expression legitimated through the sacrificial victim.

This violence is associated with consumption in so far as it is not connected with work and so is not concerned for the future. The idea of sacrifice therefore entails a particular view of time in which the present is foregrounded. The sacrificer is concerned not with what will be but with what *is* because useless consumption, the consumption of excess can only occur once concern for the future is relinquished. There is no need to hold back anything if there is no concern for the future and the person who lives in this way entirely in the present can consume all s/he possesses. Such useless consumption of the kind performed in sacrifice is a way of revealing subjectivity and intimacy to others and is a way in which the subject can connect with others. In sacrifice, for Bataille, we have a return of the thing to the order of intimacy and this return releases violence, but a violence that is contained within the ritual sphere of sacrifice, within the bacchanalian excess of the festival. In being given release, it preserves and protects those who offer the rites. As for Girard, for Bataille sacrifice protects a community from the excess of violence and from the contagion of violence. Sacrifice prevents violence from spreading through the community and, through the merging of individuals in the sacred present, allows them to communicate in future oriented, secular time. In sacrifice we have an attempt to diffuse violence, to continue the status quo, to save a community from ruin. The sacrificial victim is a surplus who is withdrawn from the realm of wealth by destruction: he becomes 'the accursed share' violently consumed who, brought back from the world of things, occupies the realm of intimacy

---

[17] Bataille, *La part maudite*, 94.
[18] Bataille, *La part maudite*, 96.

and subjectivity for a time and represents the masters who offer sacrifice, even becoming their equal in the short period before destruction. The victim is both sacred and cursed. Only destruction can rid the victim of his 'thinghood,' that is, of his usefulness, and achieve the release of violence necessary for the energy balance and restoration to a state of equilibrium.

In modern, industrial societies we do not, of course, have sacrifice in any sense akin to Aztec sacrifice. But Bataille observes that we are still subject to the loss of intimacy in the world of things and that this is indeed a loss. Sacrifice enables a return to intimacy. There is a separation between the sacrificer and the world of things, and the victim of sacrifice who joins the world of things returns to the world of intimacy and thereby restores the immanence between 'man and the world', between subject and object.[19] While Bataille does not advocate a return to violent sacrifice, he is sympathetic to the notion of a release of forces and to the irrationality of the intimate, subjective sphere, set apart from the real realm of labour and work and from the future. If sacrifice is a movement from the realm of things, of objectivity, to the realm of intimacy which facilitates the release of violence or tension in a community, then contemporary, western societies would benefit from it, if not literally then metaphorically. The excess of solar energy, on this view, is a fact about life that we cannot escape. It is only over our response to this fact that we, presumably, have power. Sacrifice as violent act has largely disappeared from contemporary western societies but the need for resolution, the need for energy release among organisms that have filled a particular space, has not. However, the catharsis model does not exhaustively explain sacrifice.

### 3. CONSUMPTION OR RENUNCIATION?

I would not wish to be overly critical of Batailles' extremely stimulating work; if he is wrong he is wrong in a very creative and interesting way. But there are, it seems to me, a number of problems with Bataille's and other cathartic models of sacrifice. There are historical questions to begin with. Firstly, it is not clear that Aztec society is prototypical of sacrificial cults; most sacrificial cults have rarely practiced human sacrifice. Secondly, we can take issue with Bataille's claim that sacrifice is necessarily linked to excess. For Bataille sacrifice is an attempted reinvigoration of intimacy through the violent release of energy brought about by the transfer of the sacrificial victim from the realm of work or the real world, to the realm of intimacy, luxury, and subjectivity. He therefore aligns the category of sacrifice with the erotic. The destruction of

---

[19] Bataille, *Théorie de la religion*, 59.

the victim in Aztec society ensures the return to intimacy, although it does so only incompletely as the victim who is a slave must remain subordinated to the sacrificer who is the master. The excess of violence channelled into the victim happens because of the victim's retrieval back into the world of intimacy from the realm of work; an event that is inevitably marked by violence as the excess energy in the system seeks release.

I now want to contrast this account with a thesis of sacrifice as refusal. My argument is that although sacrifice is a collective enterprise and experience, it is nevertheless deeply connected to subjectivity: the moral subject is transformed through refusal, which aligns sacrifice with asceticism. Both asceticism and sacrifice share in the refusal of death. In support of this claim I shall draw on historical research from India. We will also see that the transformation of the moral subject is not a form of individualism but that sacrifice is much rather conducive to the formation of a shared subjectivity realized in the sacrificial event constituted by refusal and renunciation.[20] Indeed, this is implicit in common parlance where 'sacrifice' is typically understood in terms of giving something up: a mother might sacrifice her career for a child, a soldier sacrifice his life for his country, and so on. This 'common sense' understanding points to an important dimension of moral transformation in sacrifice. The refusal of a particular kind of wealth (vegetal and animal offerings as symbols of the sacrifier's life) changes the inner condition or the status of the donor.

Could we not argue, then, that a key feature of sacrifice is less the cathartic expression of violence, which maintains the cultural status quo, and more the renunciation of material goods that gives expression to the desire for the refusal of death and nothingness? This would mean that sacrifice is not so much about the consumption of excess, which in such a society would be without hardship, but rather about the renunciation of goods or wealth created through labour, through which the community enacts the transcendence of its own mortality. On Bataille's account, sacrifice is not a giving up, not a relinquishing of anything, but the affirmation of luxury through abandoning or destroying excess. My alternative proposal suggests that rather than being about luxury and the *intimacy* of subjectivity, sacrifice is about suffering and the relinquishing of a *self-focused* subjectivity in favour of a *shared* subjectivity in which that which is most precious, a life itself, is given up in order to affirm that very life. Sacrifice, I will argue, is less about the cathartic expelling of excess or surplus energy and more about the renunciation of that which is held to be most valuable and the refusal of that which we seek to overcome. Seeing sacrifice in such terms brings out elements of a deeper, existential level that remain hidden from purely cultural functionalist views. In the following I thus seek to develop the

---

[20] Foucault has written extensively on asceticism and, drawing on Mauss, on techniques of the body but does not, to my knowledge, address sacrifice directly. See the selection of readings in Carrette, *Religion and Culture by Michel Foucault*. See also Flood, *The Ascetic Self*, 243–246.

argument that (i) sacrifice is the refusal of that which is most precious, (ii) that there is an analogy between the victim and the sacrificer, which (iii) shows the proximity of sacrifice to renunciation or asceticism and how the indexical-I of the sacrificer is analogous to the indexical-I of the renouncer. This will show (iv) sacrifice to be the refusal of death, nothingness, and meaninglessness; in fact, the refusal of time that is tragic in its necessary failure.

## (i) Sacrifice as Refusal

All sacrificial practices entail some refusal: the refusal of goods—animals and other offerings into the fire—that would otherwise be of profit. At a metaphorical level this is the refusal of a person or group for the benefit of others: the hungry mother's relinquishing of her share of bread for her children or even the ascetic's refusal to succumb to the passions. Such sacrifice of worldly attachment to what is desirable is typically geared towards higher goals specified within the tradition, such as the prosperity of a community, the attaining of heaven for the patron of the sacrifice, or the collective bond entailed in sacrificial practice that serves to reinforce social relations. The burnt oblation bears witness to the sacrificer's lack of self-interest; the gift destroyed is the pure gift, the gift that represents the transcendence of present time and space, the here-and-now. Indeed, rather than the emphasis on present time, as Bataille argues, sacrifice is concerned with the future, with piling up merit in heaven for the vedic Brahmans, and structuring the universe in an ordered way that relates the future to the present and a higher world to the lower world.

Such a giving up of goods (namely food or precious substances) for the sake of the community is linked to the refusal of death. The ethnographic record seems to support the view that what is regarded as precious is given up to death in the belief that this will somehow renew the sacrificial community. Most sacrificial societies have been agricultural, where domestic animals are important for the general economy and livelihood of the people. Evans-Pritchard, for example, writes about this with regard to the Nuer. The Nuer hold cattle in high esteem: they are the topic of most conversation and there is an identification with them in the custom of taking names from the cattle in addition to names given at birth.[21] Cattle are subject to sacrifice, which is a means of communicating with a transcendent reality (Kwoth) and substitutes for the community or particular people who make the sacrifice. This idea of substitution is attested in other areas and times: in vedic India the patron of the sacrifice is identified with the victim. In some sense, this is the case even in Christianity where Christ as sacrifice becomes the representative of humanity.

---

[21] Evans-Pritchard, *Nuer Religion*, 248–255.

That which is most precious is subjected to destruction, which is a symbolic act of substitution of the community or patron for the victim.

## (ii) The Sacrificer and the Victim

This identification of the patron with the victim is an important dimension of sacrifice that Bataille is right to emphasize. The victim of the sacrifice is an analogue of the patron of the sacrifice so that instead of the patron dying, the victim dies so that the patron might live in a renewed or refreshed way. Sacrifice is the performance of the ambiguity that killing means death and yet can mean an affirmation of life. The victim dies in order that the patron or community might live and thrive. Death is symbolically transcended through its performance and ritual containment within the boundaries of the sacrificial rite. As Bataille has highlighted, sacrifice implies a confrontation of death and in a sense we can see sacrifice as the attempt to control and ultimately transcend death: an attempt that is, of course, doomed to failure and so needs to be continually repeated in sacrificial societies. Indeed, we might see sacrifice as the ultimate tragic act: it attempts to affirm life and transcend death through embracing death which, as we all know, nonetheless remains. In sacrifice I meet my death and attempt to transcend it. The substitute dies for me and through that dying I live anew—if only for a limited time. Bataille's Aztecs clearly fall into this pattern where the victim is taken into the world of intimacy and identified with the subjectivity of the sacrificer, as the Nuer is identified with the ox through the personal name. In sacrifice I meet my death. But who is this 'I' of the sacrifice?

## (iii) Sacrifice and Renunciation

To answer this we must make a distinction between individualism and subjectivity. Individualism is a value of modernity that highlights the particular agency and creativity of the person over any social collective. What is notable about sacrificial communities is that they are all within what we might call a cosmological world-view. Sacrifice is the performance of a cosmic drama in which the structure of the cosmos is affirmed and the soteriological hope of a community expressed. The 'I' of the sacrifice, the patron who pays for the rite in the vedic case, while being a particular, individual person, should not be confused with expressing the values of individualism. The sacrificial 'I' is an index of a shared identity that expresses and gives voice to a collectivity or shared subjectivity. In such a cosmological society, such as ancient vedic India, when I symbolically meet my death in the sacrificial arena through the victim, the 'I' is a particular reference point in the here-and-now for a broader social identity. Vedic sacrifice is a fine example. Here the patron (*yajamāna*) undergoes a series of ascetic purifications and the sacrifice is performed within the 'sacred canopy' of a cosmology with a fixed order: the three levels of the universe (earth, atmosphere, and sky), the gods who inhabit those layers, and the social order of classes (*varṇa*) that corresponds to the cosmic structure. In such a society, when I perform sacrifice I am standing in for the community and enacting the socio-cosmic order. When I see my death in the victim, it is the community that sees its death through me, which is simultaneously the renewal of life (because I do not die) and the affirmation of the order of the world. The sacrifice transforms me, who am a sign of the collective identity, into a new life in the world and affirms the order of life. Sacrifice can thus only flourish in a society that is deeply cosmological in its world-view (as vedic society was).

The identification of the sacrificial 'I' with the victim brings sacrifice into proximity or alignment with renunciation. Indeed, we might say that the 'I' of the sacrificer and the 'I' of the renouncer are analogues. The ideal ethnographic location for this identification is, of course, India where sacrifice and renunciation are two poles of religious being that we need to say something about in order to develop the more general and widely applicable thesis. There is no space here to develop an entire history of Indian sacrifice, but suffice it to say that the original, central religious act of early nomadic communities in South Asia was sacrifice, in solemn and complex ritual proceedings accompanied by verses (mantras) from the revealed scripture or Veda.

The oldest, well-documented and as it happens most elaborate, sacrificial system we know about is the Brahmanical one. This is attested in the Vedas whose hymns were composed for recitation during the sacrifice. The vedic ritual sacrifice, that still on occasion takes place, has been well-documented.[22] To give a brief example, the sacrifice called the *agnicayana*, the piling up of fire, takes place over twelve days. An altar in the shape of giant bird is built of more than a thousand bricks in layers within a ritual enclose. A number of priests perform different functions and recite different mantras. The patron of the sacrifice, the *yajamāna*, along with his wife undergoes purification that involves bathing, fasting, and a 'sweat-lodge' type of enclosure. Goats are sacrificed by being tied to a pole and suffocated, their meat boiled, and the sacred drink soma is consumed. The *yajamāna* after the concluding rites on the twelfth day returns home with three fires which he installs in his home altars. He thereafter performs milk oblations into fire for the rest of his life in the evening and morning. In earlier days other animals were sacrificed, particularly the horse (*aśvamedha*). There is even mention of a human sacrifice (*puruṣamedha*), although whether this ever took place has been questioned.

---

[22] See, for example, Staal, *Rules Without Meaning*, 65–77.

These proceedings are highly formalized with great stress on correct per-formance. There is very little evidence of cathartic release of energy through killing. Indeed, the death of the victims seems simply to be part of the proce-dure along with the recitation of mantras. But what seems to be significant is the change in status of the sacrifier. He is purified through the rite and there is the idea that his faults go into the sacrificial victim, who symbolically replaces him. The sins of the sacrifier are, in a way, symbolically consumed. The focus of sacrifice is not the appeasing of a deity or explicit and overt consumption, but rather the subjective condition of the patron. In this sense Mauss' defini-tion seems quite correct. Indeed, Mauss probably derived it from the vedic sacrifice that he was so interested in and that provides the basic example of his text.

This idea of purification is later developed in the Upaniṣads where the exter-nal sacrifice is interpreted symbolically or rather the external rite becomes an internal rite.[23] The true sacrifice is the sacrifice of the breath for the higher gno-sis of recognizing one's identity with the absolute. The abstinence of the patron in the vedic sacrifice becomes the asceticism of the ascetic in the Upaniṣads. Sacrifice and renunciation become analogous. This tradition of inner renun-ciation being identified with sacrifice continues into the medieval period with the Tantras. Here we have the idea of 'yogic suicide' (*utkrānti*) where the yogi intentionally dies through starvation, transferring his consciousness out of his body to a different realm. Here the refusal of life in order to affirm and realize a higher moral condition entails the yogi's own 'sacrifice'.[24] The sacrifice of the yogi himself is not for appeasement or catharsis, but for inner transformation.

Although of course there is a change or, to use Mauss' vocabulary, a moral change occurring in the human person of the sacrifier, there is a sense in which this is occurring in a collective setting that affects the broader commu-nity. The vedic sacrifice is individualistic in some ways—it is the patron who is transformed—but it is not the affirmation of individualism. Individualism is an entirely modern value associated with self-assertion and a will that would seek to be unique. Sacrifice is clearly not individualistic in this sense as those involved seek a repetition of performance as close as possible to what went before and as they seek to wholly conform themselves to the structures of the pre-existent tradition. The vedic patron is the performer of a pre-given narrative of tradition that he is following; there is no self-assertion here in Blumenberg's sense as a characteristic of modernity. Indeed, we might even say that sacrifice is antithetical to modernist self-assertion because, on the contrary, it asserts a collective subjectivity and assertion of collective identity. The vedic patron, the yogic suicide, and the *teyyam* are sharing in a collec-tive performance in which the individual will is subsumed beneath a broader,

[23] Biardeau/Malamoud, *Le Sacrifice dans l'inde Ancienne*, 65–73.
[24] Vasudeva, *The Yoga of the Mālinīvijayottaratantra*, 437–445.

collective will. The *volo* or *icchāmi*, 'I will', becomes a sign for the broader community and the indexical 'I' becomes a carrier of a group identity. Perhaps a better way of putting this is that the performers of the sacrifice participate in a greater narrative such that the story of their own lives, the story of 'my' life, becomes transformed into the narrative of the group.

But even if this is the case, even if we need to understand sacrifice in terms of renunciation or refusal of some good to attain a higher, collective good, then we are still left with the persistent question concerning the link between human finitude and sacrifice. How does the performance of sacrifice and the renunciation of subjectivity that it entails, address human finitude? Sacrifice in terms of the accursed share does not really deal with this adequately; it does not confront the existential question, or rather answers it in a way that is inadequate for human finitude. Bataille's understanding is almost a pantheistic sense of continuous consumption or re-cycling of solar energy in an inevitable, life-driven way that leaves no room for subjective sentiment, human narrative, or transcendence. I, by contrast, propose that it is through sacrifice that communities confront the inevitability of death and attempt to control it: sacrifice refuses finitude, and death actually means life. In his actions we can almost hear the sacrifier say, through the death of this animal I am refusing death itself and affirming my own true nature as deathless.

The sacrificial patron and the renouncer share the refusal of death, which is the refusal of time and mortality. To attain the immortal (*amṛta*) the flow of time has to be reversed through ascetic practice—fixing the body in a single posture, slowing the breath, stopping the mind—and these practices have their precursor in early sacrifice. The 'I' of the sacrificer and the 'I' of the renouncer are linked in the refusal of death, time, and the world of change. For Bataille, the human Aztec victim is brought from the world of things into the world of intimacy where the patron can become identified with the victim: where they share the same substance. For the vedic sacrificial patron, we might see the external sacrificial rite as brought into the realm of intimacy in the patron's participation where his asceticism contributes to the success of the procedure. In the renouncer, the 'victim' is the renouncer himself, who sacrifices himself as an act of refusal of time and death. In renunciation, the internalization of the sacrifice, there is thus a distancing between the indexical-I of the renouncer (the subject of first person predicates) and the higher self to be realized, the goal of which is the transcending of death.

This inner sacrifice entails self-reflection and narratability. The renouncer reflects on himself in contemplative practices, turning the self into an 'object' which is analogous to the sacrificial victim. The realization of the timeless self is achieved through the inner process of practice, which is like sacrifice in that it refuses the reality of death. For Bataille, in Aztec sacrifice we have a collapse of objectivity and the world of work into subjectivity, and similarly in vedic sacrifice we have the collapse of objectivity, the victim as economic commodity, into a shared subjectivity in which the victim comes to represent the patron and thereby the community. Likewise the vedic renouncer has withdrawn from the world of work and social productivity to confront the naked aporia of his transient life. But whereas for Bataille the sacrifice plays out a cultural logic in an economy of energy exchange at a purely horizontal level, we must understand both vedic sacrifice and renunciation as having a transcendent dimension, a dimension that the tradition regards as being outside of death and outside of time but which is nevertheless expressed through the cosmic order.

### (iv) The Refusal of Death

Sacrifice, I argue, plays out the paradox of the affirmation of life through its destruction. Through death life is affirmed. The dead animal in the Vedas is only sleeping, and not really dead but ready to awaken. Likewise, the ritual patron will awaken from his own death to the realm of the ghosts (*pretaloka*) and thence to the realm of the ancestors (*pitṛloka*) where sacrifice will ensure that he does not undergo a second death (*punarmrtyu*). In turn, the renouncer will awaken to the cognition (*jñāna*) that his self is immortal. In both cases there is the recognition of the transcendence of death and of death as a kind of birth: both sacrifice and renunciation affirm the paradoxical idea that birth follows destruction and this immortality is assured for both sacrificer and renouncer.

### 4. INTERPRETATION AND EXPLANATION

As we have seen with the example from vedic India, sacrifice gives order to the world in cosmological societies. The claim about sacrifice as refusal would need to be corroborated through being 'tested' on other sacrificial societies, but its fittingness for vedic culture is highly significant: any general theory of sacrifice needs to take the vedic material into account simply because of the large scale of the vedic literature devoted to sacrifice and its interpretation, and because for many hundreds of years the Indic tradition has itself already reflected on the meaning of its sacrificial practices. Drawing an analogy with the Aztecs, Bataille could read this material in terms of his thesis, that vedic sacrifice is the consumption of surplus, of excess, whose violent expression restores order to the group. This is clearly a possibility but this is to ignore the indigenous ascetic understanding of sacrifice and to allow cultural function (the bringing about of equilibrium, the restoring of energy balance) to take precedence over existential expression. What is important about sacrifice is that it is a performance of the ambiguity of the affirmation of life through its negation and that this is a sacrificial community's confrontation with the bare life of being born and dying.

Gift exchange and catharsis models of sacrifice are not wrong but operate at one cultural level—a level of energy balance and expression in a community. There is, however, a deeper or more fundamental function of sacrifice as a practice and a metaphor that lays bare the reality of life. Sacrifice brings us into the world through creating a cosmos in which the meaning of human life, of a community, can be located. Sacrifice takes place at a more visceral cultural level and is the pre-philosophical articulation of problems that can be articulated philosophically but that can only be resolved or expressed through action. The existential level of sacrifice shows us something about ourselves. It points to mortality and it points to the human aspiration for transcending mortality and negating death and nothingness. It says that death is not final and all-consuming but that death can affirm life.

Because of the existential nature of sacrifice it requires an approach from the human sciences that accepts its multi-layered complexity. A hermeneutical approach is better suited to gaining a fuller understanding of sacrifice than a scientific approach that seeks causal explanations (such as those offered by cultural functionalist models). Sacrifice is a very ancient human institution and needs to be understood as operating at different cultural levels. Ricoeur offered an interesting approach to social phenomena. If human society displays certain characteristics that are analogous to a text, then we can 'read' human social action in ways analogous to reading a text. Thus sacrificial practices as social action can be 'read' and the reading I have presented here seeks to understand the complex phenomenon of sacrifice in terms of human existential reality, in terms of the refusal of death and the affirmation of life—concerns that have been fundamental to all human societies throughout history.

The phenomenon of sacrifice is truly complex and resists explanation in terms of any single paradigm. The causal terms that the social sciences or brain science could develop are clearly insufficient, and so we must pursue other approaches. In the study or inquiry into sacrifice, especially across cultures, we arguably need, firstly, a phenomenology that allows sacrifice to show itself, as it were, and that allows what shows itself to be seen. This is essentially an ethnographic or descriptive account (of the kind that I have briefly referred to above). We, secondly, need a hermeneutical account that generates theory from description or, rather, that uses description to offer particular interpretative angles. In one sense, of course, these kinds of understanding are also explanations, as Ricoeur has pointed out.[25] I have tried to do this here within the general thesis of sacrifice as refusal. Lastly, in our modern Western economies

---

[25] Ricoeur, 'Qu'est-ce qu' un texte?', 159–162.

where literal kinds of sacrifice are not performed (unless we count the millions of animals slaughtered in industrial meat production) we have grown unaccustomed to, and horrified by sacrifice. The world of sacrifice for us is, in Heesterman's phrase, a broken world. As David Brown argues in Chapter 12 of this volume, we need therefore a kind of human empathy or something like Heidegger's formal indication, using the fact of my being to understand the being of others, in order to partially step into the world of sacrifice. We can understand sacrifice as renunciation as a feature of all our lives that can become a formal indication of a pre-modern sense of sacrifice. The patron of the sacrifice is a sign for the community and in refusing death is affirming life for all. The existential *aporia* of human life, facing death, seems to be resolved; although perhaps in truth it is not.

# 9

## Sacrifice in Recent Roman Catholic Thought

### *From Paradox to Polarity, and Back Again?*

Philip McCosker

Sacrifice is a central element of Catholic thought and life. The Roman Catholic Church is centred on the person of Jesus Christ, and his life—from Annunciation to Ascension and beyond—must pattern the nature of the community which he founded. Indeed one way in which the Church understands its identity is as 'body of Christ'. Though clearly not identical with Christ, the Church continues in some sense his life and ministry on earth. The events of Jesus' paschal mystery—Last Supper, Cross, and Resurrection—are thus at the heart of the Church's thought and practice. This centrality is focused on the sacrament which Catholics attend most frequently and which thus defines their identity: the Mass. This sacrament represents the events of the paschal mystery, centred on the Last Supper in which Jesus asked his followers to 'do this in memory of me'. In obedience to his invitation at that foundational meal, the Church and her ministers, calling on the Holy Spirit, consecrate bread and wine, as their founder did, give thanks to the Father and unite themselves to Jesus' self-offering in proclaiming that 'This is my Body' and 'This is my Blood'. By consuming his body and blood they become his body.

The Church has always interpreted the paschal mystery in sacrificial terms—whether in Scripture or in early theological texts—and consequently sacrifice has always been part of its understanding of the representation of that mystery in the Mass. Because the Church understands itself as founded by Christ, and therefore in some complicated sense continuous with Christ, the Church must proclaim Christ's mission of salvation which scripture and tradition insist was substantially achieved by the events of the paschal mystery. Because sacrifice has been a central or governing, if not unique, mode for understanding those mysteries, sacrifice simply is central to Catholicism.

Nevertheless, anyone conversant with disputes over interpretation of the scriptures, church history, and ecumenical relations, or even petty liturgical squabbles, will know that this relatively straightforward, somewhat idealized, account of centrality is not the end of the story. Sacrifice is a riotously polyvalent term: the more scholars discuss it, the more mercurial it seems to get. It is certainly clear from this book that even our small circle of contributors is not using the term sacrifice in a straightforwardly univocal sense. Like the category 'religion', there is no one universally functional definition of sacrifice. I will operate with a basic heuristic spectrum between immolationist accounts of sacrifice, which involve the destruction of the 'victim', and oblationist accounts which emphasize the act of offering the *offerandum*, whether of self or something else. Such an optic works both with the broader discussion of kinds of sacrifice in this book—for instance, Julia Meszaros' use of sacrifice is more oblationist (Chapter 5), while the sacrifices described by David Brown, Laura Rival or Bettina Schmidt (Chapters 12, 11, and 13, respectively) tend much more to the immolationist end of the spectrum, with Johannes Zachhuber (Chapter 2) giving an account of the transition from one end to the other—as well as with the particular story of Catholicism.

In what follows I will show that what appears to hold true in general of this volume as a whole, namely, that there is no one definition of sacrifice—it is an inherently aporetic or lacunic reality—and that it is therefore a polyvalent concept with many senses, holds true in particular of its appearance in the Catholic tradition: it is this aporetic yet polyvalent configuration which I term paradoxical. And yet one consequence of such aporia and concomitant plurality is conflict between some more polarizing and exclusive ideas of sacrifice. It is my contention that a paradoxical plurality held sway in the Church until the Reformations, both Protestant and the Catholic responses, when sacrifice became a polarizing concept. In more recent Catholic thought, the main interest of this article, a return to paradoxical plurality can be perceived with a very wide range of accounts of sacrifice available in the twentieth and twenty-first centuries. There will be a practical and contemporary sting in the tale, however: contemporary Catholicism faces the resurgence of a polarizing conception of sacrifice. Pope Benedict XVI is emblematic here both by strongly accenting the paradoxical sense of sacrifice, setting it on a more capacious canvas, while having to deal with the practical difficulties attendant on the resurgence of a polarizing understanding as a function of his Petrine ministry of unity.

Modern Catholic understandings of sacrifice were heavily influenced by a constellation of three thinkers at the beginning of the twentieth century: Maurice de la Taille SJ (1872–1933), Anscar Vonier OSB (1875–1938), and Odo Casel OSB (1886–1948).[1] De la Taille's main work, *Mysterium Fidei*, proposed a thorough reworking of the theology of sacrifice prevalent in Catholicism since the Reformation debates. Following those debates the Catholic theologians, insisting that the Eucharist was indeed a sacrifice in

---

[1] Arguably a fourth member of this constellation is Eugène Masure, but space precludes treating him here.

some predefined kind of way, had then to find where the sacrifice was located. Some found it in the transformation of the elements into Christ (what more lowly existence could be imagined than to be insensate in a wafer?), others in the immolation of the consecrated elements in the mouth and stomach of the celebrant.[2] In opposition to these immolation-hunting views de la Taille reframed the discussion by emphasizing the element of oblation, of offering, as central to the Church's sacrifice. This allowed him to integrate his under-standing of soteriology, sacrifice, eucharist, grace, desire, and prayer.[3] Most significantly de la Taille insists on the unity of supper and cross as together comprising the one sacrifice of Christ's Passion. The supper-oblation is exter-nal sign of Christ's interior devotion in tendering his loving gift of himself to God, and this then is central in reframing our own desire from worldly to divine terms. In emphasizing the will in this way de la Taille appears strik-ingly modern. This key insight, linking the internal disposition, or posture, of Christ (and therefore ideally his followers) with the external outworking of that on the Cross and beyond, recurs in subsequent Catholic theology, right up to the contemporary author James Alison, as we will see.

Despite de la Taille's apparent modernity, his work was highly controversial and was soon relatively forgotten. Vonier's theology of the Eucharist, by con-trast, has arguably had a greater impact and was a tacit criticism of de la Taille. The key insight of Vonier, relying apparently on Aquinas, is made in the area of the 'link' between Calvary and the Mass by arguing that the Mass is the sac-rament of the sacrifice of Christ, a 'sacrament-sacrifice'.[4] Vonier, like Thomas Aquinas, can be described as a semiotic theologian: the sacrament of the Mass re-presents the reality of Calvary under the category of sign, transposed, as it were. This approach makes the prior category of sacrament central in seeking to shed some light on the link between the Passion and the Mass. All sacra-ments proceed by using earthly signs to denote what they contain. The signs of the Eucharist denote the sacrifice of Calvary which they thus re-present. The historical passion of Calvary however is not thereby repeated but made pre-sent in the sacramental realm or order.[5] Vonier's championing of the category of sign prefigures the work of Power and Chauvet.

This early constellation is completed by Odo Casel's remarkable *Mysterientheologie* or *Mysterienlehre*.[6] Central was the biblical and patristic

---

[2] The fullest catalogue of these now extraordinary ideas is Lepin, *L'idée du sacrifice de la messe*. A summary of some of the views can be found in Daly, 'Robert Bellarmine and Post-Tridentine Eucharistic Theology'.

[3] See Matthiesen, *Sacrifice as Gift*.

[4] Vonier, *A Key to the Doctrine of the Eucharist*, 89 and *passim*.

[5] For a criticism of Vonier's reading of Aquinas, see Kilmartin, 'The Catholic Tradition', 407–413.

[6] Casel, *The Mystery*.

idea of *mysterion* which for Casel had three main referents: God in his combination of hidden mystery and outgoing economy of salvation, Christ in the full sweep of his incarnation, life, ministry, death, and Resurrection, the revelation of the invisible Father. Finally for Casel, mystery is the term for sacramental action which makes present past deeds of redemption. In each sense of mystery, we see a paradoxical combination of revelation and hiddenness which requires faith for reception. The apostles and early Christians passed on the *mysterion* of Christ in the mysteries of the sacraments, *ta mysteria*. For Casel the God who revealed himself in Christ continues to act through Christ after his Resurrection and glorification in the liturgy of the Church. Casel wished to emphasize the real presence of those saving mysteries in the liturgical mysteries, not just as intentional re-presentation or as a (mere) communication of grace. Where 'sign' arguably downplays realism, Caselian 'mystery' does not. This presence of the economy of salvation through and in the liturgical mysteries calls on the Christian to identify with the life of Christ by reliving it in the liturgical mysteries. It can be argued that Casel's thought has subsequently influenced official Church documents substantially, both in the Catechism and the documents of Vatican II. Significantly, Joseph Ratzinger endorsed his theology of mystery as 'perhaps the most fruitful theological idea of our century.'[7]

It is worth pausing here to note that, through their various emphases on oblation, sacrament, sign, and mystery, this early constellation of Catholic theologians effectively moved theological discourse about sacrifice away from the crudely transactional, mechanistic, and ultimately idolatrous accounts which framed the Reformation disputes onto altogether more promising, because more unifying, territory. Thus twentieth-century theology has witnessed a remarkable rapprochement between Catholic theologians and theologians from other ecclesial communities on this topic.[8] So it has been possible, for example, in the twentieth century for Reformed theologians to assert the sacrificial nature of the Eucharist and our participation in it in no uncertain terms. Thus, Jean-Jacques von Allmen could say that understood as *anamnesis*, the Eucharist 'is much more than a mnemonic ceremony; it is a re-enactment of the event which the celebration commemorates' and that this 'compromises neither the uniqueness nor the sufficiency of the death of Christ...it avoids a doctrine of the Eucharist which sees in the Supper a repetition of Calvary...but...does not downgrade the celebration of the Supper into a mere memorial meal.'[9] To exclude sacrifice from one's understanding of the Lord's Supper is to 'deal a blow at the intention of Jesus when he made it a sacrament of his sacrifice' in which Jesus asks his disciples 'through their own sacrifice to share in his sacrifice...The Supper becomes in a way the channel

---

[7] Ratzinger, *Die sakramentale Begründung*, 3.
[8] See, for instance, Tillard, 'Sacrificial Terminology and the Eucharist'.
[9] Allmen, *The Lord's Supper*, 24.

of the sacrifice of Christians [cf. Rom. 12:1, Eph. 5:2], the sacrament of their sacrifice as it is the sacrament of the sacrifice of Christ.'[10] Similar statements of broad areas of agreement can be found in works of theologians of other ecclesial communities too, for instance the Methodists and Anglicans.[11] We are at a remarkable and exciting ecumenical moment in the history of sacramental and Eucharistic theology.[12]

What of more recent Catholic theology—what does it have to say about sacrifice? While these theologies of sacrifice in the first half of the twentieth century accept sacrifice and contribute various ways of thinking about the unity of Christ's Passion and the Mass, towards the end of the twentieth century and on into the twenty-first century the picture, while still very plural, is tending to become polarized, once again. A *tour d'horizon* will bear this out.[13]

David Power, pushing well beyond Vonier, draws attention to the *metaphorical* nature of the language of sacrifice hoping to press beyond a reductive (because not literal) or banally transactional (because literal) view of sacrifice by arguing that sacrifice as metaphor contains an excess of meaning which can be applied to the Christian community, Christ's death, and the Eucharistic celebration, without the implication of a literal offering of a gift to God. By 'metaphor' Power means to draw attention to the conjoining of both identity and difference, and as iconic its 'value lies in the fact that the difference shows in the affirmation of identity.'[14] Vis à vis the wider, 'history-of-religions' category of sacrifice, Christian sacrifice, for this Catholic author, sits in tensile relation: enough similarity for a connection but at the same time a greater subverting dissimilarity: an analogy in other words. Where does this lead Power?

Power situates the Eucharist firmly within thanksgiving and praise. In the Eucharist we do not add an offering to Christ's offering but our act is metaphorically called a sacrifice. Further, the self-offering of the Church is also metaphorically called a sacrifice, so that the faithful unite themselves existentially with the love and obedience of Christ. This entails for Power the startling conclusion that the literal offering of bread and wine are not necessary to the Eucharist but, when added, 'draw out' the meaning of the Eucharist in certain directions. In terms of Christ's death the metaphor of sacrifice draws out Christ's obedience, and the obsolescence of ritual sacrifice following Christ's death, as a metaphor of the expiation of sin, is a metaphor for God's love found in Christ.

[10] Allmen, *The Lord's Supper*, 91–92.
[11] On convergence between Methodists and Catholics on sacrifice see the very thorough work of Stephen Bentley Sours: 'Eucharist and Anthropology' (unpublished thesis). On the fruits of official dialogues between Anglicans and Roman Catholics on these points, see Franklin, 'ARC-USA: Five Affirmations'.
[12] See now Hunsinger, *The Eucharist and Ecumenism*, especially parts 1 and 2.
[13] Analogous surveys can be found in Journet, *The Mass*, and Schenk, 'Opfer und Opferkritik'.
[14] Power, 'Words that Crack', 159.

There is much here which resonates with the official teaching of the Church, but the account can be questioned in some ways. Power does not, at least on this account, situate sacrifice sufficiently within a Trinitarian context. Such a context would show that for real metaphor to work, literal and metaphorical cannot be played off against each other as a zero-sum game. Doing so must put one on a path to the regrettable evacuation of metaphor, feeding off a noxious disdain for the real.

While Power favours metaphor, Jean-Louis Chauvet champions 'symbol'. Strongly marked by his interaction with Heidegger's critique of metaphysics Chauvet wants to relocate the sacramental discourse outside the metaphysical, and therefore ontotheological, 'ball park'. We should replace scholastic categories of instrumental causality, with a new methodology based 'upon [sacraments] as symbolic figures allowing us entrance into, and empowerment to live out, the (arch-) sacramentality which is the very essence of Christian existence.'[15] For Chauvet the mistake of the metaphysical tradition is to think that our use of the verb 'to be' actually links language and the real, whereas the mismatch between these two must be foregrounded. A failure in this regard has led to a view of causality in sacramental theology which is 'always tied to the idea of production or augmentation,'[16] or in the terms I used above, transactional. Chauvet seems to think that all sacramental theology, until his symbolic proposal, has laboured under a far too creaturely, ontotheological, because essentially univocal, under-standing of the operation of grace and the sacraments.

For Chauvet it is Thomas Aquinas who falls most prey to the ontotheological captivity—though he admits his presentation of Aquinas is more of a caricature and that is surely right; following the work of Denys Turner and Jean-Luc Marion, it can hardly be said that Thomas is an ontotheologian but rather seriously apophatic and analogical.[17] Despite the fact that the allegation of ontotheology may not stick to Thomas this does not discount the insights of Chauvet's own 'symbolic' approach. How then does he see sacrifice?

For Chauvet sacrifice in the symbolic perspective should be seen as 'anti-sacrifice' (and Eucharistic presence, oddly, as 'ad-esse'). By this term he wishes to escape both horns of the dilemma between either 'sacrifice or non-sacrifice' in Eucharistic theology.[18] He then reinterprets the language of the Eucharistic Prayers in terms of symbolic gift exchange. He emphasizes the obsolescence of the whole Jewish cultic system: 'Christians have no other Temple than the glo-rified body of Jesus, no other altar than his cross, no other priest and sacrifice

---

[15] Chauvet, *Symbol and Sacrament*, 2.

[16] Chauvet, *Symbol and Sacrament*, 7.

[17] For a critique and correction of Chauvet's liturgical theology via Lonergan's understanding of intention, see Mudd, 'Eucharist and Critical Metaphysics' (unpublished dissertation). More positively, see Ambrose, *The Theology of Louis-Marie Chauvet*.

[18] Chauvet, *Symbol and Sacrament*, 307. This trichotomy is picked up and usefully developed in Kirwan, 'Eucharist and Sacrifice'.

than his very person: Christ is their only possible liturgy.'[19] This 'trumping' of the Jewish cultic system by the Christian order means that sacrifice must operate in a totally new way. Chauvet centres on the *todah*, thanksgiving, or offering as the appropriate context to formulate this new 'anti-sacrificial' approach (though *todah* offerings were part of the Jewish sacrificial complex). Sacrifice should be existential rather than ritual and modelled on Christ's sacrifice as kenosis understood as 'the consent to his condition as Son-in-humanity and as Brother of humanity.'[20] The Son's selfless giving is the reversal of Adam's proud, grasping, ontotheological, sin. The Son offers us an example of 'de-mastery', of 'letting-be'.[21] The Son's filial trust in the Father is his sacrifice of (his divine) self. This enables Chauvet to include elements of expiation within his overall conception of sacrifice as sacrifice of thanksgiving, in clear resonance with James Alison's Girardian proposal. The whole sacrificial order is to be approached with this filial attitude of trust, as contrasted with the ontotheological, competitive, servile attitude. Sacrifice, then, is a pedagogy which teaches us to 'acknowledge ourselves as from others and for others by recognizing ourselves to be from God and for God.'[22] Initially more promising than 'sign', it turns out that Chauvet's reading of 'symbol' carries on its work of evacuation.

Matthew Levering has taken up what appears to be a very different view of sacrifice within Catholic theology. He argues vigorously in his recent *Sacrifice and Community*,[23] that recent Catholic theology has tended to envision the Eucharist in terms of communion, with God and each other, at the expense of the Eucharist's sacrificial aspects. This has happened, he argues, both implicitly by means of a change of emphasis in Eucharistic theology but also actively in the evacuation of sacrificial categories from Eucharistic thought. He terms this stance of promoting communion at the expense of sacrifice 'Eucharistic idealism'.

Significantly, Levering argues that to downplay or even excise sacrificial categories from our understanding of the Eucharist is not only unfaithful to scriptural presentations of the paschal mystery, but also ultimately supersessionist in its total rejection of the sacrificial matrix within the Old Testament and Judaism. To argue that Christ's Eucharist is simply a sacrament of communion is to repudiate Christ's Jewishness and to sunder the New Testament from the Hebrew Bible in a quasi-Marcionite way. Interestingly, Levering's argument here is paralleled from a Jewish perspective by Klawans, who argues that a supersessionist bias can be found in both Christian and Jewish parsings of the sacrificial elements of scripture which are over-determined by an evolutionary model of sacrifice. In this view biblical conceptions are replaced by a 'better' or

---

[19] Chauvet, *Symbol and Sacrament*, 250.
[20] Chauvet, *Symbol and Sacrament*, 301.
[21] Chauvet, *Symbol and Sacrament*, 300.
[22] Chauvet, *Symbol and Sacrament*, 314.
[23] Levering, *Sacrifice and Community*.

more 'spiritual' understanding with an inherently patronizing attitude towards those who maintain some literal sense to sacrificial language.[24]

Rather, for Levering, sacrifice and communion belong together. We are only able to celebrate communion because of sacrifice. He makes his case by a pincer movement from both the Christian and Jewish perspectives. From the *Aqedah* he argues that communion with the infinite only proceeds on the basis of self-surrender. In a self-dispossessing posture we are made ready for communion with God and one another. He goes on to explore biblical traditions of sacrifice in some detail and argues that the language of expiatory sacrifice is pervasive in these texts which together make up a pattern of 'dispossessive thanksgiving' to God, emphasizing, however, that the bodily and spiritual must go together. For Levering, Christ is the fulfilment of the Temple and his sacrifice, therefore, the culmination of all forms of Jewish sacrifice and the final restoration of the covenant between God and humanity. The Eucharist is not a different or repeated sacrifice, but the same sacrifice represented in a sacramental mode. He goes on to look at how for Aquinas charity is always framed in self-sacrificial terms. Thus Christians are to be a cruciform people in representing Christ's own self-sacrifice in their lives. In this way the Eucharist is a school of charity. Here we find a strong sense of sacrifice defended, combining Christ's immolation with our subsequent oblation.

In many publications Robert Daly has wrestled with the topic of sacrifice and his thought has evolved dramatically.[25] His final, crucial move came when he was very struck by a point Edward Kilmartin made in his massive *Eucharist in the West*—which Daly prepared for publication after Kilmartin's death—that fundamentally, Christian sacrifice must be understood in a Trinitarian optic.[26] This, for Daly is the fundamental key and was a game-changing revelation.[27] Sacrifice is articulated within the Trinitarian dynamic of mutually self-giving love of the members of the Trinity in which we participate, in and through the Holy Spirit. This understanding is a long way from the general secular understanding of sacrifice as 'giving something, usually of at least some value, in order to get something of greater value' emphasizing as it does, a transactional calculus and yielding a focus on the negative. He argues that it is very important to note the way in which such a secular understanding impinges on religious ones.[28]

---

[24] See Klawans, *Purity, Sacrifice, and the Temple*. Levering is much influenced by John Paul II's repeated insistence on the continuing validity of the two covenants and the theological readjustments that implies.

[25] Daly gives an account in *Sacrifice Unveiled*, 222–237.

[26] Kilmartin, *The Eucharist in the West*, 381–382.

[27] Daly popularized this view in a series of articles and culminating in *Sacrifice Unveiled*. See Daly, 'Sacrifice Unveiled or Sacrifice Revisited', 'New Developments in the Theology of Sacrifice'.

[28] Though actually the reverse may be more interesting. It would be fascinating to investigate to what extent the early theoretical study of sacrifice, largely culturally and geographically French, and much discussed elsewhere in this book, is organically related, whether positively or

For Daly, the authentic Trinitarian account of sacrifice focuses on the fact that sacrifice is not something we do but something which originates rather in God's action. 'Sacrifice' as we see it in the Cross or the Mass is like an earthly 'snapshot' of the way God simply is. Daly sees this starting in a first 'moment' with the Father's offering of himself in the Son which then returns when the Son offers himself to the Father in the Spirit, and this latter movement encompasses the whole of Christ's redemptive incarnation from Annunciation to Ascension and sending of the Spirit, without ignoring the Cross. None of this self-offering proceeds on the basis of compulsion or need but is loving and free. Sacrifice continues to come into being, as it were, when we are caught up into that movement of self-giving offering in the Spirit into the Trinity. One can see how for Daly sacrifice and Trinitarian theosis are interlinked. By participating in Christian sacrifice in this broader sense we are being transformed into the body of Christ and included in the movement of divine self-offering, a movement of love. This is all really symbolized in the Mass and lived out existentially in lives of self-offering in the world. Daly moves sacrifices onto a broad, Trinitarian, oblationist canvas.

Joseph Ratzinger's theology of sacrifice has been forged, it can be argued, by engagements on two different fronts. Early on he was very marked by Luther's critique of the sacrifice of the Mass, and grants the 'profound theological weight' of Luther's concerns, and indeed says that it would be easy to 'set Luther aside and derive similar ideas directly from the New Testament itself'—especially of course in the *ephapax* of the Letter to the Hebrews.[29] Ratzinger stresses the positive in Luther's critique and argues that two elements of Luther's views help the Christian find an answer. First, the emphasis on the *ephapax* is vital: 'Christ's sacrifice is offered once and is sufficient for all time' and in it God shows us the fruitlessness of our various cultic systems. Secondly, our worship cannot consist merely in offering our own gifts, but in 'thankful acceptance...of Christ's salvific action'.[30] All this must mean that the Mass cannot be seen as 'a self-sufficient, independent sacrifice'.[31] Ratzinger then stresses, in concert with the theologians I explored towards the beginning of this contribution, that Christ's sacrifice cannot be considered something simply past but rather becomes present for us in the sacramental ceremony. Thus for Ratzinger here thanksgiving and sacrifice cannot be separated: one is thankful for the redeeming presence of Christ's all-sufficient sacrifice. He then goes on to contrast two groups of texts which contain the words of institution at the Last Supper, going on to align one group

negatively, to a particular French Catholic understanding of sacrifice. For an argument in this direction, see Strenski, *Contesting Sacrifice*, supplemented with Despland, *Le recul du sacrifice*.

[29]	Ratzinger, 'Is the Eucharist a Sacrifice?', 35.
[30]	Ratzinger, 'Is the Eucharist a Sacrifice?', 36.
[31]	Ratzinger, 'Is the Eucharist a Sacrifice?', 36.

(Matthew and Mark) with a Mosaic understanding of sacrifice represented by the covenantal theology of cultic ritual described in the Torah, and the other group (Luke and Paul) with the critique by the Prophets of that very cultic system in pointing to Jeremiah's 'new covenant'. He then argues that the theme of the Suffering Servant unites these two seemingly exclusive trajectories. The new covenant doesn't simply interiorize the old cultic ritual of the Temple but is rather embodied in the selfless giving of the Servant who suffers 'for many'. From this context of exile there was no possibility of Temple worship and so Israel has come to see herself, in the corporate personality of the Servant, as a sacrifice. Here the 'new type of sacrifice is martyrdom'.[32] Christ picks up this new view of worship of God and offers himself. Christ has become the ritual and 'it is in this sense that the Eucharistic supper is a sacrifice'.[33] In our remembrance of it, it becomes present to us. Ratzinger stresses here that in this way past and present, from our perspective, are in some sense porous to each other and he relies on the (then) recent research on the idea of 'memorial' in biblical texts to show that this was a sense deployed by biblical authors. But he adds that we must not forget the future either: insofar as the Eucharist is an eschatological act it also points to its consummation at the end of time: 'it is a summons to put hope and trust in what is to come'.[34] In proclamation of God's deeds in time we recall them and make them present and it is in this way for Ratzinger that 'there is no antithesis between Word and Sacrament'.[35] Ratzinger can be seen here to be close to Casel's understanding of the making present of the one Sacrifice of Christ in the Church's worship, but expanding the concept biblically and eschatologically.

Later in his career, Cardinal Ratzinger, as he then was, addressed the topic of sacrifice again during a conference on liturgy at the Abbey of Notre Dame de Fontgombault.[36] The interesting battle line here is not with old Reformation disputes but, fascinatingly, with something of an internal polarizing Catholic equivalent: the critique of the *novus ordo* of the Mass brought into Church life after the Second Vatican Council by the Lefebvrist organisation, the Society of St Pius X, and the concomitant promotion of the Mass of St Pius V.[37] The critique, simply put, is that the Caselian approach to the Paschal Mystery—meaning the mystery of Christ's sacrifice taken in its multifarious and 'stretched out' form in the whole sweep of Christ's life, death, Resurrection, and Ascension, as represented in the Eucharist—actually

---

[32]  Ratzinger, 'Is the Eucharist a Sacrifice?', 38.
[33]  Ratzinger, 'Is the Eucharist a Sacrifice?', 39.
[34]  Ratzinger, 'Is the Eucharist a Sacrifice?', 39.
[35]  Ratzinger, 'Is the Eucharist a Sacrifice?', 39.
[36]  Ratzinger, 'The Theology of the Liturgy', in Reid, *Looking Again*, especially 23–25.
[37]  Their position can be found in Aa. Vv., The Society of Saint Pius X, *The Problem of the Liturgical Reform*. For a contemporary presentation of the Tridentinist take on sacrifice, see Lucien, 'Le sacrifice rédempteur'.

downplays the expiatory sacrifice of Christ on the Cross. By attempting to set the Cross within a wider context one is minimizing or even denying the reality of what was achieved on the Cross. Very oddly, a zero-sum is perceived between the full economy of salvation and the narrow sacramental economy. This cannot be right.

In his response Ratzinger sets sacrifice within the context of love. Passover cannot be separated from sacrifice, the two are scripturally intrinsically related. It is thus the narrow approach of the Lefevrists which does an injustice to the picture given in revelation, just as the narrowness found in the Reformation debates on both sides did the same. Relying on Augustine, Ratzinger accents the positive cast of Christian sacrifice. This is no 'standard' sacrifice: 'destruction does not honour God'.[38] Rather, consonant with the prophetic critique of cultic ritual, Christian sacrifice lies in the transformation of humanity. This is a process of conforming to God and a human being is 'conformed to God when he becomes love'.[39] Or as Augustine puts it: 'true sacrifice is every work which allows us to unite ourselves to God in a holy fellowship'.[40] For Augustine all sacrificial systems prior to Christ refer to him and are figures of the love of God and neighbour. Sacrifice is at once individual and communal in this view. Ratzinger highlights here how it is we who thus become the sacrifice for Augustine: 'the sacrifice is ourselves'.[41] Ratzinger here links sacrifice to the early Christian tradition of theosis and goes as far as to say that sacrifice consists 'in the abolition of difference—in the union between God and man, between God and creation: "God all in all"' (1 Cor. 15:28).[42] Sacrifice is a practice of participation. He goes on to highlight that in the Christian tradition, in contrast to some others, this union is achieved in a differentiated way without the loss of our integrity (or that of God). Although difference may in one sense be overcome, this is in fact achieved without loss of difference, by virtue of a higher union of love as found in the archetypical Trinitarian relations—a union which respects, even highlights, the difference of those thereby united. Ratzinger is keen to point out that this location of sacrifice within love (cf. Hos. 6:6) is not a facile opposition between 'ethos and worship' which might lead to a simplistic moralism, but rather a response to God's prior action and love.[43] 'It is the love with which God loves, which alone makes our love towards Him increase.'[44] And of course this love has a name: Jesus Christ.

[38] Ratzinger, 'The Theology of the Liturgy', 25.
[39] Ratzinger, 'The Theology of the Liturgy', 25.
[40] Augustine, *City of God*, X.6: 'uerum sacrificium est omne opus, quo agitur, ut sancta societate inhaereamus Deo'.
[41] Augustine, *City of God*, X.6:, 'sacrificium nos ipsi sumus'.
[42] Ratzinger, 'The Theology of the Liturgy', 25.
[43] Ratzinger, 'The Theology of the Liturgy', 26.
[44] Ratzinger, 'The Theology of the Liturgy', 26.

Finally, Ratzinger explores the meaning of *logike thusia*, which Paul exhorts the Roman believers to become (cf. Heb. 13:15). In and through our bodies we offer God a sacrifice of praise with our words that reflects our interior disposition towards God: word and action are not separate, just as word and sacrifice are not opposed but intimately related. He concludes by saying that he thinks the error of Luther is a false sense of historicity and poor understanding of unicity.[45] Ratzinger's theology of sacrifice is significant for its reliance on theologians like Casel, its location of sacrifice in the prior context of love, and its contrast with the theology of sacrifice of John Paul II.[46]

James Alison's conception of sacrifice grows out of René Girard's understanding of mimetic desire: we each desire what the other desires. Our competing, mimetic, desires lead us to rivalrous violence which is cast off by transfer to a scapegoat. What Jesus did, in Girard's view, is to reveal this scapegoating mechanism for what it was, and thus end the cycle of rivalrous desire and violence and point us to an economy of non-rivalrous coexistence.

Alison, in various writings, puts this insight in startlingly fresh language. In one of his earliest works, *Knowing Jesus*, he looks at sacrifice through the lens of victimhood. For Alison it was Jesus' life of complete freedom in the form of totally free self-giving which led to his death: '... the self-giving is prior, anterior to the sacrifice, and the sacrifice is incidental, accidental to the self-giving. So, Jesus did give himself so as to be a victim, but did not want this at all. Immolation was an accidental outcome of oblation. There was no death-wish in Jesus.'[47] Christ's life and being are 'an ascesis of desire' which help us move 'human desire out of a pattern of relating to others from rivalry, a relationship based on death, to a relationship based on the pacific imitation of Jesus, leading to a relationship with others based on gratuity, service.'[48]

Alison highlights that because God offers himself as the victim and thus undoes the rivalrous relationship practitioners had had towards the victim thus far, and reveals an optic of seeing God in the victim rather than 'over against, or by exclusion of, the victim.'[49] Sacrificial systems based on a transactional, 'grasping', logic cannot produce unity, and they are the 'direct inverse of the self-giving up to death of Christ, which permits the forming of a sociality

[45] Ratzinger, 'The Theology of the Liturgy', 29.
[46] This topic merits further attention. John Paul's theology of sacrifice is much more marked by Trent, and less theologically developed than his successor's, but one must remember the different remits of magisterial documents and personal theological writings. Close attention to John Paul's letter to the world's bishops, *Dominicae Cenae* (1980), and his encyclical *Ecclesia de Eucharistia* (2003), suggests that he tried to emphasize sacrifice rather more, or at least differently, than his successor and to the implied exclusion, or at least relativization, of other elements of the Mass. This is not unrelated to his teachings on the ministerial priesthood.
[47] Alison, *Knowing Jesus*, 49.
[48] Alison, *Knowing Jesus*, 56.
[49] Alison, *Knowing Jesus*, 71.

without any "over against"...'[50] In the Mass we 'celebrate the being-set-free from sacrifice by repeating with gratitude the way Jesus chose to make his self-giving apparent, which is simultaneously not a sacrifice at all, in the world-religions sense of the word, and the one true sacrifice, since it blows apart the world of sacrifice.'[51] Strikingly, Alison describes the celebration of the Mass as a secularizing move: the 'relocation of the Temple onto Jesus' own body, the replacement of Temple sacrifice with a single human "sacrifice" to be re-presented continuously as a way of inhabiting the time in which the sacred is in perpetual collapse.'[52] For Alison, then, Christ's sacrifice is a 'sacrifice in which God sacrifices himself to us, and we discover that we are the wrathful divinity in the equation', reconfigures us, shows us how to be free, and reveals God's true nature: 'Jesus is God's living interpretation of himself to us at our level, not *over against us* in any way at all, but *for us* in the way that only God can be, as something coming out of nothing.'[53] For Alison the sacrifice of the Mass is vital for reordering Christian desire as the body of Christ, assuming Christ's oblationary posture to live beyond bad sacrifice in non-rivalrous relations with all.

Our *tour d'horizon* of the theme of sacrifice in modern Catholic theology has built a cumulative argument. We started out from the assertion that sacrifice is a central part of Catholicism. We noted that neither the decrees of the Council of Trent, nor subsequent ecclesial documents, have actually defined sacrifice. In many ways then the history of sacrifice in Catholic thought has been that of a central concept seeking understanding, a specific form of Anselmian *fides quaerens intellectum*. This surprising aporia has been for me a positive outcome of this investigation: Catholic theology is remarkably free, within the very broad terms of Scripture, conciliar, and ecclesial documents (of varying levels of normativity), to form its own 'fleshing-out' of the sacrificial skeleton. At the same time, one might find it perplexing that one of the most central ideas in Catholicism lacks a fully worked-out understanding. But, if one is fully alive to the nature of the Christian God, especially the nature of his transcendence as Creator, and the eschatological nature of his reality and our interaction with him, it is no wonder, indeed it is vital, that Catholic theology recaptures this necessarily 'lacunic', or apophatic, nature of its theological and ecclesial activity.

Significantly, this highlights the sadness of the Reformation debates, focused as they were on both sides on a narrow, transactional view of sacrifice, locked within an essentially creaturely conception of theology and God and his interactions with us. But the freedom found in more recent ecclesial documents, paradigmatically and ironically also in those of Trent, means that in recent

---

[50]  Alison, *The Joy of Being Wrong*, 252.
[51]  Alison, *The Joy of Being Wrong*, 123–124.
[52]  Alison, *The Joy of Being Wrong*, 124.
[53]  Alison, *Undergoing God*, 8.

years remarkable ecumenical advance has been achieved on the topic of sacrifice such that to a large extent sacrifice has been rehabilitated on the theological scene. Through a reinvigoration of the biblical concept of 'remembrance',
the one sacrifice of the cross and the celebration of the Eucharist are no longer
seen as locked in a zero-sum, the one neither competing with, nor showing the
insufficiency of the other.

In looking at two constellations of Catholic thinkers, one early and the
other more recent, we noted a number of features of modern Catholic thinking on sacrifice. The early constellation was important in helping along the
loosening of the oppositions bequeathed by the Reformation and opening
up new vistas. The fruitless battle of the debate on sacrifice conducted on
the turf of transactional conceptions could only fail. Casel's textured understanding of mystery helped here, but it also helps situate the issue of sacrifice
within the sweep of Christ's whole (continuing) life event and relates the
topic of sacrifice to the nature of the God with whom it seeks union. His
emphasis on mystery stresses, too, the necessarily partial, or failing, nature
of our theological discourse—partly picked up one-sidedly later by Power
and Chauvet in different ways. De la Taille helped ease the sole focus on the
event of Jesus' death by drawing our attention to the Supper and the offering,
controversially arguing that, at the Supper, Jesus was offering the sacrifice of
the Cross. Significantly he also, in ways we were not able to explore, argues
for the sacrificial 'shape' of several theological doctrines, for instance grace
and prayer. By integrally relating Eucharist and theology in this manner, he
thus reminds us of the age-old adage *lex orandi, lex credendi*: the way we
pray should influence the way we believe and the way we articulate the faith.
Finally, Vonier insists, in a way that also helps to assuage the Reformation
stand-off, that the Eucharist is the sacramental re-presentation of the sacrifice of the Cross and by virtue of that *is* the same sacrifice, not a new or
repeated one. Unfortunately, to my mind, in doing so he accented the metaphorical nature of the sacrifice of the Eucharist, whereby he helps to undo
his own argument. As always, paradoxical concepts are uneasy and tend to
contain the seeds of their own undoing.

Our more modern constellation showed great variety, a variety only possible given the concept's 'lacunic' core. On the one hand, Power and Chauvet
continue the seeds of Vonier's approach: by overly stressing the disjunct
between our sacrifice and that of Christ they loosen the unity and threaten the
ecumenical gains. Power does this by arguing for the essentially metaphorical nature of sacrifice (and clearly using a weak understanding of metaphor),
whereas Chauvet relocates the whole discourse to the realm of symbol, thereby
accenting the gap between words and reality. While the attempt to avoid onto-
theology is highly to be commended, this way of doing it seems to sow a seed
which can only threaten any purchase on the reality both authors clearly wish
to attain. I would suggest that a strong understanding of analogy might help

here, but equally it is possible that stronger understandings of metaphor and symbol could also do this work.

We then saw how Levering insists on the central place of sacrifice in Eucharistic theology against what he terms 'eucharistic idealism', the tendency to play up the communion at the expense of the sacrificial. Rightly Levering sees that doing away with sacrificial elements too easily threatens the loss of the authentically Christian sense of sacrifice: there is a fine line between the non-sacrificial (and metaphor and symbol too easily push in this direction) and the anti-sacrificial which sees Jesus' sacrifice as the culmination (and not the supersession) of the Jewish cultic system. It is only in terms of the latter that the former can be clearly seen.

This connection is not lost on the final three theologians, who each set the sacrificial discourse on, differing but related, broad canvases. Daly has 'discovered' the Trinitarian setting of sacrifice, emphasizing the mutual self-offering of the Triune God, into which dynamic we are inscribed by imitating the dispossesive posture in the Eucharist. Sacrifice is then a movement of God from God to God, which runs via creation and Incarnation, including us within it. For Ratzinger sacrifice is ultimately about love and theosis. Again, by imitating the Son's life of self-giving which climaxed on the Cross but continues in Heaven we become his Body and offer ourselves to God. James Alison's take on sacrifice, heavily influenced by Girard, focuses on sacrifice as anti-sacrifice and, like Ratzinger, portrays Christian sacrifice as the end of the cultic system, because it reveals the non-rivalrous relations between God and ourselves through God's offering of himself to us in Christ. In the victim on the cross who yet lives we see the triumph of an anti-sacrificial way of relating, ironically made manifest in a sacrifice. By constantly attending to the representation of that sacrifice we learn to follow God's model and in so doing draw closer to him and to one another.

# 10

## Using Hubert and Mauss to think about Sacrifice

### Nick Allen

[The 1899 essay by Hubert and Mauss] still provides the best starting point from which sophisticated and possibly adequate theories of ritual can be derived.[1]

Whether or not one accepts this grand claim (made by a senior and well-recognized Vedic scholar), the early study by Hubert and Mauss is widely regarded by students of sacrifice as a classic. However, like most classics, it does not yield all its riches on first reading. Moreover, it needs to be situated within the life and thought of its authors, and it will be read and judged differently by those who come to it from different points of view. Assessment is complicated by the joint authorship, but since the two authors collaborated over the course of a decade, and were close and lifelong friends, this source of difficulty is less weighty than one might fear. Despite the alphabetic ordering of the authors' names, I start with the better known of the two.

Marcel Mauss (1872–1950), nephew of the great Durkheim (1858–1917), was brought up in a Jewish family in Alsace. After studying sociology with his uncle (then at Bordeaux), he moved to Paris to study philology, religious studies, and Indology, especially Sanskrit. Arguably his life's work was as much inspired by the great Indologist and humanist Sylvain Lévi (also Jewish), as by Durkheim's sociology.[2] Anyway, he helped Durkheim to found (in 1898) the important yearbook, the *Année sociologique* (henceforth *Année*), and a few years later was appointed to teach on 'Religions of Non-civilized Peoples'. After Durkheim's death, returning from the war, he struggled to develop the academic tradition that his uncle had founded. Having dominated French anthropology for twenty years, he retired at the start of the Second World War and could achieve little thereafter.[3]

---

[1] Staal, *Ritual*, 150.
[2] Allen, 'Mauss and India'.
[3] Fournier, *Mauss*.

Though Mauss himself, notoriously, never published a single-author free-standing book, his bibliography runs to fifty-five pages in Fournier's biography. Four posthumous volumes collect 2,500 pages of his anthropological writing and a fifth collects his political journalism (he was a moderate socialist, favouring the Cooperative Movement). In addition, his valuable *Manual of Ethnography* (1947) was compiled by a student from students' lecture notes taken in the 1930s. Of all his texts the most celebrated is undoubtedly his classic study, *The Gift*, which has come to be almost as widely read outside anthropology as within it. Mauss' work (both lectures and writings) exercised considerable influence on such major post-war figures as Lévi-Strauss, Dumont, Dumézil, and Evans-Pritchard, and to judge from secondary literature and translations from the French, his reputation is still growing. Quite apart from the quality of his insights and the range of topics on which he wrote, his (at first sight) unsystematic cast of mind, allusive style, and fragmented production constitute both an invitation and a challenge to define and develop his ideas and relate them one to another.

Henri Hubert (1872–1927) was an equally enthusiastic follower of Durkheim, though he was neither related to him nor Jewish. A Parisian by birth and education, more self-disciplined than Mauss, he interested himself in sociology, history, and archaeology, with special reference to pre-Christian Europe and West Asia.[4] He met Mauss in 1896 and was promptly enrolled in the team of contributors to the *Année*; Mauss called him his professional twin (*jumeau de travail*). Their collaboration, which started with the 1899 essay on sacrifice (henceforth *Sacrifice*), continued with a joint essay on magic in 1904, and two years later with an 'Introduction to the Analysis of Certain Religious Phenomena'.[5] In 1909 they published together the *Mélanges d'histoire des religions*, which apart from the jointly-signed 'Introduction' and *Sacrifice* included two individually signed articles: a second paper by Mauss on magic, and Hubert's *Time* (his best known paper).[6] But whatever the signatures, the whole book was based on collaboration.

The 'Introduction' gains prominence from the position that Karady gave it in his edition of the *Oeuvres*—right at the start of the first volume (entitled *The Social Functions of the Sacred*). Unfortunately it remains untranslated, and the vagaries of translation history have fragmented the *Mélanges*, which the authors saw as essentially a single enterprise. But it was a single enterprise within the Durkheimian project, and a few words are needed on this project.

---

[4] Isambert, 'Introduction'; Hubert, *Time* (with selective bibliography 97–100).
[5] Mauss, *Oeuvres*, vol. 1, 3–39.
[6] Fournier, *Mauss*, 147–148 (fuller in the French original, 312–317).

## 1. RELIGIOUS PHENOMENA

Durkheim's purpose was to change the map of learning. He wanted to establish *sociologie* (including what is now social anthropology) as a serious academic discipline, distinct from (in particular) philosophy, psychology, and history. Two years after his thesis (*Division of Labour*, 1893), he presented his manifesto.[7] The new discipline was to be a science of social facts, that is, of social phenomena viewed objectively. Like other sciences, it needed to classify the phenomena it studied, organizing them into carefully defined taxa. No scholar could cover the whole field in detail, and Durkheim proposed that Mauss specialize in religious facts—which accorded with the nephew's own preferences.[8] He deliberately avoided the term 'religion'.

That Hubert and Mauss shared Durkheim's theoretical position is clear not only from *Sacrifice* but also from the encyclopaedia article that Mauss wrote with another *Année* colleague in 1901, and from the 'Introduction' that Hubert contributed in 1904 to a manual for students of History of Religions.[9] Above all, then, their study will view sacrifice as a social fact, one that conforms to the accounts they give of what makes a phenomenon a social one. Thus sacrifice will be studied as manifesting the specific traditions of specific societies, and not the proclivities of a generalized human nature—an approach that would belong to psychology. As to what makes a social fact a religious one, the key to their thinking lies in the word 'sacred', as we shall see in more detail later. Definitions of religion along the lines of belief in spiritual beings, gods, or the Absolute were unsatisfactory. Their shortcomings included underemphasis on behaviour and the awkward fit with a religion like Theravada Buddhism, in which gods are of secondary significance.

As is shown by the title and contents of *Mélanges*, Hubert and Mauss included magic among religious phenomena, albeit in a subordinate position. In his *Manual* Mauss formulates the matter as follows:

> Just as aesthetics is defined by the notion of beauty, techniques by technical efficacy, just as economics is defined by the notion of value and law by the notion of property, *religious or magico-religious phenomena are defined by the notion of the sacred.*[10]

In the first instance this applied to religious facts in the strict or narrow sense. Religion in the broader sense embraced magic and divination, and around this broader realm lay a halo of folklore or popular beliefs, sometimes labelled superstitions.

[7] Durkheim, *Rules*.
[8] Mauss, 'Self-portrait', 35.
[9] Fauconnet/Mauss, *Sociology*; Hubert 'Introduction' (on which, see Mauss, *Oeuvres*, vol. 1, 46).
[10] Mauss, *Manual*, 162 (original italics), 165.

This concentric schema was only one of various ways recognized by Durkheimians to classify the religious phenomena in a society. Another was according to the way the phenomena relate to social structure, that is, to the groups or categories that make up a society. A fundamental distinction, more useful for our purposes, was between rites or practices on the one hand, and myths or representations on the other—behaviour versus cognition, as we might now say. These too could be subdivided. Among the practices, positive rites like sacrifice contrasted with negative rites or ritual prohibitions—expressions that Mauss preferred to 'taboos'; and among the positive rites, oral ritual contrasted with manual ritual ('manual' as in 'manual work', which involves physical or bodily actions not necessarily confined to the hands).

This last distinction is particularly relevant to *Sacrifice*. While Mauss was working on it, he was also working on his thesis, which was to be on prayer. In 1911 he circulated privately the first quarter of the work,[11] but he never completed it. However, we know what he planned from the account of his academic work which he prepared in 1930 for his (successful) candidacy for a position at the Collège de France. He was originally intending to treat Vedic oral literature in the second volume.[12] This explains why *Sacrifice* concentrates on manual ritual and de-emphasizes the verbal presentation of victim to deity. It explicitly omits discussion of invitations to the gods, hymns, the description of the victim, and the statement of the results expected from the ritual.[13]

Other background assumptions of the Durkheimian school can be left until after the presentation of the argument of *Sacrifice*. My précis tries to extract what is most relevant in the present context.

## 2. THE ARGUMENT OF 'SACRIFICE: ITS NATURE AND FUNCTIONS'

**Introduction.** The authors plan to put forward a provisional hypothesis that builds on recent work but goes beyond it. For Tylor, sacrifice was originally a gift to supernatural beings, given in the hope of a return, but subsequently it became a homage to them (return not expected), and thereafter self-denial and renunciation. Such an approach is generally accepted by ordinary folk and is part of the whole picture, but Tylor's position hardly amounted to a theory. Robertson Smith, writing of the Semitic world, put the emphasis on the consumption of animal victims, whose sacredness derived from totemism. He

---

[11] Mauss, *Prayer*.
[12] Mauss, *Self-portrait*, 38.
[13] Hubert/Mauss, *Sacrifice*, 126, n. 182.

knew that sacredness can be ambiguous—valued or devalued, and in the second case the victim could be destroyed without being consumed. Frazer drew attention to sacrifices *of* rather than *to* gods, and connected them to seasonal agrarian cults (in the first edition of his *Golden Bough*).

These British writers are severely criticized. They allocated their emphases arbitrarily, took for granted a link between sacrifice and totemism, conflated different types of sacrifice, and derived one type from another without adequate historical evidence. Another fault of method was to accumulate data hugger-mugger, rather than studying particular societies in depth. *Sacrifice* would focus primarily on the Vedas and the Bible (especially the Pentateuch), where the ritual was presented by the practitioners themselves at length and in their own language. Neither Greco-Roman nor ethnographic data were of comparable depth, though they are introduced occasionally.

1. **Definition and Unity of the Sacrificial System**. Though 'sacrifice' and 'consecration' are etymologically linked, their meanings overlap only in part. Every sacrifice includes consecration of an offering, but consecrations also occur outside of sacrifice. A distinction may be needed between, on the one hand, the sacrifier, an individual or collectivity, who benefits from the effects of the ritual, and on the other, the sacrificer, who actually performs it (perhaps for pay). The benefit may radiate from the sacrifier to other entities, whether material (a house or field) or immaterial (an oath or alliance). The thing consecrated stands between the earthly beneficiaries and the deity. Though some consecrated offerings (ex-votos, firstlings) are similarly placed, the rituals in which they occur are not naturally labelled 'sacrifices'; the offering needs to be destroyed. On the other hand, whether it is animal or vegetable is not crucial. Hebrew, Greek, and Vedic rituals assimilate the two.

In this way the authors arrive at their preliminary or external definition. (As throughout the chapter, although I cite pages of the English versions, I sometimes retouch the published translations.) *Sacrifice is a religious act which, via the consecration of a victim, modifies the condition of the moral person who performs it or of certain objects in which that person is interested.* The word 'victim' reflects their remark about destruction; 'moral person' covers collectivities as well as individuals; the person and object together can be thought of as the 'beneficiaries'.

To define sacrifice is to grant a certain unity to a phenomenon that can vary enormously. The combination of unity and variety is illustrated by the neat indigenous typology of Vedic rituals and the less neat Hebrew one.

2. **The Scheme of Sacrifice**. The account will be based primarily on Vedic animal sacrifice, and will only make secondary use of other Vedic sacrifices (which are vegetarian) or of comparisons from outside India. It falls into three sections—entry, victim,[14] and exit. What starts as profane must first be

---

[14] Helpfully distinguished by Karady (Mauss, *Oeuvres*, vol. 1, 630–631) and Halls, the middle section is less clearly distinct in the original.

consecrated or purified. This applies to sacrifier, sacrificer, the place where the ritual is held, and the ritual apparatus. Vedic sacrifice takes place not in a temple but on a specially prepared patch of ground, and it is to be performed in a special state of mind characterized by confidence or faith. Of the apparatus the most sacred items are the altar (dug out, not built up) and the adjacent sacrificial post, with which the sacrifier is identified.

The victim is carefully selected, pacified verbally and consecrated progressively, but cannot simply be deified since it has to link the sacred with the sacrifier; victim and sacrifier fuse. The immolation, a sort of sacrilege or murder, frees the divine principle in the victim (i.e. its life), but leaves behind a carcase. This too has two possible destinations. It can be attributed to beneficent gods (or, as a scapegoat, to maleficent demons), or to humans, who typically consume it. Vedic *iḍā* refers to a special portion of meat for priests and sacrifier, but also (Sanskrit scripts lack capital letters) to Iḍā, a goddess of abundance who is invoked into the meat. This is 'a veritable transubstantiation', comparable to what happens in the Christian mass. Overall, the sacrality concentrated in the victim is released to supernaturals and to humans.

Finally the exit phase reverses the entry, returning everything to the profane world and atoning for any ritual errors.

3, 4. **Variations from the Abstract Scheme.** In an initiation or ordination the aim may be to sacralize a being that starts off as profane. The entry rites are then emphasized, the exit ones minimized, and sacrality passes from victim to sacrifier. Conversely, the aim may be to desacralize. Since the sacred can be bad or negative as well as good, the starting point may be an undesired level of sacrality, which needs to be eliminated or expelled. Religious thought tends to associate illness, death, and sin with the bad sacred, so such rituals can be therapeutic or expiatory. But they can also be held for the Hebrew *nazir*, to release him from his period of extreme purity; and they can be held for things rather than persons. The sacred quality of a harvest may be concentrated in the firstlings, whose sacrifice frees up the remainder for ordinary consumption. The ambiguity of the sacred explains the similarities between sorts of desacralizing rituals that may seem fundamentally opposed, as well as between sacralizing and desacralizing rituals (nowadays sometimes contrasted as conjunctive and disjunctive).

If one source of variety among the rituals is the difference between sacralization and desacralization, another is the variety of beneficiaries. If the beneficiary is an individual, he may be 'reborn' and take on a new name, or gain post-mortem benefits, while a collectivity may gain socially or politically. If the beneficiary is a thing, as in an 'objective sacrifice', the entry and exit rites are minimized, and the emphasis of the middle phase is on creating a spirit, for instance the guardian spirit of a new house. Agrarian rituals are particularly complex since the farmer needs not only to expel a potentially angry spirit (so as to desacralize the harvest), but also to recreate or resurrect it with a view to future fertility. Moreover, other purposes and meanings are often amalgamated, so that the ritual contains an expiatory or scapegoat element.

5. **Sacrifice of the God.** This is among the most evolved forms of the sacrificial complex. Mannhardt and Frazer connected it with agrarian rituals but without emphasizing the role of mythology in the connection. A corn spirit tends to be barely individualized—little more than a sheaf of corn—until it is named and given an animal or human incarnation, together with a myth of sacrificial apotheosis. The development from victim to god was helped by the annual repetition of the ritual, one year's victim being identified with next year's.

Where the ritual has a god who is also the victim, myth often has a god (or his priest) whose death founds the cult. Sometimes the god himself is split, producing two opponents in a great theomachy (Marduk versus Tiamat, etc.), one or both of whom dies. The opponents' original unity explains their mutual resemblance.

Myth acts back on ritual, taking the god far from his agricultural origins. But the repetitive rhythms of nature mean that the myth includes rebirth as well as death. Sometimes a second sort of split occurs, reintroducing the victim–god duality, making the victim into either a gift or an evil enemy. This analysis applies to the particularly elaborate Vedic sacrifices *of soma* or Soma, king of plants, *to* Soma. If certain gods are born from sacrifice, all of them are sustained by the nourishment it provides; so sacrifice becomes cosmogonic, as in the case of Puruṣa. But the initial defeat of cosmic chaos/moral evil may need repetition, and the original sacrifice of the God therefore is perpetuated in regular cultic sacrifices. The latter is still the case in Christianity. The consecrations, the concentration of sacrality in the bread and wine and its dispersal among the congregation, the rhythm of expiation and communion, bring the mass astonishingly close to agrarian sacrifice.

6. **Conclusion.** Despite the variety of abstract types of sacrifice and the multiple functions served by a particular ritual, the underlying procedure has enough unity to allow of definition. '*[It] consists in establishing communication between the sacred and profane worlds through the mediation of a victim—that is, of something destroyed in the course of the ceremony.*'

*Contra* Robertson Smith, the victim does not enter the ritual already sacred; it needs to be consecrated. The procedure can equally well sacralize or desacralize; it sets in motion sacred forces. An intermediary is necessary because the sacred is dangerous to the sacrifier. Every sacrifice contains an element of redemption, of liberation from threat, and after their dealings with the sacred humans have to operate in the profane world. From the other side, the gods need the victims given by the humans, whence the contractual element in sacrifice. The two parties exchange services. However, the sacrifice of the god, which is necessarily mythic, lacks this selfish dimension. Superimposing the roles of sacrifier, victim, god, and sometimes sacrificer, it constitutes the acme of self-denial.

Non-believers may be surprised that humanity has put so much effort into communicating with something, namely the sacred, which does not exist. But religious ideas, such as gods, *do* exist, objectively, as social facts. Social facts both transcend individuals and are immanent in them. So from this point of view sacrifice addresses and reinforces something real outside the individual. At the same time it provides the support of society to individuals engaged in their everyday activities and problems.

Let us turn now to the 1909 introduction to *Mélanges*.


## 3. THE AUTHORS LOOK BACK

In 1900, in the second edition of his *Golden Bough*, Frazer had focused on the figure of the king-priest-god who is sacrificed, but Hubert and Mauss, working on prayer and myth, had already treated the topic in 1899. Mauss had come to it by asking how far the effectiveness of prayer derived from manual ritual, i.e. from sacrifice in the Vedic and Hebrew cases, while Hubert was wondering about the Semitic origins of Christian belief in sacrifice of a god.[15] Myths needed to be taken seriously as religious phenomena, and myths about dying gods often accompany sacrifices. Moreover, myths and rituals have in common religious emotions (*sentiments* in French), which also need study.

A major criticism of Robertson Smith had been his derivation of sacrifice from totemism. Such a connection seemed implausible since the two institutions are so seldom found together, and new publications on totemism since 1899 did not refute this criticism. However, *soma* is not cultivated and the sacrifice of the god could go back further than had perhaps been suggested—to before the domestication of plants and animals. But, outside Chapter 5, their main aim in *Sacrifice* had been schematic rather than genealogical (synchronic not diachronic, or typological not evolutionary, as we might say).

Naturally, a phylogenetic approach is also needed, and the *Essay* had helped them to position sacrifice within the general field of ritual. Sacrifice is not close to human origins, being far too complicated. In particular, it presupposes a clear separation between profane things and sacred ones, the latter being divinities, i.e. more or less personalized. A totemic clan, being identified with its totem, has no need for a victim to mediate between itself and the totem. Sacrifice is a social phenomenon, through and through, in various senses; everything about it relates to the sacred. As in the second definition of sacrifice in 1899, it is '*a means for the profane to communicate with the sacred via a victim*.'

---

[15] Hubert/Mauss, 'Introduction', 4; Mauss, 'Self-portrait', 39.

*Sacrifice* is often cited simply for its definitions, but why does it offer two definitions of sacrifice? It is because the first is preliminary. It conforms to Durkheim's methodological demands: 'the first step for a sociologist has to be to define the things he is discussing.'[16] Actually, Durkheim, writing in June 1898 from Bordeaux, to Mauss, who was in Oxford, offered him a draft initial definition, as follows. 'An operation or set of operations that form part of a system of religious rites and have as outcome the destruction (consumption, punishment, sacrifice into fire, etc.) or the elimination from ordinary use (offerings) of one or several objects, whether animate or inanimate.'[17]

But let us compare the two definitions published in *Sacrifice*. The first refers to a religious act that consecrates a victim so as to change the condition of a beneficiary; the second refers to a procedure that uses a victim to establish communication between sacred and profane. So the first takes for granted the notion of religion (sacrifice is a *religious* act), and the sacred appears only in the verb 'consecrate'. After marshalling and analysing their evidence, they sum up the results in the second definition. This introduces the notion of communication (a two-way process), and incorporates religion in the guise of the sacred–profane opposition. Their second formula expresses the *nature* of sacrifice, and is followed by their treatment of its *function* (the italicized terms appear in the first sentence of *Sacrifice*, as well as in its title).

The final two paragraphs of the 1909 section on sacrifice are extremely rich in ideas.[18] The authors had started from Robertson Smith's conception of the sacred as set apart and prohibited, combined with the Durkheimian conception of sacred things as social things; but they could now go further. People conceive as sacred everything that, for the group and its members, characterizes society. Gods may fade away, but they are replaced by human social values, such as Nation, Property, Work, or the Individual (I paraphrase a somewhat poetical passage).[19] So Robertson Smith's narrow concept of the sacred needed to be filled out with emotions such as respect, love, repulsion, and fear (*crainte*).[20] Understood in this sense, the sacred was the core around which rites and myths developed. Speaking personally, the most reliable advance they had made in *Sacrifice* had been to clarify their joint aim: it was to understand 'the identity of the sacred and the social'. An important clarification comes a few pages later, in their discussion of Mauss' article on magic. Languages may not have a single word meaning 'sacred', but this does not imply that the speakers lack the concept.[21]

---

[16] Durkheim, *Rules*, 74; similarly, Durkheim, 'Definition', 74–75.
[17] Durkheim, *Lettres*, 144.
[18] Hubert/Mauss, 'Introduction', 16–17; 'characterize' translates French *qualifier*.
[19] Allen, *Categories*, 118.
[20] Also Hubert/Mauss, 'Introduction', 38.
[21] Hubert/Mauss, 'Introduction', 21.

After Hubert's death Mauss took further his criticism of the binary schema that the early *Année* workers, including himself, had derived from Robertson Smith. Their notion of religion had been extremely narrow, in its focus on the sacred. In many contexts one needed to envisage a complex of interrelated positions, powers, and purities having six or seven components—the four cardinal points, the above and below, and often the centre.[22] Mauss himself does not relate this cosmological insight to *Sacrifice*, and it is difficult to see exactly what he had in mind. I like to think that one could approach his position by viewing Vedic sacrifice in the light of the pentadic theory of Indo-European ideology,[23] which is something that in any case I hope to attempt elsewhere.

The opening of Mauss' thesis on prayer contains a further insight. His view of *sociologie* was deeply 'evolutionist' (a label often used pejoratively by social anthropologists unconcerned with, or hostile to, the study of world history), and he is here asking himself about the rise and fall of different types of religious phenomena. The system of food prohibitions is characteristic of elemental religions (which would certainly include totemism—theriomorphic cults practised by clans), and has tended to regress, virtually disappearing in certain protestant traditions. Sacrifice, characteristic of religions at a certain stage of development, has also tended to decline qua ritual, though surviving in Christian myth and symbolism. In contrast, prayer, starting out as rudimentary formulae and magico-religious chants, has flourished so vigorously as virtually to monopolize religious life in liberal Protestantism.[24] Thus world history has seen food prohibitions decline and prayer grow, while sacrificial ritual flourished in the middle ranges.

In 1913 Mauss and his uncle co-signed a review contrasting two books on totemism.[25] Having criticized Frazer's, they turn briefly to a summary of Durkheim's *magnum opus* of 1912, noting its claim that 'all the essential elements of sacrifice' are present in a certain type of ritual (*intichiuma* or 'increase rituals'), reported from central Australia. This is indeed what Durkheim claims in his first chapter on 'positive cults', though he recognizes that in Australia the component principles are not yet articulated or organized.[26] Thus, oblation and alimentary communion are both present, even though they may be separated by an interval of weeks. Whereas Frazer regarded totemism as a disorganized heap of magical superstitions, Durkheim of course saw it as religion, and was therefore inclined to emphasize the continuity between the Australian rituals and sacrifice. Though Mauss undoubtedly agreed with much in *Elementary*

---

[22] Mauss, *Oeuvres*, vol. 2, 143–148; Allen, *Categories*, 120.
[23] Allen, 'Indo–European Background'.
[24] Mauss, *Prayer*, 23.
[25] Mauss, *Oeuvres*, vol. 1, 183–189.
[26] Durkheim, *Elementary Forms*, 340, 343.

*Forms*, one wonders how far he accepted this aspect of his uncle's argument. However, the relationship between *Elementary Forms* and the earlier works of Hubert and Mauss (not only *Sacrifice*) is a complex matter. Given the amount of oral interaction among the main *Année* contributors, it will never be totally clarified, but the debts certainly went both to and from Durkheim.

## 4. OTHER USERS OF HUBERT AND MAUSS

In raising the question of Durkheim's use of *Sacrifice*, we have already moved towards the final substantive part of the chapter. This will consist in a gesture towards reception theory, which studies 'the reading, interpretation, (re)fashioning, appropriation, use, and abuse of past texts.'[27] I say 'gesture' because *Sacrifice*, both in its original form and as incorporated into Durkheim's *Elementary Forms*, has been so widely read that any sort of completeness is out of the question. The literature on sacrifice is enormous, and I write less as a student of that topic than as a Maussian (a position that risks doing less than justice to Hubert). The writers I discuss are only those who, for one reason or another, have come to my attention and about whom I hope I can say something relevant and worthwhile.

Chapter 1 of *Sacrifice* asked whether the sacrificial system formed a definable topic, and the question remains live. A recent book on Greek religion takes as starting point for a chapter on sacrifice 'a robust but not unsubtle announcement', to the effect that any attempt to offer a general theory of sacrifice is misguided.[28] Parker is referring to Paul Veyne, writing in 2000, whom he cites. 'Learned discussions of "the" true meaning of sacrifice will continue without an end and without a purpose...Sacrifice is very widely distributed across centuries and across societies because this practice is sufficiently ambiguous for everyone to find in it their own particular satisfaction.'[29] Warnings against reifying our analytical categories will always be needed, but Hubert and Mauss could have responded to the implicit charge that they were wasting their time. Firstly, they might say, any science needs its taxa, the sociology of religion no less than others. Secondly, just as they preferred to talk of societies rather than society and of religious facts rather than religion, so they had taken care to tie down the facts they cited about sacrifice to particular times and places. Thirdly, they had not been seeking 'the' meaning of sacrifice, being fully aware of the variety of meanings, purposes, and functions that it could be made to serve, within the general framework of communication.

---

[27] Martindale/Hardwick, 'Reception'.
[28] Parker, 'Killing', 125–126, 151, 164.
[29] Veyne, 'Inviter', 22.

Chapters 3 and 4 of *Sacrifice* had in fact dealt precisely with the variety of types of sacrifice. A less abstract approach than theirs is presented in a couple of encyclopaedia articles.[30] Drawing on information from all across the world, both writers survey the range of variation under the following six headings (which may overlap): who makes the offering; what is offered; with what ritual; where and when; to whom; why.

Since there is no recipient for the offering, Henninger regards scapegoat rituals as falling outside sacrifice. Here Hubert and Mauss would have disagreed. They did not attach great importance to the absence of a clear recipient since they saw scapegoats as resembling other victims in being made to embody the sacred. It was of course the undesired form of the sacred, so scapegoat rituals could be seen as acts of desacralization, lying close to acts of expulsion and expiation.[31] In some senses *Sacrifice* foreshadows Mauss' *The Gift*, but in others the two texts are about very different phenomena: a gift presupposes a recipient, but a sacrifice need not. This is not always recognized. Thus Testart understands Hubert and Mauss to be claiming that the ritual always has three terms—sacrifier, victim, and recipient (gods or equivalent beings).[32]

Veyne's reference to the wide distribution of sacrifice raises another issue. Hubert and Mauss are clear that the institution, as they envisage it, is not universal, and they detect a degree of incompatibility between it and totemism.[33] Totemism itself they saw as a widespread and early form of religion, which cannot be demonstrated to have been universal (they say nothing about its possible rivals in early times—shamanism, possession?).[34] Durkheim, as we saw, thought he could recognize elements of sacrifice in Australian increase rituals, thereby virtually pushing back the institution into the pre-neolithic past.

In this Durkheim is not alone. Girard sees the violence of sacrifice as embedded in human nature as such. Though he cites *Sacrifice* on the first page of *Violence and the Sacred*, he shows little interest in Eastern religions, Vedic or other, let alone in totemism, which he views through the lenses of Freud and Robertson Smith; and his criticism of *Sacrifice* is too slapdash to merit detailed discussion.[35] A similar emphasis on violence, aggression and ancient biological roots is found in the work of Burkert, the eminent Hellenist who (following Karl Meuli), interpreted Greek sacrifice as continuing the behaviour of Palaeolithic hunters. However, as is argued by Parker, the Greek sources provide little evidence of emphasis on violence or on the moment of killing.[36] The same criticism is one of several fired against Girard by Heusch, writing on

---

[30]  Flaherty, 'Sacrifice'; Henninger, 'Sacrifice'.
[31]  Hubert/Mauss, *Sacrifice*, 38–39, 53–56.
[32]  Testart, *Dons*, 27.
[33]  Hubert/Mauss, 'Introduction', 11.
[34]  Mauss, *Oeuvres*, vol. 1, 163 (from 1905).
[35]  Girard, *Violence*, 89–90.
[36]  Burkert, *Homo Necans*, esp. 1–48; Parker, 'Killing', 159–165.

Africa;[37] and it applies no less to Vedic animal sacrifice, where the victim's death (by strangulation), though necessary, is far less salient than the offering of its body parts into the fire.

Among those on the opposite side of the argument, closer to Hubert and Mauss than to Durkheim, I shall mention only two authors. Testart writes about Australia as follows. 'Sacrificial practice is obviously absent from this continent'; 'The Dream-time beings receive neither sacrifices nor offerings'; in these religions there exist 'neither gifts not requests nor communication of any sort' between humans and Dream-time beings.[38] My other author is Lévi-Strauss, who discusses the 'traditional problem' of the relationship between totemism and sacrifice, even though, like Mauss,[39] he is uneasy with the term 'totemism' and tends to put it in inverted commas. Having ignored *Sacrifice* in his introduction to the first posthumous collection of Mauss' essays,[40] he does not refer to it in the passage in question (where he mentions Mauss only in vague terms, and Robertson Smith and Durkheim not at all).[41] However, the contents of the passage makes it clear that he is engaging with *Sacrifice*, and the bibliography includes both *Mélanges* and *Elementary Forms*.

Lévi-Strauss starts by expressing surprise that the History of Religions has sometimes viewed totemism as the origin of sacrifice, when the two institutions stand in contrast and are incompatible—'as Mauss, not without hesitation and afterthought, was often led to affirm.'[42] His arguments for the two systems being mutually exclusive are characteristically abstract, and I summarize only one strand in his remarks. Both totemism and sacrifice related humans and natural species, but they do so in totally different ways. Totemism selects certain species (say animals) so as to give a finite set $A, B, C \ldots N$; it allots humans to clans $a, b, c \ldots n$; and it then relates the two sets. Lévi-Strauss sees the essential relation as being between the contrasts or gaps within the two sets ($A$ versus $B$ versus $C\ldots$, and $a$ versus $b$ versus $c\ldots$) rather than between $A$ and $a$, $B$ and $b\ldots$, i.e. between totem and clan. So totemism emphasizes the discontinuities within nature and correlates them with the discontinuities within society. In contrast, sacrifice, at this level of abstraction, is not concerned with discontinuities of either type. It is about relating humans to the divinity (Hubert and Mauss would say the sacred), and uses animals as intermediaries to fill in the gap. Species differences are not crucial, and one species may substitute for another—as is illustrated by a passage taken from Evans-Pritchard, on the cucumber that may replace an ox among the Nuer. The gap between sacrifier and divinity may be

---

[37] Heusch, *Africa*, 16–17.
[38] Testart, *Dons*, 50, 51, 53.
[39] Allen, *Categories*, 25.
[40] Lévi-Strauss, *Introduction*.
[41] Lévi-Strauss, *Savage Mind*, 223–228.
[42] Lévi-Strauss, *Savage Mind*, 223.

crossed in either direction, depending on whether the ritual is one of expiation or communion (cf. desacralization and sacralization in *Sacrifice*).

Lévi-Strauss ends his discussion with a paragraph on the non-existence of recipients of sacrifice, as contrasted with the existence of the totemic species. He does not take up the contrary proposal, made near the end of *Sacrifice*, namely that the sacred *does* exist, because communal beliefs are social facts and part of the real world that science must study. But, as the authors recognized more clearly in 1909, fundamentally the sacred exists because it is a conceptualization of society, with all that that entails. The sacred was not merely set apart and prohibited, it was filled with content. If their older view had been negative, their newer one was positive, and it was to contribute importantly to *Elementary Forms*.[43]

The Durkheimian conception of the sacred has accumulated a vast literature, which I cannot address. More immediately relevant is a book on sacrifice in Africa, a continent whose ethnography is cited only in the final footnote of *Sacrifice*. Luc de Heusch, an experienced Africanist, presents his work as a critical response to the famous study of Hubert and Mauss, which he mentions both in his first sentence and at the start of his final section 'Provisional Conclusions'. Like many others, he is unhappy with the concept of the sacred. 'The sacred/profane opposition is clearly a misleading starting point for the analysis of ritual'; it is one of the two aporias in their 'failure'.[44] He detects in *Sacrifice* a degree of Indo-European ethnocentrism, and traces the problem to the authors' archaic vocabulary, especially Latin *sacer*. The authors would have replied that the issue of vocabulary was one they had precisely addressed.[45] The second aporia Heusch identifies is the relationship between sacrifice in general and sacrifice of the god/king.[46] It is true that there is a tension between the typological approach of the first few chapters of *Sacrifice*, as announced in the 1899 introduction, and the explicitly evolutionary argument of Chapter 5 (perhaps because the latter was first drafted by Hubert?).

Whatever one makes of Heusch's rather abrupt dismissal of Chapter 5, it is obviously right that *Sacrifice* be brought into relation with African material. Hubert and Mauss present themselves as putting forward a theory that is better than its predecessors, but it is emphatically no more than a provisional hypothesis—a synthesis based on the knowledge at their disposal, but one that would need modification as new information became available.[47] Heusch's book contains interesting critical discussion of the use of *Sacrifice* by Evans-Pritchard, and a vigorous dismissal of the 'metaphysical excesses' of Girard

---

[43] Strenski, *Durkheim*, 77.
[44] Heusch, *Africa*, 5, 213.
[45] Hubert/Mauss, 'Introduction', 21, as at n. 21 above.
[46] Heusch, *Africa*, 14–15, 213.
[47] Hubert/Mauss, *Sacrifice*, 1.

('the expediting system of the scapegoat is peripheral to the sacrificial pattern. It does not constitute the centre of gravity for all sacrifice.'). Both writers are too much influenced by their Christianity. However, the verdict on *Sacrifice* itself is muted. It apparently remains relevant to Vedic India and, despite deconstructionists, its topic remains a viable one. What Heusch proposes is new perspectives, not a new overall theory to replace the one he has challenged.[48]

Another anthropologist with an Africanist background has proposed a general theory of ritual and includes a chapter on sacrifice. Bloch naturally cites *Sacrifice*, contrasting its 'communication' theory with the gift theory ('which goes back to Plato'), and discussing various aspects of its reception. But my comment concerns his more embracing project, which is to identify 'a minimum irreducible structure which is common to many rituals and other religious phenomena' (incidentally he does not cover totemism). This structure rests on the view of human life held by most societies, namely that it occurs within a framework that transcends the ordinary biological processes of life, and often inverts them. Ritual joins the everyday or here-and-now to the other life which it evokes, or to the transcendental units which it creates. The ritual process is conceived in terms of the three-stage model of rites of passage proposed by van Gennep in 1909, and much emphasis is placed on the double role of violence. In the special case of sacrifice, the initial violence involved in immolation 'rebounds' when the sacrifier and his community consume the victim and gain the vitality that facilitates military aggression. Contrasting his approach with those of Girard and Burkert, Bloch sees violence not as innate but as resulting from 'the attempt to create the transcendental in religion and politics.'[49]

One wonders how Hubert and Mauss would have reviewed Bloch's book in the *Année*. They were aware of having neglected the political aspect of sacrifice, claiming that the topic belonged under general sociology;[50] and whatever they would have made of Bloch's very broad conception of violence, they would surely also have welcomed his general framework—albeit with a comment on his terminology. Bloch's framework is based on the relation between two concepts. The transcendental (the word is used thirteen times on page five), associated with what is outside, external, or beyond, has to be linked with the here-and-now (a phrase used six times), which is associated with this world, the present life, the mundane. The terms 'sacred' and 'profane' are avoided, but it is not clear why.

This limited and unsystematic sampling of the reception accorded to *Sacrifice* has ignored Indologists. However, having opened the chapter with an epigraph from a Vedicist, I end it by mentioning another Sanskritist, Madeleine

---

[48] Heusch, *Africa*, 6–14 (cf. Allen, 'Brāhmaṇas'); 15–17, 211 (Girard); 213.
[49] Bloch, *Prey into Hunter*, 1–7 (general aim); 27–30 (sacrifice); 6–7 (violence).
[50] Hubert/Mauss, *Sacrifice*, 145, n. 374.

Biardeau, whose substantial study of 'Sacrifice in Hinduism' mentions *Sacrifice* in its very first line. However, subsequent references are few, and one is inaccurate: Mauss does not ignore the famous and fundamental Vedic hymn about the cosmogonic sacrifice of Puruṣa.[51] *Sacrifice* is so packed with facts and ideas that no one can find it easy to absorb as a whole.

## 5. IN CONCLUSION

Students of anthropology sometimes think that, if their subject is a proper science, what matters to them is the literature of the last couple of decades—that work from the nineteenth century belongs to the history of the subject and is unlikely to offer much help with their research. Theologians are no doubt less presentist. In any case, the nature of the sacred is not a question on which consensus is likely to be reached in the near future, and Hubert and Mauss still seem to have plenty of life in them; they still offer stimulus and inspiration to students of sacrifice. An impressive achievement from two twenty-seven year olds.

---

[51] Biardeau, *Sacrifice*, 14, n.1; cf. Hubert/Mauss, *Sacrifice*, 92.

# 11

## The Aztec Sacrificial Complex

### Laura Rival

> There is no moral act that does not imply sacrifice [...] Because society
> surpasses us, it obliges us to surpass ourselves and to surpass itself a being
> must to some degree depart from its nature.
>
> E. Durkheim, *The Dualism of Human Nature and its Social Conditions*,
> 328, 338.

The fact that an anthropologist is willing to offer a new analysis of the Aztec
sacrificial complex some 450 years after the first Spanish accounts were written and exactly 90 years after the publication of Frazer's abridged version
of the *Golden Bough*[1] is a testimony to its enduring significance for modern
thought. Sacrifice is not only a foundational part of anthropological theory,
but, as *human* sacrifice, it also continues to challenge modern ontological
premises, as well as our deepest held values. A specialist of lowland South
America, I have long been fascinated by Mesoamerican shamanism and warfare and the questions they pose: do native Mesoamericans postulate a radical
difference in mind and consciousness between humans and animals—as we
do, or does their animism create a sacrificial continuity between human and
non-human persons—as seems to be the case in Amazonia? To what extent
were pre-Columbian cultures of sacrifice ontologically transformed with
the introduction of Catholicism? Should we follow Eric Wolf[2] in differenti-
ating 'auto-sacrifice' from 'allo-sacrifice,' or is such a contrast fundamentally
ethnocentric?

I am ultimately interested in finding out whether classic anthropological
theories of sacrifice elaborated on the basis of Judeo-Christian and Vedic religious practices are applicable to the ritual killing of humans in the pre-modern
world. However, for the purposes of this chapter, I will content myself with

[1] See Codex Florence, Durán, *Historia de las Indias*, Sahagún, *Psalmodia Christiana*, and
Frazer, *The Golden Bough*.
[2] Wolf, *Envisioning Power*.

examining the political and religious contexts in which the Aztecs immolated some of their enemies and fellow citizens to their gods. I will show that human sacrifice in pre-Columbian Mexico was characterized by two contrastive ritual practices: the sacrifice of warriors caught in battle, and the immolation of slaves and women who impersonated the gods of the Aztec pantheon. I shall then explore the links between such ritual practices and native ideas about personhood and its cosmic, rather than human, nature.

## 1. PAYING WHAT IS OWED TO THE SUN, THE LORD OF THE EARTH

The Aztecs[3] or Tenochca (literally, 'cactus stone/heart people') were a late-coming and ethnically diverse population that rose to prominence in the second half of the fourteenth century and expanded their vast and powerful empire throughout the fifteenth century. Tenochtitlan, their city-state, was founded between 1325 and 1345. At the time of the Conquest, the city's socially heterogeneous and ethnically composite population amounted to approximately 200,000 inhabitants. The population in Mexico's central valley had grown close to two million, having increased by a factor of ten between 1200 and 1520.[4] This demographic increase was linked to an extraordinary cultural efflorescence which saw the intensification of lakebed agriculture, the construction of dams, causeways, canals, and aqueducts, the development of a vast market network, and state-sponsored long-distance trade.[5] As many commentators have pointed out, the beauty, civilizatory development, and wealth of Tenochtitlan under Aztec rule was also linked to ceaseless military activity, imperial conquest, tribute extraction, and the intensification of human sacrifice. The political and ideological processes by which the Aztec gained prominence, forced the unification of the forty small polities that peopled the valley at the time of their arrival on the great lake's western shore, centralized their administrative structures, and monopolized power by reinterpreting the past and by homogenizing a vast and cosmopolitan cultural heritage are

---

[3] Nahuatl-speakers are commonly referred to as Mexica when referring to pre-Columbian times, and as Nahua when referring to post-Conquest history or to the present. It would be erroneous to see the Mexica as an ethnic group, for they were composed of peoples with many different origins, identities, and mother tongues. The Aztecs were the descendants of one of the northern tribes that migrated to central Mexico in the course of the twelfth century. They became the most powerful section of the Mexica people. They are also referred to as Tenochca, in reference to their city-state, Tenochtitlan, although some would argue that their direct rivals, the inhabitants of Tlatelolco, were also Aztec.

[4] Wolf, *Envisioning Power*, 157.

[5] Brumfield, 'Aztec State Making'.

well documented—a testimony to Western intellectual fascination with state formation.[6] Scholarly attention to the meaning and performance of human sacrifice, however, is more recent.[7]

The classic Aztec sacrificial rite was laid out between 1440 and 1468, during the reign of Moctezuma I.[8] It involved an elaborate calendar of festivities punctuated by spectacular human sacrifices during which enemy warriors were offered to the Sun and, on the calendric anniversary of certain deities, Mexica women and slaves immolated. The intensification of human sacrifice under Moctezuma I, Ahuitzol and Moctezuma II was a response to historically documented crises such as the repeated earthquakes that occurred between 1455 and 1513, the great famines of 1454 and 1502, and the major floods of 1486 and 1502, when Technotitlan was partly destroyed, thousands of people died of hunger and many more fled away, and large sections of the nobility sold themselves in bondage in order to survive.[9] It also corresponded to the consolidation of the Tenochca hegemonic order, which started with Itzcoatl's destruction of pre-Aztec calendric records,[10] and its profound reconfiguration of prevailing ideas about tutelary gods, cultural heroes, city founders, and visionary priests. Itzcoatl's vast ideological reworking of Mexica myth-history culminated in the imposition of the Aztec patron-god Huitzilopochtli as the supreme, over-ruling super-god.[11]

Mythology offered a justification for both the practice of human sacrifice and the political dominance of the Aztecs. Huitzilopochtli legitimized the use of the rewritten mythology by Moctezuma I to stage the large-scale public performance of human sacrifice. From the middle of the fifteenth century onwards, festivities played as important a role as war did in Tenochtitlan. If war ensured the expansion of the empire, festivities secured victory by advancing cultural homogenization. Religious celebrations were organized almost continually throughout the year,[12] and human sacrifice formed an integral part of the permanent theatre constituted through religious celebrations.[13] It is through such lived performances that myth became action, and that the multitude of deities comprising the complex and ever expanding Aztec pantheon were brought to life. Human sacrifice was modelled on the sacrifice of the deities who had made life on earth possible by throwing themselves in the great primordial fire through which the fifth sun was created and given motion. Their hearts

---

[6] Soustelle, *La vie quotidienne*, Brumfield, 'Aztec State Making', Wolf, *Envisioning Power*, McEwan and López Luján, *Moctezuma*.

[7] Duverger, *La fleur léthale*, Clendinnen, Aztecs, Carrasco, *City of Sacrifice*, Graulich, *Le sacrifice humain*.

[8] Duverger, *La fleur léthale*, 209.

[9] Wolf, *Envisioning Power*, 155–156.

[10] Nash, 'Gendered Deities', 339.

[11] Wolf, *Envisioning Power*, 146–147.

[12] Soustelle, *La vie quotidienne*, 173–174.

[13] Graulich, *Le sacrifice humain*, 97.

had transformed into stars. The cosmos, which had taken on a new structure with the twin birth of the fifth sun and of the new human race, threatened to undergo further cycles of creative destruction. Continued renewal through human blood and heart offerings would ensure the persistence of the fifth sun structure and delay, if not prevent, the unavoidable entropic decay.[14]

Sacrifice in Nahuatl, *uemanna* (from *huentli*, 'offering' and *mana*, 'pat out a maize tortilla to make it flat and smooth') literally means 'the spreading out of an offering'. The generic term for priest, *tlamacazqui*,[15] literally means 'the one who offers food by bringing it to the table', or the 'provider of offerings'. Nahuatl texts describe the function of war in very similar terms—'to serve drink and food at table to Sun and to Earth'. Duverger mentions another term for blood sacrifice, *nextlaualli* (from *ixtlaua*, 'to pay what is owed'), which evokes the repayment of a debt.[16] Many forms of offerings and sacrifices were performed beside human sacrifice during official religious ceremonies.[17] Priests, warriors, and members of the ruling elite would offer their own blood in small recipients, or on a variety of objects such as maguey thorns, strings, twigs, or paper strips. An infinite number of art objects and materials, including minerals, feathers, or precious stones would also be offered. Several of the regular ceremonies described in the Florentine Codex involved the 'sacrifice' by heart excision and decapitation of giant bread dolls or mountains made of dough.[18] Deer, rabbits, wolves, coyotes, birds, especially quails, were commonly decapitated and offered, as well as snakes, jaguars, and eagles.[19] It is clear that these 'minor' sacrifices had been practised for many centuries in Mexico, and that they continued to be practised by the population at large during communal or private ceremonies. Penance, fasting, and drawing blood from one's own body in front of a sacred image were commonly practised by all at certain times of the year, or when illness or misfortune struck. These ritual acts were practised with more frequency by the elite, who increased their power and prestige through self-bleeding.[20]

Exclusively state-sponsored, human sacrifices occurred in centrally located state buildings (pyramids, temples, and military schools), as well as in neighbourhood temples and schools. On special occasions, sacrificial ceremonies took place on top of mountains and at the centre of the great lakes surrounding Tenochtitlan. Priests, warriors, and the ruling elite had full monopoly over human sacrifice; no one could immolate humans outside of the state-regulated

---

[14] Duverger, *La fleur léthale*, Wolf, *Envisioning power*.
[15] Or *tlamacazque* in the plural form for priesthood. Blood offering is often described in Nahuatl texts as *tlaxcaltiliztli*, or literally, the offering of maize tortillas (*tlaxcalli*).
[16] Duverger, *La fleur léthale*, 162.
[17] Graulich, *Le sacrifice humain*, 101–128.
[18] Graulich, *Le sacrifice humain*, 106.
[19] Duverger, *La fleur léthale*, 210–212.
[20] Graulich, *Le sacrifice humain*, 319.

religious festivities.[21] All human sacrifices required the express consent of state officials, and executions could only be performed by priests sent by the ruler himself. As city-states complexified and cults linked to professional corporations multiplied, the state was faced with increased demands for the public performance of human sacrifices. Long-distance trade merchants, in particular, lobbied hard to have the right to offer human beings in sacrifice as warriors did.[22] As the empire expanded, more and more divinities of conquered peoples had to be integrated into the Aztec pantheon and be fed with human blood, resulting in more and more slaves and prisoners being killed.

## 2. COMMUNICATING WITH THE GODS THROUGH SACRIFICE

The descendants of Aztec rulers repeatedly told Sahagún (their main ethnographer) that sacrificial offerings to *Tonatiuh Tlaltecutli*, 'the Sun, the Lord of the Earth', and to its doubles Eagle and Jaguar had to be human, for no other kind of offering was precious enough. To understand the many forms of ritual killings that existed in the late Aztec empire, we therefore need to pay as much attention to the specific meanings embedded within ritual practice as to ideology and political expediency. Humans became the sacrificial animal par excellence in a cultural system that combined the mystery of life contained in the human body with the wonders of scale, quantity, and extreme intensity. Laden with cosmological significance, the human body was a privileged instrument to communicate with supernatural powers. This cultural system, I wish to contend, is best explored by comparing and contrasting two major types of human sacrifice, the immolation by heart-excision of Nahuatl-speaking warriors captured on the battlefield (*teomiqui*, 'he who dies in godlike fashion') and the ritual killing by decapitation of Mexica women and slaves who impersonated particular deities (*ixiptla*, literally, a 'stand-in for god'). As I argue below, the warrior and the god impersonator represent two distinct and complementary aspects of the human condition, defined by the dynamic and unstable fusion of divine fire and earthly flesh.

---

[21] This was also the case for 'accompanying deaths' and forms of ritual immolation that we know had existed in the region for a very long time, and which Testart ('Doit-on parler') differentiates from human sacrifice per se. Ragot indicates that those who died accompanying rulers and nobility were called 'those who died facing the lord to accompany him' (*teixpan miquiz temicaltin*) (Ragot, 'Les au-delàs aztèques', 65). If we adopt Testart's definition of human sacrifice, it is then unclear whether the mass killings through flooding, burning, or throwing from a cliff that multiplied with imperial expansion should be understood as human sacrifices, although the term seems appropriate to describe the ritual killing of infants and young children (i.e. humans who had never eaten maize), who were offered to Tlaloc, the rain god.

[22] Duverger, *La fleur léthale*, 111–122.

## (i) Dying like a god does

The most highly valued sacrifice was that of a valiant Nahuatl-speaking warrior who had been captured live on the battlefield. Wars between rival cities sharing the same culture and the same language, and whose elites often intermarried, were considered sacred. Led by an intense desire to impose their unifying militarism on all neighbouring city-states, the Aztec had moved from their initial status as mercenaries to that of leaders of a 'triple alliance' in which rival cities had agreed to respect each other's autonomy and to combat ritually in 'flowery wars' (*xochiyaoyotl*),[23] with the objective of capturing enemies in hand-to-hand combat. Armies were led to the battlefield by priests, and offerings and sacrifices were practised before, during, and after battle. War captives were brought to their captors' home city, where they were offered to the ruler (*tlatoani*). Prisoners could be kept in military houses for months before being sacrificed. The ruler, who was also chief military commander, rewarded military prowess with gifts, such as jewellery, fine clothing, and feather adornments obtained as tribute from allied or subjected communities. Commoners demonstrating courage in battle and achieving victory were rewarded by the state, although they could never achieve the same wealth or status as noble warriors.[24] Noble warriors carrying bundles of aromatic flowers were compared to 'dancing flowers', and blood was called 'flower water'. Success in war was associated with the beauty of flowers, itself symbolically and poetically linked with eroticism, sexuality, food, and life.[25]

Captors and their relatives would look after the war captives with great care and consideration. The relationship between captor and captive was assimilated to that of a father (captor) and a son (captive).[26] During the weeks—sometimes the months—preceding their execution, captives were made to rehearse the sacrificial ceremony, including a mock heart excision. Prized war captives (those of equal noble rank and those of demonstrated courage) were made to fight in gladiatorial games before being brought to the temple. They were presented to the tribal god Huitzilopotchli and displayed in the royal palace, where they had to stand facing the supreme ruler, while priests would pronounce lengthy speeches detailing their forthcoming death. The night before their death, captives were kept awake, their warrior hair locks cut off. The locks were handed to the captors as trophies and preciously kept to be burnt on their funerary pyres. The captives' bodies were painted white with chalk or covered

---

[23] From *yaotl* ('enemy') and *yaoyotl* ('adversity'); 'warfare' in religious language was called 'water and fire' (*atl, tlachinolli*).

[24] Duverger, *La fleur léthale*.

[25] Duverger, *La fleur léthale*, 103; see also Brown, 'Human Sacrifice', Chapter 12, in this volume.

[26] Soustelle, *La vie quotidienne*, 127. In other words, men who were potential brothers-in-law became through war ritual agnatic kin.

with white down, eagle feathers, and ornaments made of white bark cloth, all of which were burnt once the sacrifice was completed. In the hours preceding the sacrifice, captives had to participate in a number of games, races, and acts of torture aimed at heating their bodies up. Bodies were brought to the brink of exhaustion, a process that the priests controlled carefully. Gladiatorial games were especially prolonged, causing the lacing of the skin with blood, and ensuring that the heartbeat would reach its maximal speed. It is in such a state of exhilaration and exhaustion that the captives were made to climb the steep steps towards the sacrificial stone, the bravest shouting, singing, and praising their home city.[27]

Upon reaching the top of the pyramid, the captive was seized by five priests who laid him onto the sacrificial stone, each firmly holding hands, feet, and head. The senior priest, dressed in the full regalia of the deity he incarnated, incised the thorax, just below the last ribs. He plunged the sacrificial knife in the cavity, cutting the veins, and tearing the beating heart off. The heart (called *quauhnochtli* or 'eagle's precious cactus fruit') was raised to the Sun. These sacrifices took place in the late morning, before being deposited in an eagle or jaguar shaped vessel. After having collected litres of blood from the victim's thorax, the priest threw the corpse unceremoniously down the steep slopes of the pyramid, where another priest cut the head.[28] Old men working as temple attendants and standing at the base of the pyramid collected the cadavers and dispatched them throughout the city. The captor was given three of the four limbs—the fourth being offered to the supreme ruler. The skull was cleaned and slung on one of the skull racks (*tzompantli*) that were stacked to form imposing public displays. The torso was fed to carnivorous animals in the royal zoo appended to the main temple. The skins of renowned and particularly brave captives, full of potent healing powers, were flayed and lent out by the captors to whomever wished to don them. The limbs were prepared in the captor's house and served with a tomato and pepper stew. This meal was shared by residents and guests, but not by the captor.[29] Only elite and merchant families were allowed to consume cooked, sacrificed human flesh, although surpluses might have been sold on the market. Harner argues that once the heart had been severed from the sacrificed body, it became desacralized, and the captive's flesh treated as ordinary meat.[30] Díaz contends that priests ate the cooked flesh of sacrificed victims, and possibly their hearts as well.[31]

---

[27] Duverger, *La fleur léthale*, 131–152, Clendinnen, *Aztecs*, 94.
[28] Duverger, *La fleur léthale*, 130–155.
[29] Harner, 'The Ecological Basis'.
[30] Harner, 'The Ecological Basis', 126.
[31] In Harner, 'The Ecological Basis', 122, 124. For contrasting interpretations of cannibalism, see Saez ('O canibalismo asteca') and Isaac ('Aztec cannibalism').

## (ii) Giving life to, and dying with, the gods

*Teteo imixiptlahuan* ('men who receive in their breast the force of a god as living images and representing the divinity on earth'[32]), in short, *ixiptla*, are best understood as containers of cosmic personhood, as I argue below. Attended by old women who looked after them until death, *Ixiptla* who impersonated the gods connected with the divination and the solar calendar were adulated by the public.[33] They were 'slaves', that is, non-Tenochca prisoners caught in expansionary wars (rather than in ritual battle), or Tenochca citizens who had lost their citizenship through debt or immoral behaviour. Before being fit to stand in for gods, slaves had to be redeemed and purified through ritual bathing to erase all trace of their low status, marginality, and own identity.[34] For months, they were taught by priests all the arts and demeanours of the gods they were to become. The closer they were to the day of sacrifice, the more they danced, sang, and drank alcoholic beverages. Having become 'ambulant images of the sacred ones',[35] these women and men were described as having lost all consciousness and control over their own movements and thoughts. They danced for days and nights, the lavish consumption of alcohol and drugs enhancing their altered state of consciousness and their closeness to death. Haggard and wild looking, the poor creatures were 'no more than a puppet body animated by an alien mystical force.'[36] Graulich discusses a number of cases of women who embraced the glorified helplessness of the *ixiptla* and chose to be put to death as embodiments of divinities of fertility deities and maize and earth goddesses appearing in the religious calendar, especially in celebration of the wet season and sowing.[37] Male impersonators embodied male characteristics of the maize plants associated with male gods.

Little is said about their actual execution, which, compared to that of war captives, seems to have happened at night, rather than during the day, and to have involved beheading, rather than heart excision. We only know that upon death *ixiptla* did not go to the house of the sun (*tonatiuh ichan*), or to any of the three other afterlife destinations,[38] but, instead, to the places in the

---

[32] López Austin, *The Human Body*, 294.

[33] Clendinnen, *Aztecs*, 77.

[34] Duverger, *La fleur léthale*, 121.

[35] Clendinnen, *Aztecs*, 89.

[36] Clendinnen, *Aztecs*, 79, 92–93

[37] Graulich, *Le sacrifice humain*, 212–216. Summary descriptions of these sacrifices can be found in Duverger, *La fleur léthale* (pp. 168–173), Carrasco, *City of Sacrifice* (pp. 188–210), and Graulich, *Le sacrifice humain* (pp. 101–128, 245–248, 296–301, and 328–329), who all use the second book of the Florentine Codex (Sahagún, *Psalmodia Christiana*).

[38] The place of death (*mictlan*), where those who died of a natural death went; Tlaloc's place (*tlalocan*), where those who drowned, died from an illness related to water, or from a skin disease went; or the maize house (*cincalco*), which was reserved for children who died very young and those who committed suicide.

universe where the incarnated divinities were most likely to dwell.[39] The complex association of maleness and femaleness was most spectacularly staged during *ochpaniztli*, the ritual with which the sacred year cycle started, and during which Toci, the earth goddess, was put to death. It is on her way to the nuptial chamber mounted on the back of a priest in the middle of the night that Toci was beheaded. The priest who had reincarnated Toci by killing Toci's first impersonator and then donning her flayed skin now stood in front of the temple dedicated to the sun to give birth to Cinteotl, the god of ripe corn. The piece of skin from the thigh of Toci's first impersonator partly covered his face as he stood. It was subsequently taken by warriors to be thrown on the military frontier at the border of the empire.

For Duverger, sacrificial decapitation is a form of torture akin to copulation exclusively reserved to women, who, he argues, are sacrificed as brides.[40] For Graulich, sacrifice by decapitation is historically linked to ancient rites, especially ball games, which encouraged the alternating of seasons. Graulich[41] also mentions that whereas heart excision, which was performed with a flint knife (flint contains sparks from heaven), corresponds to a sacrifice to the Sun, beheading, which was performed with an obsidian knife (the black, cool, and nocturnal stone that comes from the entrails of the earth and which is also used for dismembering), is associated with sacrifice to the telluric divinities of Earth and Maize.[42] If both Duverger's and Graulich's explanations offer important insights, they pay insufficient attention to the *abandonment* and *possession* that are so characteristic of death by decapitation, and which stand in such stark contrast with the courage and bravery demonstrated by those who die of heart excision. To grasp the contrast between 'dying as a god' and 'dying with a god' in all its meaningful difference, we need to turn to indigenous constructions of personhood, including their political and historical dynamism.

## 3. DEATH AND BECOMING

Staged to both impress a large and composite public and humiliate rivals, the theatre of sacrifice intensifies to the limits of the possible the productivity of the human body by decomposing its energy and multiplying it through ritual action. Hair locks, heartbeat, blood, limbs, trunk, skull, flayed skin, fingernails, the weeping of parents, the screams of infants, the priests' incantations—all acquire and generate a force of their own. Power and vitality also emanate from

[39] Graulich, *Le sacrifice humain*, 215.
[40] Duverger, *La fleur léthale*, 172–173.
[41] Graulich, 'Les mises à mort doubles', 52.
[42] Graulich, *Le sacrifice humain*, 320.

the innumerable artefacts, sacred objects, and precious materials that adorn, represent, or complement the human body, and constitute the material culture of war and sacrifice. Sacrifice works on the body's resistance to pain and to fatigue; it exacerbates the possibilities of life in the human body. Yet, the sacrificial death of warriors and god impersonators mobilizes different ways of treating the body and of relating to the supernatural. The body of the warrior and that of the bathed slave are prepared and destroyed in ways that highlight two opposed and complementary aspects of mortality, as illustrated by Figure 1.

**Fig. 1.** Contrast between the death of a warrior and the death of a god impersonator.

|  | warrior | god image |
|---|---|---|
| provenance or origin | from an allied city (so of noble rank and equal status) | from a conquered, non-Nahuatl speaking region, or a Nahuatl-speaker who has lost status or citizenship |
| selection | captured in one-to-one combat | selected from a mass of victims for his or her personal qualities, beauty, or youth |
| association | owned by the captor fusion, identity, and asymmetry expressed as a relation between 'owner' (father) and 'owned' (son). In time, the father/captor will become son/captive of another warrior | owned by the slave merchant identification of the human victim and the god s/he impersonates, fusion between spirit (superior animating principle) and body undergoing ecstatic experience |
| treatment before sacrifice | captive loved and cared for by captor, captor parades captive, public display and rehearsal of the sacrifice | impersonator loved by the public, long training to become the god. Rehearsal of demeanour, impersonation through use of sacred regalia |
| preparation of the body | hair lock cut the night preceding the sacrificial ritual (so no longer a warrior), on the day, dons white feathers and chalk (and so does the captor) | slaved is ritually bathed with holy water to wash away status face washing = purification sedation = sacralization of the face, becomes receptive to the divinity's spirit |
| qualities cultivated | bravery, courage, physical strength, achieving unity of body and mind in full consciousness | physical grace, skills, and social docility through long training to become someone else, someone more powerful, more sensuous, and more alive |
| sacrifice | death through heart excision at mid-day with flint knife on altar at top of pyramid | death through decapitation at dusk or night with obsidian knife in dark parts of the temple |

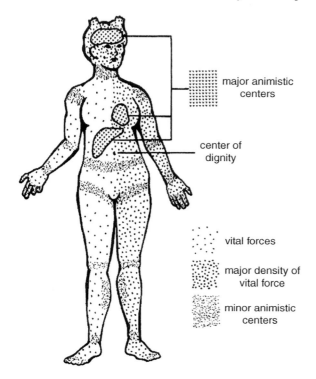

major animistic
centers

center of
dignity

vital forces

major density of
vital force

minor animistic
centers

Fig. 2. The human body with the major animistic centres and vital forces. Reproduced from López Austin, *The Human Body*, p. 200. Reprinted with the permission of the University of Utah Press.

Why would self-mastery be associated with execution by heart excision and the surrender of the self with death by decapitation? I would like to suggest that a consideration of Nahua conceptualizations of the person, body, and soul illuminates the grammar of Aztec sacrifice. Thanks to the path-breaking work of López Austin[43] and other anthropological studies of personhood among ancient and modern Nahuatl-speaking peoples, we know that each individual person is inserted in a socio-cosmic web through various 'souls' or animistic centres.[44] As shown in Figure 2, one of these 'souls', *tonalli* (literally, 'sun's heat'), is lodged in the head and links the person to the rest of the universe. A second 'soul', *teyolía* (literally, 'it makes one live', 'it beats'), builds up within the physical heart and works through its associated animating quality. A third 'soul', *ihíyotl* (literally, 'breath', 'night-air' or 'dirty vapour') is found mainly in the liver. A strong, moral, and healthy person is characterized by a

---

[43] López Austin, *The Human Body*.
[44] See also McKeever Furst, *The Natural History*.

perfect balance between the three souls, while physiological, psychological, or emotional disorders are almost always attributed to an internally or externally caused imbalance between them. Although *tonalli, teyolía,* and *ihíyotl* are concentrated within head, heart, and liver respectively, they also circulate throughout the human body, the natural environment, and the cosmos.

A seed of energy inserted into the pregnant woman's womb by the Lord of Heaven (Ometecutli), the *tonalli* is highly unstable. Susceptible to loss and predation, it can also be increased through moral conduct, penance, and discipline. In ancient Mesoamerica, *pipiltin* (nobles) were thought to have received from the gods more *tonalli* than *macehuales* (commoners, artisans, cultivators) had. The *teyolía,* which causes the body to grow, only separates from the body upon death. It is the main soul, the vital centre of the person, the centre of human consciousness, and, for many communities, the collective mark of inherited identity associated with a patron god, often the founder of the community. The *teyolía* is closely related to *yollotl* (the palpitations of the heart) and *ollin,* which refers to abrupt movements, such as the kicking of the foetus, the throes of abortion, or the tremors of earthquakes. In pre-Columbian times, the *ihíyotl* was closely linked to passion, personal courage, vitality, and artistic qualities. Individuals of great personality (men-gods, elder rulers, artists, inventors, or diviners) were all said to have *yolteotl,* or divine force.[45] López Austin has recently argued that while *tonalli,* the domain of the highest cosmic layers, is linked to the father as head of the household, *ihíyotl,* the subterranean domain of the underworld is linked to motherhood; as for *teyolía,* it belongs to the domain of stars, meteorites, and children.[46]

On the basis of this anthropological understanding of Nahua personhood, I wish to argue that dying of heart excision favours the amplification of the soul through the fusion of *tonalli* (conquered destiny and courageous mind) and *teyolia* (individual energy, intensified spark of life), or mind and heart. Beheading, by contrast, allows the third soul, *ihíyotl,* to take centre stage in persons whose *tonalli* has been entirely colonized by divine presence. I find support for this interpretation in López Austin's discussion of the relationship between *ihíyotl,* the animistic centre concentrated within the liver; *ix* which means 'perception' or 'emotion'; and *ixtli,* which means face.[47] *Ihíyotl* is closely linked to passion, personal courage, vitality, and artistic qualities, and often used as a synonym for face, *ixtli,* the prime organ of perception and sensation.[48] Individuals of great personality (such as men-gods, elder rulers, artists, inventors, or diviners) were said to have *yolteotl,* or divine force; they had 'perfected, wise face, and good heart' (*in ixtli in yollotl*), and were capable

45 López Austin, *The Human Body*; McKeever Furst, *The Natural History*.
46 López Austin, *Breve historia*; 'The Natural World'.
47 López Austin, *The Human Body*, 170–172.
48 López Austin, *The Human Body*, 171.

of sound judgment and sentiment.[49] For López Austin, the expressions *in ixtli in yollotl*, which he translates into English as 'the eyes, the heart,' was used as a metaphor to signal that great persons had succeeded in amplifying their animistic force.[50] The face with the eyes was the place from which the vital force of breath issued to the outside, a breath charged with emotion, feeling, and moral values. This made 'the face a mirror of individual qualities.'[51] López Austin also remarks that a sorcerer was defined as someone who turned people's *ixtli* around, and distorted her vision.[52]

This semantic exploration clarifies that *teixiptla* or 'images of the divine' were more than mere images, covering, or wrapping. By containing a deity's animistic forces and centres, the *ixiptla* was also giving a visible and public personality to the deity; upon death, her mortal envelope had fully become the deity's body. Deities could materialize in a wide range of material supports, such as paper, stones, sculpted wood or sculpted stones, pottery effigies, bread dolls, or insignia, which could all become the abode of their 'fire'. Although the divine fire or *tonalli* could lodge in any natural or man-made object, it is only within a human body that deities could acquire a face and a personality, and *feel* life. As complex and ubiquitous entities who could divide up, their inner essences multiplying ad infinitum, divinities were thought to be both subjected to and limited by cosmic rules; to wear out as they journeyed the universe; and to feel an intense desire for sensuous, humanly, earthly ways of being.[53] This is perhaps why Nahua pictography did not differentiate between the image of a god, the priest consecrated to the god, or the bread dough presented as an offering to the god.[54] Rulers and temple priests wearing the insignia of the deities they served were god impersonators too. In other words, the immolators were god impersonators every bit as much as their sacrificed victims.

A full understanding of *ixiptla* immolation by decapitation requires that we take into account the ways in which Nahua personhood was being reconstituted under Aztec rule. There are, as I see it, two important aspects to this question, the status of tutelary gods and the mutual implication of social ranking and personality. Space, however, allows me to comment only on the second one. In the new order created under Aztec rule, humanity was ordered according to a new continuum of moral worth, and ranked. As already mentioned, ruling elites (*pipiltin*) received at birth more *tonalli* than commoners (*macehualli*) did,[55] although anyone could increase his *tonalli* through personal moral conduct, such as, for instance, fasting, drawing blood from his body, or

---

[49] Léon-Portilla, *La pensée aztèque*, 165.
[50] López Austin, *The Human Body*, 196.
[51] López Austin, *The Human Body*, 171.
[52] López Austin, *The Human Body*, 196.
[53] López Austin, 'The Natural World'.
[54] Anders/Maarten/Jansen, *Introduction to the Facsimile of the Codex Laud*, 88.
[55] López Austin, *The Human Body*, 189.

excelling at his occupation. Weaknesses (e.g. drinking, sexual licence, laziness, stealing, gambling, or indebtedness), on the other hand, decreased one's *tonalli*. High-ranking men were said to be easily recognizable through their faces. Animated by breath (*ihiyotl*), the face and the eyes (*ixtli*), the noblest part of the body, 'revealed the reflection of vitality heightened by honour'.[56] The diminished or damaged organic functions (heart and head) of the insane were equally mirrored on their faces. Madness amounted to a loss of consciousness, and a loss of control over *ixtli*, the organ of perception.

Slaves, whether foreign war captives or Mexica debt slaves (*tlatlacotin*), occupied the bottom of the social ladder not only because of their servile condition, but also because their bodies were considered denatured, damaged, or degraded, hence the need for them to recover their integrity through the performance of special rites. Duverger develops a fascinating theory of self-imposed slavery as a form of escape from the duties of Technoca citizenship.[57] A slave (*xolotl*) is first and foremost a dependant worker, who has renounced his or her destiny and related responsibilities. Slaves were named after Xolotl, a dog deity and twin figure of Quetzalcoatl. In a well-known myth, Tezcatlipoca forced his rival Quetzalcoatl to flee the kingdom of Tula over which he ruled, mainly because of the former's opposition to human sacrifices. Quetzalcoatl agreed with blood offerings from scarification, as well as with the sacrifice of snakes, birds, and butterflies, but he opposed the immolation of human beings. To escape from his pursuers, he transformed himself into a maize deity, then into a maguey deity, and, finally, into a kind of salamander known as *axolotl*, a strange animal with the extraordinary property of being able to reach adulthood without metamorphosis, and to reproduce while still in a larval state.[58]

By contrast with their masters, slaves no longer paid taxes, and they were no longer required to take part in the activities dictated by the state. They were nevertheless assured of adequate living conditions thanks to their masters who fed and sheltered them and who were not allowed to sell them, unless they had committed a crime or did not work hard enough. In short, they pursued a life similar to that of ordinary citizens, and, one might add, a freer one, at least, in Duverger's rendering of slavery as a happy, if under-dignified, state of dependency. We should not forget, however, that the many high-ranking citizens who had to sell themselves or their children into servitude during the great famines[59] may have suffered the stigmas of slavery much more than other sections of the population. The conflict opposing slave merchants and the Aztec nobility further illustrates the way in which the status of slave plays out in human sacrifice. Whereas merchants insisted that the male slaves they

[56] López Austin, *The Human Body*, 171–172, 200.
[57] Duverger, *La fleur léthale*, 89–91, 108.
[58] Duverger, *La fleur léthale*, 91.
[59] Wolf, *Envisioning Power*.

brought back to Tenochtitlan as part of their long distance trade activities be sacrificed by heart excision in the same way as warriors captured on the battlefield were, the nobility, especially the warriors, indignantly opposed the practice, insisting that slaves who were not captured but given in tribute be kept exclusively for impersonating the gods connected with the divination and the solar calendars.[60] As argued by Duverger, it is likely that the merchant corporation was anxious to assimilate slaves to war captives in order to, by the same token, raise the status of their profession to that of the politically powerful warrior class, thereby receiving the same honours, prestige, and recognition as the warriors. But why would the warrior class consider 'bathed slaves' as pure enough to die as god images, but not sufficiently so to die as warriors?

From the warriors' point of view, I wish to argue, the *teyolia, ihíyotl, tonalli,* and *ixtli* of slaves were not noble or strong enough to be offered to the sun or to participate in its animation. Moreover, the tutelary gods of the communities from which slaves originated had not yet been fully absorbed into the Aztec pantheon, an absorption which, as it turns out, could only be done through decapitation. We know that Mexica conquerors used decapitation to sever the relationship that the people they defeated had to their land and to their ancestors.[61] For instance, when a forebear of Acamapichtli, the first Aztec ruler to be enthroned at Technochtitlan married a Colhuacan princess in the 1260s, Huitzilopotchli declared that she should be sacrificed and turned into a new Aztec goddess, Yaocihuatl. The princess was thus beheaded and her skin flayed. Her father, who had been invited to the wedding, was asked upon arriving at the palace to pay homage to Yaocihuatl. Ignoring the relationship between the goddess and his daughter, he entered the temple with his offerings of paper covered with liquid rubber, copal, flowers, tobacco, and maize tortillas. It was only when beheading quails in honour of the *ixiptla* before whom he was standing that he realized that the *ixiptla* was a priest donning his daughter's skin.[62]

To summarize, we are faced with a universe in which sacrificial victims are put through various ordeals and extreme sensuous experiences according to the ranked socio-ritual category to which they belong, which is determined by the perceived intensity and integrity of their three animistic centres. Four such categories stand out. Infants and young children, who are pure need, cold blood and breast milk, tears and cries, soft bones and undeveloped personality, with no will of their own to be directed, controlled, or conquered, personify utter hopelessness. God impersonators, perform the invaded body, dance and sing in erotic, drunken abandon, lost in emotions of voluptuousness and

[60] Duverger, *La fleur léthale*, 111–122.
[61] Graulich, *Le sacrifice humain*, 365.
[62] Johansson, 'Le spectacle', 238–239, Nash, 'The Aztecs', 351–352, McEwan/López Luján, *Moctezuma*, 29.

sleeplessness, which highlight the pleasures and emotions of living. Warriors and political rulers perform the male, aggressive body in all its splendour, force, bravery, and self-control with the focused, sharp senses of the fighting body. The ethic and aesthetic of this political elite relies on the physical accomplishment and excellence of a well developed and well exercised human body pushed to the extremes of competition, resistance, and performance. As to the priests, who must ensure through careful control that they will not die from their intensive programme of fasting and self-bleeding, they embody maximal deprivation and suffering. By drawing blood profusely from their own bodies before each sacrifice, they partake in the deaths of their victims. By drawing blood from the ears and penis of newborn boys, ordering others to bleed themselves, and mixing their blood with that of others, they regulate the universal circulation of human blood through the empire and the cosmos.

## 4. CONCLUSION

I have argued in this chapter that there were two contrastive types of human sacrifice amongst the Aztec. While war captives were associated with execution by heart excision, god impersonators met their death by decapitation. Whereas control and self-mastery characterized the warrior who met his death willingly, the surrender of the self was typical of the god impersonator. Although widely shared by the ethnically and linguistically diverse communities that inhabited the central valley of Mexico between the twelfth and sixteenth centuries, the values, complex cosmic vision, and ritual practices briefly outlined in this chapter collapsed with the demise of Aztec priesthood and nobility in the aftermath of the Spanish Conquest. However, the humbler and more ordinary substrate of Nahua ideas about personhood has endured to this day, as illustrated by countless ethnographies. Rooted in peasant concerns for maize, rain, sunlight, and life, it survives in many Mesoamerican rural communities.[63] Contemporary Nahualt-speakers continue to imagine the human person as made of two separate substances, flesh and spirit, each with its own temporality and qualities. The body, at once flesh, corn, and food[64] still constitutes the envelope in which a spark of cosmic energy (sun heat, sun ray, fire) is lodged; and blood, with its fertilizing power and flow of vital energy is still thought to link body and soul together in a fragile and unstable state of unity.

It is this profoundly animistic and dualistic philosophy of life that the Aztec co-opted in their implacable search for political ascendency. In their superhuman efforts to establish, maintain and reproduce an expanding empire, they

[63] Rival (unpublished manuscript).
[64] López Austin, *The Human Body*, 162.

chose to sacrifice the body to the soul. The high value they placed on ritual violence and killing was rooted in 'cosmological understandings of the creative and transformative capacities of violence, as well as of the use made of these ideas in imperial ideology.'[65] They constructed and projected 'ensembles of ideas that strived to connect power with visions of life', in a search to intensify 'vitality even if the price of doing so was death', a search that we cannot fully understand without taking into account the crises of expansion that affected society, leadership and individuals, as Wolf forcefully argues.[66] Wolf's focus on political ideology and Duverger's emphasis on the syncretic function of sacrifice have provided a solid ground on which to draw parallels between modes of relating to the supernatural, modes of ritual execution, and modes of integrating the great cosmopolitan civilization over which the Aztec aspired to rule imperially. If the Aztec sacrificial complex does not easily fit the cross-cultural category envisaged by Hubert and Mauss[67] in terms of the nature or function of sacrifice, it does at least fit their theory of the evolution of religious transcendence, for human sacrifice among the Aztec was anything but 'savage' or 'primitive'. We are limited in our ability to know what the Nahua thought and felt in the fifteenth century, but there is still value in considering—and perhaps reimagining—what we do know about their rituals, cosmologies and social systems. There is no end to cultivating the art of listening to native voices.

[65] Wolf, *Envisioning Power*, 193.
[66] Wolf, *Envisioning Power*, 193.
[67] Hubert/Mauss, *Sacrifice*.

# 12

## Human Sacrifice and Two Imaginative Worlds, Aztec and Christian

### *Finding God in Evil*

David Brown

### 1. INTRODUCTION

Although this is to over-simplify matters, the end of the twentieth century saw a particular type of theology dominant that was suspicious of lessons to be learnt from wider culture. Instead, what merits there were elsewhere (and these were acknowledged), it was argued that they must always be carefully viewed and assessed through the prism of biblical revelation. Barth on the Protestant side and Balthasar on the Catholic were the two most commonly conjured names, with the more open approach of theologians such as Tillich or Rahner very much in abeyance. Not that this was in any sense equivalent to cultured versus uncultured. Of the four Balthasar was undoubtedly the most widely read. Yet he was altogether too ready to impose Christian patterns on that reading. Although sometimes absurdly narrow in his interests, Tillich by contrast did seem to evince real concern to hear the distinctive voice of those beyond the Christian community. It is on the Barthian side of the divide that we find 'religion' treated in essentially negative terms as unlike Christian revelation a purely human search for God rather than any real waiting on divine grace.

Although also concerned to defend the specific tenets of Christian belief, in much of my own recent writing I have argued for the minority view, maintaining that genuine experience of God is to be found across religions and cultures and that it could on occasion even legitimately critique the content of biblical revelation.[1] Of course, such a position is hardly without its problems. Numerous questions flood in. What does it mean to experience God? Why is there such variety across the religions? On what basis should Christianity

---

[1] That is, undermine the predominance of texts, even if still brought under some more fundamental scriptural principle.

sometimes yield to insights from elsewhere? And so on. Across three volumes on religious experience I sought to indicate how the natural world and artistic creation might generate aspectival experience of the divine: potentially complementary rather than necessarily conflicting attributes.[2] Depending on context, the aspect identified might be generosity, order, simplicity, immanence, infinity, fecundity, otherness, compassion, love, playfulness, intimacy, and so on. Again, in two volumes that explored the nature of revelation, I argued that content cannot be isolated or divorced from placement within the developing tradition of a particular community.[3] So, just as Christianity cannot be understood apart from the history of the texts within the biblical canon and their subsequent exegesis across the centuries, so this is true also for other religions. Comparing rival texts from, for example, the Bible and Qur'an is thus pointless unless due care is taken to explore the subsequent role they played within the two competing traditions. None of this is to imply the removal of all conflict but it might at least lead to its lessening and, perhaps more importantly, also to greater mutual self-understanding. So, for example, on a key Christian claim such as justification by faith it is important for Christian theologians to concede that Paul represents a radical departure from the original meaning of the key texts in the Hebrew canon to which he makes appeal. Jews are thus quite right that their own tradition represents better continuity in interpretation of the relevant passages that once spoke of something significantly different: faithfulness in action.[4] So in any contemporary dialogue that more complex reality would need to be heard.

While some would argue that any such concessions necessarily undermine the exclusive claims of Christianity, I would contend that such an approach is in fact endorsed by the pattern of divine action to be found in Christianity's central doctrine of the incarnation, of complete divine enmeshment in the contingencies of history.[5] But it does mean that Christianity has no automatic claim to superiority over another religion. Instead, a more complex story needs to be told, with sometimes, as in the example above, Christians needing to learn as well as inform. Nor does this point apply only to the 'advanced' world religions of the contemporary world. Because on my view divinity is present and accessible everywhere in the world, like the water in a sponge (to use Augustine's familiar image),[6] there might also be important things to learn even from more 'primitive' contexts. However, rather than taking some innocuous example such as the attitude to the land among Australian Aborigines,

---

[2] Brown, *God and Enchantment of Place*; Brown, *God and Grace of Body*; Brown, *God and Mystery in Words*.

[3] Brown, *Tradition and Imagination*; Brown, *Discipleship and Imagination*.

[4] For the argument, Brown, *Tradition and Imagination*, 213–237, esp. 218–219. Key texts include Gen.15:6 and Hab. 2:4.

[5] Especially if a kenotic model is adopted, as I do in Brown, *Divine Humanity*.

[6] Augustine, *Confessions* VII, 5.

I want to illustrate my theme by an extreme case, that of human sacrifice at its apparently most barbaric among the Aztecs and related cultures. What I want to suggest is that even here genuine religious experience can be detected, with God engaging with all the messiness of life and so even with what we might now describe as unqualifiedly wrong.

Before proceeding, however, one common objection to such a comparative process needs to be faced. In our postmodern world it is frequently contended that such judgments on the loci of religious experience and of divine action are impossible, with a variety of arguments deployed from the philosophical to the anthropological. Obviously there is not the space to expand upon such larger issues here. All I can do is note why I do not view the task as impossible despite the undoubted difficulties involved. Let me make two points. The first concerns the common objection that any such implicit assertion of universal values must inevitably tend to undervalue the integrity of 'the other' by in effect not allowing that very otherness to emerge fully. In the companion essay to this one Laura Rival argues for what she herself admits is a highly original interpretation of the background to Aztec beliefs, and to human sacrifice in particular. The scale of the numbers involved, the extent to which cannibalism was associated with the prac-tice of human sacrifice, a graded scale of value with children at the bottom and warriors at the top, the extent to which divinity was assumed by human beings, a complex ontology of soul/body relations, are all contentious matters that would not be universally endorsed by every writer on the subject. This is not to say that Rival is wrong on any particular item but it does mean that she presents a much stranger society than the one I offer here. The danger in my taking only what would be universally agreed on the topic is that I make the imaginative task I have set myself much easier than it really is. But the danger in hers is that 'the other' is made so strange that they may be left without anything significant to say to us. It is surely precisely by admitting both sameness and difference that a true dia-logue can begin in which superiority is guaranteed for neither side. But, secondly and more substantially, there can in any case be no such thing as total differ-ence. This is because human beings have emerged from a particular process of evolution with definite psychological and social needs and brain structures that include both rational and imaginative capacities of a certain definite kind.[7] So the choice is not limitless. In analytic philosophy Donald Davidson's assertion of a 'principle of charity' over against Quine's total incommensurability thus seems to me exactly right.[8] We need to presume that, however different the beliefs and practices of the other culture are, some sense can be made of them because after all they spring from individuals with essentially the same basic inherited frame-work of needs and aspirations as ourselves. So, although very much more work is ahead of me should aspects of Rival's suggested interpretation become more

---

[7] For left and right brain hemisphere activity, see McGilchrist, *The Master and his Emissary.*

[8] Helpfully expounded in Ramberg, *Donald Davidson's Philosophy of Language,* 64–82.

widely accepted, I suggest for the moment the reader enter into the spirit of Aztec society as I present it here and see what conclusions may be drawn. There is after all a core on which we do agree.

The discussion is divided into three parts: first, an attempt to engage imaginatively (and sympathetically) with its particular cultural context; secondly, an analysis of what it might mean to attribute veridical experience of the divine to such culture; then, finally, some observations on how the process might be reversed, and Mesoamerica address the Judaeo-Christian tradition.

## 2. HUMAN SACRIFICE IN PRE-CONQUEST AMERICA

The basic facts about Aztec sacrificial practice are well known. At the heart of their impressive capital city, Tenochtitlan (with a population of perhaps a quarter of a million and thus five times the size of Henry VIII's London) lay a great temple that, had it survived, would now dominate and tower over Mexico City's impressive cathedral.[9] Jointly dedicated to Tlaloc, god of rain, and Huitzilopochtli, god of war, the sight of victims' hearts rent out on its high platform above and their bodies then cast down the steep steps of its pyramids must have been truly awesome and terrifying to behold. Even contemporary tourists can sense something of the horror, as their eyes suddenly confront the *tzompantli*, the skulls of adult victims exhibited in rows in the excavated ruins, just as they once were in the city's heyday.[10] Fortunately, none of those currently exhibited include the children whom Tlaloc preferred. Although the invading Spanish conquerors almost certainly deliberately exaggerated the number of victims in order to exculpate their own behaviour, there can be little doubt that the volume was considerable.

What, however, has come to light in more recent years is the extent to which such practices were reflected in pre-Conquest America as a whole. Although in some ways it might still be legitimate to describe the Incan culture of South America (1200–1532) as somewhat gentler, this was by no means entirely so, for, while Andean society was undoubtedly much less militaristic than its neighbours further north, nonetheless it too engaged in ritual human sacrifice. However, while Pachamama, their earth goddess, only received llamas and guinea pigs in sacrifice, the Sun, we now know, expected rather more. Here child sacrifice seems to have been the norm, with children between about the age of ten and twelve being routinely offered.[11]

---

[9] For an illustration of their relative scales, Moctezuma, *Great Temple of the Aztecs*, 11.
[10] For illustration, Coe, *Mexico: From Olmecs to Aztecs*, 144.
[11] Stone-Miller, *Art of the Andes*, 134–136.

Further north, it is the longevity of human sacrifice that perhaps occasions most surprise. The ancient Olmec culture (perhaps best known for their gigantic sculpted heads) began to crystallize as early as 1200 BCE, yet already they were producing many of the features that are characteristic of much later Mesoamerican life. So, for instance, the survival of perforators demonstrate the existence of ceremonial bloodletting, while some carvings also show the disembowelling of sacrificial victims.[12] Even the practice of the sacred ball game with its characteristic use of the thigh rather than hands or feet that in its Aztec form required the sacrifice of the losers had already made its appearance.[13] Nor were the Aztecs' immediate predecessors any different. Their magnificent ruins near Mexico City to which the Aztecs gave the name Teotihuacan ('city of the gods') have disclosed a society to which human sacrifice was just as integral as it had been with the Olmecs, or would now be with the Aztecs.

For much of the twentieth century under the influence of the work of Sir Eric Thompson the Maya on the Yucatan peninsula were seen as a cultured and peace-loving society that was to be set in marked contrast to the bloodthirsty Aztecs. However, increasing success in deciphering Maya hieroglyphics from the 1960s onwards has forced recognition of a much more complex reality.[14] One historian even goes so far as to suggest that in reality the Aztecs may have been the more merciful of the two societies.[15] For another, Thompson's work was flawed precisely because his romantic High Anglican views had misled him into projecting onto the Maya his own love of ritual and the quiet pursuit of scientific interests (in their case astronomical observation).[16] Caustically put, Thompson thought of 'the Classic Maya as Anglicans like himself, chanting antiphonal psalms in the quiet calm of an evensong service.'[17] Sadly, there is now evidence in abundance (from burial sites, for example) to suggest a different reality in frequent human sacrifice. There are also indications that the Maya, like the Aztecs, used war as a means of obtaining the necessary sacrificial victims. Note too needs to be taken of the fact that the Maya appear to have subjected their captives to extensive bloodletting rituals before they were sacrificed.[18] A particularly gruesome example from the Bonampark murals is of blood dripping from fingers where the nails have been pulled off.[19] So, although in what follows I will primarily use material from Aztec culture, illustrations from what we know of the Maya and other groups will not be inappropriate.

[12] Benson/De la Fuente, *Olmec Art,* 214, 259–260.
[13] Benson/De la Fuente, *Olmec Art,* 90.
[14] Described in Coe, *Breaking the Maya Code.*
[15] Schele, *The Blood of Kings,* 217; cf. Coe, *Breaking the Maya Code,* 4.
[16] Coe, *Breaking the Maya Code,* 2.
[17] Schele, *The Blood of Kings,* 2.
[18] Benson/Boone, *Ritual Human Sacrifice in Mesoamerica,* 212–213.
[19] Illustration no. 122 in Stierlin, *The Art of the Maya.*

In considering what underlies the practice of sacrifice in general, scholars have over the last hundred years or so again and again sought for a single explanation, whether we take discussions from the end of the nineteenth century such as those of EB Tylor or Robertson Smith or more recent approaches such as those of Walter Burkert or René Girard. Several of these positions are discussed elsewhere in this volume, such as in Nick Allen's and in Wolfgang Palaver's respective contributions (Chapters 10 and 6). There is therefore no need for me to pursue the matter here except to protest against any one single explanation. Irrespective of the theory canvassed, the very range of types differentiated in Hebrew law and elsewhere should have alerted such advocates to the difficulty of any unified, all-encompassing theory,[20] something in any case confirmed by the sheer range of options still being explored.[21] The truth is that the institution has in fact been harnessed to a very great range of purposes, from appeasement to communion, from fear to thankfulness, from expiation to imitation, from gift to substitution, and so on. Likewise, then, in the context of human sacrifice it would be foolish to narrow matters down to a single account. No doubt the practice was sometimes encouraged for the worst of motives in undiluted sadism, kindness used as a means simply to infantilize victims, and gods hated even as they were appeased. But there are also signs of other motives afoot, and it is to these that I wish to draw attention here.

Perhaps the best way to enter sympathetically into the attitudes of such cultures is by trying to construct a defence on their behalf. Fortunately, in respect of the Aztecs the task has already been undertaken for us in the form of a newspaper report, allegedly written up at the time:

The foreigners call us cruel because we sacrifice people to our gods. But what do they know about our beliefs? They don't realize how, at the very beginning of our history, the gods sacrificed themselves so that we could live. And neither do they seem to understand that if we don't repay our gods for this selfless act, the earth will be destroyed. Is it not obvious that if we fail to honour our gods and goddesses with our blood, they'll become angry and turn their backs on us? Huitzilopochtli must be constantly fed with blood and prayers, or he will leave us. And if this happens, who will then protect us? And if we stop sacrificing children to Tlaloc in the spring, their tears will no longer bring the rain to make the crops grow. If the Spaniards can't understand how vital it is for us to give blood to the gods, how can they understand what an honour it is to be chosen as a sacrifice? How can they say we are cruel to send someone to a carefree life after death? After all, the reward for those chosen is the same as that given to a man who dies in battle, or to a woman who dies in childbirth. They become the companions of the Sun. Then, after four years, they return to earth as butterflies or hummingbirds.

---

[20]  For the Hebrew picture, e.g. Vaux, *Ancient Israel*, 415–423.
[21]  Well represented in Carter, *Understanding Religious Sacrifice*.

Only those who have died such heroic deaths are honoured in this way. When the rest of us die we have to go to Mictlan, the place of darkness.[22]

That notion of reciprocity between the gods and human beings, of something given and something returned, runs deep through all the myths of these cultures. Consider first the Maya. According to their beliefs, the gods had shed their own blood in the creation of the world and now human beings were required to reciprocate if the world was to continue functioning properly.[23] Indeed, so honoured was this human contribution that even a captive whose life had been taken by force was envisaged as given, by way of recompense, at the very least eternal life, or even divinized.[24] The gods required blood as food and the earth children's tears, but it was recompense and shortage that demanded this, not any vicious delight in cruelty for its own sake. Much is made of sacrifice as the consequence of the ball game in the Maya's most significant literary survival *Popol Vuh* or 'Council Book'. After recounting the story of the creation, it tells of the various heroic adventures of two warriors, the Twins, in the Underworld. Although they are eventually sacrificed, they are envisaged as returning to life five days later; so life once more emerges out of death.[25]

The Aztecs too had a myth of the gods sacrificing themselves to initiate this world, the fifth to exist.[26] As part of their origin myth, however, the Aztecs did speak of one king who had attempted unsuccessfully, to banish sacrifice.[27] This suggests that, despite the uniform pattern of earlier dominant cultures, the Aztecs saw themselves as having made a deliberate choice. That mythic choice implies that something of much wider importance was at stake. It was a deliberate decision to enter into what was seen as a terrible responsibility, to maintain the fabric of the world, at whatever the cost. So, while it is entirely proper for us to recoil in horror from the evidence of child sacrifice to Tlaloc, and from the practice of tearing out adult hearts even if the victims may have been anaesthetized, it is important that such revulsion be set in the context of false beliefs generated by the easy failure of crops, and not by delight in suffering for its own sake.[28] Such beliefs, no doubt initially generated by the nature of agriculture and its recurring shortages in that part of the world, had now lasted for at least two millennia. So we should not underestimate the difficulty

---

[22] Steele, *Aztec News*, 18.

[23] For Maya gods performing bloodletting, including perforation of the penis, see Stierlin, *Art of Maya*, 181, 193, and 206.

[24] Stierlin, *Art of Maya*, 274.

[25] *Popol Vuh*, 126–129, 133–141.

[26] Baquedano, *Los Aztecas*, 66–68.

[27] Topiltzin, ruler of Tula, subsequently identified with the divine feathered serpent, Quetzalcoatl.

[28] On the possible use of anaesthetics, Benson/Boone, *Ritual Human Sacrifice in Mesoamerica*, 57, 97.

for the Aztecs in extricating themselves from such a belief, not least given the lack of contact with any quite different cultures.

As I have already noted, given any institution such as this, it was of course quite probable that some at least would be attracted to the priesthood precisely because of their sadomasochistic tendencies. But, that said, it is important to note at the same time how far these cultures tried to guard against any such results. In particular, priests and the nobility were also made subject to blood rituals that meant that they too had some conception of what it was that they were putting their noble captives through. While there is little to suggest that native kings, priests, or nobles ever went so far as to offer their own lives, there is no doubt that Aztec and Mayas also subjected themselves to precisely the same kind of bloodletting rituals which their captives endured. These included the men perforating the penis to draw blood, and the women the tongue. The blood thus drawn appears to have been collected in little slips of paper and then burnt.

Of course, none of this makes what the Aztecs did right, but it does mean that, although it may sometimes have degenerated into this, it was not usually done out of a gratuitous delight in suffering or violence. What happened with the inauguration of a new king is especially illuminating in this connection. The noble concerned was offered no great ritual demonstration of power but rather required to spend four days fasting naked in the main temple.[29] That same general perception emerges from the kind of preparations that we know the Aztecs engaged in prior to human sacrifice. In general their sacrificial captives seem to have been treated well, despite the horrific nature of their eventual end. Perhaps the most extraordinary case is that of the young captive chosen annually to impersonate one of their main gods, the warrior Tezcatlipoca, opponent of Quetzalcoatl. For a full year he was given every honour the state could muster before finally being sacrificed in the traditional manner.[30] Even the rite that involved wearing the victim's skin for twenty days began with him being addressed as 'beloved son' and included various rituals in which victor and captive acted very much like kinsmen.[31]

It is of course possible to object that I am being altogether too accommodating in the way I am presenting such practices. Indeed, one commentator argues at length that Aztec attitudes should in no way be confused with Christian compassion or empathy.[32] Instead, it was an essentially fatalistic culture in which victims who came from distant parts were deliberately infantilized in

---

[29] Coe, *Mexico: From Olmecs to Aztecs*, 172–173.
[30] Coe, *Mexico: From Olmecs to Aztecs*, 183. For depictions of the ceremonial, Grunzinski, *Painting the Conquest*, illus. 46–47.
[31] For details, Anker, *Aztecs*, 103–105. Contrast Hunt in *Gods and Myths of the Aztecs* where only a sense of horror emerges: 95, illus. 98.
[32] Clendinnen, *Aztecs: an Interpretation*, e.g. 66, 70, 73–74.

order to behave appropriately during the rituals.[33] While elements in her case for a totally alien society do carry conviction, the way in which the evidence from myth, art, and poetry is almost wholly ignored does seem to me to count decisively against her claims. Even beliefs about the afterlife are given only two quite short, dismissive sentences.[34] That parallels were drawn with the fate of their own warriors or women who died in childbirth is surely much more significant. They were assumed to lead a better life than average beyond the grave, and much the same was promised for the victims. Instead of the ultimate dispensability of the victim, he is assumed to become part of a new and richer life, symbolized in art as serpent, maguey, or butterfly.

Similar attitudes can also be found to lie behind the notorious ball game that was practised throughout two millennia. Although also used for other purposes such as dramatic performance or as a way of deflating social tensions, it is the deadly game for which these courts are best known. As such, the court exercised a symbolic role, in which life was depicted as emerging out of death. For the Maya this seems to have been understood largely in terms of the rising once more of the maize god, whereas among the Aztecs the allusion was rather to the rising of the sun.[35] Although war captives were forced to participate, it has been observed that at least this gave them the chance to die honourably.[36] Whether that is how they themselves saw matters or not, certainly the art associated with the courts does speak of new life for the victims, with serpents or the maguey plant growing out of their decapitated heads, or with them surrounded by butterflies, as at Teotihuacan.[37] Indeed, at Tenochtitlan the god of the ball court was Xolotl, the dualist counterpart of Queztalcoatl. His name is apparently linked linguistically to twins and deformity, and so once more makes explicit the idea of life arising out of its opposite.[38] Again, among the Incas we know that sacrificed children were believed to be elevated to a divine life, whereas what awaited the great mass of the population was nothing, neither a heaven nor a hell. Indeed, what seems to have determined the choice of children is belief in the special powers of infants who, like dwarfs and hunchbacks, were regarded as having a unique kind of access to the supernatural. While some reconstructed corpses exhibit acceptance of their fate, others show fear or even terror. So it is not that such beliefs necessarily lessened the ordeal, but they do demonstrate that the usual

---

[33] Clendinnen, *Aztecs: an Interpretation*, 90, 102–103, 107, 237–239.

[34] Clendinnen, *Aztecs: an Interpretation*, 104.

[35] For Aztec attitudes, see Uriarte, 'Unity in Duality', 41–49; for Mayan, Miller, 'The Maya Ballgame', 79–87.

[36] Uriarte, 'Unity in Duality', 44.

[37] For illustrations, see various essays in Whittington, *Sport of Life and Death*, 47, 75, 256, 258, 260.

[38] Uriarte, 'Unity in Duality', 42, 46.

motive was far from sadistic delight in pain, or any undervaluing of what or who was offered.

So, initial appearances notwithstanding, it does become possible to imagine such an institution generating religious experiences of a kind that the major religions of the modern world, including Christianity, might comprehend, and indeed endorse. But did they occur?

## 3. RELIGIOUS EXPERIENCE IN SUCH A CONTEXT

Consider first self-inflicted bloodletting. Some iconography suggests that the pain involved helped induce a religious vision. Whether common or infrequent, what the possibility indicates is how different the sacrifice itself could also be viewed. It might be tempting to offer an entirely natural explanation in the resultant physical weakness but even the most bigoted atheist could scarcely be content with that explanation alone. The nature of the visions will in part have been determined by antecedent beliefs, and so that is why butterflies or serpents could be seen.[39] However, it is far from clear to me that the Christian believer should stop at this point: in a secularized world shared with the non-believer. The reason is that much Christian experience could then be subject to similar reductionism. Think, for instance, of the Desert Fathers or medieval mystics such as St Catherine of Siena, and the role that sensory deprivation also played in their experience, occasioned of course in their case largely by fasting. Could we not say that sensory deprivation provided the stimulus or trigger that in both cases permitted a genuine religious experience, through the temporary suppression of physical needs allowing greater openness to the spiritual? Any inclination to concede this much would of course depend upon what sort of evaluation is made of the kind of spiritual perception that the Inca and Maya nobility had along with their bloodletting. So far as I determine, it was an experience of being drawn closer to the fundamental character of reality, both of the world and of the divine, in the bloodletter sharing, however fleetingly, in the sacrificial foundations of both: new life through costly self-giving.

Now of course, no matter how much it was disguised in their treatment prior to death, the highest costs were borne not by the nobles but by others who were given no choice in the matter. So the question becomes rather different when we ask whether either for observers or perpetrators genuine religious experience could ever result from participation in human sacrifice. Such evidence as there is comes from poetry rather than art. Despite the savagery of

[39]  Schele, *The Blood of Kings*, 46–47, 178.

their altars, the Aztecs may well have been the first people in the world to have had universal schooling.[40] The result was poetry widely acknowledged to be of a very high quality. The imagery is rich, the content also often deeply reflective. Certainly, it is much less monochrome than prior prejudice might lead modern readers to expect. Doubts about the precise nature of the afterlife occur alongside affirmations.[41] There are also tentative monotheistic explorations.[42]

As in their painting, the aim of Aztec poetry was to capture not just superficial appearance but the deeper essence of the world, in the divine reality behind it:

> Truly earth is not the place of reality.
> ...................................................
> Beyond is the place where one lives.
> ...................................................
> No, O Lord of the Close Vicinity,
> it is beyond, with those who dwell in your house
> that I will sing songs to you, in the innermost of heaven.[43]

But it is a spiritual reality that also makes itself felt in our world, in a way not dissimilar to Augustine's familiar analogy for nature as 'the second book' of revelation.

> With flowers you write
> O Giver of life;
> With songs you give colour
> ...................................................
> You live only in your book of paintings,
> here, on the earth.[44]

Surprising to us, the language of flower and poetry is intimately connected with our central theme of blood, for it is often a related word that is used for all three. So, when the poet declares:

> God sent me, I possess his flowers:
> my duty to weave love chains on the earth[45]

it is in effect a claim to enjoy the same intimacy with the divine as the priest. Again, in an engagingly direct poem addressed to Xippe Totec, the poet's intimacy with the god, the fragility of the rising corn, and the blood necessary to renew the earth are all skilfully and beautifully woven together into a single, potent unity.

---

[40]  Coe, *From Aztecs to Olmecs*, 170.
[41]  Léon-Portilla, *Native Mesoamerican Spirituality*, 179, 183.
[42]  For the terminology employed, de Sahagún, *Psalmodia Christiana*, xxv–vi.
[43]  Léon-Portilla, *Native Mesoamerican Spirituality*, 186–187
[44]  Léon-Portilla, *Native Mesoamerican Spirituality*, 244.
[45]  Kissam/Schmidt, *Flower and Song*, 16, 37.

> You drunken cock, god, you drink the still night.
> It's the blood you need to live.
> ....................................................
> I am the shoot of corn.
> My heart is as fragile and as precious as jewels
> but it waits for the rainburst,
> the gold shining through the rain.
> ....................................................
> I am the tender corn.
> Your god is coming to you
> from your mountains, over the ridge.[46]

Nor is it unknown to find poetry that addresses the issue of how the cult might be justified:

> It was the doctrine of the elders
> that there is life because of the gods;
> with their sacrifice they gave us life.
> In what manner? When? Where?
> When there was still darkness.[47]

Some poetry draws an even closer connection, in language that sounds distinctly liturgical. Children are given appropriate words with which to lament the necessity of their death in order to satisfy the corn god, Tlaloc:

> Now it is time for you to weep.
> Alas I was created
> and for my god
> festal bundles of blood-stained ears of corn
> I carry now
> to the divine hearth.

An answering choir is then assigned this reassuring promise:

> In four years
> comes the arising among us
> ....................................................
> in the place of the fleshless,
> the house of quetzal feathers,
> is the transformation.
> It is the act of the Propagator of men.[48]

What such poetry suggests to me is that the typical response to the bloody rituals was quite different from what our own culture might lead us to expect. So

---

[46] Kissam/Schmidt, *Flower and Song*, 68–69.
[47] Léon-Portilla, *Native Mesoamerican Spirituality*, 215.
[48] Léon-Portilla, *Native Mesoamerican Spirituality*, 194–195.

far from encouraging delight in violence and brutality, such deeds remained restrained and contained by their context, and so in general the Aztecs, far from being wholly brutalized by such bloody sacrifices, looked upon them more as a sad religious duty that nonetheless brought them closer to the divine. As one commentator observes, 'to the Aztecs gentleness had to come out of violence, in exactly the same way as life came out of death.'[49]

Such observations, however, still leave some key questions unanswered, most obviously the precise sense in which God has engaged with the evil involved. Is the good that emerges just incidentally correlated with the practices involved, or is there some more intimate connection? In other words, might the situation be parallel to a Nazi Commandant who lays claims to religious experience while his concentration camp victims are playing Bach (where the victims' suffering in no way contributes to the power of the music) or is there something about the very nature of some institutions in Mesoamerica that helped to make the religious experience possible? Despite the initial shock in envisaging this, my own inclination is to suggest the latter, not of course in the sense that God endorsed such cruelty but that there was something about its form as other-directed sacrifice that made it possible for individuals to draw closer to the divine. That is to say, while its specific brutal content was wrong, its basic structure or form did point to something integral to religious perception: that sacrifice is built into the nature of reality as God intended it. While there is not the space to develop the idea here, in defence it could be argued that shortages and the very precariousness of life in pre-industrial societies helped generate the basic notion, and that this has now been reinforced by what we know of the pattern evolution takes.[50] Put thus, however, only an intellectual perception as such might be in play. What would transform it into religious experience would be some sense of being drawn closer to the divine as a result. Yet that is surely precisely what the poetry suggests: the individual being allowed to participate in the fundamental nature of reality, what a Christian might describe as an experience of grace. Moreover, on occasion the experience might even be identified as revelatory, not least where a tension was felt in the sacrifice being something less than the offering of one's own self, something I suggested did indeed happen in the practice, for example, of bloodletting.

## 4. REVERSING THE DIALOGUE: CHRISTIANITY THROUGH MESOAMERICAN EYES

As noted earlier, sacrifice can of course be used to express and convey a quite different experience of the divine, the God of plenty found in a feast of good

[49]  Hunt, *Gods and Myths of the Aztecs*, 102.
[50]  For the latter, Henry Scott Holland, *Logic and Life*, 83–85, 101, 126–127, 137.

food and wine. But ancient peoples also discovered the divine in situations of want, hunger, and anxiety, in a creation where harvests are not always guaranteed, where the good does not always triumph. Mesoamerica intuited a divinity that recreates and transforms through costly activity, and their religious ritual was designed to reflect that reality. It is this fact that helps explain why the Christian missionaries found such a ready audience. What was exhibited of God in Christ was not wholly unlike what they had already discovered for themselves. So, for example, even to this day among the Tseltal (a group descended from the Maya), Christ is compared to the Twins who sacrificed themselves and went down to the underworld to defeat the powers of darkness, only once more to rise again into the heavens.[51] However macabre it may seem, the victims were truly honoured. This is why I find David Carrasco's application of Girard's scapegoat mechanism to Aztec culture so implausible, even without his dubious preference for post-Conquest Spanish sources over pre-Conquest art and archaeology.[52] Indeed, it even seems to be possible to draw a legitimate element of critique of Christianity from the Mesoamerican side. Although I shall begin with some moral observations, my ultimate intention is to suggest a re-evaluation of two elements in the Judaeo-Christian revelation itself.

Take first the question of how warfare was conducted. Here moral critique of the Christian invaders not only became common at the time but continues apace into our modern world as in Peter Schaffer's 1964 play *The Royal Hunt of the Sun*. Although Cortés did attempt various moral justifications for his conduct in Mexico, there is no doubt that his own behaviour in the massacre of Cholula tells a rather different tale, as does the butchery ordered by his deputy, Pedro de Alvarado, upon unarmed dancers at a feast in honour of Huitzilopochtli. In his classic account of the invasion Bartolomé de Las Casas suggests that the latter might well be taken to rival anything that could have been perpetrated by the natives in honour of this god,[53] while his judgement on Pizarro's actions in Peru is not much different ('another great villain').[54] If his statistics at times cannot be judged other than as wild exaggerations, there seems no reason to doubt the general thrust of his assessment of incidents that included torture, rape, the murder of children, and sometimes the imposition of cannibalism.[55] Even the enslaving of the natives in which the more obviously pious Christopher Columbus engaged contrasts unfavourably with the Aztecs' relatively mild treatment of their own slaves who apparently retained their basic rights: apart, that is, from having to serve without pay.[56]

---

[51] Marzal, *The Indian Face of God*, 30.
[52] Carrasco, *City of Sacrifice*.
[53] Las Casas, *A Short History*, 45–56.
[54] Las Casas, *A Short History*, 107–115.
[55] For some extreme examples, Las Casas, *A Short History*, 15–17, 19, 22, 26, 62–63, 93–94.
[56] Crosfield, *Columbus*, 130–139, 157, 207. For Aztec rules, Anker, *Aztecs*, 138–139.

Aztecs had in general to be much more circumspect in their conduct of war than their opponents since, in order to secure victims acceptable to the gods, these had not to be mutilated in any way. In addition, it appears that there was an insistence that such captives had to have been fairly won. Attempts were, therefore, made to ensure what looked like a more equal match with opponents. One periodic form of battle with their Tlaxcalan neighbours (known as the War of the Flowers) was fought by the Aztecs according to very strict rules without hope of conquest, and exclusively in order to guarantee fresh sacrificial victims.[57]

Yet such moral comparisons do not really get to the heart of the imaginative exercise I am proposing. Spanish actions could all so easily be attributed to human sinfulness rather than any intimate connection with how God has been understood within Christianity. Hence it is important to note the way the Bible is itself partly to blame. Friar Diego de Landa, the chief written source for our knowledge of Maya culture, may be used by way of illustration. As justification for Spanish conduct he mentions the 'great cruelties' done by the Hebrews in their own entry to the promised land,[58] meaning thereby passages such as Deut. 7:1–6 and 20:10–18 which portray extermination of the native population as part of the divine plan. Nor were Israel's greatest prophets or even the New Testament itself immune from the dreadful effects of such exclusivism. For the prophets other nations may share in Israel's glorious future but only in a firmly subservient role,[59] while the foundations for anti-Semitism are already there in two of the gospels.[60]

I say this not to undermine the Scriptures as revelation (however fallible), but to rebel against the tendency of professional theologians no less than of those in the pew to give Scripture too easily the benefit of the doubt in a way that would be firmly resisted were it another religion in question. In the case of the *herem* of Deuteronomy, for instance, two strategies are common: the older one of assuming it was conditional on lack of change in the native peoples and so in actual fact never carried out, or, more recently, the claim that its present scriptural context transforms the command into a purely metaphorical image for absolute commitment.[61] To my mind neither proposal seems likely. Instead, I would suggest the presence of a parallel problem to what emerged in respect of Aztec sacrifice, with dubious content attached to a correct formal insight. That is, ancient Israelites correctly perceived that the ultimate reality that is divinity requires absolute commitment but wrongly applied this in terms of their own self-advantage and to the detriment of others. So, rather

---

[57] So Hunt, *Gods and Myths*, 94.

[58] Landa, *Yucatan*, 46–47.

[59] E.g. Contrast Isa. 56:6–8 with 60:10–14.

[60] Mt. 27:25; John, more generally.

[61] For the former, e.g. *Sifre Deuteronomy* 202: 'if they perform repentance, they shall not be killed.' For the latter, with Deut. 7 interpreted in the light of Deut. 6:4: Moberly, 'Towards an Interpretation', 124–144, esp. 133–137.

than either defence or blanket condemnation, what we need to heed is a more complex reality: the divine element present in the evil gradually drawing individuals to a more appropriate perception of how such commitment should be applied.[62] In a similar way I would suggest that it is not the notion of jihad as such that is wrong but modern applications which show no regard for any innocent individuals involved.[63]

A second way in which an Aztec perspective might throw interesting light on Christianity's own traditions is on the question of how self-sacrifice was to be evaluated in relation to the practice of sacrifice in general. As already noted, there are some reasons for believing that, despite obvious aspirations for high quality in the human sacrifices offered, they were nonetheless viewed as second-best. Several Mesoamerican myths spoke of the gods sacrificing themselves rather than others, while the painful process of self-bloodletting surely demands an explanation beyond simply the amount of blood donated. Much greater qualities could after all be much more easily secured by yet more human sacrifice. So it looks as though the objective was a form of vicarious identification, something that could be achieved without going to the ultimate extreme of offering one's own life. That would also help explain why the message of Christ's own self-sacrifice received such a ready audience.

But, if so, such contextualization throws an interesting light back on the Bible. On the basis of some puzzling texts in Exodus, Ezekiel, and Kings, a number of scholars, most notably Jon Levenson, have suggested that the sacrifice of the first born was once quite common in ancient Israelite religion.[64] If so, there would be a dreadful paradox in Christian haughty dismissal of Aztec religion when a darker reality of appeasing a jealous deity lay hidden in its own earlier roots. But the irony may well run still deeper. For if I am right that Mesoamerica was struggling towards a view of the superiority of self-sacrifice over the sacrifice of others, the irony would be that this was a position to which all three Western monotheistic religions had in fact advanced in their own interpretation of their texts until modern tendencies towards literalism threw them back once more upon an earlier view.

Elsewhere I have explored at length the traditions of exegesis associated with Genesis 22, the story of Abraham's sacrifice of Isaac.[65] There is no need to repeat details here except to note their general thrust. In the case of Judaism, the focus moved from concentration on Abraham's dilemma to taking Isaac's self-offering as the heart of what became known as the *Akedah* and was seen as one of the principal defining moments of Jewish self-understanding. As the

---

[62] So this is equally to reject the pure evil interpretation found in Lüdemann, *The Unholy in Holy Scripture*, 55–75 esp. 73.

[63] In Islamic law jihad shares features with the Christian notion of the just war, and is set about with conditions in the Qur'an itself: e.g. 22.40–42.

[64] Levenson, *Death and Resurrection of the Beloved Son*, esp. 3–17.

[65] Brown, *Tradition and Imagination*, 237–260, esp. 251ff.

story was retold, Isaac came to be treated as a heroic, self-consenting adult, and given accordingly various ages, sometimes as much as thirty-seven years.[66] Nor was the trajectory in Christianity any different. Under the influence of Jesus' own choice of the Cross, the early fathers of the Church were quick to see in Isaac a type of Christ, and so the passage was read with a new emphasis on the son's contributing role. Clement of Rome, for instance, informs us that because 'Isaac knew with confidence what was about to happen, it was with gladness that he was led forth as a sacrificial victim', while Irenaeus urges us 'take up our cross as Isaac took up his bundle of sticks'.[67] Islam followed essentially the same course. Although the boy is unnamed in the Qur'an, tradition quickly identified him with Abraham's older son, Ishmael, the ancestor of the Arabs, but also once more because of his age able to offer his full consent.

Although Kierkegaard is the best-known Christian writer to return the focus to Abraham, he is in fact quite typical of wider currents in all three religions that have sought meaning in original contexts rather than continuing currents of tradition.[68] To my mind that pattern is quite sad since, just as it is hard to feel any sympathetic imaginative identification with the Aztecs without entering into their developing traditions, so it is hard to make sense, as one Old Testament scholar observes, of what could justify 'the private hell initiated by these words: Take your son and offer him as a burnt offering'.[69]

## 5. CONCLUSION

Christian theology has had a long history of interpreting generously its own foundational documents while assuming the worst for what lies beyond their compass. The sheer nastiness of, for example, the conclusion of Psalm 137 or much of the Book of Revelation needs to be fully acknowledged.[70] Yet, just as this is quite compatible with continuing to find the action of God in these texts, so the same needs be acknowledged of the myths and practices of Mesoamerica. By imaginatively entering into such 'alien' cultures we will find not only authentic religious experience even in the midst of great evil but also through that imaginative exercise an ability to turn back on the Christian faith and hear a critique from that world in its turn.

[66] For the *Genesis Rabbah* argument, see Brown, *Tradition and Imagination*, 249.
[67] Clement, *1 Corinthians*, 31; Irenaeus, *Adversus Haereses*, IV 10 (both my transl.).
[68] Rabbinic Judaism is now less popular than it once was, just as many Muslims pay less heed to *hadith*, the oral traditions of the Prophet.
[69] Crenshaw, *Theodicy*, 8.
[70] For Revelation, see my *Discipleship and Revelation*, 158–160. In the case of Psalm 137 already with Augustine 'Edom' has become 'all that is carnal,' and the 'children thrown against the rocks' for Jerome merely 'evil thoughts'.

# 13

## Blood Sacrifice as a Symbol of the Paradigmatic Other

### *The Debate about Ebó-Rituals in the Americas*

Bettina E. Schmidt

Susan Sered describes sacrifice as a cultural process of embodiment and dis-embodiment 'in which certain groups or individuals are modified, marked, defined, set off, or classified.'[1] Nowhere is this process more visible than in the case of blood sacrifice, which is probably the most dramatic form of sacrifice. The persistence of animal sacrifice, particularly in the twenty-first century, in highly urbanized and industrialized societies such as the USA is a paradox. One of the results of the Enlightenment is the rejection of sacrifice as Zachhuber outlines in this volume (Chapter 2); however, blood sacrifice remains integral to religious worship in many traditions. In indigenous belief systems, life is regarded as the most precious gift that anyone could offer to God. Blood is often considered necessary for cleansing and renewing the contract between humans and deities, for reaffirming the bond that is the source of the power of the individual and the community. 'Blood sacrifice assures', as Kaplan writes about the Benin indigenous religion, 'the continuity essential for social communion, cohesion, and life itself'.[2] This link has survived the transatlantic slave trade and the inhumane institution of slavery during the colonial period, and has become an essential part of the religious practice of Afro-American religions in the Caribbean and Brazil. To this day, blood continues to be spilled upon altars to propitiate the deities and ancestors, who are regarded as the source of all life and power. Blood sacrifice remains a moral imperative for devotees of the African deities in the Americas. It is essential for the various rites of passage, but is also performed in many other rituals. The comments of Evans-Pritchard concerning the Nuer are particularly pertinent: blood

---

[1] Sered, 'Gendered Typology', 14.
[2] Kaplan, 'Sacrifice', 184.

sacrifices are concerned with social relations, but also with the moral and physical well-being of the individual and the community. Offering blood to the deities and ancestors signifies the mark of membership to a community since only members of the community are allowed to perform these rituals. Even attendance is often restricted to members of the community, although guests can also be invited. Thus, blood rituals can serve to mark the cultural identity and religious tradition of the group.[3]

On the other hand, blood sacrifices are perceived as barbaric, especially where these are human sacrifices, but even in the case of animal sacrifices. 'Blood impresses the imagination', as McCarthy writes; 'its loss means weakness and death. It can, therefore, easily be identified with strength. But blood also arouses fear and repulsion.'[4] The colonial conquest of America was justified with gory descriptions of human sacrifice performed by the 'savages', particularly after the conquest of the Aztec empire.[5] It was conveniently overlooked, however, that the victims of the European conquest outnumbered the human sacrifices of the Aztec and Incan empires, as well as other Amerindian people. Human sacrifice was perceived as so barbaric that the practitioners needed to be defeated, permanently.

The same attitude characterized the colonial rule in other parts of the world. In West Africa, for instance, the colonizers believed that the colonial rule would replace cruelty and human sacrifice with Christian virtues and worship. Kaplan describes how the Benin religion was decried as 'barbaric' at the end of the nineteenth century, the same time Africa was being divided among the European powers. When British forces invaded the Benin kingdom in 1897, they 'painted a gory picture of bloody brutality' and the capital was even nicknamed 'City of Blood' because of the reports about human sacrifices.[6]

Colonial rule replaced human sacrifice with animal sacrifice, which remains an important sacrificial ritual to this day, despite decades of colonial rule, Christianization and modernization of the Benin kingdom. In public discourse about these rituals, however, animal sacrifice is seen as a relic, belonging to an archaic past and out of touch with modern society. In this rejection of sacrifice, we can trace the influence of the world-view of Western modernity, associated as it is with the ideals of the Reformation and Enlightenment, which are essentially anti-ritualistic and anti-sacrificial. Modern accounts of sacrifice have been informed, as Zachhuber argues in this volume, by the absence of ritual sacrifice from the practices of Western societies. Consequently, communities that still perform blood sacrifices are perceived as archaic, pre-modern, and even savage. The sacrificial ritual, particularly blood ritual, becomes

---

[3] Evans-Pritchard, 'Sacrifice', 21.
[4] McCarthy, 'Symbolism', 166.
[5] See Rival and Brown, Chapters 11 and 12, respectively, in this volume, for details about the ethnographic reality of human sacrifice among the Aztec people and the perception of it.
[6] Kaplan, 'Sacrifice', 181.

the marker of the paradigmatic other, even within one's own society. Conflict arises in particular, 'when representatives of a world religion insist...followers reject dual loyalties.'[7]

In the case of Benin, as Kaplan highlights, the Christian notions of sacrifice and sanctity associated with Christ were originally not regarded as irreconcilable with traditional beliefs. For several centuries the ruling *obas* (traditional kings, regarded as sacred) allowed their people to practice Roman Catholicism, for combining modernity (identified with Christianity) with traditional beliefs and practices was not seen as a problem. Even today most Benin people can accommodate both traditions simultaneously: 'They equate Christianity with modernity, and indigenous religion with their cultural identity, tradition, and the Oba.'[8]

However, other studies suggest that this coexistence might change in the near future. While Kaplan does not elaborate further on the impact of the various Christian Pentecostal and Evangelical churches, other scholars have shown in their studies of neighbouring countries how the hostility that is expressed by these churches against indigenous beliefs and practices changes the relationship between Christianity and traditional beliefs.[9] A similar process is visible in the Americas. After a more or less unproblematic coexistence of Roman Catholicism and Afro-American religions, which gave to each individual the power to determine the degree of identification with Christianity and the Afro-American tradition respectively, migratory flows and the spread of new Charismatic religions have provoked new conflicts. By focusing on animal sacrifice in Afro-Brazilian and Afro-Cuban religions, I will discuss how the migration from a Roman Catholic environment (Cuba) to a predominately Protestant environment (USA), as well as the spread of new forms of Protestantism in Brazil, has influenced the perception of sacrificial practices in these countries.

For an understanding of this process it is helpful to look at René Girard's theory of sacrifice. Girard stresses the dichotomy between Christianity and the religions that Girard labelled 'primitive', mainly indigenous religions. In his influential book *Violence and the Sacred*, he restricted sacrificial rituals to these so-called 'primitive' religions, but later reassessed his position, as he explains in an interview with Rebecca Adams:

> I say at the end of *Things Hidden*—and I think this is the right attitude to develop—that the changes in the meaning of the word 'sacrifice' contain a whole history, religious history, of mankind. So when we say 'sacrifice' today inside a church or religious context, we mean something which has nothing to do with primitive religion. Of course I was full of primitive religion at the time of the writing of

[7] Kaplan, 'Sacrifice', 196.
[8] Kaplan, 'Sacrifice', 196.
[9] See, e.g., Meyer, 'Devil', about Ghana.

the book, and my main theme was the difference between primitive religion and Christianity, so I reserved the word 'sacrifice' completely for the primitive.[10]

This excerpt indicates that Girard, despite the revision of his position, maintains the distinction between the 'sacrifice of Christ' and 'archaic sacrifices', as Palaver highlights in this volume. Palaver argues, however, that the difference 'does not have to be understood as a radical separation negating any connection between archaic religions and the Judeo-Christian revelation' because Girard promotes 'a paradoxical unity of all that is religious'.[11] Nonetheless, and as Palaver makes clear, modern men usually reject this idea of unity—with terrible consequences. Palaver interprets, for instance, the killing of indigenous people in America, which was justified with the rejection of human sacrifice, as 'the result of this moralistic attitude of a *corruptio optimi pessima*, a corruption of the best always leading to the worst'.[12] Palaver recognizes in Girard's 'paradoxical unity of all that is religious' an interreligious perspective that overcomes the unbridgeable separation of Christianity and other religions. Although 'archaic' and Christian concepts of sacrifice are, according to Girard, radically opposed to each other, they are nonetheless inseparable. In order to overcome the violence of these 'archaic' sacrifices, one needs to transform violence into suffering. Palaver sees here the foundation of Girard's Catholic theory of sacrifice and argues that sacrificial Catholicism should not so easily be rejected as false. He refers at this point to the post-Enlightenment condemnation of sacrifice that characterizes our world today, mentioning, for instance, Habermas' critique of the traditional cult of sacrifice.[13] Palaver argues that Girard offers a way of maintaining a fundamental difference as well as a connection between Christian and other forms of sacrifice.

Girard's position sheds light on the main theme of my article: the reason why Afro-American religions are facing an increasingly hostile situation in the USA and Brazil. I will show that the growing number of Evangelical churches in Brazil and the Protestant mainstream environment with which the Cuban immigrants are confronted in the USA, affect the understanding of sacrifice and the relationship to communities practising sacrificial rituals. While the 'affinity between Catholic liturgical and sacramental structures and West African religious ritual'[14] had enabled Afro-American religions in Catholic environments to maintain sacrifices, the situation today is different. I argue here that blood sacrifice defines not only the boundary between members of a religious community and outsiders, between 'us' and 'them', as described above; it also signifies the process of 'othering' by illuminating the contested

---

[10] Girard/Adams, 'Violence, Difference, Sacrifice', 29.
[11] Palaver, 'Sacrificial Cults', Chapter 6, in this volume.
[12] Palaver, 'Sacrificial Cults', Chapter 6, in this volume.
[13] Habermas, *Time*, 46.
[14] Camara, 'Syncretism', 299.

boundary between perceived ideals of being 'civilized' or 'savage', 'modern' or 'archaic'. In this sense, sacrificial rituals work on various levels. They express what we are (in relation to sacrifice) and how we perceive the other within the debate about modernity, but also how modernity itself is perceived.

## 1. THE UNDERSTANDING OF EBÓ WITHIN THE FIELD OF SACRIFICE-STUDIES

During my time in the 'field' as an anthropologist I have been present at several sacrificial ceremonies, the first time in Ecuador and later in New York City and São Paulo. In a rural context people are still used to the slaughter of animals; even the slaughter of a large animal such as a cow does not cause a problem, whereas urban settings have created a distance between living animals and the food we consume. Slaughter has become an unfamiliar practice and people respond to the killing of animals, particularly ritual killings, with revulsion and anxiety. Nonetheless, sacrifice still has a place in our imagery.[15] The focus in our perception of sacrificial rituals remains on the victim, whether it is a human being or an animal, which is often perceived as a substitution for the human being performing the sacrifice. As Fiddes points out, in the modern debate sacrifice is regarded as 'violence done to a victim in order to establish order in society and meaning in the realm of language.'[16] The cultural context of the ritual is usually ignored despite its importance for the understanding of the ritual, as Brown highlights in this volume.[17] It is therefore important to connect the debate about animal sacrifice to the tradition that is at the core of any given case study. Therefore, I will begin by discussing the meaning of the African ritual from which the Afro-American religions have derived within the wider debate about sacrifice.

My focus in the present chapter is on the *ebó*-rituals practised in Brazil and the USA. The term *ebó* derives from the West African Yoruba language. *Ebó* can be translated as sacrifice and is always used in a religious context. It thus follows the narrow definition of sacrifice as a religious act in distinction from an offering as a 'presentation of a gift'.[18]

Sacrifice among the Yoruba people is at the core of worship in their traditional religion. It is a means 'to establish, renew, and maintain communication with the supernatural beings and to share and enjoy communion with them' in order to please the spiritual powers.[19] In this sense, it is a thanks offering

---

[15] Hedley, *Sacrifice Imagined*.
[16] Fiddes, 'Sacrifice, Atonement, and Renewal', Chapter 4, in this volume.
[17] Brown, 'Human Sacrifice', Chapter 12, in this volume.
[18] Henninger, 'Sacrifice', 7997.
[19] Awolalu, 'Yoruba Sacrificial Practice', 82.

to the supernatural beings, the *orishas*, embedded in the belief that they have
human-like qualities and needs. Human beings have to please them by regularly offering the things that they like. Only if this is done adequately, will
favours be granted. Thus, the offerings can be 'an expression of gratitude for
benefits received', but also a 'means of securing the favour of the divinities and
of establishing right relationship with them.'[20]

To an extent, the Yoruba evidence confirms Marcel Mauss' and Henri
Hubert's theory of sacrifice. They challenged Tylor's definition of sacrifice as
a gift to deities, a simple business transaction based on the principle *do ut
des* (I give so that you will give in return). While Tyler perceived the origin
of sacrifice in a bribe, an activity without special moral significance, Hubert
and Mauss argued that the exchange of gifts always contains an obligation,
since it aims to establish a contractual relationship between the giver and the
recipient. For them, therefore, *do ut des* contains a deeper meaning and is not
simply a pure transaction. In this sense, Mauss and Hubert saw sacrifice as a
means of mediation between the profane and the sacred because the act of
sacrificing changes the nature of the sacrificial victim from profane to sacred.[21]
They also strongly disagreed with creating a firm opposition between gift and
communion; instead, they offered a third reading by describing sacrifice as
a religious act during which the profane communicates with the sacred via
the consecrated victim. Summarizing Hubert and Mauss, Evans-Pritchard
describes sacrifice as:

> a symbolic enactment of the relation in which the individual stands to society.
> From society, for which the god is a symbol, the individual draws the strength and
> assurance he needs in his undertakings and the redemption of his faults; and in
> return he renounces his possessions, the value of the renunciation being not the
> worth of the possessions but in the act of submission and abnegation before the
> collective personality of the social groups. The act recalls to individual minds the
> presence of collective forces and serves to maintain them.[22]

Although their idea of a separation between the sacred and the profane has
been challenged[23] and cannot be applied to the Yoruba religion (or any other
African tradition), Mauss' and Hubert's relational approach to sacrifice does
reflect the Yoruba sacrifice with its complex of sacrificer (performer of the
sacrifice), sacrifice (regardless of the kind of material used), beneficiary of the
sacrifice (whether an individual or a group) and the supernatural beings to
whom the sacrifice is offered, in our case deities and ancestors. The kind of
offering used in *ebó* varies depending on the circumstances, the divinity, and

---

[20] Awolalu, 'Yoruba Sacrificial Practice', 82.
[21] See Allen, 'Using Hubert and Mauss', Chapter 10, in this volume, for a discussion of this
theory.
[22] Evans-Pritchard, 'Sacrifice', 25.
[23] E.g. Bloch, *Prey into Hunter*, 28.

the function. However, the material does not reflect the value of the sacrifice since the material consists of things used in everyday life, 'ranging from
the smallest living and non-living things to the biggest domestic animals, like
a cow'; Awolalu even mentions human sacrifices 'in some very special circumstances', although he later states that this practice was abolished by British
colonial rule in the nineteenth century.[24]

*Ebó* signifies all kinds of sacrifice, irrespective of the material used and is
not restricted to sacrificial killing. The crucial aspect of *ebó* is the sincerity of
intention, the giving itself, as Evans-Pritchard explained with regard to sacrifice among the Nuer people in Sudan. 'If a man is poor he will sacrifice a
goat, or even a cucumber, in the place of an ox, and God will accept it.'[25] In
this respect, the kind of sacrifice holds no significance for the one receiving it.
With reference to Mauss, Evans-Pritchard interprets sacrifice as 'the creation
and maintenance of a relationship':

> When Nuer give their cattle in sacrifice they are very much, and in a very intimate
> way, giving part of themselves. What they surrender are living creatures, gifts more
> expressive of the self and with a closer resemblance to it than inanimate things,
> and these living creatures are the most precious of their possessions, so much so
> that they may be said to participate in them to the point of identification.[26]

This is also the case among the Yoruba. As already mentioned, the greatest
possible sacrifice among the Yoruba used to be a human being, which is similar to the practice among the Aztecs discussed by Rival in this volume. Human
sacrifice was performed for the good of the community, usually at times of
national crisis and disaster: 'It was considered necessary that the highest and
the best must be offered to a divinity who gave protection to a whole community or to assuage the anger of one who had brought calamity upon the whole
community.'[27]

Nowadays, large animals are substituted for human beings. In these sacrifices, the whole animal is offered to the deity, while in most other cases the
sacrifice consists only of the blood and the head of the animal:

> Blood is regarded as an indispensable constituent of sacrifice. The life of the vic-
> tim is in the blood; and in consequence of this, the blood that is poured out is
> always given first to the divinity…In offering the blood, the Yoruba know and
> believe that they are offering the life of the animal.[28]

In this case it is customary to prepare food from the flesh of the sacrifice for
the priests, and in some cases for the community as well, although special

[24] Awolalu, 'Yoruba Sacrificial Practice', 86–87.
[25] Evans-Pritchard, 'Sacrifice', 27.
[26] Evans-Pritchard, 'Sacrifice', 27.
[27] Awolalu, *Yoruba*, 87.
[28] Awolalu, *Yoruba*, 90.

parts of the cooked food are also offered to the deity. Here one can see a connection to Robertson Smith's idea that sacrificial meals establish or reinforce
the communion between the worshippers and the divine.

## 2. EBÓ IN THE AMERICAS

The two religions I am about to turn to, the Cuban Orisha religion (also called
Santería, although this term has recently been perceived as discriminatory)
and the Brazilian Candomblé, are both largely derived from the Yoruba tradition discussed above. Animal Sacrifice is part of a wider category of offering
to the gods that is practised in both traditions. As in the Yoruba tradition the
offerings are various and have different functions, depending on the supernatural recipients and the religious context of the ritual. Nivaldo Léo Neto and
his co-authors write that the main purpose of the sacrifice is the fortification
and feeding of the deities. When the sacrifice is conducted successfully, the
requests and desires of the devotees will be met. According to the authors,
the interviewees use the verb 'to eat' when describing the sacrifice. However,
this expression needs to be understood in a symbolic way since the deities do
not actually eat the flesh but feed off the energy of the sacrificial victim. This
energy is called *axé* (derived from Yoruba) and refers to 'a mystic force that is
present in some places, objects, or certain parts of the animal body, such as the
heart, liver, lungs, genitals, riverbeds, stones, seeds, and sacred fruits.'[29] Blood
is especially important since it is thought to transport *axé* in a living being. The
purpose of the sacrifice is to provide energy to the deities so that the energy
will return as gifts to the practitioners of the sacrifice. Consequently, the harmony between the world and the deities is preserved.

Sacrificial rituals have to be performed on a regular basis. All devotees,
whether they have just passed the first step of initiation or are experienced
priests and priestesses, have to fulfil certain obligations regularly in order to
honour the lifelong link between deity and devotee. These rituals are often part
of the religious calendar. For instance, once a year every religious congregation
should celebrate a special feast for each of the main deities. Sponsoring such
a feast is regarded as an important *ebó* of the 'children' of that deity which is
honoured by the feast (every initiate member is called the son or daughter of
the deity to whom he or she belongs). Furthermore, in a personal crisis, for
instance, people can also 'negotiate', via the priest, a favour from the deities in
exchange for a special offering.

The sacrifices are usually divided into two categories—warm and cold, with
'warm' referring to a blood sacrifice and 'cold' referring to other gifts, such as

---

[29] Neto/Brooks/Alves, 'From Eshu to Obtala', 3.

perfume, alcohol, sweets, flowers, and candles. Deities can also demand a special deed such as praying every day for a certain amount of time or avoiding certain food as a sacrifice for spiritual support. It is also possible that a devotee might be told by the priest to give up drinking or smoking or sweets or something else because the deity has requested it. Wearing certain jewellery can be another obligation or even the initiation to a higher grade. Animal sacrifice, however, is regarded as the most powerful deed.

The most common animals to be selected as victims are chickens, pigeons, guinea fowls, and goats, but I have also seen sheep being sacrificed.[30] Parts of the animal (for example, the head) as well as some of the other offerings of fruits or vegetables are presented to the deities on especially prepared shrines or altars. At the end of the ceremony (sometimes after days or weeks) these parts are buried somewhere in the earth (often but not always near open water). Other parts of the *ebó* are used to prepare a meal for the members of the community and sometimes also for visitors who attended the public part of the ceremony.

While the meal for human consumption is often prepared alongside the sacrificial meal (albeit separately, sometimes even in different kitchens), it includes a special dish that is prepared with the same ingredients as the food for the deities. Eating this dish is regarded as a special blessing that creates a communion between the devotees and the deities, as the devotees and the deities share the energy of the sacrifice. Neto and his co-authors compare this meal with the Christian Holy Communion. They further state that the communal meal 'reinforces the interconnectedness of the community of adherents, and therefore plays a significant role in the maintenance of the Candomblé religion.'[31] The same can also be said about sacrifice in the Cuban Orisha religion.

## 3. FIRST EXAMPLE: THE LEGAL BATTLE OF THE CUBAN ORISHA RELIGION IN THE USA

In the wake of the Cuban Revolution in 1959, the Orisha religion spread to the USA. White Cuban refugees, who often opposed the practice in Cuba, began to embrace the worship of the *orishas* as part of their Cuban (exile) identity in Florida. This development caused a *blanqueamiento* ('whitening') of the Orisha religion that subsequently caused serious tension within the Cuban community, when the second wave of refugees arrived during the 1980s.[32]

---

[30] See: Neto/Brooks/Alves, 'From Eshu to Obtala', 5–6 for a list of animals slaughtered in sacrificial rituals, based on their interviews with eleven priests and priestesses in Brazil.

[31] Neto/Brooks/Alves, 'From Eshu to Obtala', 4.

[32] See Brandon, *Santería*, for the history of the religion.

Together with the *blanqueamiento* came the need to accommodate the religion to the new environment. Although all efforts to organize the autonomous religious houses within one federation had so far failed, some priests managed to transform their congregations into churches. One such example is Ernesto Pichardo, the founder and leader of the Church of Lukumi Babalu Aye. In 1986, he leased a property to build a house of worship in order to establish his congregation as an official registered church. The neighbours opposed this, however, and alerted the city council. During an emergency public session, the council prohibited animal sacrifice in a resolution.[33]

With the spread of the Orisha religion to the USA, animal protection groups became aware of *ebó* and began to target Cuban communities. In the USA, it is illegal to kill animals for a purpose other than food consumption. As a result, animal protection groups managed to disrupt and consequently invalidate sacred ceremonies by sending in the police to rescue animals and prevent the sacrificial slaughter from taking place. As it was impossible for most of the political refugees to visit Cuba and perform the ceremonies in their homeland, the constant interruptions not only desecrated several temples but also made impossible the performance of important rituals, such as the initiation of new priests (animal sacrifice being part of the these rituals).

Things only began to change when the Cuban exiles became politically more influential and took legal steps to protect their religious tradition. Pichardo appealed against the resolution of the city council on the grounds of the First Amendment which grants the free exercise of one's religion. The city responded that residents were concerned because the practices were inconsistent with public morals, peace, and safety.[34] It prohibited the sacrificial rituals based on Florida's animal cruelty law and argued that animal sacrifice was an unnecessary slaughter. In sum, the city firmly rejected the religious context of the ritual—and the case went through various legal stages and appeal courts.

At first, the ban was confirmed by the appeal court and the Church of Lukumi Babalu Aye lost the authority to sacrifice animals. The first federal trial even concluded that children would be psychologically affected when attending these rituals, so the community was prohibited from opening the church. The case then went to the appeal court arguing that the ruling was a violation of their rights under the Free Exercise Clause of the First Amendment. However, although the appeals court acknowledged that the ban was not religiously neutral, the District Court ruled for the city because 'compelling governmental interests in preventing public health risks and cruelty to animals fully justified the absolute prohibition on ritual sacrifice accomplished by the ordinances.'[35] Finally, the case was heard by the Supreme Court in Washington

[33] Pichardo, 'Supreme Court Ruling'.
[34] U.S. Supreme Court, *Church*, 1993.
[35] U.S. Supreme Court, *Church*, 1993.

which eventually overruled all former decisions. The judges of the Supreme Court voted unanimously in favour of the Church and reversed the former judgement because the ban of the animal sacrifice would violate the first amendment.

The ruling received much attention (even the *New York Times* reported about this 'War of the Chickens') as it acknowledged that the group did indeed represent a religion.[36] Consequently, it strengthened the position of the Cuban Orisha priesthood and of other Caribbean religions in the USA that are confronted with similar stereotypical objections concerning their rituals. Within the Caribbean Diaspora in the USA countless ceremonies take place every year that could result in fines (plus high legal costs) for participants or even in their imprisonment.

When, in *The Times*, I read about the ruling of the Supreme Court while conducting research about the Orisha religion in Puerto Rico, I celebrated it as a victory for religious freedom in the USA. However, nothing is ever so straightforward, and, as I found out, the struggle continues today. Peñalver states that 'the treatment of adherents of the Santeria religion by some local communities provides a[n]…example of the vulnerability of minority religious groups to persecution through the majoritarian political process.'[37] In addition to the aforementioned case, he refers to other legal controversies prompted by these rituals as well as to an alleged anti-Santería bias of the State Department, which, in August 1997, denied thirty-one Cuban *babalawos* (high priests) entry into the United States for a conference in San Francisco.[38]

The most recent case is still ongoing: In 2006, Jose Merced, a priest of the Orisha religion in Texas, was told that animal sacrifice was against the city ordinance. When he applied for a permit to legally sacrifice animals referring to the Florida case, the city rejected the application—and he filed a lawsuit. The city argued that this case was different from the Florida one, as it does not concern land law but health and safety law. The city also had a problem with the perception that by permitting the sacrifice, they would endorse the tradition as an official religion.[39] As a compromise the city offered to allow the sacrifice, but only under certain conditions, for instance, by restricting sacrifices to birds and by limiting the size of the audience to twenty-six. However, these restrictions would have prevented a proper performance of the ritual and Merced rejected the offer.

Ultimately, it is not only the opposition of animal protection groups that affects the Caribbean religions. In the perception of most people animal sacrifice is just one step away from human sacrifice, a fact highlighted by the

---

[36] Peñalver, 'The Concept of Religion', 793.
[37] Peñalver, 'The Concept of Religion', 806.
[38] Peñalver, 'The Concept of Religion', 806, n. 106.
[39] Robinson, 'Santeria'.

so-called Matamoros incident. In 1989, the bodies of over a dozen murdered men were found in Matamoros, Mexico, near the border to Texas. The media immediately blamed these killings on Satanists, Witches, Voodoo priests, and so-called 'Santerians' (derived from Santería, the common label for the Orisha religion). Although the police investigation concluded that the killings were orchestrated by an individual hired by a criminal gang of drug runners and had nothing to do with any Caribbean religion, there was indeed a connection: the gang members had reportedly many times watched *The Believers* (1986), a movie that presents a random mixture of elements from the Orisha religion taken out of context, including human sacrifice.[40] To this day the popular media is full of false portrayals of Caribbean religions (for example, in countless episodes of US TV shows such as *Law and Order, CIS,* and *Bones*), which inevitably influence the audience in their perception of these religions.

## 4. SECOND EXAMPLE: THE HOLY WAR IN BRAZIL

A growing number of Brazilians belong to one of the numerous Protestant, mainly Charismatic and Evangelical churches (already slightly above fifteen per cent in the 2000 national census).[41] This demographic shift from Roman Catholicism to Protestantism, particularly Pentecostalism, affects the Afro-Brazilian religions insofar as it confronts them with an increasingly hostile attitude. Mainstream, mission-related churches have been relatively disinterested in local traditions and Brazilians usually have no problems with practising an Afro-Brazilian religion while belonging to the Roman Catholic Church. However, this coexistence of religious practices became problematic or even impossible when the neo-Pentecostal churches started their crusade against non-Christian rituals.

The largest neo-Pentecostal organization is the Igreja Universal do Reino de Deus (Universal Church of the Kingdom of God, short form: UCKG). The UCKG was founded in Rio de Janeiro in 1977 by Edir Macedo Bezerra who continues to be its leader. Today, the UCKG owns several TV and radio stations in Brazil and has more than three million members.[42] Several delegates of the Federal Congress, the Constituent National Assembly and other legislative assemblies at national and local level are UCKG members. But the UCKG is no longer only a Brazilian phenomenon; it is international and is currently active in more than thirty countries. Scholars regard the UCKG as

---

[40] Robinson, 'Santeria'.
[41] The figures for the religious self-identification of the 2010 census have not been announced yet.
[42] Oliva, *Ação Diabólica e Exorcismo*, 2–3.

the largest and most important new church in the so-called developing world today.[43]

At the centre of the UCKG theology is the idea that Satan and the demons constantly disturb 'the mental, physical, and spiritual order'.[44] The UCKG sees Satan and the demons as responsible for all the misery and evil in the world and it is the duty of everyone to 'liberate' the world—and oneself—from these demons by exorcizing them. All other religions, especially Afro-Brazilian religions, are guilty of bringing demons into the world. It is therefore crucial to convert everyone to the UCKD and to undermine other religions, particularly by putting an end to the Afro-Brazilian ceremonies.

An important element of the crusade against the Afro-Brazilian religious practices is the visual shock of blood sacrifice, hence the confrontation with photos of animal sacrifice. In a strategy similar to that used by Western animal protection groups, Macedo included in his manifesto *Orixás, caboclos & guías: deuses ou demônios?* colourful illustrations of altars and ceremonies of Afro-Brazilian religions with the intention of shocking the readers with images of blood and slaughtered animals, the 'Achilles heel' of Afro-Brazilian religions as Gonçalves da Silva writes.[45] In the book, Macedo outlined his doctrine and stated, for instance, that anyone who attends these ceremonies is an 'easy target' for demonic attacks. In support of his claims he adduced testimonies of converts to the UCKG who previously had attended Afro-Brazilian ceremonies. The book's biggest impact, however, was due to the photos of Afro-Brazilian rituals. Taken out of context, they confirmed the prejudice that Afro-Brazilian religions were 'bloody' and 'primitive', the paradigmatic other. Macedo even implied that not only animals were being sacrificed but human beings as well.

Although he had to remove some photos from a revised publication later on, they had a dramatic impact on the way the wider public perceived the Afro-Brazilian religions. Members of the UCKD attack members of the Afro-Brazilian religions in an increasingly aggressive manner. They try to intimidate participants in Afro-Brazilian rituals and prevent them from entering the compound where these rituals are performed: stones are thrown over the wall into the compound; hymns are broadcast via mobile loudspeakers outside the compound; occasionally, worshippers have even been kidnapped.[46] While there is currently no legal restriction to animal sacrifice in the course of religious ceremonies, the public perception of Afro-Brazilian religions increasingly associates them with 'savage', bloodthirsty, and demonic rituals.

Similar to the Orisha priesthood in the USA, Afro-Brazilian religious leaders have been using legal procedures to fight back even though these procedures

---

[43] Corten/Dozer/Oro, 'Introdução', 13.
[44] Oliveria, *Ação pastoral*, 112.
[45] Gonçalves da Silva, 'Neopentecostalismo e religiões afro-brasileiras', 214.
[46] See Gonçalves da Silva, 'Neopentecostalismo e religiões afro-brasileiras' for more details.

are time-consuming and costly. Nonetheless, some small victories have dem-onstrated the power of legal resistance and encouraged other priests to indict local Pentecostal pastors in court.[47]

## 5. ANIMAL SACRIFICE AS A SYMBOL OF THE PARADIGMATIC OTHER

These two examples present religious traditions in which animal sacrifice still plays an integral role. During their initiation, every new member has to learn the precise procedure of the sacrifice with all its gestures and body movements. The bodily reproduction of socially prescribed behaviour such as takes place in the sacrifice expresses the relationship between members of the community and their relationship with the spiritual beings.[48] Following a new initiate (to whom he refers as 'Carter') into the Orisha religion, Mason writes that 'while the initiation is the first time that Carter has witnessed the sacrifice of birds, he now is religiously bound to make regular sacrifices himself.'[49] During his initiation he has to acquire an understanding of how the gestures are used. If he succeeds, then he will begin 'to act socially within this religious commu-nity.'[50] Thus, this culturally specific behaviour marks an important distinction between initiated devotees and non-members, and expresses the collective identity of the community.

This community's interaction with other groups depends on the level of understanding—and of tolerance towards other religious practices. And here we need to turn back to the Christian perception of sacrifice, particularly its rejection during the Enlightenment. While Catholicism has shown some affin-ity to the ritual practice of West African religions and offered a framework for the creation of Afro-American religions, Protestantism did not demonstrate a similar tolerance. Camara even highlights 'the underlying Calvinist attitude of distrust of the world' that condemns all forms of religion that are structur-ally similar to Catholicism.[51] During the period of slavery in the USA, the evangelists, who were deeply influenced by the Calvinist world-view, almost inevitably perceived the West African religions with their complex rituals, cult

---

[47] One priest in Recife told me in 2010 that when he was initiated, he insisted on a bloodless initiation as he would otherwise become sick because of the smell of blood. His congregation performs rituals with cold offerings such as fruits, beverages, and fish as substitutes for warm (blood) sacrifice. However, this is an exception and has nothing to do with the crusade against Afro-Brazilian religions. The vast majority of communities still perform blood sacrifices.

[48] Mason, 'I Bow My Head', 35.

[49] Mason, 'I Bow My Head', 30.

[50] Mason, 'I Bow My Head', 31.

[51] Camara, 'Afro-American Religious Syncretism', 313.

of the dead, sacrifice, and mediation by religious intermediaries as a form of 'popery' and considered them 'to be heathenism of the worst sort', as Camara puts it.[52] Camara continues that:

> the stern character of Calvinism, with its avoidance of all undisciplined behaviour and sensorial gratification, coupled with the apostolic zeal, would seem to have led the Calvinist-oriented ministers and preachers of the Old South to oppose vigorously the this-worldly religious practice of the Africans, particularly in its more sensorially stimulating aspects, such as dancing.[53]

While Camara specifically looks at the attitude in the South of the USA during the nineteenth century, he argues that a similar opposition prevailed in other Protestant settings, for instance in the British part of the Caribbean. Despite the later revival of African patterns of worship, such as the cultivation of religious ecstasy in certain Protestant circles, Camara insists that 'it remains a fact that Protestantism hindered the survival on American soil of well defined, readily recognizable, full-blown retentions of African worship.'[54] While Brazilian Catholicism—and the same can be said about Spanish Catholicism during the colonial time in Cuba or French Catholicism in Haiti—allowed the coexistence of Christian and African religious content, particularly at the level of ritual and liturgy, Protestantism made it difficult from the beginning. Camara continues by stating that the ritual life of Brazilian Catholicism supported the 'preservation of ethnic identity for the minority group, within the larger process of national consolidation.'[55]

We therefore have two different cultural environments in the Americas: On the one hand, there is the (Catholic) attitude which, due to the recognition of ritual resemblance, allowed the upholding of sacrificial rituals throughout colonial suppression until modern times. On the other hand, there is the (Protestant) condemnation of ritual practices, including sacrificial rituals and the devotion to saints (or African deities which took their place in Afro-American religions), on the grounds of their resemblance to Catholic practices. In the USA, it is this latter attitude which has dominated.

However, people and their religions are no longer restricted to specific environments. People move and take their religious beliefs with them, as the Cuban Diaspora shows. In a new environment, immigrants may be confronted with an antagonistic attitude towards a ritualistic life that focuses specifically on sacrificial rituals. But religions migrate also and change the religious composition of a society, as the data about religious affiliation in Brazil indicates. Again, the outcome is the confrontation with an increasingly aggressive stance

---

[52] Camara, 'Afro-American Religious Syncretism', 314.
[53] Camara, 'Afro-American Religious Syncretism', 314.
[54] Camara, 'Afro-American Religious Syncretism', 315, n. 7.
[55] Camara, 'Afro-American Religious Syncretism', 316.

against ritualistic religious practices that even provokes open hostility towards minority religions. In both situations animal sacrifice presents a 'perfect' target for the antagonism with which devotees of Afro-American religions are confronted.

During the European conquest of America and other parts of the world, human sacrifice, often combined with cannibalism, which was seen as the sign of the 'barbaric other', played a central role in the colonial discourse.[56] The conquerors were not interested in the religious content of the rituals, but used the image of slaughtered human beings to create an unbridgeable distinction between the 'civilized' Europeans and the 'barbaric' others. The objective of the colonial discourse was 'to construe the colonized as a population of degenerate types on the basis of racial origin, in order to justify conquest and to establish systems of administration and instruction'.[57]

A similar construction of the other is now underway in the two exemplary cases discussed above. Stories about blood sacrifice provoke images playing with the 'terror of blood'—and as a consequence lead to the demarcation between 'us' and 'the other'. When Columbus arrived in the Caribbean, he encountered—as he expected—stories about cannibalism, but never found the cannibals: the natives always directed him to other islands, to other indigenous groups. In the end, the characterization of some groups as 'cannibals' and other groups as 'peaceful' became coterminous with the distinction between 'good natives' and 'bad natives'—the latter being the ones who resisted the European conquest.[58]

The history of encounters between Europeans and non-Europeans is full of such demarcations between 'us' and 'them', between the 'civilized' and the 'savages'. Today, animal sacrifice has taken over the role as the mark of the savage other. In a way, the antipathy of Protestantism towards ritualistic religions that was characteristic of the USA in the nineteenth century[59] laid the foundation for the increasing tendency to marginalize adherents of Afro-American religions, not only in the USA but also in Brazil where North American Pentecostalism fell upon fertile ground and developed escalating Brazilian versions.

In this process, the association of modernity with the rejection of sacrifice comes to the fore, particularly with respect to Brazil. Belonging to a country which some still regard as a threshold country, even though its economic power has already overtaken several industrialized nations, Brazilians, especially the aspiring middle classes, highlight their firm commitment to modernity whenever possible. This strong need to be seen as educated, modern, and civilized, encourages people to join the new Protestant churches in vast numbers.

---

[56] See Hulme, *Colonial Encounter*.
[57] Bhabha, 'The Other Question', 154.
[58] Hulme, *Colonial Encounter*.
[59] Camara, 'Afro-American Religious Syncretism'.

Alencar classifies these new Brazilian churches as 'modern Protestantism', and strictly distinguishes them from the Protestantism of the immigrants, the Protestantism of the missionaries, as well as Pentecostal Protestantism.[60] To be 'modern' in this sense means to be educated, neoliberal, anti-Catholic—and against the Afro-Brazilian rituals, particularly sacrifice.

In her study of the Ewe people in Ghana, Meyer outlines a similar associa-tion between modernity and a specific type of Christianity. She argues that the defining features of Ewe Christianity throughout the twentieth century have been education, the Christian religion, and 'civilization', and states that these elements 'were conceptualized as synonyms'.[61] Heaven is even depicted in a popular picture called *Judgement Day* 'as the ultimate fulfilment of moder-nity'.[62] In order to proceed forward towards modernity, one needs to move away from the traditional past and its rituals.

A similar attitude characterizes the situation in the USA where the continu-ing practice of rituals seemingly rooted in the past tests the limits of religious freedom. In this regard, the Brazilian context and the US context are identical. People oppose animal sacrifice not because they have actually attended such a ritual, but because they classify the ritual as 'savage', the sign of the other. By distancing themselves from these rituals, they are able to emphasize their own difference from the past and instead associate themselves with modernity.

However, those who oppose animal sacrifice often overlook that their under-standing of Afro-American religions and their adherents does not correspond to reality. Among the supporters and devotees of Afro-American religions are highly educated individuals, committed to defending their beliefs and prac-tices in every possible manner, as the many court cases conducted in the USA (and recently also in Brazil) demonstrate. While some are attracted precisely to the subversive otherness of Afro-American religions, most practitioners fight for the acceptance of their practices as a normal part of the religious pluralistic modernity. From a Brazilian perspective, therefore, their country can appear today as more committed to religious freedom and the rights of the individual—two important aspects of modern societies—than European countries. As one of my interviewees put it: In Brazil it is possible nowadays to practice one's faith while in Greece [the country of his forefathers] sacrificial rituals are prohibited.[63]

---

[60] Alencar, *Protestantismo Tupiniquium*, 151, appendix 1 with an overview.
[61] Meyer, *Translating the Devil*, 213.
[62] Meyer, *Translating the Devil*, 214, a copy of the picture is on the frontispiece inside Meyer's book.
[63] Interview in May 2010.

# 14

## Apocalypse and Sacrifice in Modern Film

### *American Exceptionalism and a Scandinavian Alternative*

#### Jon Pahl

Sacrifice offers a paradox.[1] On the one hand, a sacrifice is an ending. Something is selected to be burned, obliterated, killed, given up, or consumed. On the other hand, a sacrifice asserts a continuity. Some association, identification, *telos*, purpose, or rationale is asserted, and someone enacts the rite in light of that association or rationale.

A range of sacrifices exists in the history of religions that might be plotted on a continuum. On one end are physical sacrifices—food, animal, and human offerings or gifts, usually enacted within a ritual process. On the other end are rhetorical sacrifices—literary, imaginative, or psychological offerings (renunciation, self-giving, and so forth) that are invoked (in language or practice) for some broader purpose (see Hughes and Meszaros, Chapters 15 and 5, in this volume). Most sacrifices stretch across the continuum with varying emphases: the physical destruction of something is shrouded in rhetorically-laden explanations, incantations, or exhortations. The modern world, as many commentators note in this volume, has privileged rhetorical over physical sacrifice. Moderns have disdained the violence of so-called 'primitive' practice while simultaneously invoking 'sacrifice' for a host of causes. Often, what has been 'sacrificed' in the supposedly 'rational' sacrifice-that-is-not-a-sacrifice of modern cultures, in a way ironically reminiscent of the most primitive and appalling of archaic practices, is a human life, usually in battle on behalf of a nation and its 'glory'. But in any event

---

[1] I follow here especially Kathryn McClymond in 'The Nature and Elements of Sacrificial Ritual', who posits four elements of a sacrificial process that may be involved: selection, substitution, elimination, and identification. See for more detail my essay 'Sacrifice', in *The Routledge Companion to Religion and Film*.

the paradox of sacrifice endures: something must be destroyed (given up, offered, renounced) in order to secure some continuity (purpose, rationale). How does this paradox change when that which is ending, that which is sacrificed, is the world itself?

Obviously, any such 'sacrifice' exists on the imaginative or rhetorical end of the sacrificial continuum—although modern military capacities and persistent environmental exploitation have rendered such thought more literal than at any time in history. Yet the idea of the sacrifice of the world, which is one way to understand apocalypse, has been a persistent strain in religious thought around the globe.[2] For the sake of argument, two broad schools at the conjunction of sacrifice and apocalypse can be posited. The first—triumphal apocalyptic sacrifice—imagines the end of the world as a 'glorious appearing', a millennial horizon of triumph and glory where the sacrifice establishes some durable (if not infinite) continuity for the sacrificial community. The second—tragic apocalyptic sacrifice—posits an absolute ending. Only the moment of obliteration itself, the process of sacrifice, is real—and the sacrificial community is caught up in the killing or consumed in the process along with the rest of the world. Needless to say, both of these modes of thought depend upon the basic features of sacrifice (if not of religion), namely compression and displacement, or (more neatly), upon substitution: the world ends symbolically through the substitution of some object or icon (or, in the case of self-sacrifice, a subject) that depicts (enacts) the obliteration while paradoxically presuming an audience upon whom the substitution as enacted or narrated has an effect.[3]

Not surprisingly, given the power of both sacrifice and apocalyptic thought in the history of religions, these two dramatic alternatives have been vividly played out in modern cinema.[4] In the United States, the triumphal apocalyptic sacrifice has been dominant. From among many possible candidates, we shall trace a trajectory through *The Birth of a Nation* (1915), *Dr Strangelove* (1963), which reinforces the point through its satire, to *Armageddon* (1998) and the *Left Behind* trilogy (2001, 2002, 2005). In these movies, film-makers advocated for (or in the case of Kubrick's *Dr Strangelove*, critiqued—but in any event *engaged with*) what I have called elsewhere American 'innocent domination'.[5] That is, there are no real *victims* of either sacrifice or apocalypse. The sacrificed is either evil and guilty and thereby deserving of obliteration, or the sacrificed (or sacrificial community) is innocent, and in any

[2] On defining 'apocalypse', I follow Bernard McGinn of the University of Chicago, who puts it succinctly: 'Visions of the End—visions of terror and dread, visions of peace and of glory. Such is the stuff of apocalyptic tradition.' *Visions of the End*, 1.

[3] See Pahl, *Empire of Sacrifice*, for this methodological approach to 'religion'.

[4] I here move beyond the theological boundaries of Ostwalt, 'Apocalyptic'. See also his *Secular Steeples*, where he employs a more capacious approach.

[5] See again *Empire of Sacrifice*.

event emerges from the sacrificial apocalypse triumphant and in glory—as a hero if not as a god. In both versions, however, the sacrificial community is not *implicated* in the obliteration or violence or in any way morally responsible for it. Dominance is innocent. Transcendence trumps finitude. By way of contrast, Scandinavian film-makers have (perhaps in contradistinction to the American penchant for happy endings), stressed the mode of tragic apocalyptic sacrifice. From Ingmar Bergman's *The Seventh Seal* (1957), through Andrei Tarkovsky's *Offret* (1986), to Lars von Trier's *Melancholia* (2011), the inexorability of ending, and the complicity and powerlessness (if not responsibility) of humanity in the sacrificial obliteration, has been emphasized. Domination is not innocent (although it might be natural), and when it is unleashed it is absolute. Fragments endure, if anything. What the apocalypse unveils is not any glorious appearance or triumph through sacrifice, and certainly not some transcendence that trumps cataclysm. Sacrifice is costly, even total. The immanent frame, to use the famous phrase of Charles Taylor, is all.[6]

In the United States, as Harvard's President Drew Gilpin Faust has recently argued, 'death created the modern American nation'.[7] That is, out of the trauma of the Civil War, a civil religion emerged in America that systematically denied, sanitized, and in effect rendered 'innocent' the policy-based killing and total war that consumed the nation (yet, ironically, established its continuity). It is not surprising, then, that rhetorics and ritualized enactments of sacrifice 'upon the altar of the nation', as Yale's Harry Stout put it, became the prevailing trope to explain this trauma.[8] The religious language of 'sacrifice' shrouded dominance in sacred innocence; sanitizing an exercise of total war through what Wolfgang Palaver has aptly described in this volume (see Chapter 6) as the tendency *corruptio optimi pessima* ('the corruption of the best produces the worst'). This innocent domination dispersed, as I contend in my latest book *Empire of Sacrifice*, throughout American culture in the twentieth century. In Europe, aside from the fragmented nature of Continental (not to mention Scandinavian) history, there is lived memory of contested terrain; sacrifices for the nation have not produced glorious triumph, but brutal devastation. These broad trajectories hardly encompass a full historical explanation of the cinematic differences between American and Scandinavian sacrificial apocalypses. They do, however, raise fascinating theological and ethical questions about the operation of sacrifice in the context of modern thought, to which I shall return, briefly, at the end of this chapter.

[6] Taylor, *A Secular Age*.
[7] Faust, *This Republic of Suffering*.
[8] Stout, *Upon the Altar of the Nation*.

## 1. AMERICAN EXCEPTIONALISM AND TRIUMPHAL SACRIFICIAL APOCALYPSES

*The Birth of a Nation* was the first US blockbuster.[9] Produced and directed by D.W. Griffith and released in 1915, the film featured explicit language of 'sacrifice' that culminates in an apocalyptic vision of triumph where whites rule over blacks in a united American civil religion (with strong Christian imprint). The film, over three hours long, is in roughly two equal parts. Part One depicts scenes from the Civil War; Part Two treats Reconstruction. It was wildly popular with white audiences (while protested by the just-emerging NAACP). [10] Even more, *The Birth of a Nation* established the basic operation of sacrifice in American film, and the basic apocalyptic vision of triumph. It clarified cinematic conventions by which American dominance would be depicted as innocent that have largely endured to the present. Since I have written about it at length elsewhere, I shall summarize the plot here.[11] Three sacrifices mark the film. The first—of two white soldiers on the battlefield, one Northern, one Southern, Griffith depicts as a 'bitter, useless sacrifice' of war.[12] The second, of the virginal Flora—who leaps to her death to escape the amorous advances of 'Gus', a black suitor, Griffith calls a 'priceless sacrifice on the altar of an outraged civilization.'[13] Flora's death is consequently memorialized by the KKK (the heroes of the film) in a bloody flag ritual that sanctifies her death on behalf of innocence and purity. The third sacrifice, then, is that of 'Gus'. He is lynched by the KKK.[14] These various sacrifices lead to the climax of the film: a double wedding. Northerners marry Southerners, whites marry whites, and the film closes with an apocalyptic image of a wedding banquet presided over by a diaphanous Christ, as the title card reads: 'Liberty and union, one and inseparable, now and forever.' And ' "THE BIRTH OF A NATION or The Clansman." THE END.'[15]

Of course, D.W. Griffith did not invent the idea of sacrifice for the nation to produce peace, or of a triumphal sacrificial apocalypse. And, it should also be obvious that this trajectory of 'innocent domination' would take a long and convoluted course in American culture, with many permutations. But its durability can be made evident in the way it appears in a 1963 satire of the American civil religion—Stanley Kubrick's *Dr Strangelove: Or How I Learned to Stop Worrying and Love the Bomb*. The title is ironic. Kubrick was in fact quite worried about the bomb; the film ends with multiple scenes of exploding

---

[9] 'The Birth of a Nation'.
[10] Stokes, *D. W. Griffith's THE BIRTH OF A NATION*.
[11] See again Pahl, 'Sacrifice'.
[12] 'The Birth of a Nation', 63.
[13] 'The Birth of a Nation', 128.
[14] 'The Birth of a Nation', 120–128.
[15] Lang, 145. See also Salter, 'The Birth of a Nation as American Myth'.

thermonuclear devices. This apocalyptic outcome eventuates through a series of strategic blunders by the US military that stem from the willing sacrifice, albeit motivated by paranoia—of a single soldier. The film is a cutting satire of anti-communism and what Richard Hofstadter called (in an Oxford lecture) the 'paranoid style in American politics'.[16] And yet, as we shall see, the film invariably reinscribes links between sacrifice and apocalypse that renders US dominance innocent—while attempting at the same time to subvert that conjunction through what is in effect an American jeremiad.

The basic plot of the film traces how a rogue US General, Jack D. Ripper (Sterling Hayden), has sent a secret code to launch nuclear-armed B-52 bombers toward the Soviet Union. Ripper has also locked down the US Air Force base he commands (motto: 'Our Job is Peace'), cutting it off from communication and making it impossible to stop the attack unless he reverses the code. His second in command, Group Captain Lionel Mandrake (Peter Sellers), is a British Officer assigned to Ripper's base who eventually (after an attack on the base by US Army commandos) secures the code when Ripper kills himself (a cinematic 'sacrifice'). Mandrake then deciphers and sends the code (in a hilarious collect call from a phone booth to the White House) to the US President, Merkin Muffley (also played by Sellers). Muffley and his administration are gathered in the Washington, DC, 'war room', which is dominated by the jingoistic anti-communist ranting of General Buck Turgidson (George C. Scott). Over Turgidson's objections (he calculates that a pre-emptive attack by the US against the Soviets would lead to the deaths of 'ten million, twenty million, tops!' of US citizens), Muffley is able to negotiate a deal with the Russians to shoot down or otherwise stop the planes from delivering their payloads. But one plane (flown by Major T.J. 'King' Kong—played by Slim Pickens) is only damaged, not destroyed, and it approaches unabated one of the slated targets inside Russia. When the bomb bay of his B-52 jams, Pickens, cowboy hat on his head, climbs into the bay and, sitting astride the warhead in a now iconic image, unleashes it and rides it downward toward its target in yet another giddy cinematic sacrifice that triggers eventually the closing scene of nuclear annihilation. In the meantime, the Muffley Administration has turned for advice to Dr Strangelove, a former (and quite unrepentant) Nazi (also played by Sellers). Strangelove counsels that the US can build underground communities for public elites (such as those gathered in the war room) in deep mineshafts that will survive until the fallout dissipates. Each community will feature a ratio of one male to ten females, to insure ample breeding, with the females selected for their 'sexual attributes and attractiveness'.[17]

Now, the film's satire is rich. The apocalypse will come through a combination of policy and an accident, but will depend upon the willingness of soldiers

[16] Hofstadter, 'The Paranoid Style in American Politics'.
[17] *Dr. Strangelove* (DVD). See also Chernus, *Dr. Strangegod*.

(and others) to sacrifice for the national cause. The policy here under critique is of course nuclear 'deterrence'. The accident is the deployment of technology against humanity that allows a General like Ripper to gain control of the system. Yet what motivates Ripper—undoubtedly the oddest element in the film to most viewers—is the key to its sacrificial motif. Ripper is convinced that the Russians are poisoning Americans' 'precious bodily fluids' through fluoridation of US water sources. Motivating the apocalypse—the sacrifice of the world, is a purity system. The entire arms race is risking the sacrifice of the world on behalf of ideological (and biological) purity. Put more vividly: the arms race leading to Armageddon is a massive phallic undertaking (the imagery is simply unmistakable throughout the film) to assert male control over 'female' bodily fluids. Hence, the utopian continuity that Dr Strangelove recommends as a secular version of the kingdom of God—ten attractive females for every male in the 'deep mineshafts' of former coal mines (evoking the 70 virgins of Islamic lore decades later)—is no coincidence. Such a 'vision' is in fact the logic of the whole. The film thus concludes not only with the images of exploding thermonuclear devices, but to the soundtrack of a romantic ballad, 'We'll Meet Again'. The song was made famous by Vera Lynn in 1939, as an ode to soldiers going off to fight in the Second World War.

Inevitably, in other words, *Dr Strangelove* reinscribes American 'innocent domination' and exceptionalism, albeit with an important twist. If in the typical plot of exeptionalism, America is exceptionally good, in this version, America is exceptionally bad (stupid, incompetent, etc). Inverting the dualistic paradigm does not change it, as Sacvan Bercovitch argued many years ago in *The American Jeremiad*.[18] Jeremiads seldom solve the problem they identify. They do serve to support the righteousness of the Jeremiah (as in fact this film did for Stanley Kubrick—in effect establishing his reputation as an *auteur*). The moral superiority of the film-maker trumps the stupidity and/or moral craveness of military and political leaders. Yet within *Dr Strangelove* any moral responsibility for averting apocalypse remains uncertain; viewers are given no clear strategic (or religious) alternatives. The 'sacrifice' of their cash in exchange for the thrill of entertainment (or joy at the folly of others) renders the apocalypse cinematically spectacular but not emotionally cathartic in any but an ironic sense. Essentially a nihilist satire, for all of its self-righteous critique *Dr Strangelove* leaves its viewers (most of them Americans) quite contentedly alive and well. Every viewer who laughed at the film's humor in 1963 could still enjoy the booming benefits of life in a burgeoning empire with expanding military (and market) might. The triumphal sacrificial apocalypse—the innocence and purity underneath American dominance—endures, albeit now in the cultural product of a film rather than directly through policy, civil religion, or traditional religions (the latter being all but absent from the film).

---

[18] Bercovitch, *The American Jeremiad*.

Consequently, after the end of the Cold War, American film-makers struggled to identify a new enemy, but the paradigm of the triumphal sacrificial apocalypse remained largely unchanged. For one example, consider briefly the sci-fi thriller *Armageddon* (1998), which revives and reapplies the old 'birth of a nation' paradigm in quite direct ways.[19] An asteroid headed toward Earth threatens humanity with annihilation in eighteen days. The only solution, NASA astrophysicists conclude, is to land a crew on the asteroid, drill into its core (800 feet down), plant a nuclear device, and detonate it. This will split the asteroid into bits that will bypass the earth and drift harmlessly into space. To implement this solution, NASA (with ample help from the US military, the FBI, and even the Russians) enlists Harry Stamper (Bruce Willis) and his team of oil-rig operators. Harry proves to be up (so to speak) to the task: he designs and deploys a drill that, carried in a space shuttle along with his crew through many and various perils, lands on the asteroid and creates the hole in which a nuclear device can be placed. But due to damage from a collision in space, the nuclear device cannot be remotely detonated. One individual must remain behind on the asteroid to detonate the bomb. Harry tricks his future son-in-law, A.J., with whom he has been wrapped in a ceaseless (and annoying) Oedipal struggle regarding his young daughter, the theologically named Grace (Liv Tyler), into allowing him to remain behind. As the shuttle escapes the asteroid, Harry valiantly sacrifices himself by detonating the weapon—saving all 'mankind', as the film frequently reminds viewers. The movie then concludes with the wedding of A.J. and Grace, complete with an iconic image of Harry placed beside the altar in the church bestowing his remote, if not eternal, blessing on their union.

Now, starting with the end of the film, the continuity between *The Birth of a Nation* and the genre of triumphal sacrificial apocalypse in *Armageddon* is evident enough. Both films conclude with weddings—a standard (Christian) apocalyptic metaphor (heaven as a wedding banquet). Both proceed through sacrifices—Harry's self-sacrifice is joined by the loss of three other expedition members, along with countless nameless others who are all but forgotten in the glory of triumph (the film depicts massive asteroid fragments devastating first New York City, then Southeast Asia, and finally Paris). Both films celebrate the civil religion. *Armageddon* is replete with images of American flags, red, white, and blue patches, soldiers and astronauts, and all of the trappings of US military power and technological sophistication. And while the enemy in *Armageddon* is merely a 'natural' catastrophe, as opposed to the moral catastrophe of war depicted in *The Birth of a Nation*, the religious resources mobilized to 'save' the world remain sacrifice on behalf of the nation (empire/world), now not only through white, masculine power to preserve domestic purity, but also through the nation's 'innocent' (and even salvific) nuclear weapons!

[19]  *Armageddon* (DVD).

If *Armageddon* can show how durable the genre of triumphal sacrificial apocalypse is in America, even in its 'secular' form, the *Left Behind* series (2000–2005) can show the ongoing appeal of the traditional religious version. In *Left Behind: The Movie* (2001), *Left Behind II: Tribulation Force* (2002), and *Left Behind: World at War* (2005), the basic plot mechanisms of triumphal sacrificial apocalypse are evident.[20] In all three films Kirk Cameron stars as the journalist (and recent convert to Christianity) 'Buck Williams'. Williams' nemesis is no less than the Antichrist, Nicolae Carpathia (played by Gordon Currie). Journalist Williams is joined by pilot Rayford Steele (Brad Johnson), and his daughter, Chloe (Chelsea Noble), among others, in the 'Tribulation Force'. The 'Tribulation Force' is the clandestine cadre of those 'left behind' after the Rapture. All of them have converted to Jesus after becoming convinced that they are living in the 'last days'. Their mission is now to battle against the Antichrist. The apocalyptic frame is obvious. Within the first twenty minutes of the first film, all those who profess Jesus Christ as Lord (and believe it in their heart) are raptured from the earth—leaving behind their clothes and their loved ones. Among the raptured are all children under the age of thirteen or so, who are declared 'innocent'. Those left behind were somehow stuck in sin. The *Left Behind* series features the classic apocalyptic theme of dualism: Christians must do battle against evil.

If these films are obviously apocalyptic, the way they operate sacrificially might need clarification.[21] There is, first, a process of selection. All non-Christians (and Christians are a very narrowly-defined, 'evangelical' type) are suitable for sacrifice—are 'left behind' to become pawns (or opponents) of the Antichrist. This includes all believers in religions other than Christianity, and especially Jews.[22] There is, second, substitution at the core of the plot. All actors (and viewers) must decide: do they confess 'Jesus Christ as Lord' or do they seek 'peace' through the promises of the Antichrist? At core, actors and viewers are asked to identify with a particular symbolic mode of transcendent authority. Do they side with 'God' or with 'Satan'. That 'God', conveniently, operates largely through US citizens, while Satan identifies largely with vague agents of globalization renders this choice a rather easy one for most American Christian viewers. Nevertheless, third, the film invites its audience to consider the possibility that God requires sacrifice—even the sacrifice of the entire world. The key (Christian) actors must all give up something tangible (family, comfort, security) in exchange for their eternal reward—while those actors who depict the legions supporting the Antichrist imagine that they are fulfilling their self-interest when (of course) they are in fact participating in

---

[20] *Left Behind* (DVD); *Left Behind II: Tribulation Force* (DVD); *Left Behind: World at War* (DVD).
[21] Following McClymond (see n. 1).
[22] See Ariel, 'How Are Jews and Israel Portrayed'.

their own damnation—not to mention bringing about a Third World War. Literally millions die in these films. The last two films were released post 9/11 and clearly evoke this American trauma, with posters of the 'missing' and shrines set up in churches to mourn the loss. Yet the sacrifice God requires is even subtler than these massive acts of genocide and war-making: 'Christians' all must parrot key phrases (especially biblical verses about 'prophecy') that signify their 'acceptance' of Jesus. Their independence (autonomy, will, reason) is subsumed under projections of transcendent authority (discourses) that demonstrate their new status as Christians. Finally, the films seek to produce a catharsis within or identity-solidarity among viewers (an entire documentary has traced 'conversions' due to the novels and films, and the website associated with the series invites 'testimonies' from visitors about how the series has 'changed your life').[23] The films compress fear of globalizing economic (and military) forces, while reassuring viewers that the United States will, with God's help, triumph over evil (the last convert in the series of films is the US President). The sacrifices will have been worth it, because they bring about (after the seven years of Tribulation) the millennial rule of God's chosen—the kingdom of God.

Now, to recognize the ways in which these films reinforce American exceptionalism and innocent domination should not take much deciphering. President George W. Bush (and before him Ronald Reagan) consistently depicted the United States pitted against an 'axis of evil', or an 'evil empire', respectively. Americans (if not their government) are, like every child in the *Left Behind* series, innocent. And yet at the disposal of this 'Tribulation Force' (largely Americans) are rather astonishing weapons. The characters lie, steal, misrepresent their intentions, and (in the last film especially) have recourse to weapons that belie any actual innocence, and in fact produce domination through force. As Amy Johnson Frykholm has put it, 'The world's believers embrace without question American Protestant language, methods, and beliefs. When a character becomes a part of the Tribulation Force—whether he or she is Chinese, Egyptian, or Greek—the Tribulation Force's bunker in the United States becomes his or her second home.'[24] These 'Christians', furthermore, are technologically adept, strategically sophisticated, and because their end is innocent (nothing less than 'God's kingdom') can use any means necessary to insure their triumph. And if, by chance, they fail—some supernatural remedy will miraculously appear to intervene. The world is suitable for sacrifice. The Third World War rages—with the deaths (presumably) of millions, if not more, as the film series ends. But good Christians will inevitably be safe and endure—even eternally. Theirs is a triumph that transcends time. One might even call it a manifest destiny.

---

[23] *Left Behind*, official website.
[24] Frykholm, 'What Social and Political Messages', 176.

## 2. TRAGIC SACRIFICIAL APOCALYPSES IN
## SCANDINAVIAN FILM

In contrast to this triumphalist scenario, we can turn to several films produced in Scandinavia. As I have argued elsewhere, any death on a screen can be a sacrifice, since it represents a substitute (an actor) whose selection (by the filmmaker) to be killed is symbolically offered to the audience to compress and channel their desires and/or fears. This displacement of emotion into the vehicle of the cinematic plot, and any resulting catharsis—which includes identification with (or abhorrence at) the victim or object *and* association of some emotion or attribute that serves as motive or rationale for the killing—serves both to stabilize social order and (selectively) to critique and transform it. Reel sacrifices, no less than 'real' ones, offer an ending and a continuity.[25]

It is important to recall the durability of this sacrificial paradox as we turn to three Scandinavian films that pose a stark contrast to the triumphal sacrificial apocalypses traced in the American films above. The first film, *The Seventh Seal* (1957), is widely regarded as Ingmar Bergman's masterpiece.[26] Its plot is famous (and subject to satire by Monty Python and many others).[27] A medieval Knight, Antonius Block, and his squire, Jons, have just returned to their native Sweden from the Crusades. Sweden is beset by the Black Plague, and on their way home to Block's castle the two negotiate various encounters. Most notably, Block meets a figure dressed in black who announces himself as 'Death'. Block challenges 'Death' to a chess match—and the plot proceeds to its inevitable ending.

The apocalyptic theme is announced in the opening moments of the film. Ominous and discordant trumpet chords (from the soundtrack by Erik Nordgren) crescendo to a tympani roll and a choir singing in fortissimo: '*Dies irae, dies illa*' ('Day of Wrath, That Day'). This thirteenth-century Latin hymn was used in the Roman Catholic *Requiem Mass* until Vatican II. A voice-over then intones a passage from the Apocalypse of John (8:1–2): 'And when the lamb opened the seventh seal, there was silence in heaven about a half an hour. And the seven angels which had the seven trumpets prepared themselves to sound.' This cryptic passage will be repeated in the penultimate scene of the film, in Block's castle where he and Jons and all but three of the other main characters in the film are met by 'Death' which claims them once and for all. Bergman's theme is the end of the world (as various characters proclaim throughout the film).

---

[25] See Pahl, 'Sacrifice'. For further insight along these methodological lines, see Miles, *Seeing and Believing*; and especially Lyden, *Film as Religion*.
[26] Bergman, *The Seventh Seal* (DVD). Among the literature on Bergman, I found particularly helpful Blake, 'Ingmar Bergman, Theologian?'
[27] See my interpretation of Monty Python's *Quest for the Holy Grail* in Pahl, *Shopping Malls*, 48–50.

If the theme of apocalypse announces itself directly in *The Seventh Seal*, the way the film operates sacrificially is apparent more indirectly. Obviously, with the Crusades as background, the idea of killing, dying, or giving up something for God is present in the film. Yet contrary to the American penchant to glorify sacrifice (or ridicule it), Bergman's film questions it. The key character here is the squire, Jons. He describes his time as a Crusader: 'For ten years we sat in the Holy Land and let snakes bite us, flies sting us, wild animals eat us, heathens butcher us, the wine poison us, the women give us lice, the lice devour us, the fevers rot us—all for the glory of God. Our crusade was so stupid that only a real idealist could have thought it up!'[28] Sacrifice is folly. It cannot produce triumph over death. The ending is absolute. Jons' last words in the film, as he dies, are: 'I shall be silent, but under protest.'[29]

But the most directly sacrificial scene in the film (aside from the penultimate scene in the castle) is the sacrifice of a 'witch'.[30] As René Girard has contended, scapegoating and sacrifice have close connections, and this scene lends itself particularly well to a Girardian reading.[31] The Knight and Jons first encounter a young girl chained outside a church, where they learn that she is accused of 'carnal intercourse with the Evil One', and is to be burned 'to keep the Devil away from the rest of us.' She is a scapegoat—one selected for sacrifice whose killing is to be protective (we will see this theme again in *Offret*). Then, in a later scene, Jons and Block are present for the sacrifice. The girl, who Block learns is fourteen, is hoisted on a ladder to a pyre that is lighted. The girl moans, Block offers her a 'potion' to kill the pain, and Jons then initiates the crucial dialogue with the Knight:

Jons: What does she see? Can you tell me?

Knight: (shakes his head) She feels no more pain.

Jons: You don't answer my question. Who watches over that child? Is it the angels, or God, or the Devil, or only the emptiness? Emptiness, my lord!

Knight: This cannot be.

Jons: Look at her eyes, my lord. Her poor brain has just made a discovery. Emptiness under the moon.

Knight: No.

Jons: We stand powerless, our arms hanging at our sides, because we see what she sees, and our terror and hers are the same. (an outburst) That poor child.
I can't stand it, I can't stand it![32]

---

[28] *Seventh Seal, The Script*, 8–9, 12.
[29] *Seventh Seal, The Script*, 47.
[30] DVD, 35:–37:00; 72:–75:14.
[31] See among his many writings, Girard, *Violence* and *Scapegoat*.
[32] *Seventh Seal, The Script*, 36.

Jons' repulsion is intended to be the viewer's. The cinematic sacrifice unveils the way religion sacrifices innocence to illusions of purity in an attempt to stabilize the social order. The scapegoating is not only violent and unjust, but sadistic and cruel. It is as morally repellent as it is ineffective. Facing the end, even war heroes are powerless.

So the film aptly moves toward its conclusion: the death of the Knight and his squire in a castle, as the Knight's wife reads from the Apocalypse of John. This is another sacrifice, at least implicitly, and it is definitely a revelation. The final scene of the film (one of the most famous in the history of cinema) is thus a vision by the character Jof, who is an actor—a substitute within the substitutions. It is a *danse macabre* across a cloudy ridge. Death leads a procession, and Jof explains 'I see them, Mia! I see them! Over there against the dark, stormy sky. They are all there...and Death, the severe master, invites them to dance....They dance away from the dawn and it's a solemn dance toward the dark lands, while the rain washes their faces and cleans the salt of the tears from their eyes.'[33] This aquatic apocalyptic image (see Apocalypse of John 21:4) is as close as the film gets to transcendence, along with an earlier pastoral (eucharistic) scene when Jof and Mia shared some wild strawberries and milk with the Knight and Jons. Yet even this 'triumph' is undercut in the end. As Jof shares with his wife what he sees, Mia utters the last words in the film, while smiling: 'you with your visions and dreams.'

The film thus reveals a universal fate—an absolute ending. It evokes not only the end of each individual, but also the end of the world. The actors quote directly from the most famous of Christian apocalyptic sources, and several actors throughout remind viewers that 'the plague' of death, no doubt in part a metaphor used by Bergman to evoke both the *Shoah* and the threat of nuclear weapons—is ruthless in its selection. The sacrifice of the world is the dread Bergman wants to invoke. And the film operates through sacrifice. It substitutes actors with whom viewers are invited to identify (or to reject) who 'die' on the screen, and it does so in ways which invite associations that compress and displace fear and desire in the context of a cinematic plot. To be sure, this tragic sacrificial apocalypse asserts a continuity along with the ending: the film endures, and it presumes an audience existing to view it! But the continuity is hardly triumphal. It is not that innocence is cathartically restored, much less that dominance is masked or legitimized. What endures are moments, or perhaps art itself—and even that is, in the end, recognized as a matter of 'visions and dreams'. Or as Bergman put it in his memoirs: 'I believe a human being carries his or her own holiness, which lies within the realm of the earth; there are no other-worldly explanations.'[34] There is only the immanent frame; any sacrifice is costly, and moments constitute the only millennium.

---

[33] *Seventh Seal, The Script,* 47.
[34] Bergman, *Images,* 238.

In *The Sacrifice* (Swedish—*Offret*, 1986), Russian director Andrei Tarkovsky (filming in Sweden with Swedish actors) reinforces this genre. The plot of the film features an aging actor, Alexander (Erland Josephson), who faces the end of the world in a nuclear war. The film opens with credits playing over a close-up of Leonardo da Vinci's *The Adoration of the Magi*, while Bach's *St. Matthew Passion* plays on the soundtrack. A religious context is clear. The next scene shows Alexander planting a 'tree' on the Swedish coastline along with his young, mute son (called 'Little Man'). In fact, though, the 'tree' is dead—and Alexander and his son merely prop it up on the beach with stones. Alexander then tells his son a story about a Russian Orthodox monk who did something similar with a dead tree, and then told his protégé to water the 'tree' every day. After three years, it came to life. The father and son are then visited by a philosophically-inclined postman on a bicycle, Otto (Allan Edwall). After a lengthy conversation, Alexander adjourns to his beloved but secluded beach house, where he is to celebrate his birthday with his family and friends. While in the house, Alexander and his family are startled by bright lights and the sounds of jets flying over. This signals the beginning of a nuclear war, which is also announced on radio and television before communication and electricity ceases. The characters respond very differently to this news, and through a series of dreams, prayers, and conversations, Alexander becomes convinced that if he sleeps with a local 'witch' (who happens to be one of his servants), and then sacrifices everything he loves, he can prevent the apocalypse. He follows this plan. He sleeps with the 'witch', after threatening to kill himself if she refuses him, and when his dream to forestall the apocalypse appears to have succeeded the next morning (electricity has returned), he then creates a diversion to send his family away from the house. After the house is empty of people, Alexander follows through on his sacrifice by setting the house on fire in a conflagration that consumes it and all of its contents. As the film ends, Alexander is taken away in an ambulance, now himself mute (apparently by choice). The 'Little Man' is then seen watering the 'tree', and he breaks his silence to utter the last words in the film: 'In the beginning was the Word. Why was that, Papa?'

Now, on a literal level, the sacrifice appears effective: the end of the world is avoided. In his memoirs, Tarkovsky explained the film as follows:

> Has man any hope of survival in the face of all the patent signs of impending apocalyptic silence? Perhaps an answer to that question is to be found in the legend of the parched tree, deprived of the water of life, on which I based this film which has such a crucial place in my artistic biography: The Monk, step by step and bucket by bucket, carried water up the hill to water the dry tree, believing implicitly that his act was necessary and never for an instant wavering in his belief in the miraculous power of his own faith in God. He lived to see the miracle: one morning the tree burst into life, its branches covered with young leaves. And that 'miracle' is surely no more than the truth.[35]

---

[35] Tarkovsky, *Sculpting in Time*, 229, as cited by Tolleson, 'Materialism and the Messiah'.

Tarkovsky clearly had apocalypse on the mind (he was terminally ill while making the film, and died shortly after completing it). And as the title of the film suggests, its theme is sacrifice: 'I am interested above all in the character who is capable of sacrificing himself and his way of life.'[36] Yet as this quote reveals, this is the characteristically modern notion of sacrifice—of *self*-sacrifice.[37] Such a tragic outcome is hardly a triumph. A more patient viewing of the film, then (and it does require patience—only 120 cuts, less than one per minute, mark the more than two-hour film), reveals its tragic apocalyptic dimensions. It is no coincidence that Tarkovsky called his memoirs *Sculpting in Time*.[38] His cinema bears the quality of a sculpture—*mise en scène* replaces *montage* as the critical cinematic device. Every image is a potential tableau or icon. 'Art', the film-maker wrote, 'is called to express the absolute freedom of man's spiritual potential.'[39]

Yet this freedom to sculpt is *in time*; indeed, is fixed by it. The crucial cinematic sacrifice is, of course, the final scene—the burning of the house. It is a famous scene; in the first take, the camera jammed as the fire blazed, and the house had to be rebuilt hastily on set. According to Bart Tolleson, the scene clarifies the main point of the film: Tarkovksy thinks Westerners have been deadened by 'materialism', and must give up attachment to things in order to encounter spirit.[40] There is much to commend in this reading of the film, but it is also a bit too parochial. Technology does invariably interfere with human realization. Tarkovsky lingers throughout the film on lamps, telephone poles, bicycles—the tools that humanity uses. When the planes fly over signalling the coming end, though, Tarkovsky uses a simple symbol to represent what is lost. A pitcher of milk sitting on the edge of a hutch is rattled by the sonic boom. It slides over the side, and crashes on the hard wood floor. The milk slowly spreads out in a white stain—innocence lost—against the black floor. This is not matter as evil; this is matter lost—matter sacrificed; matter broken. This cinematic sacrifice thus precedes Alexander's pledge to give up everything he loves to forestall the apocalypse in what is, in fact, a prayer. But this prayer of an atheist is inherently destructive. He pledges to destroy in order to save. The point is complex. Tarkovsky seems to be saying that desire for life (even altruistic) destroys; every gift is a sacrifice (see scene three in the film). Human beings can't simply let things be; the drive to control, to fix, to dominate is too insistent. Hence, to get his way, Alexander contrives to have sex with his servant, the iconically named Maria. He does so by threatening suicide with a pistol. The act itself is a moment of transcendence in the film: the couple literally levitate while making

[36] Tarkovsky, *Sculpting in Time*, 217.
[37] See Meszaros, 'Sacrifice and the Self', Chapter 5, in this volume.
[38] Tarkovsky, *Sculpting in Time*.
[39] Tarkovsky, *Sculpting in Time*, 237.
[40] See again Tolleson, 'Materialism and the Messiah'.

love. But it is all founded on coercion and delusion. Maria seems moved by pity—
*and* moved to keep Alexander from killing himself with the gun. And Alexander
thinks he is having sex with a witch (a variation on the theme of the witch sleeping with Satan that appeared in *The Seventh Seal*). He is, furthermore, betraying
his wife (there are intimations earlier in the film that his wife has also betrayed
Alexander). Alexander's sacrifice thus preserves a continuity, but it is founded in
tragedy: delusion, betrayal, and destruction. He destroys his house and silences
himself. The survivors are left to pick up for themselves in the midst of fragments,
afterward, with only a dead tree to 'water'. and a question: 'In the beginning was
the Word; why was that, Papa?' This is a fragile hope, indeed.

Tarkovsky worked, of course, in a material medium: film is light, a form of
matter, on celluloid. And the film-maker is too self-aware (some critics think *far*
too self-absorbed) to forget this fact. Rather than just a critique of materialism,
then, Tarkovsky's film affirms the tragic dimension of art. A miracle is the result
of hard work, persistence, attention to detail—watering a parched tree every day
in the hope that it will bloom. There is spiritual truth *in the process* of living, but
any triumph beyond tragedy is a fragile bloom. There is da Vinci, and Bach, and
Tarkovsky—but even sculpting in time is, finally, *in time*: Alexander's sacrifice has
an immanent horizon, and the apocalypse reveals the inexorability of finitude.
There is no nation or hero, much less any transcendent authority, and certainly no
technology, that saves the world. It is even unclear in the end whether Alexander's
sacrifice might be nothing more than a futile, and quite crazy, gesture; a 'beginning' (or continuity) that is mere words, mere acting, mere art—as witness to the
inexorable fate that is the lot of all the living. What is 'revealed' in the film is the
viewer's *perception* of sacrifice (and indeed of art itself)—and dread at the end of
it all, with only a 'perhaps', a fragile hope, at best. The last words of Tarkovsky's
memoirs sum it up well:

> Finally, I would enjoin the reader—confiding in him utterly—to believe that the one
> thing that mankind has ever created in a spirit of self-surrender is the artistic image.
> *Perhaps* the meaning of all human activity lies in artistic consciousness, in the point-
> less and selfless creative act? *Perhaps* our capacity to create is evidence that we our-
> selves were created in the image and likeness of God? [emphasis added][41]

*Offret* is the film-maker's requiem. It is a warning to humanity to live respon-
sibly and creatively, to be open to fragile hope, even while always being aware
of one's own capacity for (and complicity with) destruction, deceit, betrayal,
and delusion. The potential to stoke apocalyptic fire is woven into the heart of
even the best that humanity can do—the altruistic self-sacrifice on behalf of
another.

These same themes appear in vivid form in Lars von Trier's recent film
*Melancholia*. As of this writing, the film has not yet been released on DVD, so

[41] Tolleson, 'Materialism and the Messiah', 241.

careful study of it is difficult, and our reading of it will be brief, but the significance of the film as a variant on the genre of tragic sacrificial apocalypse
is evident. [42] That the film is a tragedy is announced in its first sequence. Von
Trier depicts the end of the world in super slow motion. No one will survive this
ending. A rogue planet, previously hidden behind the sun, named 'Melancholia',
will collide with Earth, destroying all life. This is clarified through a long opening sequence in which the film speed is slowed to such a pace that the actors
do not seem to be moving, but almost imperceptibly do so. Each of the main
turning points in the film is foreshadowed: a wedding banquet that goes hor-
ribly wrong; a trust in science that will prove errant; and a cataclysm that will
obliterate everything. 'Melancholia', the planet, is a Kierkegaardian metaphor
for the experience of dread, depression, and fear. And such dread will meet all
the living: each will meet an ending in a 'dance of death', as the film explicitly
announces (invoking Bergman). That viewers survive, of course, is the beauty
of the film: the end is coming—all will be sacrificed on the screen, but the film-
maker depicts it with such skill that one is carried along despite knowing how
it is going to end, enthralled by the grace of the moment, the play of light on
screen, and the actors who compress a variety of responses to the end and invite
the viewer's identification. Any 'catharsis' that the film promotes, then, is simply
the experience of beauty that the film can convey. One knows the ending from
the beginning. It is the process, the immanent frame, that is the product that
the viewer is invited to invest in and enjoy. There is no nation, no savior, on the
horizon—only the moment of beauty, and the possibility (perhaps) of being (for
a time) a co-creator, through the substitutions of art and the invitation to recognize our mutual fragility.

## 3. SACRIFICE AND APOCALYPSE IN MODERN CINEMA: THE MOBILITY OF RELIGION

These films all arose along with the American empire, which for the last decade
has been entwined in the so-called 'Global War on Terror'. In this policy, nothing less than terror itself, dread, melancholia, the fear of death and evil, is the
enemy. And 'sacrifice', notably of soldiers in war, has been the requisite means
to the stated, apocalyptic end: the triumph of good over evil.[43] In America, a
civil religion has arisen that is driven by what sociologist Richard Fenn has
identified as 'dreams of glory: a global crusade against evil, in which victory is
always imminent ... is a fantasy ... that dies hard.'[44] As we have seen, a stream

---

[42]  See Pahl, "Melancholia".
[43]  See among others Denton-Borhaug, *U.S. War—Culture, Sacrifice and Salvation*.
[44]  Fenn, *Dreams of Glory*, 1.

of popular films in America has reinforced this fantasy of apocalyptic glory through sacrifice, while another stream—evident above all in Scandinavian films—has countered it by accenting the tragic elements at the conjunction of sacrifice and apocalypse. This is not to suggest that Scandinavians occupy some moral ground above history. It is to suggest that film-makers can be self-critical in their productions, as can viewers, and produce (and consume) works that do not sell a cheap innocence or conform to fantasies of dominance.[45]

Over the past century, film-makers have come to function as shamans. This points us to the mobility of religious discourses and practices. Sacrifice—once restricted to archaic and traditional religions, now operates on behalf of the nation, and through the media of film. It is surely the case, as Johannes Zachhuber has offered in this volume (Chapter 2), that 'Sacrifice represents religion as we no longer know it.' But as Marcel Gauchet has suggested, 'We have broken away from religion only by finding substitutes for it at every level.'[46] Film can uncritically promote myths (and rituals) as brutal as any of the most 'primitive' practices. We need, in short, reasoned arguments (and entertaining ones are the best of all) for the ways religious traditions (including sacrificial and apocalyptic constructions) might best interact with public life and policy. Given such reasoning—in print, film, television, and all other forms of media—we then have some grounds on which to choose what kind of a society we want to live in. It is unlikely through this critical process of difficult choices that we will find some apocalyptic revelation of a final solution. More likely are quotidian triumphs; where we discover how blessed is the ordinary—how light, image, and sound on screen can communicate the truth of our mutual fragility, and yet also convey the possibility of grace, to those with eyes to see, and ears to hear.

---

[45] See on this theme Stout, *Democracy and Tradition*.
[46] Gauchet, *Disenchantment of the World*, 6.

# 15

## Human Sacrifice and the Literary Imagination[1]

### Derek Hughes

At a recent conference on the work of René Girard, Jon Pahl repeatedly described the USA as 'sacrificing' its enemies in Afghanistan and elsewhere.[2] While I have no quarrel with this usage, it seemed to me to be new. Granted, the Aztecs and many other cultures sacrificed their prisoners of war, but has not our own culture understood sacrifice in battle as the noble selflessness of those who die for their country? As an expression of the principle that it is sweet and fitting—*Dulce et decorum*—to die for one's country? During the First World War, *The Times* was full of stories of sacrifice in battle, but not of the enemy. For example, the headline 'The Sacrifice of the Peerage' laments the death in battle of forty-five heirs to noble titles and estates.[3] Yet this, in turn, showed a shift in the use of the term. The idea of self-immolation in battle has, of course, a venerable ritual precedent in the Roman practice of *devotio*, in which a general vows in advance to sacrifice his own life in battle along with that of an enemy. As far as British traditions are concerned, however, it reaches an apogee at this time. In *Times* reports of the Crimean War, sixty years earlier, we do to be sure find references to noble sacrifice, but not as something sacramental and almost desirable. 'Sacrifice' then calibrates the ratio of loss and gain: 'very little sacrifice of life', 'he might have sustained longer, but only at a great sacrifice of life'; 'the gallant but abortive sacrifice of the British Light Cavalry Brigade.'[4] By contrast, in 1916 we read: 'we should count every sacrifice a privilege', 'inspire them to deeds of self-sacrifice'; the 'young beauty of

---

[1] Several topics in this chapter are discussed in far greater detail in my book *Culture and Sacrifice*.

[2] Pahl/Wellman, 'The Origins of Nations and Religious Violence: Imagining Trans-Atlantic "America"; Interrogating Evolution', at: 'Surviving our Origins: Violence and the Sacred in Evolutionary-Historical Time', 27 to 28 May 2011, St John's College, Cambridge.

[3] 15 February 1916, 8.

[4] 10 August 1854, 8; 5 September 1854, 6; 20 November 1854, 6.

sacrifice and its horror'; 'facing the world proudly in the knowledge that he has made the great sacrifice. He has lost two sons in the North Sea.'[5] These First World War examples are all taken from a single week: the first week of the Battle of the Somme. Now the usage has changed again: it is the enemy who are sacrificed.

The First World War passages represent one extreme in the appropriation and sentimentalizing of the idea of sacrifice. Of course, reaction set in at once. The greatest poet of that war, Wilfred Owen, famously dismissed 'Dulce et decorum est' as 'The old Lie',[6] and in 'The Parable of the Old Man and the Young' he addressed a newer version of that lie: the idea of war as noble sacrifice. Commanded by the angel to spare Isaac, Abraham nevertheless 'slew his son,/And half the seed of Europe, one by one' (p. 42). One by one: the collective slaughter is stretched out into an endless sequence of individually experienced tragedies and individually perpetrated crimes.

In popular and even non-technical professional use, therefore, sacrifice is a shifting and malleable term. Despite its flexibility, however, it remains an indispensable though now almost invariably pejorative term in our discussion of killing. It denotes any form of killing outside society's norms; any use of life as currency in the pursuit of a dubious goal. Voluntary self-sacrifice may—by contrast—still be noble, though even that can be deluded or wasteful. Modern productions of Wagner operas tend to undercut his portrayals of redemptive self-immolation.

The scholar who is studying images of sacrifice in literature or popular culture, therefore, is doing something quite different from the theologian who explores its essential meanings, or the anthropologist who studies its many real manifestations, and perhaps finds structural elements uniting the practices of widely separated cultures. The literary critic is dealing with the imagining of sacrifice: an imagining that may have scant connection with actual practice, and that is usually rooted in the preoccupations of the writer's own society, and the traditions from which its literature has grown. In the case of human sacrifice, the literary influences are primarily Greek: sacrificial plots in post-Renaissance European literature to a large degree chart a changing understanding of Greek texts—and, in particular, of Euripides.

Greek literature is permeated by human sacrifice. At the funeral of Patroclus in Book XXIII of the *Iliad*, Achilles slaughters twelve Trojan prisoners of war, and human sacrifice is a theme in fourteen of Euripides's nineteen surviving plays. Blood sacrifice of animals was central in Greek religion and had a structural role in affirming the position of humanity between the gods and the animals: between the animals (who eat flesh raw) and the gods, who do not eat

---

[5] 1 July 1916, 11; 3 July 1916, 10; 6 July 1916, 9; 3 July 1916, 11.
[6] 'Dulce et Decorum Est', in *Collected Poems of Wilfred Owen*, 55. The quotation is from Horace, *Odes* 3.2.13.

mortal food.[7] Sacrifice of human victims would confound this chain of being and was therefore a powerful and self-evident symbol for the breakdown of order. Evoking the great temple at Jerusalem, Edward Burnett Tylor describes what is true of any major sacrificial centre: a temple as a shambles, crowded with living animals, 'the drain beneath [the altar] to carry off the streams of blood.'[8] But what if the blood were human? When, in the *Odyssey*, Telemachus reaches the palace of Nestor, as part of his journey to adult social responsibility, his entry into a pious and ordered society is confirmed by the fact that he arrives in the middle of a sacrifice of five hundred oxen. Arrival in the midst of a mass sacrificial feast upon of human victims would obviously have a quite contrary effect—as, indeed, anthropophagy does in other parts of the poem. On Odysseus' travels, the city of the cannibalistic Laestrygonians forms the boundary at which he passes from the world of human culture into that of the monstrous and marvellous. When, beyond this boundary, he encounters cannibalism again, in the one-eyed giant Polyphemus, it is in a primitive milieu without social organization, without cultivation of crops, and without sacrifice. In a later age, in his satyr play *Cyclops*, Euripides was to turn Polyphemus into a practiser of human sacrifice, but for Homer cannibalism is not an alternative form of sacrifice but a negation of its structure and principles. The two earliest works of Western European literature thus lay the foundation for seeing anthropophagy and human sacrifice as negations of civilized community.

During the Middle Ages, however, these topics largely disappear from European literature, along with the disappearance of literal blood sacrifice as an official religious rite (however much it survives in folk customs such as foundation sacrifice). They were rediscovered in the sixteenth century through contact with Aztec and Peruvian cultures, but it was not the sacrificial element in their ritualized violence that initially made the greatest impact on European writers: rather, it was cannibalism—its impact enhanced by the instances of anthropophagy closer to home, during the Wars of Religion, when human flesh was consumed, and indeed exposed for sale.[9] When, in *Gerusalemme Liberata* (1580), Tasso looks beyond the First Crusade to prophesy the civilizing of the New World, it is through the abolition of cannibalism: of 'abominevoli vivande'.[10] Tasso remained an important model for lesser epic poets throughout the seventeenth century, and his imitators retained his concern with the missionary enlightening of savage cultures. By the mid-seventeenth century, however, there is a change of emphasis, the civilizing process becoming specifically associated with the abolition of human sacrifice: examples

---

[7] Vernant, *Myth and Society*, 197–198.
[8] Tylor, *Primitive Culture*, vol. 2, 387.
[9] De Léry, *History of a Voyage*, 122–133.
[10] Tasso, *Gerusalemme Liberata*, Canto 15, stanzas 28–32. Translations from foreign texts are my own unless otherwise stated.

are Girolamo Graziani's *Il Conquisto di Granata* (1650), George de Scudéry's
*Alaric* (1654), Pierre Mambrun's *Constantinus* (1658), and Pierre Le Moyne's
*Saint Louys* (1658).[11]

At the same time, human sacrifice becomes a regular topic on the tragic
and operatic stage, notably in plays derived from Euripides' two plays about
Agamemnon's daughter Iphigenia. In *Iphigenia in Aulis* (408–406 BCE) the
Greeks are becalmed at Aulis and unable to sail to Troy because of the anger
of Artemis. They, and eventually Agamemnon himself, are willing to obey her
command to sacrifice Iphigenia, in order to secure winds. Some earlier versions of the myth narrate that Iphigenia was spared by the miraculous last-
minute substitution of a deer, others that the sacrifice was performed. The
original play may well have ended with Iphigenia's departure for sacrifice, but
in surviving texts her exit is followed by a messenger's speech, probably added
by a later hand, narrating the miraculous substitution. It is as a celebration of
sacrifice averted that the play has largely influenced later writers, but even with
its happy ending it unsparingly lays bare the greed, venality, and arrogance of
all the celebrated heroes. *Iphigenia in Taurica*, an earlier play of uncertain date
(possibly 414–12 BCE), shows us Iphigenia after her rescue, acting as priestess
of Artemis in the Crimea, in a cult that practises human sacrifice. The cult is
abolished, but only after Iphigenia has come dangerously close to sacrificing
her own long-lost and unrecognized brother.

There had been sporadic adaptations and translations of *Iphigenia in Aulis*
before, but a sustained post-classical Iphigenia tradition first appears in the
mid-seventeenth century, with Jean de Rotrou's tragedy *Iphygénie* (1641),
which appeared just as human sacrifice was gaining prominence in the historical epic. In Le Moyne's *Saint Louys*, indeed, there is an obvious reworking of
the Iphigenia story, in which the Sultan of Egypt sacrifices his daughter in an
attempt to gain victory.[12] Conversely, Racine's *Iphigénie en Aulide* retains the
shadow of cannibalism when Clytemnestre accuses Agamemnon of wishing to
re-enact the Thyestean banquet: 'there only remains for you to make a horrible
feast of her for her mother' ('il ne vous reste enfin/Que d'en faire à sa mère un
horrible festin').[13] In the epics, human sacrifice becomes the moral antipodes
to the self-oblation of the Crucifixion and of Christian martyrdom (especially
in Mambrun). In tragedy, the implications are often more secular, in that the
sacrificial plots explore the rights and value of the individual in relation to
systems of political authority. This is not a problem that is directly formulated
in (for example) Shakespeare, but it comes to the fore in the decades after his
death, not only on the stage but in the political arena, in mid-century attacks
on monarchic authority in Britain, Holland, France, and Naples. In Racine's

---

[11]  See Hughes, *Culture and Sacrifice*, 56–58.
[12]  Le Moyne, *Saint Louys*, 156–167.
[13]  IV.iv.1251–52, in Racine, *Œuvres complètes*.

*Iphigénie en Aulide*, the life of Iphigenia is set in the balance against 'l'honneur et la patrie' and 'l'état' (I.i.74–77). Here, as in most plays on this subject from Euripides onwards, the figure of Ulysses is used to promote, and unwittingly discredit, the transactional subordination of life to political expedience. In recent versions, there has also been a tendency to see the values of honour and country as specifically male ones. In Pizzetti's opera *Ifigenia* (1950) the baritone chorus leader intones the words 'onore, gloria, patria', which Ifigenia repeats 'as if dazed' ('quasi smarrita').[14] In Hans Schwarz's *Iphigeneia in Aulis* (1947), similarly from the immediate postwar period, it is the hideous Thersites, the man no woman would have, who trumpets the values of honour, friendship, and country ('Ehre, Freunde, Volk').[15] In Michael Cacoyannis' 1977 film *Iphigenia*, male mobs repeatedly chant 'Sacrifice! Sacrifice!' ('Θυσία! Θυσία!') and the final shots alternate massed men converging on the ships with the brooding, vengeful, full-screen face of Clytemnestra.

Racine's version, the most famous Iphigenia play of the seventeenth century, manages both to spare Iphigenia and retain the accomplishment of sacrifice, in that the demands of the oracle are fulfilled by a second woman, who turns out to be Iphigenia's namesake, and who is driven to suicide by her passionately uncontrolled nature. In general, however, adaptors of the Iphigenia plays preferred the total rejection of human sacrifice, and by the early eighteenth century it had been abolished in Aulis, or Taurica, on the stages of England, France, Germany, Italy, and Spain. The celebration of human progress continued throughout the eighteenth century, with other exemplary plots joining the repertory: for example, Metastasio's sacrifice-averted libretti *Alessandro nell'Indie* (1729) and *Demoföonte* (1733) were both set many times, their last outings being in, respectively, 1824 and 1836. From the 1770s onwards, audiences from Italy to Sweden watched operatic and balletic treatments of the story of Alonso and Cora from Marmontel's novel *Les Incas* (1777): the story of an unchaste vestal spared from sacrifice, and shorn of the eventual unhappy ending which Marmontel gave it. At times, an evening at the theatre might treat audiences to a double dose of averted sacrifice. Salvatore Rispoli's setting of *Idalide* (1786), a version of the Alonzo and Cora story, contained a ballet entitled *I barbari sacrifizj distrutti*, and Paisiello's setting of *Demoföonte* (1775) had *Iffigenia in Tauride* as one of its balletic interludes. As the eighteenth century proceeds, sacrifice-averted plays and libretti attracted religious sceptics (such as Marmontel): Frederick the Great collaborated on an operatic *Ifigenia in Aulide* (1748), set by Carl Heinrich Graun; his friend Count Algarotti wrote an *Iphigenie en Aulide* (1755); and Voltaire wrote *Les loix de Minos* (1773), about the abolition of a sacrificial ritual in ancient Crete. In

---

[14]  Pizzetti, *Ifigenia*, 160.
[15]  Schwarz, *Iphigeneia in Aulis*, 84.

addition, the fashion for plays about the ending of human sacrifice coincides with the growth of secular interpretations of the story of Abraham and Isaac. For example, the English deist Thomas Chubb dwelt on its difficulties, Voltaire on its absurdity and barbarity.[16]

What is notable is the total absence in this period of any adaptation of Euripides' grimmest portrayal of a sacrificial subject: *The Bacchae*, in which the new god Dionysus punishes Thebes for denying his divinity. The women of the city are afflicted with a malign version of the ecstatic possession associated with his rites and, in her madness, the mother of the king participates in the hunting and dismemberment of her son in the belief that she is sacrificing an animal. In its portrayal of destructive collective hysteria, this play was, along with *Oedipus Rex*, one of the two Greek tragedies that most appealed to twentieth-century adaptors. Its view of the fragility of civilization, however, had no appeal for the eighteenth century; conversely, recent writers have been more interested in Iphigenia sacrificed than Iphigenia saved.

What is also missing in the eighteenth century is any elaborate anthropology or psychology of sacrifice. Voltaire's treatment of sacrificial themes in plays such as *Mahomet* (1741) and *Les loix de Minos* is related to his concern with fanatical religious cruelty in his own society. He stresses the role of the mob in encouraging such savagery, but attempts to explain the psychology of sacrifice are at this stage crude. Volney's *Ruines, ou méditations sur les révolutions des empires* (1791) deplores the role of superstition and fanaticism in bringing about the decline of civilizations, but he merely interprets sacrifice as an attempt to appease elemental forces.[17] In the same period, Marmontel traces the forms of religion back to man's primitive, pre-agricultural state. Whereas a few revered the peaceful aspects of nature, most were in awe of its destructive aspects: the tiger, the lion, the vulture. 'After imagining cruel and bloody gods, it was necessary to give them a cult as barbarous as they were' ('Après avoir imaginé des dieux cruels et sanguinaires, il fallut bien leur rendre un culte barbare comme eux'). The cult naturally involved human sacrifice.[18]

The origins of modern literary approaches to sacrifice are, however, to be found later in the nineteenth century. As in the sixteenth century, European imperialists were confronted with actual sacrificial practices. Colonial authorities attempted to suppress widow-burning and other forms of funerary sacrifice: Samuel Charters Macpherson documented the fertility rituals of *sparagmos* practised by the Khonds of Orissa, and the inconclusive attempts to suppress them.[19] Meanwhile, in an odd cultural disjunction, audiences of

[16] Chubb, *A Collection of Tracts*, 240–246; Chubb, *Four Tracts*, 84–119; Voltaire, *La Bible enfin expliquée*, vol. 1, 53–56.
[17] Volney, *Les ruines*, 140.
[18] Marmontel, *Les Incas*, vol. 1, 185.
[19] MacPherson, *Memorials of Service in India*, 113–131, 146–157.

Wagner and many lesser opera composers—Meyerbeer, Delibes, Lalo, for example—were invited to applaud heroines who fulfilled their sex's supposed instinct for self-immolation.[20] According to Wagner, woman's child-bearing role hardwires her to the role of willing sacrificial victim:

> A woman who truly loves sets her virtue in her pride and her pride in her sacrifice: that sacrifice with which she surrenders, not one part of her being, but rather her total being in the richest fullness of her capability. That is, when she conceives.

> Ein Weib, das wirklich liebt, seine Tugend in seinen Stolz, seinen Stolz aber in sein Opfer setzt, in das Opfer, mit dem es nicht einen Theil seines Wesens, sondern sein ganzes Wesen in der reichsten Fülle seiner Fähigkeit hingibt, wenn es empfängt.[21]

Crude as such a conception is, it shows an advance in exploring how the idea of sacrifice was implicit in the structure of the human brain—an exploration carried forward, in quite different terms, by Frazer.

Interest in the mental structures of sacrifice complements a far wider change in the way in which the structure of myth was imagined: as a composite of quasi-geological or archaeological layers, whose excavation would yield truths about the original, prehistoric stages of human culture or racial development, or the primitive layers of the human mind. In his monumental *Das Mutterrecht* (1861), Johann Jakob Bachofen detected four universal stages (*Stufen*) in the evolution of culture: a primal stage of universal promiscuity, in which women were the indiscriminate sexual prey of predatory males, a subsequent stage of female dominance, in which women wrested control by means of religion, and then progress to an Apollonian state of patriarchy by an intermediate Dionysian stage of civilization. This evolutionary pattern leaves its imprint upon the structure of myth: the element of incest in the Oedipus myth, for example, preserves a memory of the primal state of promiscuity, while Oedipus' remarriage to Euryganea, recorded in some forms of the myth, recalls the evolution to a settled system of matrimony.[22]

There are two factors of interest in this approach to myth. One is the new prominence that Bachofen gives to Dionysus, who in preceding centuries had been reduced to a jolly wine god. The other is the emphasis on layering: on the primitive remaining as a residue in more advanced developments of the narrative. For Bachofen, there was evolution to a higher state of religious and social enlightenment, but other theorists of myth gave more stress to the persistence of the primitive. While documenting the evolution of 'stages of

---

[20] Sacrificial female death occurs in Wagner's *The Flying Dutchman* (1843), *Tannhäuser* (1845), *Tristan and Isolde* (1865), *Götterdämmerung* (1876), and *Parsifal* (1882), in Berlioz' *Les Troyens* (1863), Meyerbeer's *L'Africaine* (1865), Delibes' *Lakmé* (1883), and Lalo's *Le roi d'Ys* (1888), and as late as Albert Roussel's *Padmâvatî* (1923). Sacrifice is averted in Bizet's *Les pêcheurs de perles* (1863).

[21] Wagner, *Oper und Drama*, in Sämtliche Schriften und Dichtungen, vol. 3, 319.

[22] Bachofen, *Mutterrecht*, 120.

culture', Tylor also conceded that 'we may draw a picture where there shall be scarce a hand's breadth difference between an English ploughman and a negro of Central Africa' (1:7).'[O]ur resemblances to the savage', warned Frazer, 'are still far more numerous than our differences from him.'[23] Whereas the eighteenth-century Iphigenia texts propose a decisive evolution beyond the superstitions of the past, Frazer invites us to contemplate the fundamental identity of our own most prized religious beliefs with those of barbaric and ancient cultures: belief in the sacrificed and resurrected god, for example. Under Frazer's influence, Jane Harrison investigated the 'primitive stratum' of Greek religion, and Gilbert Murray traced the origins of tragedy, traditionally the highest literary form, to Dionysiac ritual: an enactment of the death and rebirth of vegetation one stage of which is 'a Pathos, or disaster, which very commonly takes the shape of a *Sparagmos*, or Tearing in pieces; the body of the Corn God being scattered in innumerable seeds over the earth; sometimes of some other sacrificial death.'[24] *The Bacchae* can thus be seen as a representation of its own generic and cultic origins. In *The Origin of Attic Comedy*, F.M. Cornford postulated a similar genesis for the comic genre. With a frisson of excited horror, we began to see the outlines of human sacrifice in art forms which for earlier generations had constituted the acme of serene harmony.

A key figure in the rehabilitation of Dionysus is Richard Wagner. For the ill-fated Paris production of *Tannhäuser* (1861), he added an orgiastic ballet in the Venusberg—a 'Bacchanale'—but found it impossible to win over the decorous choreographer Petipa to his 'bold and savagely sublime' vision of Maenads and Bacchants: the result, Petipa objected, would be 'a cancan, and we should be lost'.[25] Wagner's plans were, however, honoured after his death in his widow Cosima's Bayreuth production of 1891, which portrayed the Venusberg as 'an incarnation of Dionysian antiquity'.[26]

It is appropriate that Wagner should have been the subject of Nietzsche's *The Birth of Tragedy* (1872): a key text in restoring the cultural centrality of Dionysus, and consequently ensuring that *The Bacchae* became one of the twentieth century's favourite Greek tragedies. Famously, Nietzsche sees Greek tragedy as holding in balance the Apollonian and the Dionysiac: the former the image-building and individuating faculty and the latter an imageless, collective intoxication, a breakdown of cognitive forms, seen in Bacchic Greek choruses and in Medieval movements such as the St Vitus's dance. The Dionysiac can manifest itself in the cruel and sensual orgies but can also renew the bond between human beings, in the way celebrated in Schiller's 'Ode to Joy'. After receiving Nietzsche's book, Wagner became particularly preoccupied by what

[23] Frazer, *The Golden Bough*, 218.
[24] Harrison, *Prolegomena to the Study of Greek Religion*, 16; Murray, *Euripides and his Age*, 30.
[25] Borchmeyer, *Drama and the World of Richard Wagner*, 136, citing Wagner, *Über das Dirigieren, Sämtliche Schriften*, vol. 8, 315.
[26] Carnegy, *Wagner and the Art of the Theatre*, 140.

he saw as the Dionysian element in Beethoven's seventh symphony. He repeatedly describes it as representing a Dionysian festival: the procession, the sacrifice of the god, a rustic celebration.[27] In Wagner's mind, the seventh symphony becomes a foreshadowing of Stravinsky's *The Rite of Spring*.

By what channels is the sacrificial instinct assumed to persist in modern society? One further line back to the primitive is provided by the racial theory that emerged during the nineteenth century and exercised such a terrible influence on the twentieth. According to the social Darwinian Georges Vacher de Lapouge:

> Each of us, on coming into the world, brings into it a mentality which is his own, but which is also a synthesis of an infinite number of ancestral mentalities. That which thinks and acts in it is the innumerable legion of ancestors buried beneath the earth; it is everything which has felt, thought, and desired in the infinite line, bifurcating in each generation, which links the individual, across millions of years and countless billions of ancestors, to the first lumps of matter to reproduce themselves.

> Chacun de nous venant au monde apporte sa mentalité à lui, qui est sienne, mais qui est la synthèse d'un nombre infini de mentalités ancestrales. Ce qui pense et agit en lui, c'est l'innombrable légion des aïeux couchés sous terre, c'est tout ce qui a senti, pensé, voulu dans la lignée infinie, bifurquée à chaque génération, qui rattache l'individu, au travers de millions d'années et par des milliards innombrables d'ancêtres, aux premiers grumeaux de matière vivante qui se sont reproduits.[28]

Psychoanalysis was at this time beginning to see the structure of ancient myth as contained in the modern brain, but racial theory provides an earlier basis for explaining the persistence of the atavistic and primitive. For Count Gobineau, the practice of human sacrifice arises from a people's racial composition: the sacrificial barbarity of the Aztecs, for example, resulted from the double current of black and yellow which had formed the race ('résultait naturellement du double courant noir et jaune qui avait formé la race').[29] Similarly, among the diverse racial mixtures of France, Bretons retained an unusual amount of Druid blood, the ancestral instinct for human sacrifice being now expressed in its modern equivalent of killing and plundering shipwreck victims.[30] According to Gustave Tridon, Judaism and its epigone Christianity are rooted in the Semitic cult of Moloch,[31] and Houston Stewart Chamberlain similarly argues that 'we find human sacrifice only where (as in Phoenicia) the Semitic element strongly predominated' ('Da wir Menschenopfer nur dort eingebürgert sehen, wo (wie in Phönizien) das semitische Element stark überwog').[32]

---

[27] Wagner, *Cosima Wagner's Diaries*, vol. 1, 604–605, 850, vol. 2, 205, 253.

[28] Vacher de Lapouge, *L'Aryen. Son role social*, 350–351.

[29] Gobineau, *Essai sur l'inégalité*, vol. 2, 512.

[30] Gobineau, *Essai sur l'inégalité*, vol. 1, 44.

[31] Tridon, *Du Molochisme Juif* (1884). The work was published posthumously, Tridon having died in 1871.

[32] Chamberlain, *The Foundations of the Nineteenth Century*, vol. 1, 395; *Die Grundlagen des neunzehnten Jahrhunderts*, 377.

Many grounds, therefore—psychological, racial, evolutionary—have been evoked to demonstrate that the impulse to this stereotype of archaic barbarity remains alive in modern man. It is significant that many modern theorists of civilization need to postulate a primal condition of human sacrifice as a starting point. René Girard's sacrificial crisis is well known and discussed by several contributors to this volume.[33] Human sacrifice and cannibalism also form a hypothetical cultural beginning in Adorno and Horkheimer's *Dialectic of Enlightenment*, in which they address the question of how the civilization of Kant could also manifest itself as that of Hitler. Enlightenment, they argue, has through its very methods of abstraction an intrinsic potential to produce its own opposite, for these methods dissolve the unique and particular and promote the interchangeability, expendability, and alienation of the individual. An early example of such abstraction is the substitution of animal for human victims, 'the hind offered up for the daughter' again implying the interchangeability of what was previously unique.[34] Sacrificial origins occur yet again in the work of Jean Baudrillard. Taking the inevitable starting point of a completely hypothetical prehistoric state of nature, Baudrillard postulates a movement from a 'sacrificial' to an 'economic' social organization. In earliest times, prisoners of war were originally killed on the spot. Later, they were instead enslaved. Later still, they became paid labour. Labour is, thus, deferred death.[35]

Human sacrifice also plays a well-known role in the genesis of modernist music. 29 May 1913 witnessed the first performance of one of the most influential works of early twentieth-century music, Stravinsky's *The Rite of Spring*. This depicts a quasi-Dionysiac human sacrifice to promote the renewal of the earth. Indeed, it has human sacrifice as its formal principle, since the victim—the Chosen One—dances herself to death, the work of art itself becoming the sacrificial instrument. *The Rite* is a portrayal of psychological collectivity, in which ritual itself assumes an identity more powerful than that of its individual participants, and is thus quite different from the works of maiden sacrifice associated with the Romantic period. The idea of the dance to death is not new—it is averted in *Giselle* and carried to conclusion in Puccini's *Le Villi*, on both occasions with a male victim—but the transformation of the entire work into a sacrificial ritual is at once revolutionary and in keeping with its epoch.

Like most classic works, *The Rite* has lost some of its original raw shock. The startling musical innovativeness remains, but less so, perhaps, the astonishment at being invited to observe a barbaric rite with objective, aesthetic appreciation. For Adorno, the *Rite* reflected the depersonalization of the industrial age,

[33] See in particular the contributions of Wolfgang Palaver, Paul Fiddes and Jessica Frazier, Chapters 6, 4, and 7, respectively, in this volume.
[34] Adorno/Horkheimer, *Dialectic of Enlightenment*, 10.
[35] Baudrillard, *Symbolic Exchange and Death*, 39.

foreshadowing the slaughter in the Great War,[36] and aestheticized violence was in the air: witness the callow posturing of the *Manifesto del Futurismo* (1909), with its glorifying of 'war, the only way of cleaning the world' ('la guerra—sola igiene del mondo').[37] The previous year saw the appearance of Gustave Sorel's *Refléxions sur la violence*, which Mann in *Doktor Faustus* stigmatized as 'the book of the epoch' ('das Buch der Epoche') in its rejection of parliamentary procedures and exaltation of mythic fictions as means of 'unchaining political energies' ('die politischen Energien zu entfesseln').[38] Mann names this as one of the prize texts of the Kridwiss circle, a group of minor intellectuals who gathered in 1913–1914 to devote themselves to the aesthetic glorification of violence, exemplified in the enthusiasm for blood sacrifice of the Jewish intellectual Chaim Breisacher (based on Oskar Goldberg), unaware of what horror he is helping to foreshadow.[39]

Several Futurists changed direction after the experience of the First World War, but the appetite for sacrificial scenes survived. An example is provided by Egon Wellesz's balletic cantata *Die Opferung des Gefangenen* (*The Sacrifice of the Prisoner*) of 1925, based on a Mayan ritual. In D.H. Lawrence's short story 'The Woman Who Rode Away' (1925), a young American woman rides into the Mexican heartland, not at first understanding her own purpose, but finding fulfilment when she becomes the victim of a Native American human sacrifice. We find a reaction against such developments in the virgin sacrifice to the Golden Calf in Schoenberg's incomplete opera *Moses und Aron* (1930–1932; first performed 1954). In Richard Begam's words, this scene 'is a savage rewriting of Stravinsky, *Le Sacre du Printemps* purged of its primitivist stylizations and restored to the dark and bloody breast of Dionysus.'[40]

Along with the provocative aestheticization of barbarism, however, is a simpler idealization of Dionysus, under the influence of Nietzsche: works inspired by *The Bacchae*, but simplifying it into a sheer celebration of a liberating miracle-worker, triumphing over the sacrificial barbarity of others. In Karol Szymanowski's opera *King Roger* (1926), a Dionysiac stranger initiates the king and queen of Sicily into a new and liberating religion. Whereas versions of *The Bacchae* generally show a collapse of individual motive into collective mob madness, Szymanowski reverses the normal pattern, creating a movement from the opening impersonal ritual chants in a Byzantine church to a process of individual self-realization in a ruined Greek theatre, in which Queen Roxana assumes the guise of a Maenad. Here, it is the ordered, ritualistic church that embodies collective violence, unsuccessfully inciting the mob to stone the stranger. In Erich Korngold's *Das Wunder*

---

[36] Adorno, *Philosophy of Modern Music*, 146–147.
[37] Cassinelli, *Futurismo*, 30. The *Manifesto* was first published in *Le figaro*, February 20, 1909, 1.
[38] Mann, *Doktor Faustus*, 486–487.
[39] See especially Goldberg's *Die Wirklichkeit der Hebräer*, 157–173.
[40] Begam, 'Modernism as Degeneracy,' 33.

*der Heliane* (1927), very similarly, a mysterious stranger offers to restore sexual vitality to a tyrannically repressed kingdom. Instead of the savagery of Euripides' conclusion, there is a double resurrection, of the executed hero and the tyrant's wife, who had been jealously murdered by her husband.

More ambiguous is Egon Wellesz's opera *Die Bakchantinnen* (1931), for which he wrote the libretto. Wellesz outdoes Euripides by directly representing the death of Pentheus, and the massed, torch-bearing Maenads who advance on him may represent the gathering forces of National Socialism.[41] Yet Wellesz saw the sacrificers of Pentheus as false worshippers of the God,[42] and Dionysos himself is less suspect than his Euripidean model. For example, he does not trick Pentheus into going to Cithaeron or into disguising himself as a woman, and Wellesz omits the maenads' bare-handed dismemberment of a herd of cattle, terrifyingly described by the messenger in Euripides' play.

Soon Wellesz and Korngold would be exiles from Nazism, fleeing from as terrible an outburst of Dionysiac frenzy as history is likely to afford. Thereafter, *The Bacchae* gained in popularity as a subject for adaptation, but, for a long time, in versions very different from the expurgations of Szymanowski, Korngold (and Nietzsche). Adaptations for the first time not only equalled but outdid Euripides in savagery. A prime example is Giorgio Ghedini's opera *Le Baccanti*, composed in 1941–1944 and first performed in Milan 1948, with a libretto by Tullio Pinelli, who was later famous for his work on Fellini films such as *La Dolce Vita*. It alters Euripides' structure by concentrating all the seemingly beautiful aspects of Dionysus in the early part of the opera, so as to falsify them the more emphatically later. For example, halfway through Euripides' play a messenger describes a scene of magical beauty, in which the Bacchanals bring forth milk and honey from the earth. Beauty turns to horror, however, when they realize that a man is observing them, and start dismembering cattle and even bulls with their bare hands. Wellesz (and Nietzsche) cite the beautiful miracle and omit the grim *sparagmos*. Ghedini and his librettist, by contrast, accentuate the element of grimness. The conjuring of milk from the earth is mentioned early and is immediately ambiguous, so that we are not allowed even a brief mirage of pure beauty. The earth will, Diòniso affirms, bring forth milk—but also blood; flowers—but also serpents.[43] Moreover, this combination of beauty and menace is followed by the wild sacrificial dismemberment of a goat and the impalement of its head on a thyrsus: not in a messenger's speech but on the stage; not in the wilds of Cithaeron but in the centre of the city. It is in the context of this bloody rite that the chorus proclaim that the earth has brought forth milk and wine.[44] Whereas Euripides' Pentheus

---

[41]  Symons, *Egon Wellesz*, 71.
[42]  Symons, *Egon Wellesz*, 69, n. 35.
[43]  Ghedini, *Le Baccanti*, 8–10.
[44]  Ghedini, *Le Baccanti*, 58–59.

preaches against rites he has neither seen nor understood, this barbarity is seen not only by Penteo but by citizens and the priests of Apollo, who attempt to purify the blood-stained steps with water. For the first time in the history of *Bacchae* adaptations, Apollo is invoked as a counterbalance to Dionysus, as part of a vain attempt to prevent the collapse of civilization into collectivist barbarism. At the end of the opera, the impalement of the goat's head is re-enacted in that of Penteo himself.

The most persistent exploration of the Dionysiac is, however, in the work of Thomas Mann. *Death in Venice* (1912) and *Doctor Faustus* (1947) both portray an Apollonian artist's fatal encounter with Dionysus, the latter work exploring the dialectic of forces in German culture that made possible the Third Reich. The Mann novel which most specifically engages with the idea of human sacrifice, however, is *The Magic Mountain*, the title of course alluding to that seminal discussion of the Dionysiac, Nietzsche's *The Birth of Tragedy*. Writing of the dark, pre-Olympian stages of Greek religion, Nietzsche had written 'Now, as it were, the Olympian magic mountain opens up and shows us its roots' ('Jetzt öffnet sich uns gleichsam der olympische Zauberberg und zeigt uns seine Wurzeln'). Those great Hellenists Goethe and Schiller had not, finally, been able to enter 'the Hellenic magic mountain' ('den hellenischen Zauberberg').[45]

Like *The Bacchae*, *The Magic Mountain* involves a journey from a city to a mountain. The young engineer Hans Castorp leaves his native Hamburg to visit his tubercular cousin in the sanatorium in Davos, on the boundary of untameable snowy wastes beyond the reach of civilization. The ostensibly brief visit turns into a seven-year stay, which traces the descent of European culture into the First World War. It concludes with a *sparagmos*: bodies being blown apart by shells. Three quarters of the way through the novel, moreover, Hans makes the acquaintance of an embodiment of Dionysus, the Javanese planter Pieter Peeperkorn: a man from the East, and a figure of heroic exuberance and excess, like 'Bacchus himself' ('Bacchus selbst').[46] He is, however, an elderly Bacchus, committing suicide when he realizes that the hero, Hans Castorp, slept with his mistress some years before. He is like a Frazerian god-king, killing himself when his potency declines. The death of this Dionysus figure is the death of a form of symbolic explanation: it precedes the descent into the carnage of the First World War, of which no mythic figure is an adequate representation. Old cultural symbols are no longer sufficient to describe the new configurations of civilization.

It is the last of a sequence of encounters with impersonal and massively destructive forces, beyond the representative scope of myth, which both call forth and redefine the image of sacrifice. The first is the geological catastrophe of the Lisbon earthquake. Voltaire, the Enlightenment rationalist Settembrini

---

[45] Nietzsche, *Die Geburt der Tragödie*, 12, 116.
[46] Mann, *Der Zauberberg*, 517.

says, 'protested in the name of the intellect and reason against that scandalous irrationality of nature, to which thousands of human lives fell sacrifice' ('Er protestierte im Namen des Geistes und der Vernunft gegen diesen skandalösen Unfug der Natur, dem...Tausende von Menschenleben zum Opfer fielen').[47]

The idea of human sacrifice is most directly confronted in another confrontation with the impersonal mechanisms of nature. Lost in the snow, Hans Castorp falls into a hallucinatory state, seeing a landscape which, seemingly, reverses the sterile wastes in which he is lost: a classical, Mediterranean landscape, inhabited by beautiful youths and manifesting every early category of culture except crop-growing and writing. Yet this formal perfection of culture is as grounded in death as the lifeless symmetry of the snow. There is a temple at whose entrance stand statues of a mother and daughter—evidently Demeter and Korê, alluding to the Eleusinian mysteries. Inside, however, is a pair of figures diametrically opposed to the Hellenic fertility goddesses: two old hags, dismembering a child and talking in an ugly Hamburg dialect. Here, Hans Castorp gazes into the depths of Nietzsche's Magic Mountain and sees the heart of darkness in Hellenism, and the societies which pattern themselves upon it.

Why this particular image? An answer perhaps lies in the essay 'Demeterfest' by Wilamowitz: an exponent, of course, of an anti-Nietzschean view of Hellenism. This opens with a discussion of Schiller's poem 'Das Eleusische Fest' (1798), which, according to Wilamowitz, schoolboys were required—under protest—to learn by heart. It is a poem, he says, which retains the optimistic faith in brotherly love inspired by the early days of the French Revolution, long after its descent into bestiality. In it, Ceres roams the earth looking for her lost daughter and arrives in a land without culture, where a tribe of cannibalistic hunters offer her a human sacrifice. She refuses it, and brings culture and humanity to the land, beginning with the growing of corn and concluding with the construction of a temple at whose altar she preaches the values of freedom and humanity. The poem is an Enlightenment text portraying the purging of civilization through the transcendence of human sacrifice. A text that Hans Castorp would have learned as a schoolchild. A text outmoded in its optimism even when written, and deeply irrelevant now.[48]

Operatic and dramatic adaptations of *The Bacchae* continued to proliferate: by Harry Partch, Hans Werner Henze, Joe Orton, Wole Soyinka, Richard Schechner, Roy Travis, John Buller. Some adaptations move ecstasy away from the political sphere: Partch's *Revelation in the Courthouse Park* (1960–1961) interweaves the ancient Euripidean story with a modern rethinking of it, in which Dionysus is a pop musician, and Schechner's *Dionysus in 69* explores

---

[47] Mann, *Der Zauberberg*, 230.
[48] Schiller, *Sämtliche Werke*, vol. 1, 194–200; Wilamowitz-Moellendorff, *Reden und Vorträge*, 271.

the psychology and consequences of the sixties' sexual revolution (though politics re-enter at the end when Dionysus stands for US president).

The proliferation of *Bacchae* imitations is matched by a reduction in Iphigenia's profile. *Iphigenia in Taurica* has, in particular, failed to regain its eighteenth-century prominence, though Helen Gifford's operatic version, *Exile,* became the first opera to be released specifically for iPad. Adaptations of *Iphigenia in Aulis* continue, without great confidence in human progress, but it does not rank as one of the defining Greek tragedies of the twentieth century, as *The Bacchae* (like *Oedipus Rex*) does. *Jertfirea Ifigeniei* (*Iphigenia's Sacrifice*) (1968), an impressive opera by the Romanian composer Pascal Bentoiu, stresses the nobility of the heroine's sacrifice, but scepticism has more frequently been the recent mode. In André Obey's *Une fille pour du vent* (1953), for example, an intelligent piece of weather forecasting nearly enables the priest Calchas to synchronize the sacrifice of Iphigenia with the return of wind. But his deception does not work, since the wind starts to blow before the sacrifice—which goes ahead anyway. The wind similarly blows prematurely in Michael Cacoyannis' 1977 film *Iphigenia.* The opening of Kenneth Rexroth's *Iphigenia at Aulis* (1951) introduces us to a crowd including 'a street prostitute' and Iphigenia, 'dressed like the prostitute, but without the jewellry and make-up'.[49] Iphigenia and Agamemnon have been lovers, and she is now in love—and sleeping—with Achilles, who had originally been intended as a mere shield to cover the affair with Agamemnon. No virgin sacrifice, then: rather, Iphigenia dies under the knife of the father who had sexually initiated her. Nevertheless, she takes the lead in seeing sacrifice as her inner destiny.

Even versions which retain the traditional happy ending can do so ironically. The most complex and pessimistic twentieth-century rewriting is that of Gerhart Hauptmann, written as part of his *Atridentetralogie,* and staged in Vienna in 1943, during the nadir of German civilization. Hauptmann portrays a Greece taken over by dark, chthonic gods and mob passions. A ship with blood-red sails, used to transport sacrificial victims to Taurica, lies in the harbour, and Artemis' will is expressed in savage, anthropophagic terms as a desire for human flesh ('Menschenfleisch').[50] Hauptmann uses last-minute substitution of the deer, yet even this contributes to the horror, for Agamemnon is too carried away to understand, and furiously kills the animal in the belief that it is his daughter. At the end of *The Bacchae*, a mother kills her child in the belief that he is an animal. Here, a father kills an animal in the belief that it is his child. This seems rather worse. Hauptmann was writing in Hitler's Germany, under a regime with which he had compromised, but the play nevertheless mirrors the horrors of its period. Like Ghedini's *Le Baccanti*, written in the same period, it takes Greek tragedy to new levels of savagery.

[49] Rexroth, *Iphigenia in Aulis*, 59–60.
[50] Hauptmann, *Die Atriden-Tetralogie*, 10.

In 1998 the Swiss author Jürg Amann published *Iphigenie, oder Operation Meereswind* (*Iphigenia, or, Operation Sea Wind*), obviously alluding to the codename for the First Gulf War: Operation Desert Storm. The main part of the play follows Euripides quite closely, with the addition of commentary from a CNN reporter, Linda Xenakis, digesting the action into trivial sound bites, the culminating one being 'Miraculous Rescue of Iphigenia' ('Iphigenie durch Wunder gerettet').[51] The play suggests that the appetite for news creates war, and it provides a novel view of the transformation that occurs in the act of sacrifice. Iphigenia, spared, is transmuted into a headline.[52]

Other recent works continue to demonstrate the enduring fascination of human sacrifice: the film *The Wicker Man* (1973), Achebe's novel *Things Fall Apart* (1958), Peter Ackroyd's *Hawksmoor* (1985), and James Macmillan's opera *The Sacrifice* (2007). Despite its persistence in significant works, however, one cannot assemble from the postwar years sacrificial works as great and semi-nally influential as *The Rite of Spring*, *The Magic Mountain*, or *Moses und Aron*. In general, the emphasis has shifted from the individuated consciousness of sacrificer and sacrificed to the blind action of the mob. A work which is often mentioned as portraying human sacrifice is Shirley Jackson's powerful short story 'The Lottery' (1948), portraying an annual custom in which a member of a village community is chosen by lot to be stoned by the other villagers. The word 'sacrifice', however, is never used. Even in Henze's *The Bassarids* (1966), probably the greatest reworking of *The Bacchae*, there is no sacrifice: Pentheus is, simply, the victim of a hunt.

Perhaps the most significant recent treatment of human sacrifice has been Margaret Atwood's novel *The Blind Assassin* (2000). *The Blind Assassin* is the title not only of the novel but of an embedded novel, which in turn contains a fictional narrative, based on pulp science fiction by the political activist for whom the two central characters—sisters—are rivals, both in the primary novel and in the elusively glimpsed embedded one. The inmost narrative is about virgin sacrifice on an alien planet (with prior prostitution of the 'virgins'), and it is transparently a commentary on the events of the main novel: for example, the narrator, Iris Chase, is sacrificed in marriage to a ruthless industrialist in a vain attempt to save her father's business. It is also, however, a sensationalizing of them by an author who cannot face up to the challenges of socially realistic fiction, and in this respect it has something in common with the other major image of sacrifice in the novel: the First World War.

[51] Amann, *Iphigenie*, 73.

[52] Other versions of *Iphigenia in Aulis* include Jean Moréas; *Iphigénie* (1904), a paraphrase of Euripides. Hans Schwarz's *Iphigeneia in Aulis* (1947) explores the different values of men and women and repudiates human sacrifice. Ildebrando Pizzetti's opera *Ifigenia* (1950), also depicts a clash of male and female values. After the performance of the sacrifice, a mysterious voice asks 'Why' in various languages. *Iphigenia by Euripides*, adapted by Edna O'Brien (2003) also explores the different values of men and women and concludes with the sacrifice and a rain of blood.

The heroines' father Norval, who has been badly maimed in the war, commissions a memorial to the fallen. The townsfolk, however, are unimpressed by the unheroic weariness of the resulting statue. They want ennobling fiction rather than truth. They want sacrifice, demanding that the statue bear the inscription 'For Those Who Willingly Made the Supreme Sacrifice'.[53] Sacrifice here becomes a distorting cliché, willed and imposed by those who did not participate, prettifying events which it cannot describe. Norval, however, refuses to back down: 'if they didn't watch out he'd go in for bare-naked realism all the way and the statue would be made of rotting body fragments, of which he had stepped on a good many in his day'.[54] No more the 'young beauty of sacrifice'. The war is a *sparagmos*, but not a sacrifice. No fiction or metaphor can impose coherence on the pieces of mangled flesh. The term 'sacrifice' is as alien to them as the stone which celebrates them.

It seems unlikely that sacrifice will ever be exhausted as a literary topic, as long as social organizations have to make decisions about the value of individual life, as one hopes they always will. If we have lost the faith in rational progress of some eighteenth-century texts, so we have the lost the early twentieth-century taste for beautiful barbarism. The term continues its mutations of meaning, and it is no longer inevitably necessary to describe the destructive hysteria of the mob. Yet the topic retains its power and, outside the world of fiction, we must like earlier generations still confront sacrificial cultures that challenge our own, and whose boundaries are now less distinct: our Other is now not the sacrificial priest in Taurica, or Tenochtitlan, or Orissa, but the suicide bomber on the Circle line.

---

[53] Atwood, *The Blind Assassin*, 148.
[54] Atwood, *The Blind Assassin*, 148.

# Bibliographical References

Adams, Rebecca, 'Loving Mimesis and Girard's "Scapegoat of the Text": A Creative Reassessment of Mimetic Desire', in: Swartley, Willard (ed.), *Violence Renounced: René Girard, Biblical Studies, and Peacemaking*, Ontario (Pandora Press) 2000, pp. 277–307.

Adorno, Theodor W., *Philosophy of Modern Music*, transl. Mitchell, Anne G. Blomster, Wesley V. London (Sheed & Ward), 1973.

——/Horkheimer, Max, *Dialectic of Enlightenment*, transl. Cumming, John, London (Verso), 1979.

Alencar, Gedeon, *Protestantismo Tupiniquium: Hipóteses sobre a (não) contribuição ão evangélica à cultura brasileira*, São Paulo (Arte Editoral), 2005.

Algarotti, Francesco, Count, '*Iphigenie en Aulide*', in: *Saggio sopra l'Opera in Musica*, Livorno (Marco Coltellini), 1763, pp. 97–157.

Alison, James, *Knowing Jesus*, London (SPCK), 1988.

——, *The Joy of Being Wrong: Original Sin Through Easter Eyes*, New York (Crossroads), 1998.

——, *On Being Liked*, London (DLT), 2003.

——, *Undergoing God: Dispatches from the Scene of a Break-In*, London (DLT), 2006.

——, 'Sacrifice, Law, and the Catholic Faith', in: Alison, James, *Broken Hearts and New Creations: Intimations of a Great Reversal*, London (DLT), 2010.

Allen, N. J., *Categories and Classifications: Maussian Reflections on the Social*, Oxford (Berghahn), 2000.

——, 'From the Brāhmaṇas to *Nuer Religion*: One Strand in Studies of Sacrifice', in: Berger, Peter et al. (eds.), *The Anthropology of Values: Essays in Honour of Georg Pfeffer*, Delhi (Dorling Kindersley), 2010, pp. 249–59.

——, 'The Indo-European Background to Greek Mythology', in: Dowden, Ken/Livingstone, Niall (eds.), *A Companion to Greek Mythology*, Oxford (Blackwell), 2011, pp. 341–56.

——, 'Mauss and India, and Perspectives from World History', in: *Journal of Classical Sociology* (forthcoming).

——, 'Durkheim's Sacred-Profane Opposition: What should we make of it?' in: Hausner, Sondra (ed.), *Durkheim in Dialogue. A Centenary Celebration of The Elementary Forms of Religious Life*, Oxford (Berghahn).

Allmen, Jean-Jacques von, *The Lord's Supper*, transl. W. Fletcher Street, Philadelphia (Newman), 1966.

Amann, Jorg, *Iphigenie, oder Operation Meereswind*, Düsseldorf (Eremiten), 1998.

Ambrose, Glenn P., *The Theology of Louis-Marie Chauvet: Overcoming Onto-Theology with the Sacramental Tradition*. Farnham (Ashgate), 2012.

Anders, Ferdinand/Maarten, E. R. G. N./Jansen, N., *Introduction to the Facsimile of the Codex Laud*, Mexico (Fundo de Cultura Económica), 1994.

Anderson, Pamela Sue, 'Liberating Love's Capabilities: On the Wisdom of Love', in: Wirzba, Norman/Benson, Bruce Ellis (eds.), *Transforming Philosophy and Religion: Love's Wisdom*, Indianapolis, IN (Indiana University Press), 2008, pp. 201–26.

Anderson, Pamela Sue, 'Transcendence and Feminist Philosophy: On Avoiding Apotheosis', in: Howie, Gillian/Jobling, Jannine (eds.), *Women and the Divine: Touching Transcendence*, New York (Palgrave), 2009, pp. 27–54.

——/Bell, Jordan, *Kant and Theology*, Philosophy for Theologians series, London/New York (Continuum), 2010.

——, 'The Lived Body, Gender and Confidence', in: Anderson, Pamela Sue (ed.), *New Topics in Feminist Philosophy of Religion: Contestations and Transcendence Incarnate*, Dordecht/London/New York (Springer), 2010, pp. 163–80.

——, 'The Weakness of our "Messianic Power": Kristeva on Sacrifice', in: Bradley, A./Fletcher, P. (eds.), *The Politics to Come. Power, Modernity and the Messianic*, London (Continuum) 2010, pp. 111–29.

——, *Re-visioning Gender in Philosophy of Religion: Reason, Love and Epistemic Locatedness*, Aldershot, Hants (Ashgate Publishing Ltd.), 2012.

Andolsen, Barbara Hilkert, 'Agape in Feminist Ethics', in: *The Journal of Religious Ethics*, 9 (1981), pp. 69–83.

Anker, C., *Aztecs: Reign of Blood and Splendor*, Alexandria, VA (Time-Life Books), 1992.

Anspach, Mark R., (ed.) *René Girard*, Cahiers de l'Herne, Paris (Edition L'Herne), 2008.

Ariel, Yaakov, 'How Are Jews and Israel Portrayed in the Left Behind Series? A Historical Discussion of Jewish-Christian Relations', in: Forbes, Bruce D./Kilde, Jeanne H. (eds.), *Rapture, Revelation, and the End Times: Exploring the Left Behind Series,* New York (Palgrave/Macmillan), 2004, pp. 131–66.

Atwood, Margaret, *The Blind Assassin*, London (Bloomsbury), 2000.

Augustine, *De civitate dei libri XXII*, (ed.) Dombart, B./Kalb, A., Stuttgart (Teubner) 1981, ET: *St. Augustine's City of God*, transl. Dods, M., 2 vols., Edinburgh (T&T Clark), 1871.

——, *Confessions*, transl. Chadwick, Henry, Oxford (Oxford University Press), 2008.

Awolalu, J. Omosade, 'Yoruba Sacrificial Practice', in: *Journal of Religion in Africa*, 5:2 (1973), pp. 81–93.

Bachofen, Johann Jakob, *Das Mutterrecht: eine Untersuchung über die Gynaikokratie der alten Welt nach ihrer religiösen und rechtlichen Natur*, Stuttgart (Krais and Hoffmann), 1861.

Badiou, Alain, *In Praise of Love*, with Truong, Nicolas, transl. Bush, Peter, London (Serpent's Tail, an imprint of Profile Books Ltd.), 2012.

Balthasar, Hans Urs von, *Mysterium Paschale*, transl. Nichols, A., Edinburg (T&T Clark), 1990.

——, 'The Glory of the Lord. A Theological Aesthetics', Vol. VII, *Theology: The New Covenant*, transl. McNeil, Brian, Edinburg (T&T Clark), 1989.

——, 'Theo-Drama. Theological Dramatic Theory', Vol. IV, *The Action*, transl. Harrison, G., San Francisco (Ignatius Press), 1994.

Baquedano, Elizabeth, *Los Aztecas*, Mexico City (Panorama), 1992.

Baudrillard, Jean, *Symbolic Exchange and Death*, transl. Grant, Iain Hamilton, London, (Sage), 1993.

Barth, Karl, *Church Dogmatics*, transl./ed. Bromiley G. W./Torrance, T. F., 14 Volumes, Edinburgh (T& T Clark), 1936–77.

Bataille, Georges, *La part maudite*, Paris (Les Éditions de Minuit), 1967.

——, *Théorie de la religion,* Paris (Gallimard), 1973.

Beattie, Tina, *New Catholic Feminism: Theology and Theory,* London (Routledge), 2006.

Begam, Richard, 'Modernism as Degeneracy: Schoenberg's *Moses und Aron',* in: *Modernist Cultures* 3 (2007), pp. 33–56.

Belangia, Sherwood, 'Metaphysical Desire in Girard and Plato', in: *Comparative and Continental Philosophy,* 2:2 (2010), pp. 197–209.

Belayche, Nicole, 'Sacrifice during the "Pagan Reaction"', in: Baumgarten A.I. (ed.), *Sacrifice in Religious Experience,* Leiden (Brill) 2002, pp. 101–26.

Bell, David A. *The First Total War: Napoleon's Europe and the Birth of Warfare as We Know it,* Boston (Houghton Mifflin Co.), 2007.

Bellarmine, Robert, 'De Missa', in: Bellarmine, Robert, *Disputationes de controversiis Christianae fidei,* vol. 3, Naples (Giuliano), 1838, pp. 469–576.

Benson, E. P./Boone, E. H., *Ritual Human Sacrifice in Mesoamerica,* Washington, DC (Dumbarton Oaks), 1979.

——/De la Fuente, B., *Olmec Art of Ancient Mexico,* Washington, DC (National Gallery of Art), 1996.

Bentoiu, Pascal, *Jertfirea Ifigeniei. Operă radiofonică,* conducted by Baci, Ludovic, Romania (Electrecord), *c.*1969 [Sound recording].

Bercovitch, Sacvan, *The American Jeremiad,* Madison (The University of Wisconsin Press), 1978.

Bergman, Ingmar, *Images: My Life in Film,* transl. Ruuth, Marianne, New York (Arcade Publishing), 2011[1994].

Berlin, Isaiah, *The Crooked Timber of Humanity: Chapters in the History of Ideas,* New York (Vintage Books), 1992.

Beutler, Christian, *Der älteste Kruzifixus: Der entschlafene Christus,* Frankfurt (Fischer), 1991.

Bhabha, Homi K., 'The Other Question: Difference, Discrimination, and the Discourse of Colonialism', in: Barker, Francis et al. (eds.), *Literature, Politics and Theory: Paper from the Essex Conference 1976–1984,* London (Methuen), 1986, pp. 148–72.

Biardeau, Madeleine and Malamoud, Charles. *Le sacrifice dans l'inde Ancienne,* Louvain-Paris (Peeters), 1996.

Biviano, Erin Lothes, *The Paradox of Christian Sacrifice: The Loss of Self, the Gift of Self,* New York (Crossroads), 2007.

Blake, Richard, 'Ingmar Bergman, Theologian?', in: *America* (27 August 2007), online at <http://www.americamagazine.org/content/article.cfm?article_id=10155>, accessed 25 June 2012.

Bloch, Maurice, *Prey into Hunter: The Politics of Religious Experience,* Cambridge (Cambridge University Press), 1992.

Blum, Larry et al. 'Altruism and Women's Oppression', in: Gould, Carol C./Wartofsky, Marx W. (eds.), *Women and Philosophy: Towards a Theory of Liberation,* New York (Pedigree Books), 1976, pp. 222–47.

Borchmeyer, Dieter, *Drama and the World of Richard Wagner,* transl. Ellis, Daphne, Princeton/Oxford (Princeton University Press), 2003.

Bradley, Arthur/Fletcher, Paul (eds.), *The Politics to Come: Power, Modernity and the Messianic,* London (Continuum), 2010, pp. 111–27.

Brandon, George E., *Santería from Africa to the New World: The Dead Sell Memories*, Indianapolis (Indiana University Press), 1993.

Brandt, Richard, 'Rationality, Egoism and Morality', *The Journal of Philosophy*, 69 (1972), pp. 681–97.

Bronkhorst, Johannes, *Greater Magadha: Studies in the Culture of Early India*, Leiden (Brill), 2007.

Brown, David, *Tradition and Imagination*, Oxford (Oxford University Press), 1999.

——, *Discipleship and Imagination*, Oxford (Oxford University Press), 2000.

——, *God and Enchantment of Place*, Oxford (Oxford University Press), 2004.

——, *God and Grace of Body*, Oxford (Oxford University Press), 2007.

——, *God and Mystery in Words*, Oxford (Oxford University Press), 2008.

——, *Divine Humanity*, Waco, TX (Baylor University Press), 2011.

Brumfield, Elizabeth, 'Aztec State Making: Ecology, Structure and the Origin of the State', in: *American Anthropologist*, 85 (1983), pp. 261–84.

Buber, Martin, *I and Thou*, Edinburgh (T&T Clark), 1937.

——, *Between Man and Man*, London (Collins), 1961.

Burkert, Walter, *Homo Necans: The Anthropology of Ancient Greek Sacrificial Ritual and Myth*, transl. Bing, P., Berkeley (University of California Press), 1983.

Bushnell, Horace, *The Vicarious Sacrifice: Grounded in Principles of Universal Obligation*, New York (Scribner), 1871.

Butler, Judith, *Gender Trouble: Feminism and the Subversion of Identity*, London (Routledge), 1990.

Calvin, Jean, *Institutes of the Christian Religion*, McNeill, J. T. (ed.), 2 vols., Louisville/London (Westminster John Knox Press), 2006.

Camara, Evandro M., 'Afro-American Religious Syncretism in Brazil and the United States: A Weberian Perspective', in: *Sociological Analysis*, 48/4 (1988), pp. 299–318.

Carnegy, Patrick, *Wagner and the Art of the Theatre*, New Haven/London (Yale University Press), 2006.

Carrasco, David, *City of Sacrifice: The Aztec Empire and the Role of Violence in Civilisation*, Boston (Beacon Press), 1999.

Carraud, Vincent, 'De la destruction. Métaphysique et idée du sacrifice selon Condren', in: *Archivio di filosofia*, 76 (2008), pp. 331–48.

Carrette, J. R., *Religion and Culture by Michel Foucault*, Manchester (Manchester University Press), 1999.

Carrithers, Michael et al., 'Ontology is Just Another Word for Culture', in: *Critique of Anthropology*, 30/2 (2010), pp. 152–200.

Carter, Jeffrey (ed.), *Understanding Religious Sacrifice: A Reader*, London (Continuum), 2003.

Casel, Odo, *The Mystery of Christian Worship and Other Writings*, ed. Neunheuser, Burkhard, London (Darton, Longman & Todd), 1962.

Cassinelli, Paola, *Futurismo*, Florence (Giunti), 1997.

Cavanaugh, William T., *Torture and Eucharist: Theology, Politics, and the Body of Christ*, Oxford (Blackwell), 1998.

——, 'The World in a Wafer: A Geography of the Eucharist as Resistance to Globalization', in: *Modern Theology*, 15/2 (1999), pp. 181–96.

——, 'Eucharistic Sacrifice and Social Imagination in Early Modern Europe', in: *Journal of Medieval and Early Modern Studies*, 31/3 (2001), pp. 585–605.

——, *Being Consumed: Economics and Christian Desire*, Grand Rapids, MI (Eerdmans), 2008.

Celsus, *Alethes Logos*, in: Bader, R. (ed.), *Der Ἀληθὴς λόγος des Kelsos*, Tübingen (Kohlhammer), 1940.

Chamberlain, Houston Stewart, *The Foundations of the Nineteenth Century*, transl. Lees, John, 2 vols, London/New York (Lane), 1911.

——, *Die Grundlagen des neunzehnten Jahrhunderts*, 10th ed. Munich (Bruckmann), 1912.

Chauvet, Louis-Marie, *Symbol and Sacrament*, transl. Madigan, Patrick and Beaumont, M. Collegeville (Liturgical Press), 1995.

Chemnitz, Martin, *Examen Concilii Tridentini* (1566), Frankfurt (Sande), 1707.

Chernus, Ira, *Dr Strangegod: On the Symbolic Significance of Nuclear Weapons*, Columbia (University of South Carolina Press), 1986.

Chubb, Thomas, '*The Case of* Abraham, *with Regard to his Offering up* Isaac *in Sacrifice Reexamined*', in: *A Collection of Tracts on Various Subjects*, London (T. Cox), 1730, pp. 240–6.

——, 'The Case of *Abraham*, With Respect to His Being Commanded by God to Offer His Son *Isaac* in Sacrifice, Farther Considered', in: *Four Tracts*, London (T. Cox), 1734, pp. 83–119.

Clendinnen, I., *Aztecs: An Interpretation*, Cambridge (Cambridge University Press), 1991.

Coakley, Sarah, 'Kenosis and Subversion: On the Repression of "Vulnerability" in Christian Feminist Writing', in: *Powers and Submissions: Spirituality, Philosophy and Gender*, Oxford (Blackwell), 2002, pp. 3–39.

——, 'Visions of the Self in Late Medieval Christianity: Some Cross-Disciplinary Reflections', in: *Powers and Submissions: Spirituality, Philosophy and Gender*, Oxford (Blackwell), 2002, pp. 72–88.

——, *Sacrifice Regained: Reconsidering the Rationality of Religious Belief*, Cambridge (Cambridge University Press), 2011.

——, '*Sacrificed Regained: Evolution, Cooperation and God*', Gifford Lectures, University of Aberdeen, April–May 2012.

Codex Florence (Testimonios de los informants de Sahagún). *Facsimile elaborado por el gobierno de la república Mexicana*, Mexico (Giunte barbera), 1979.

Coe, M. D., *Mexico: From the Olmecs to the Aztecs*, 4th ed., London (Thames & Hudson), 1994.

——, *Breaking the Maya Code*, rev. ed., Harmondsworth (Penguin), 2000.

Condren, Charles de, *L'idée du sacerdoce et du sacrifice du Jésus-Christ*, new revised ed., Vitry-le-François (Hurault), 1849.

Corten, André/Dozer, Jean-Pierre/Oro, Ari Pedro, 'Introdução', in: Oro, Ari Pedro/ Corten, André/Dozon, Jean-Pierre (eds.), *Igreja Universal do Reino de Deus: Os novos conquestadores da fé*, São Paulo (Paulinas) 2003, pp. 13–45.

Cornford, Francis Macdonald, *The Origin of Attic Comedy*, London (Edward Arnold), 1914.

Crenshaw, J., (ed.), *Theodicy in the Old Testament*, London (SPCK), 1983.

Crenshaw, Kimberlé, *On Intersectionality: The Essential Writings of Kimberlé Crenshaw*, New York (The New Press), 2012.

Crosfield, R., *Columbus: A Discoverer and his Conscience*, Kirstead, Norfolk (Frontier), 1998.

Cudworth, Ralph, *Discourse Concerning the True Notion of the Lord's Supper* (1670), in: Cudworth, Ralph, *The True Intellectual System of the Universe*, vol. 4, new ed., London (Priestley), 1820.

Dalferth, Ingolf U., 'Self-sacrifice: From the Act of Violence to the Passion of Love', in: *International Journal for Philosophy of Religion*, 68 (2010), pp. 77–94.

Daly, Mary, *Beyond God the Father: Toward a Philosophy of Women's Liberation*, Boston (Beacon Press), 1973.

Daly, Robert, 'Robert Bellarmine and Post-Tridentine Eucharistic Theology', in: *Theological Studies*, 61 (2000), pp. 239–60.

——, 'Sacrifice Unveiled or Sacrifice Revisited', in: *Theological Studies*, 64 (2003), pp. 24–42.

——, 'New Developments in the Theology of Sacrifice', in: *Liturgical Ministry*, 18 (2009), pp. 49–58

——, *Sacrifice Unveiled: The True Meaning of Christian Sacrifice*, London (T&T Clark), 2009.

Dawkins, Richard, *The God Delusion*, Boston (Houghton Mifflin Company), 2006.

Denton-Borhaug, Kelly, *U.S. War-Culture, Sacrifice and Salvation*, London (Equinox), 2011.

Derrida, Jacques, 'Signature, Event, Context', in: Derrida, J., *Margins of Philosophy*, transl. Bass, A., New York (Harvester Wheatsheaf), 1982.

Despland, Michel, *Le recul du sacrifice. Quatre siècles de polémiques françaises*, Quebec (Presses de l'Université de Laval), 2009.

Detienne, Marcel, 'Culinary Practice and the Spirit of Sacrifice', in: Detienne, Marcel Vernant, J. P. (ed.) *The Cuisine of Sacrifice Among the Greeks*, Chicago (Chicago University Press), 1989.

*Didache Apostolorum*, Wengst, K. (ed.), *Schriften des Urchristenstums*, vol. 2, Darmstadt (Wissenschaftliche Buchgesellschaft), 1984, pp. 1–100.

Donoso Cortés, Juan de, *Essay on Catholicism, Liberalism & Socialism: Considered in Their Fundamental Principles*, transl. Vinton Goddard, Madeleine, Albany (Preserving Christian Publications, Inc.), 1991.

Dostoevsky, Fyodor, *The Brothers Karamazov*, transl. Avsey, Ignat, Oxford (Oxford University Press), 1998.

Dupuy, Jean-Pierre, 'The Self-Deconstruction of the Liberal Order' in: *Contagion: Journal of Violence, Mimesis, and Culture*, 2 (1995), pp. 1–16.

Durán, Fray Diego, *Historia de las Indias de Nueva España y Islas*, ed. Ramirez, J. F., Mexico (Edit. Nacional. de Tierra Firme), 1951.

Durkheim, Émile, *On Morality and Society: Selected Writings*, ed. Bellah, Robert N. Chicago (University of Chicago Press), 1973.

——, 'Concerning the Definition of Religious Phenomena', transl. Redding, J./ Pickering, W. S. F., in: Pickering, W. S. F. (ed.), *Durkheim on Religion: A Selection of Readings with Bibliographies*, London (Routledge), 1975 (orig. 1899), pp. 74–99.

——, *The Rules of Sociological Method, and Selected Texts on Sociology and its Method*, transl. Halls W. D., London (Macmillan), 1982 (orig. 1895).

——, *The Elementary Forms of Religious Life*, transl. Fields, K. E., New York (Free Press), 1995 (orig. 1912).

——, *Lettres à Marcel Mauss*, presented by Besnard, P./Fournier, M., Paris (PUF), 1998.

Duverger, Christian, *La fleur léthale. Economie du sacrifice aztèque*, Paris (Eds du Seuil), 1979.

Elliott, Peter, *Sacrifice in the Mass*, London (Catholic Truth Society), 2011.

Euripides, *Bacchae: Iphigenia at Aulis; Rhesus*, ed./transl. Kovacs, David, Cambridge, MA (Harvard University Press), 2002.

Eusebius of Caesarea, *De demonstratione evangelii*, in Heikel, I. A. (ed.), *Eusebius Werke*, vol. 6, Leipzig (Hinrichs), 1913.

——, *De preparatione evangelica*, in: Mras, K. (ed.), *Eusebius Werke*, vol. 8, Berlin (Akademie Verlag), 1954–56.

Evans-Pritchard, E. E., 'The Meaning of Sacrifice Among the Nuer', in: *The Journal of the Royal Anthropological Institute of Great Britain and Ireland*, 84:1–2 (1954), pp. 21–33.

——, *Nuer Religion*, Oxford (Oxford University Press), 1956.

——, *Theories of Primitive Religion*, Oxford (Oxford University Press), 1965.

Farley, Margaret, 'New Patterns of Relationship: Beginnings of a Moral Revolution', in: Burkhardt, W. (ed.) *Woman: New Dimensions*, New York (Paulist Press), 1977, pp. 51–70.

——, *Just Love: A Framework for Christian Sexual Ethics*, New York (Continuum), 2006.

Fauconnet, Paul/Mauss, Marcel, *The Nature of Sociology*, New York, Oxford (Durkheim Press), 2005 (orig, 1901).

Faust, Drew Gilpin, *This Republic of Suffering: Death and the American Civil War*, Cambridge (Harvard University Press), 2008.

Fenn, Richard C., *Dreams of Glory: The Sources of Apocalyptic Terror*, Hampshire/ Burlington (Ashgate), 2006.

Feuerbach, Ludwig, *The Essence of Religion*, transl. Loos, Alexander, Amherst (Prometheus Books), 2004.

Fiddes, Paul S., *Past Event and Present Salvation: The Christian Idea of Atonement*, London (Darton, Longman and Todd), 1989.

——, *The Creative Suffering of God*, Oxford (Oxford University Press), 1992.

Flaherty, Robert L., 'Sacrifice', in: *Encyclopaedia Britannica*, vol. 16, Chicago (Benton), 1974, pp. 128–35.

Flood, Gavin, *The Ascetic Self: Subjectivity, Memory and Tradition*, Cambridge (Cambridge University Press), 2004.

Foucault, Michel, 'About the Beginning of the Hermeneutics of the Self: Two Lectures at Dartmouth', in: *Political Theory*, 21 (1993), pp. 198–227.

Fournier, Marcel, *Marcel Mauss: A Biography*, Princeton (Princeton University Press), 2006 (orig. 1994).

Franklin, William, 'ARC-USA: Five Affirmations on the Eucharist as Sacrifice', *Worship*, 69/5 (1995), pp. 386–90.

Frazer, James G., *Golden Bough: A Study in Magic and Religion*, abridged, London (The Macmillan Press), 1922.

Frazer, James G. *The Golden Bough: A Study in Magic and Religion. A New Abridgement from the Second and Third Editions,* ed. Fraser, Robert, Oxford and New York (Oxford University Press), 1994.

Frazier, Jessica, *Reality, Religion and Passion: Truth and Ethics in Hans-Georg Gadamer and Rupa Gosvami,* New York (Lexington Books), 2008.

Freeman, Rich, 'The Dancing of the Teyyams', in: Flood, Gavin (ed.), *The Blackwell Companion to Hinduism,* Oxford (Blackwell), 2003, pp. 307–26.

Freud, Sigmund, *Totem and Taboo,* transl. Strachey, James, reprinted in: Freud, Sigmund, *The Origins of Religion,* ed. Strachey, James/Dickson, Albert, London (Harmondsworth: Penguin) 1985, pp. 43–224.

———, *An Outline of Psycho-Analysis,* transl. Strachey, James, New York (W.W. Norton & Co.), [1939] 1949.

———, *The Future of an Illusion,* transl. and ed. Strachey, James, New York (W.W. Norton & Co.), 1961.

Frykholm, Amy Johnson, 'What Social and Political Messages Appear in the Left Behind Books? A Literary Discussion of Millenarian Fiction', in: Forbes, Bruce D./ Kilde, Jeanne H. (eds.), *Rapture, Revelation, and the End Times: Exploring the Left Behind Series,* New York (Palgrave/Macmillan), 2004, pp. 167–96.

Gauchet, Marcel, *The Disenchantment of the World: A Political History of Religion,* transl. Oscar Burge, Princeton (Princeton University Press), 1997.

Ghedini, Giorgio, *Le Baccanti,* Milan and New York (Ricordi), [1948].

Gill-Austern, Brita, 'Love Understood as Self-Denial: What Does It Do to Women?', in: Moessner, J. S. (ed.), *Through the Eyes of Women: Insights for Pastoral Care,* Minneapolis (Fortress), 1996, pp. 304–21.

Girard, René, *The Scapegoat,* transl. Freccero, Y., London (Athlone Press), 1986.

———, *Things Hidden Since the Foundation of the World: Research Undertaken in Collaboration with J.-M. Oughourlian and G. Lefort,* transl. Bann, S./Metteer, Michael, London (Athlone Press), 1987, pp. 326–51.

—— and Rebecca Adams, 'Violence, Difference, Sacrifice: A Conversation with René Girard', in: *Religion & Literature,* 25 (1993), pp. 11–33.

———, *Quand ces choses commenceront... Entretiens avec Michel Treguer,* Paris (Arléa), 1994.

———, 'Mimetische Theorie und Theologie' in: Niewiadomski, Józef/Palaver, Wolfgang (eds.), *Vom Fluch und Segen der Sündenböcke: Raymund Schwager zum 60, Geburtstag,* Thaur (Kulturverlag), 1995, pp. 15–29.

———, *The Girard Reader,* ed. Williams, James G., New York (Crossroad), 1996.

———, 'Desire and the Unity of Novelistic Conclusions' (From *Deceit, Desire, and the Novel*), in: Williams, James G. (ed.), *The Girard Reader,* New York (Crossroad), 1996, pp. 45–61.

———, 'Freud and the Oedipus Complex', in: Williams, James G. (ed.), *The Girard Reader,* New York (Crossroad), 1996, pp. 225–42.

———, 'Sacrifice as Sacral Violence and Substitution' (From *Violence and the Sacred*) in: Williams, James G. (ed.), *The Girard Reader,* New York (Crossroad), 1996, pp. 69–94.

———, 'Triangular Desire' (From *Deceit, Desire, and the Novel*) in Williams, James G. (ed.), *The Girard Reader,* New York (Crossroad), 1996, pp. 33–44.

——, *Celui par qui le scandale arrive*, Paris (Desclée de Brouwer), 2001.

——, *I See Satan Fall Like Lightning*, transl. Williams, J. G., Leominster (Gracewing) 2001.

——, *Violence and the Sacred*, transl. Gregory, Patrick, London (Continuum), 2005.

——, 'Ratzinger is Right', in: *New Perspectives Quarterly*, 22/3 (2005), pp. 42–8.

——, *De la violence à la divinité*, Paris (Bernard Grasset), 2007.

——, *Evolution and Conversion: Dialogues on the Origin of Culture. With Pierpaolo Antonello at João Cezar de Castro Rocha*, London (Continuum), 2008.

——, *Battling to the End: Conversations with Benoît Chantre*, transl. Baker, Mary, Studies in Violence, Mimesis, and Culture Series. East Lansing, MI (Michigan State University Press), 2010.

——, *Sacrifice*, transl. Pattillo, Matthew/Dawson, David, East Lansing, MI (Michigan State University Press), 2011.

—— and Sandor Goodhart, 'Mimesis, Sacrifice, and the Bible: A Conversation with Sandor Goodhart', in: Astell, Ann W./Goodhart, Sandor (eds.), *Sacrifice, Scripture, and Substitution: Readings in Ancient Judaism and Christianity*, Notre Dame, IN (University of Notre Dame Press), 2011, pp. 39–69.

Gobineau, Arthur, Comte de, *Essai sur l'inégalité des races humaines*, 2 vols, 4th ed., Paris (Firmin-Didot), 1940.

Goldberg, Oskar, *Die Wirklichkeit der Hebräer: Einleitung in das System des Pentateuch*, Erster Band, Berlin (David), 1925.

Goldstein, Valerie Saiving, 'The Human Situation: A Feminine View', first published in: *The Journal of Religion*, 1960, reprinted in: Christ, C. and Plaskow, J. (eds.), *Womanspirit Rising*, New York (Harper and Row), 1980, pp. 25–42.

Gombrich, Ernst H. *Aby Warburg: An Intellectual Biography*, 2nd ed., Oxford (Phaidon), 1986.

Gonçalves da Silva, Vagner, 'Neopentecostalismo e Religiões Afro-Brasileiras: Significados do Ataque aos Símbolos da Herança Religiosa Africana no Brasil Contemporâneo', in: *Mana*, 13/1 (2007), pp. 207–36.

Graulich, Michel, 'Les mises à mort doubles dans les rites sacrificiels des anciens mexicains', in: *Journal de la Société des Américanistes*, 68 (1982), pp. 49–58.

——, *Le sacrifice humain chez les aztèques*, Paris (Fayard), 2005.

Graun, Carl Heinrich [composer]/de Villati, Leopoldo/and Frederick II of Prussia [librettists], *Ifigenia in Aulide*, Berlin (Haude and Spener), 1748.

Gray, G.B., *Sacrifice in the Old Testament*, Oxford (Clarendon Press), 1925.

Grunzinski, S., *Painting the Conquest*, Paris (Flammarion), 1992.

Habermas, Jürgen, *Justification and Application: Remarks on Discourse Ethics*, transl. Cronin, Ciaran, Cambridge, MA (MIT Press), 1993.

——, *The Postnational Constellation: Political Essays*, transl. Pensky, Max, Cambridge, MA (MIT Press), 2001.

——, *Time of Transitions*, transl. Cronin, Ciaran/Pensky, Max, Cambridge (Polity Press), 2006.

—— and Ratzinger, Joseph, *The Dialectics of Secularization: On Reason and Religion*, transl. McNeil, Brian, San Francisco (Ignatius Press), 2006.

——, *An Awareness of What is Missing: Faith and Reason in a Post-Secular Age*, transl. Cronin, Ciaran, Cambridge (Polity Press), 2010.

Halbertal, Moshe, 'The Goldstone Illusion', in: *New Republic*, 240/21 (2009), pp. 22–7.

Halbertal, Moshe, *On Sacrifice*, Princeton (Princeton University Press), 2012.

Halbfass, W., *Tradition and Reflection*, Albany (SUNY Press), 1991.

Hamerton-Kelly, R. G. (ed.), *Violent Origins: Walter Burkert, Rene Girard and Jonathan Z. Smith on Ritual Killing and Cultural Formation*, Stanford (Stanford University Press), 1987.

Hampson, Daphne, *Theology and Feminism*, Oxford (Blackwell), 1990.

Hans, James, *The Fate of Desire*, Albany (State University of New York Press), 1990.

Harner, Michael, 'The Ecological Basis for Aztec Sacrifice', in: *American Ethnologist*, 4 (1977), pp. 117–35.

Harrison, Jane Ellen, *Prolegomena to the Study of Greek Religion*, London (Merlin Press), 1962.

Hauptmann, Gerard, *Die Atriden-Tetralogie*, Berlin (Suhrkamp), 1949.

Hedley, Douglas, *Sacrifice Imagined: Violence, Atonement, and the Sacred*, London (Continuum), 2011.

Heesterman, Jan, *The Broken World of Sacrifice: An Essay in Ancient Indian Ritual*, Chicago (Chicago University Press), 1993.

Hegel, G. W. F., *Lectures on the Philosophy of Religion*, transl. Speirs, E. B. New York (Humanities Press), 1962.

Henninger, Joseph, 'Sacrifice', in: Jones, Lindsay (ed.), *Encyclopedia of Religion*, 2nd ed., vol. 12, Farmington Hills (Thomson Gale), 2005, pp. 7997–8008.

Heusch, Luc de, *Sacrifice in Africa, a Structuralist Approach*, transl. O'Brien, L./ Morton, A., Manchester (Manchester University Press), 1985.

Hill, Thomas, 'Servility and Self-Respect', in: *Monist* 57/1 (1973), pp. 87–104.

Hobbes, Thomas, *Leviathan*, Cambridge (Cambridge University Press), 1991.

Hofstadter, Richard, 'The Paranoid Style in American Politics', in: Hofstadter, R./ Wilentz, S. (eds.), *The Paranoid Style in American Politics: And Other Essays*, Cambridge, MA (Harvard University Press), 1996 [1964], 3–40.

Holland, H. S., *Logic and Life*, London (Longmans, Green & Co.), 1911.

Hollaz, D., *Examen theologicum acroamaticum universam theologiam thetico-polemicam complectens* (1707), Teller, R. (ed.), Stockholm/Leipzig (Breitkopf), 1750.

Hubert, Henri, 'Introduction à la traduction française', in: Chantepie de la Saussaye, P. D. (ed.), *Manuel d'Histoire des Religions*, Paris (Armand Colin), 1904, v–xlvii.

——, *Essay on Time: A Brief Study of the Representation of Time in Religion and Magic*, transl. Parkin, R./ Redding, J., Oxford (Durkheim Press), 1999 (orig. 1905).

—— and Mauss, Marcel, *Mélanges d'histoire des religions*, Paris (Alcan), 1909.

—— and Mauss, Marcel, 'Sacrifice: Its Nature and Functions', transl. Halls, W. D., London (Cohen and West), 1964. (First published in French as 'Essai sur la nature et la function du sacrifice', in: *L'année sociologique* 2 (1899), pp. 29–138.)

Hughes, Derek, *Culture and Sacrifice: Ritual Death in Literature and Opera*, Cambridge (Cambridge University Press), 2007.

Hulme, Peter, *Colonial Encounters: Europe and the Native Caribbean, 1592–1797*, London (Methuen), 1986.

Hunsinger, George, *The Eucharist and Ecumenism: Let us Keep the Feast*, Cambridge (Cambridge University Press), 2008.

Hunt, N. B., *Gods and Myths of the Aztecs*, London (Brockhampton Press), 1996.

Irigaray, Luce, *An Ethics of Sexual Difference*, transl. Burke, C./Gill, G. C., Ithaca (Cornell University Press), 1993.

——, 'Divine Women', in: *Sexes and Genealogies*, transl. Gill, Gillian C., New York (Columbia University Press), 1993, pp. 57–72.

Isaac, Barry, 'Aztec Cannibalism: Nahua versus Spanish and Mestizo Accounts in the Valley of Mexico', in: *Ancient Mesoamerica*, 16 (2005), pp. 1–10.

Isambert, François-André, 'Introduction', in: *Hubert, Essay on Time: A Brief Study of the Representation of Time in Religion and Magic*, transl. Parkin, R./Redding J., Oxford (Durkheim Press), 1999 (orig. 1905).

Jay, Nancy, *Throughout Your Generation Forever: Sacrifice, Religion and Paternity*, Chicago (University of Chicago Press), 1992.

Johansson, Patrick, 'Le spectacle de la mort sacrificielle chez les aztèques', in: Albert, Jean-Pierre and Midant-Reynes, Béatrix (eds.), *Le sacrifice humain en Egypte et ailleurs*, Paris (Soleb), 2005, pp. 234–47.

Jones, Robert Alun, *The Secret of the Totem. Religion and Society from McLennan to Freud*, New York (Columbia University Press), 2005

Journet, Charles, *The Mass: The Presence of the Sacrifice of the Cross*, transl. Szczurek, Victor, South Bend (St Augustine's Press), 2008.

Juergensmeyer, Mark, 'Sacrifice and Cosmic War', in: *Terrorism and Political Violence*, 3/3 (1991), pp. 104–17.

Julian 'the Apostate', *Contra Galileos*, in: Wright, W. C. (ed.), *The Works of the Emperor Julian*, vol. 3, London/New York (Loeb), 1923, pp. 319–427.

Justin Martyr, *Dialogus cum Tryphone*, in: Goodspeed, E. J. (ed.), *Die ältesten Apologeten*, Göttingen (Vandenhoeck & Ruprecht), 1915, pp. 90–262, ET: *The Anti-Nicene Fathers*, Robertson, A. and Donaldson, J. (eds.), vol. 1, Grand Rapids, MI (Eerdmans), 1885, reprint: 1985.

Kant, Immanuel, *Groundwork of the Metaphysics of Morals*, (ed. and transl.) Gregor, Mary J., in: *Practical Philosophy*, Cambridge (Cambridge University Press), 1996.

——, *The Metaphysics of Morals*, (ed. and transl.) Gregor, Mary J., with an Introduction by Roger Sullivan, Cambridge (Cambridge University Press), 1996.

——, *Religion within the Boundaries of Mere Reason*, in: *Religion and Rational Theology*, transl. Wood, Allen W./Giovanni, George di, Cambridge (Cambridge University Press), 1996, pp. 39–215.

Kaplan, Flora Edouwaye, S., 'Understanding Sacrifice and Sanctity in Benin Indigenous Religion, Nigeria', in: Olupona, Jacob K. (ed.), *Beyond Primitivism: Indigenous Religious Traditions and Modernity*, New York (Routledge), 2004, pp. 81–199.

Kearns, Cleo McNelly, 'Kristeva and Feminist Theory', in: Kim, C. W. Maggie/St. Ville, Susan M./Simonsitis, Susan M. (eds.), *Transfigurations: Theology and The French Feminists*, Minneapolis, MN (Augsburg Fortress Press), 1993, pp. 49–79.

——, *The Virgin Mary, Monotheism and Sacrifice*, Cambridge (Cambridge University Press), 2008.

Kilmartin, Edward, 'The Catholic Tradition of Eucharistic Theology: Towards the Third Millenium', *Theological Studies*, 55 (1994), pp. 405–57

——, (ed. R. Daly), *The Eucharist in the West: History and Theology*, Collegeville (Liturgical Press), 1998.

Kirwan, Michael, 'Eucharist and Sacrifice', in: *New Blackfriars*, 88/1014 (2007), pp. 213–27.

Kissam, E./Schmidt, M. (eds.), *Flower and Song: Aztec Poems*, London (Anvil Press), 1977.

Korngold, Erich Wolfgang, *Das Wunder der Heliane*, Mainz and Leipzig (Schott), 1927.

Klawans, Jonathan, *Purity, Sacrifice, and the Temple: Symbolism and Supersessionism in the Study of Ancient Judaism*, Oxford (Oxford University Press), 2006.

Kristeva, Julia, *Powers of Horror: An Essay on Abjection*, transl. Roudiez, L. S., New York (Columbia University Press), 1982.

——, *Revolution in Poetic Language*, transl. Waller, M., New York (Columbia University Press), 1984.

——, 'Exterrestrials Suffering for Want of Love', in: *Tales of Love*, transl. Roudiez, Leon S., New York (Columbia University Press), 1987, pp. 372–83.

——, *In the Beginning was Love: Psychoanalysis and Faith*, transl. Goldhammer, A., New York (Columbia University Press), 1987.

——, 'Freud and Love: Treatment and Its Discontents' in: *Tales of Love*, transl. Roudiez, Leon S., New York (Columbia University Press), 1987, pp. 40–8.

——, 'Stabat Mater', in: Toril Moi (ed.), *The Kristeva Reader*, Oxford (Blackwell), 1987, pp. 160–86.

——, *Black Sun. Depression and Melancholia*, transl. Roudiez, L. S., New York (Columbia University Press), 1989.

——, 'Women's Time', in: *Signs* 7, 1 (1981), pp. 13–35; reprinted in Moi, Toril (ed.), *The Kristeva Reader*, transl. Jardine, Alice/Blake, Harry, Oxford (Blackwell), 1986, pp. 188–213; and in: *New Maladies of the Soul*, transl. Guberman, Ross, New York (Columbia University Press), 1995, pp. 201–24.

——/Clément, Catherine, *The Feminine and the Sacred*, transl. Todd, J. M., Basingstoke (Palgrave), 2001.

Lage, Dietmar, *Martin Luther's Christology and Ethics*, Lewiston (E. Mellen Press), 1990.

Lamennais, Félicité Robert de, *Essay sur l'indifférence en matière de religion*, 4 vols., 2nd ed., Paris (Pagnerre), 1843.

Landa, Diego de, *Yucatan Before and After the Conquest*, transl. Gates, W., Mexico City (Ediciones Alducin), 1994.

Las Casas, Bartolomé de, *A Short History of the Destruction of the Indies*, Harmondsworth (Penguin), 1992.

Le Doeuff, Michèle, *The Philosophical Imaginary*, transl. Gordon, Colin, London (Continuum), 2002.

——, 'The Spirit of Secularism: On Fables, Gender and Ethics', Weidenfeld Professorial Lectures, University of Oxford, Trinity Term 2006.

Le Moyne, Pierre, *Saint Louys, ou la sainte couronne reconquise*, Paris (Louys Bilayne), 1658.

Lepin, Marius, *L'Idée du sacrifice de la messe d'après les théologiens depuis l'origine jusqu'à nos jours*, 2nd ed., Paris (Gabriel Beauchesne), 1926.

Léon-Portilla, Miguel (ed.), *Native Mesoamerican Spirituality*, Mahwah, NJ (Paulist Press), 1980.

——, *La pensée aztèque*, transl. Carmen Bernand, Paris (Eds du Seuil), 1985.

Léry, Jean de, *History of a Voyage to the Land of Brazil*, transl. Whatley, Janet, Berkeley, Los Angeles (University of California Press), 1990.

Levenson, D., *The Death and Resurrection of the Beloved Son*, New Haven (Yale University Press), 1993.

Levering, Matthew, *Sacrifice and Community: Jewish Offering and Christian Sacrifice*, Oxford (Blackwell), 2005.

Lévi-Strauss, Claude, *The Savage Mind (La pensée sauvage)*, London (Weidenfeld/ Nicolson), 1966 (orig. 1962).

——, *Introduction to the Work of Marcel Mauss*, transl. Baker, F., London (Routledge/ Kegan Paul), 1987 (orig. 1950).

López Austin, Alfredo, *Hombre-Dios. Religión y política en el mundo náhuatl*, Mexico City (UNAM), 1973.

——, *The Human Body and Ideology: Concepts Among the Ancient Nahuas*, Vols. I/II, Salt Lake City (University of Utah Press), 1988.

——, *Breve historia de la tradición religiosa mesoamericana*, Mexico City (UNAM), 2002.

——, 'The natural world', in: Breuer, David (ed.), *Aztecs*, London (Royal Academy of Arts), 2002, pp. 141–69.

Lowe, W., 'Christ and Salvation', in: Vanhoozer, K. (ed.), *The Cambridge Companion to Postmodern Theology*, Cambridge (Cambridge University Press), 2003.

Lucien, Bernard, 'Le sacrifice rédempteur de la croix et le saint sacrifice de la messe', in: *Sedes Sapientiae*, 95 (2006), pp. 15–45.

Lüdemann, Gerd, *The Unholy in Holy Scripture: The Dark Side of the Bible*, London (SCM), 1997.

Lugo, John de, *Disputationes scholasticae et morales*, New edition, Lyon (Prost), 1644.

Luther, Martin, *Werke in Auswahl*, ed. Clemen, O., 8 vols., 3rd ed., Berlin (de Gruyter), 1959–67.

Lyden, John R., *Film as Religion: Myths, Morals, and Rituals*, New York (University Press), 2003.

McCarthy, Dennis J., 'The Symbolism of Blood and Sacrifice', in: *Journal of Biblical Literature*, 88/2 (1969), pp. 166–76.

McClymond, Kathryn, 'The Nature and Elements of Sacrificial Ritual', in: *Method and Theory in the Study of Religion*, 16 (2004), pp. 337–66.

Macedo, Edir, *Orixás, caboclos & guías: deuses ou demônios?*, Rio de Janeiro (Ed. Universal), 1996 [1988].

McEwan, Colin/López Luján, Leonardo (eds.), *Moctezuma: Aztec Ruler*, London (The British Museum Press), 2009.

McGilchrist, I., *The Master and his Emissary*, New Haven (Yale University Press), 2009.

McGinn, Bernard, *Visions of the End: Apocalyptic Traditions in the Middle Ages*, New York (Columbia University Press), 1979.

McKeever Furst, Jill Leslie, *The Natural History of the Soul in Ancient Mexico*, New Haven (Yale University Press), 1995.

MacMurray, John, address to the Student Christian Movement Quadrennial Conference in Liverpool in 1929, online at <http://johnmacmurray.org/wp-content/uploads/2010/10/YE–ARE–MY–FRIENDS.pdf>, accessed 11 April 2012.

Macpherson, Sam[uel] Charters, *Memorials of Service in India*, Macpherson, William (ed.), London (John Murray), 1865.

Maistre, Joseph de, *Considerations on France*, transl. Lebrun, Richard A., Cambridge Texts in the History of Political Thought, Cambridge (Cambridge University Press), 1994.

——, *Über das Opfer*, transl. Langendorf, Cornelia, Wien (Karolinger), 1997.

Mann, Thomas, *Der Zauberberg*, Berlin (Fischer), 1964.

——, *Doktor Faustus. Das Leben des deutschen Tonsetzers Adrian Leverkühn erzählt von einem Freunde*, Frankfurt am Main (Fischer), 1990.   ·

Marcel, Gabriel, *The Mystery of Being,* Vol I: *Reflection and Mystery,* Chicago (Henry Regnery Company), 1950.

——, *The Philosophy of Existentialism,* New York (Citadel Press), 1984.

——, *The Mystery of Being,* Vol. II: *Faith and Reality,* South Bend (St Augustine's Press), 2001.

——, *Creative Fidelity,* New York (Fordham University Press), 2002.

Margalit, Avishai and Walzer, Michael, 'Israel: Civilians & Combatants', in: *New York Review of Books,* 56/8 (2009), pp. 21–2.

Marmontel, Jean-François, *Les Incas, ou la destruction de l'empire de Pérou,* 2 vols., Paris (Bibliothèque Nationale), 1895–96.

Marissen, Michael, *Bach's Oratorios: The Parallel German–English Texts with Annotations,* Oxford (Oxford University Press), 2008.

Marsh, Clive, *Albrecht Ritschl and the Problem of the Historical Jesus,* San Francisco (Mellen Research University Press), 1992.

Martindale, C. A./Hardwick, Lorna, 'Reception', in: *Oxford Classical Dictionary,* 4th ed., Oxford (Oxford University Press), 2012, pp. 1256–7.

Marzal, M. M., *The Indian Face of God in Latin America,* Maryknoll, NY (Orbis), 1996.

Mason, Michael Atwood, ' "I Bow My Head to the Ground": The Creation of Bodily Experience in a Cuban American Santería Initiation', in: *The Journal of American Folklore,* 107/423 (1994), pp. 23–39.

Matthiesen, Michon, *Sacrifice as Gift: Eucharist, Grace, and Contemplative Prayer in Maurice de la Taille,* Washington, DC (Catholic University of America Press), 2013.

Mauss, Marcel, *On Prayer,* transl. Leslie, Susan, New York/Oxford (Durkheim Press/ Berghahn), 2003 (orig. 1911).

——, *The Gift: the Form and Reason for Exchange in Archaic Societies,* London (Routledge), 1990. First published in French as 'Essai sur le don, forme et raison de l'échange dans les sociétés archaïque', in: *L'année sociologique,* N.S. 1 (1923), pp. 30–186; English translation first published in 1925.

——, *Oeuvres,* Vols I–III, ed. Karady, Victor, Paris (Minuit), 1968–9.

——, 'An Intellectual Self-portrait' in: James, Wendy/Allen, N. J. (eds.), *Marcel Mauss: a Centenary Tribute,* New York/Oxford (Berghahn), 1998, pp. 29–42 (orig. 1930).

——, *Manual of Ethnography,* transl. Lussier, D., Oxford (Berghahn), 2007 (orig. 1947).

Mazza, Enrico, 'The Eucharist in the First Four Centuries', in: Chupungco, A. J. (ed.), *Handbook for Liturgical Studies,* vol. 3: *The Eucharist,* Collegeville, MN (Liturgical Press), 2000, pp. 9–60.

Melanchthon, Philipp, *Apologia confessionis Augustanae (1530),* in: Müller, J. T. (ed.), *Die symbolischen Bücher der evangelisch-lutherischen Kirche,* 6th ed., Gütersloh (Bertelsmann), 1886, pp. 71–291.

Meyer, Birgit, *Translating the Devil: Religion and Modernity among the Ewe in Ghana,* Edinburgh (Edinburgh University Press), 1999.

Midgley, Mary, *Evolution as a Religion,* London (Routledge), 2002.

Miles, Margaret R., *Seeing and Believing: Religion and Values in the Movies,* Boston (Beacon), 1997.

Miller, M. 'The Maya Ballgame: Rebirth in the Court of Life and Death', in: Whittington, E. M. (ed.), *The Sport of Life and Death: the Mesoamerican Ballgame,* London (Thames & Hudson), 2001, pp. 78–87.

Moberly, R. W. L., 'Towards an Interpretation of the Shema', in: Seitz, C./Green-McCreight, K. (eds.), *Theological Exegesis: Essays in Honor of Brevard Childs*, Grand Rapids, MI (Eerdmans), 1999.

Moctezuma, E. M., *The Great Temple of the Aztecs*, London (Thames & Hudson), 1988.

Moréas, Jean, *Iphigénie*, Paris (Société du Mercure de France), 1904.

Mosebach, Martin, *Häresie der Formlosigkeit. Die römische Liturgie und ihr Feind*, Wien (Karolinger), 2002.

Moses Maimonides, *Guide for the Perplexed*, transl. Friedländer, M., 3 vols., London (Trübner), 1881-5.

Mudd, Joseph C., 'Eucharist and Critical Metaphysics: A Response to Louis-Marie Chauvet's *Symbol and Sacrament* drawing on the works of Bernard Lonergan', unpublished PhD dissertation, Boston College, 2010.

Murray, Gilbert, *Euripides and his Age*, with a new introduction by Kitto, H. D. F, London (Oxford University Press), 1965.

Nash, June, 'The Aztecs and the Ideology of Male Dominance', in: *Signs* 4, 2 (1978), pp. 349-62.

——, 'Gendered deities and the survival of culture', in: *History of Religions* 36/4 (1997), pp. 333-56.

Neto, Nivaldo Léo/Brooks, Sharon/Alves, Rômulo, 'From Eshu to Obatala: Animals Used in Sacrificial Rituals at Candomblé "Terreiros" in Brazil', in: *Journal of Ethnobiology and Ethnomedicine*, 5/23 (2009), online at <http://www.ethnobiomed.com/content/5/1/23>, accessed 2 June 2012.

Nietzsche, Friedrich Wilhelm, *Die Geburt der Tragödie aus dem Geiste der Musik*, Cambridge (Cambridge University Press), 2010.

——, '*Zur Genealogie der Moral*', in: Colli, G./Montinari, M. (eds.), *Kritische Studienausgabe*, vol. 5, Berlin/New York (de Gruyter), 1988, pp. 245-412.

Niewiadomski, Józef, 'Transzendenz und Menschwerdung. Transformationskraft des Opfers im Fokus österlicher Augen', in: Dieckmann, Bernhard (ed.), *Das Opfer-aktuelle Kontroversen. Religions-politischer Diskurs im Kontext der mimetischen Theorie. Deutsch-Italienische Fachtagung der Guardini Stiftung in der Villa Vigoni 18.-22. Oktober 1999*, Münster (LIT), 2001, pp. 293-306.

Obey, André, *Une fille pour du vent*, Paris (Mauclaire), 1953, transl. Whiting, John, *Sacrifice to the Wind*, in: *Three Dramatic Legends*, ed. Braddon, Elizabeth, London (Heinemann), 1964.

O'Brien, Edna, *Iphigenia by Euripides*, London (Methuen), 2003.

O'Collins, Gerald, *Jesus Our Redeemer. A Christian Approach to Salvation*, Oxford (Oxford University Press), 2007.

Oliva, Margarida Maria Cichelli, 'Ação diabólica e exorcismo. Na igreja universal do reino de Deus'. MPhil thesis, São Paulo (PUC), 1995.

Oliveira, Ivo Xavier de, 'Ação pastoral da Igreja Universal do Reino de Deus: Uma Evangelizacão inculturada?'. MPhil, São Paulo (PUC), 1998.

O'Neill, Onora, *Bounds of Justice*, Cambridge (Cambridge University Press), 2000.

Ostwalt, Conrad, *Secular Steeples: Popular Culture and the Religious Imagination*, Harrisburg/London/New York (Trinity Press International), 2003.

——, 'Apocalyptic', in: *The Routledge Companion to Religion and Film*, Lyden, J. (ed.), London (Routledge), 2009, pp. 368-83.

Oughourlian, Jean-Michel, *The Genesis of Desire*, transl. Webb, Eugene, East Lansing (Michigan State University Press), 2007.

Overvold, Mark, 'Self-interest and the Concept of Self-Sacrifice', in: *Canadian Journal of Philosophy*, 10 (1980), pp. 105–18.

Owen, Wilfred, *The Collected Poems of Wilfred Owen*, ed. Day-Lewis, C., London (Chatto and Windus), 1964.

Paisiello, Giovanni [composer], Metastasio, Pietro [librettist], *Il Demoföonte*, Venice (Modesto Fenzo), 1775.

Pahl, Jon, *Shopping Malls and Other Sacred Spaces: Putting God in Place,* Grand Rapids, MI (Brazos Press), 2003.

——, *Empire of Sacrifice: The Religious Origins of American Violence,* New York (New York University Press), 2010.

——, 'Sacrifice', in: Lyden, John (ed.), *The Routledge Companion to Religion and Film*, London (Routledge), 2010, pp. 465–81.

——, 'Melancholia', in: *The Journal of Religion and Film*, 16 (April 2012), online at <http://www.unomaha.edu/jrf/Vol16.no1/Reviews/Melancholia.html>, accessed 29 June 2012.

Palaver, Wolfgang, 'A Girardian Reading of Schmitt's Political Theology', in: *Telos*, 93 (1992), pp. 43–68.

——, 'Schmitt's Critique of Liberalism', in: *Telos*, 102 (1995), pp. 43–71.

——, *René Girard's Mimetic Theory*, transl. Borrud, Gabriel, *Studies in Violence, Mimesis and Culture*, East Lansing (Michigan State University Press), 2013.

——, 'Die Frage des Opfers im Spannungsfeld von West und Ost. René Girard, Simone Weil und Mahatma Gandhi über Gewalt und Gewaltfreiheit', in: *Zeitschrift für Katholische Theologie*, 132/4 (2010), pp. 462–81.

Parker, Robert, 'Killing, Dining, Communicating', in: *On Greek Religion*, Ithaca and London (Cornell University Press), 2011, pp. 124–70.

Partch, Harry, 'Revelation in the Courthouse Park, After The Bacchae of Euripides'. Facsimile of MS full score, Library of Congress M1500.P292.R5.1960.

Peñalver, Eduardo, 'The Concept of Religion', in: *The Yale Law Journal*, 107/3 (1997), pp. 791–822.

Pichardo, Ernesto, 'Supreme Court Ruling', in: *CLBA Journal 2000–05* (1997), reprinted from ASHE Newsletter Vol. 1: 1 (1996), online at <http://www.churchofthelukumi.com/supreme-court-ruling.html>, accessed 1 April 2012.

Pizzetti, Ildebrando, *Ifigenia*, Milan (Curci), 1961.

*Popol Vuh,* transl. Tedlock, D., New York (Simon & Schuster), 1985.

Porphyry, *De Abstinentia*, in: Nauck, A. (ed.), *Porphyrii philosophi Platonici opuscula selecta*, Leipzig (Teubner), 1886, reprint Hildesheim (Olms), 1963, pp. 85–269.

Power, David, 'Words that Crack: The Uses of "Sacrifice" in Eucharistic Discourse', in: Seasolz, R. Kevin (ed.), *Living Bread, Saving Cup*, Collegeville (Liturgical Press), 1982, pp. 157–75.

Racine, Jean, *Œuvres complètes*, ed. Clarac, Pierre, Paris (Éditions du Seuil), 1962.

Rad, Gerhard von, *Old Testament Theology*, Volume I. *The Theology of Israel's Historical Traditions*, transl. Stalker, D. M. G., Edinburgh (Oliver and Boyd), 1962.

Ragot, Nathalie, 'Les au-delàs aztèques. Approche des conceptions sur la mort et le devenir des morts', PhD. dissertation, École Pratique des Hautes Études, Section des Sciences Religieuses, Paris, 1999.

Ramberg, B. T., *Donald Davidson's Philosophy of Language*, Oxford (Blackwell), 1989.

Rampley, Matthew, 'From Symbol to Allegory: Aby Warburg's Theory of Art', in: *Art Bulletin*, 79/1 (1997), pp. 41–55.

——, *The Remembrance of Things Past: On Aby M. Warburg and Walter Benjamin*, Wiesbaden (Harrassowitz), 2000.

Ramsay, Kerry, 'Losing One's Life for Others: Self-sacrifice Revisited', in: Frank Parsons, Susan (ed.), *Challenging Women's Orthodoxies in the Context of Faith*, Aldershot (Ashgate), 2000, pp. 121–33.

Ratzinger, Joseph, *Die sakramentale Begründung christlicher Existenz*, Freising (Kyrios), 1966.

——, 'Is the Eucharist a Sacrifice?', in: *Concilium*, 3 (1967), pp. 35–40.

——, 'The Theology of the Liturgy', in: Reid, Alcuin (ed.), *Looking Again at the Question of the Liturgy with Cardinal Ratzinger: Proceedings of the July 2001 Fontgombault Liturgical Conference*, Farnborough (St Michael's Abbey Press), 2003, pp. 18–31.

Raulff, Ulrich, *Wilde Energien. Vier Versuche zu Aby Warburg*, Göttingen (Wallstein Verlag), 2003.

Rawls, John, *A Theory of Justice*, Cambridge, MA (Belknap Press), 2005.

Reinecke, Martha, 'The Mother in Mimesis: Kristeva and Girard on Violence and the Sacred' in: Crownfield, David R. (ed.), *Body/Text in Julia Kristeva: Religion, Women and Psychoanalysis,* Albany, NY (SUNY Press), 1992, pp. 67–82.

——, *Sacrificed Lives: Kristeva on Women and Violence*, Indianapolis, IN (Indiana University Press), 1997.

Rexroth, Kenneth, *Iphigenia at Aulis, in Beyond the Mountains*, New York (New Directions), 1951.

Richie, James, *A Criticism upon Modern Notions of Sacrifices: An Examination of Dr Taylor's Scripture-Doctrine of Atonement*, London (Henderson), 1761.

Richmond, James, *Ritschl: A Reappraisal*, London (Collins), 1978

Ricoeur, Paul, 'Qu'est-ce qu' un texte?' in: *Du texte a l'action. Essais d'hermeneutique II*, Paris (Éditions du Suel), 1986, pp. 153–78.

——, *Oneself as Another*, transl. Blamey, Kathleen, Chicago (University of Chicago Press), 1992.

Rispoli, Salvatore [composer]/Moretti, Ferdinando [librettist], *Idalide*, Turin (Onorato Derossi), 1786, [opera libretto].

Ritschl, Albrecht, *Die christliche Lehre von der Rechtfertigung und Versöhnung*, 3 vols., 2nd ed., Bonn (Marcus), 1881–2.

——, *The Christian Doctrine of Justification and Reconciliation: The Positive Development of the Doctrine*, transl. Mackintosh, H. R./Macaulay, A. B., 2nd ed., Edinburgh (T&T Clark), 1902.

——, *Unterricht in der christlichen Religion*, ed. Axt–Piscalar, C., Tübingen (Mohr Siebeck), 2002.

Rival, Laura, 'The Cosmic Person, Maize and Sacrifice in MesoAmerica: Comparative perspectives', unpublished manuscript.

Robinson, B.A., 'Santeria, a Syncretistic Caribbean Religion: Conflicts Concerning Santeria Sacrifices—Animal and Human; Real and Imaginary', in: *Religious Tolerance.org* (2009), online at <http://www.religioustolerance.org/santeri1.htm>, accessed 4 April 2012.

Rosati, Connie, 'Self-Interest and Self-Sacrifice', in: *Proceedings of the Aristotelian Society*, 109 (2009), pp. 311–25.

Rotrou, Jean de, *Iphygénie*, Paris (T. Quinet), 1641.

Saez, Oscar Calavia, 'O canibalismo asteca. Releitura e desdobramentos', in: *Mana*, 15/1 (2009), pp. 31–57.

Sahagún, Fray Bernardino de, *Historia general de las cosas de Nueva España*, 4th vol., ed. Garibay, Angel M., Mexico (Edit. Porrúa), 1956.

——, *Psalmodia Christiana*, Salt Lake City (University of Utah Press), 1993.

Sallustius, *De deis et mundo*, in: Rochefort, G. (ed.), *Saloustios. Des dieux et du monde*, Paris (Les Belles Lettres), 1960.

Salter, Richard, 'The Birth of a Nation as American Myth', in: *The Journal of Religion and Film* 8 (October 2004), online at <http://www.unomaha.edu/jrf/Vol8No2/SalterBirth.htm>, accessed 10 February 2012.

Schele, Linda, *The Blood of Kings: Dynasty and Ritual in Maya Art*, London (Thames & Hudson), 1992.

Schenk, Richard, 'Opfer und Opferkritik aus der Sicht römisch-katholischer Theologie', in: Schenk, R. (ed.), *Zur Theorie des Opfers: Ein interdisziplinäres Gespräch*, Stuttgart (Frommann-Holzboog), 1995, pp. 193–250.

Schiller, Friedrich, *Sämtliche Werke*, Fricke, Gerhard and Göpfert, Herbert G. (eds.) 5 vols, Munich (Hanser), 1960–66.

Schmid, H., *Die Dogmatik der evangelisch-lutherischen Kirche*, 7th ed., Gütersloh (Bertelsmann), 1893.

Schmitt, Carl, *The Concept of the Political*, transl. Schwab, George, Chicago (The University of Chicago Press), 2007.

Schopenhauer, Arthur, *Aphorisms,* transl. Hollingdale, R. J., London (Penguin) 1970.

Schwager, Raymund, 'The Theology of the Wrath of God', in: P. Dumouchel (ed.), *Violence and Truth: On the Work of René Girard*, Stanford (Stanford University Press), 1988, 44–52.

——, *Jesus in the Drama of Salvation: Toward a Biblical Doctrine of Redemption*, transl. Williams, James G./Haddon, Paul, New York (The Crossroad Publishing Company), 1999.

Schwarz, Hans, *Iphigeneia in Aulis*, Hamburg (Strom), 1947.

Sered, Susan Starr, *Priestess Mother Sacred Sister: Religions Dominated by Women*, New York and Oxford (Oxford University Press), 1994.

——, 'Towards a Gendered Typology of Sacrifice: Women & Feasting, Men & Death in an Akinawan Village', in: Baumgarten, Albert (ed.), *Sacrifice in Religious Experience*, Leiden (Brill), 2002, pp. 13–38.

Siebenrock, Roman A./Palaver, Wolfgang/Sandler, Willibald, 'Wandlung. Die christliche Eucharistiefeier als Transformation der „kotigen Wurzeln unserer Kultur. Eine Antwort auf Aleida Assmann', in: Palaver/Wolfgang/Exenberger, Andreas/Stöckl, Kristina (eds.), *Aufgeklärte Apokalyptik: Religion, Gewalt und Frieden im Zeitalter der Globalisierung*, Innsbruck (Innsbruck University Press), 2007, pp. 279–320.

Skerrett, K. Roberts, 'Desire and Anathema: Mimetic Rivalry in Defense of Plentitude' in: *Journal of the American Academy of Religion,* 71/4 (2003), pp. 793–809.

Smith, J. Z. 'The Domestication of Sacrifice', in: Hamerton-Kelly, R. G. (ed.), *Violent Origins*, Stanford (Stanford University Press), 1987, pp. 278–304.

Smith, W. Robertson, *The Religion of the Semites: The Fundamental Institutions*, ed. Black, J. S., London (Black), 1894.

Sorel, Georges, *Réflexions sur la violence*, Paris (Pages libres), 1908.

Sours, Stephen Bentley, 'Eucharist and Anthropology: Seeking Convergence on Eucharistic Sacrifice Between Catholics and Methodists', unpublished PhD thesis; Duke University, 2011.

Soustelle, Jacques, *La vie quotidienne des aztèques à la veille de la conquête espagnole*, Paris (Hachette), 1955.

Srigley, Susan, 'The Violence of Love: Reflections on Self-Sacrifice through Flannery O'Connor and René Girard', in: *Religion & Literature*, 39 (2007), pp. 31–45.

Staal, Frits, *Ritual and Mantras: Rules Without Meaning*, New York (Peter Lang), 1989.

Steele, P., *The Aztec News*, London (Walker Books), 1997.

Stierlin, H., *The Art of the Maya*, Cologne (Taschen), 1994.

Stokes, Melvin, *D. W. Griffith's THE BIRTH OF A NATION: A History of 'The Most Controversial Motion Picture of All Time*, New York/Oxford (Oxford University Press), 2007.

Stone-Miller, R., *Art of the Andes*, London (Thames & Hudson), 1995.

Stout, Harry S., *Upon the Altar of the Nation: A Moral History of the Civil War*, New York (Viking), 2006.

Stout, Jeffrey, *Democracy and Tradition*, Princeton (Princeton University Press), 2004.

Strenski, Ivan, *Durkheim and the Jews of France*, Chicago (University of Chicago Press), 1997.

——, 'Durkheim's Bourgeois Theory of Sacrifice', in: Allen, N. J./Pickering, W. S. F./ Miller, W. W. (eds.), *On Durkheim's Elementary Forms of Religious Life*, London (Routledge), 1998, 116–26.

——, *Contesting Sacrifice: Religion, Nationalism, and Social Thought in France*, Chicago (University of Chicago Press), 2002.

——, *Theology and the First Theory of Sacrifice*, Leiden (Brill), 2003.

Stroumsa, Guy G., *The End of Sacrifice: Religious Transformations in Late Antiquity*, transl. Emanuel, Susan, Chicago (University of Chicago Press), 2009. First published in French as *La fin du sacrifice. Les mutations religieuses de l'antiquité tardive*, Paris (Odile Jacob), 2005.

Sykes, Arthur Ashley, *An Essay on the Nature, Design, and Origin of Sacrifices*, London (Knapton), 1748.

Symons, David, *Egon Wellesz, Composer*, Wilhelmshaven (Noetzel), 1996.

Szymanowski, Karol, *King Roger (The Shepherd)*, Vienna (Universal Edition), 1967.

Taille, Maurice de la, *Mysterium Fidei. De augustissimo corporis et sanguinis Christi sacrificio atque sacramento, Elucidationes L in tres libros distinctos*, Paris (Beauchesne), 1924. ET: Taille, Maurice de la, *The Mystery of Faith: Regarding the Most August Sacrament and Sacrifice of the Body and Blood of Christ*, New York (Sheed & Ward), 1940–50.

Tarkovsky, Andrei, *Sculpting in Time: Reflections on the Cinema*, transl. Hunter-Blair, Kitty, New York (Random House), 1987.

Tasso, Torquato, *Gerusalemme Liberata*, Carini, Anna Maria (ed.), Milan (Feltrinelli), 1961.

Taylor, Charles, *Sources of the Self: The Making of the Modern Identity*, Cambridge (Cambridge University Press), 1989.

——, *A Secular Age*, Cambridge, MA (Belknap Press of Harvard University Press), 2007.

Tertullian, *Adversus Marcionem*, (ed. and transl.) Evans, E., Oxford (Oxford University Press), 1972.

Tessman, Lisa, *Burdened Virtues: Virtue Ethics for Liberatory Struggles*, Oxford (Oxford University Press), 2005.

Testart, Alain, *Des dons et des dieux. Anthropologie religieuse et sociologie comparative*, Paris (Colin), 1993.

——, 'Doit-on parler de "sacrifice" à propos des morts d'accompagnement?', in: *Le sacrifice humain*, Albert, J.-P./Midant-Reynes, B. (eds.), Paris (Soleb), 2005, pp. 34–57.

The Society of Saint Pius X, *The Problem of the Liturgical Reform: A Theological and Liturgical Study*, Kansas (Angelus Press).

Thomas Aquinas, *Summa Theologica*, ed. Faucher, P., 5 vols., 4th ed., Paris (Lethielleux), 1926.

Tillard, Jean-Marie-Roger, 'Sacrificial Terminology and the Eucharist', in: *One in Christ* 17 (1981), pp. 306–23.

Tolleson, Bert, 'Materialism and the Messiah: Tarkovsky's *The Sacrifice*', in: *Sync: Regent Journal of Film and Video*, online at <http://www.regent.edu/acad/schcom/rojc/tolleson.html>, accessed 15 January 2009.

Traube, Elizabeth, 'Incest and Mythology; Anthropological and Girardian Perspectives', in: *Berkshire Review,* 14 (1979), pp. 37–53.

Tridon, G[usta]ve, *Du Molochisme Juif. Études critiques et philosophiques*, Brussels (Maheu), 1884.

Tylor, Edward Burnett, *Primitive Culture: Researches into the Development of Mythology, Philosophy, Religion, Language, Art, and Custom*, 2 vols, 6th ed., London (John Murray), 1920.

Uriarte, M. T. 'Unity in Duality: The Practice and Symbols of the Mesoamerican Ballgame', in: Whittington, E. M. (ed.), *The Sport of Life and Death: the Mesoamerican Ballgame*, London (Thames & Hudson), 2001, pp. 40–9.

U.S. Supreme Court, *Church of Lukumi Babalu Aye v. City of Hialeah*, 508 U.S. 520 (1993). 1993, online at <http://laws.findlaw.com/us/508/520.html>, accessed 1 May 2012.

Vacher de Lapouge, G[eorges], *L'Aryen: son role social*, Paris (Fontemoing), 1899.

Vasudeva, Somadeva. *The Yoga of the Mālinīvijayottaratantra*, Pondichery (IFP, EFDE), 2004.

Vattimo, Gianni and Girard, René, *Christianity, Truth, and Weakening Faith: A Dialogue*, transl. McCuaig, William, New York (Columbia University Press), 2010.

Vaux, R. de, *Ancient Israel and its Institutions*, 2nd ed., transl. J. McHugh, London (Darton, Longman and Todd), 1965.

Vernant, Jean-Pierre, *Myth and Society in Ancient Greece*, transl. Lloyd, Janet, New York (Zone Books), 1990.

Veyne, Paul, 'Inviter les dieux, sacrifier, banqueter. Quelques nuances de la religiosité gréco-romaine', in: *Annales*, 55/1 (2000), pp. 3–42.

Volkmann, Stefan, *Der Zorn Gottes: Studien zur Rede vom Zorn Gottes in der evangelischen Theologie*, Marburg (Elwert), 2004.

Volney, C[onstantin]-F[rançois Chasseboeuf, Comte de], *Les ruines, ou méditation sur les révolutions des empires*, Paris (Décembre-Alonnier), 1869.

Voltaire, François Marie Arouet de, *Les loix de Minos, ou Astérie*, Geneva (Valade), 1773.

——, *La Bible enfin expliquée par plusieurs aumoniers de S.M.L.R.D.P.*, vol. 1., 2 vols, 3rd ed., London (s.n.), 1777, pp. 53–6.

Vonier, Anscar, *A Key to the Doctrine of the Eucharist*, London (Burns Oates & Washbourne), 1925.

De Vries, Hent, *Philosophy and the Turn to Religion*, Baltimore (Johns Hopkins University Press), 1999.

Wagner, Cosima, *Cosima Wagner's Diaries*, ed. Gregor-Dellin, Martin and Mack, Dietrich, transl. Skelton, Geoffrey, 2 vols, London (Collins), 1978–80.

Wagner, Richard, *Sämtliche Schriften und Dichtungen*, 16 vols, Volks-Ausgabe, 6th ed., Leipzig (Breitkopf and Härtel), 1912–14.

Walker Bynum, Caroline, *Wonderful Blood. Theology and Practice in Late Medieval Northern Germany and Beyond*, Philadelphia (University of Pennsylvania Press), 2007.

Warburg, Aby, *Images from the Region of the Pueblo Indians of North America*, transl. Steinberg, Michael P., Ithaca, NY (Cornell University Press), 1995.

——, *Tagebuch der Kulturwissenschaftlichen Bibliothek Warburg. Mit Einträgen von Gertrud Bing und Fritz Saxl, Hrsg. von K. Michels und C. Schoell-Glass*, Gesammelte Schriften, Berlin (Akademie Verlag), 2001.

——, *Der Bilderatlas Mnemosyne. Hrsg. von M. Warnke unter Mitarbeit von C. Brink.* 2nd ed. in: Bredekamp, Horst/Diers, Michael (eds.), Aby Warburg: Gesammelte Schriften, Berlin (Akademie Verlag), 2003.

——, *'Per Monstra ad Sphaeram'. Sternglaube und Bilddeutung. Vortrag in Gedenken an Franz Boll und andere Schriften 1923 bis 1925, Kleine Schriften des Warburg Institute London und des Warburg-Archivs im Warburg-Haus Hamburg*, München (Dölling und Galitz), 2008.

Warner, Marina, *Alone of All of her Sex: The Myth and the Cult of the Virgin Mary*, London (Picador), 1985.

Waterland, Daniel, *The Christian Sacrifice Explained* (1738), in: Waterland, Daniel, *Works*, vol. 5, Oxford (Oxford University Press), 1843, pp. 121–84.

Weil, Simone, *Selected Essays 1934–1943*, transl. Rees, Richard, London (Oxford University Press), 1962.

——, *Gravity and Grace*, transl. Crawford, Emma/Ruhr, Mario von der, London (Routledge), 2002.

——, *The Need for Roots. Prelude to a Declaration of Duties towards Mankind*, transl. Wills, Arthur, London (Routledge), 2002.

——, *Intimations of Christianity Among the Ancient Greeks*, London (Routledge), 2003.

Weir, Alison, *Sacrificial Logics: Feminist Theory and the Critique of Identity*, London/New York (Routledge), 1996, pp. 146–84.

Wellesz, Egon, *Die Opferung des Gefangenen*, Vienna/New York (Universal Edition), 1925.

——, *Die Bakchantinnen*, Berlin (Bote & Bock), 1930.

Wellhausen, Julius, *Prolegomena zur Geschichte Israels*, 6th ed., Berlin (Reimer), 1905.

West, Angela *Deadly Innocence: Feminist Theology and the Mythology of Sin*, London (Cassell), 1996.

Whittington E. M. (ed.), *The Sport of Life and Death: The Mesoamerican Ballgame*, London (Thames & Hudson), 2001.

Wilamowitz-Moellendorff, Ulrich von, *Reden und Vorträge*, 3rd ed., Berlin (Weidmann), 1913.

Wolf, Eric, *Envisioning Power: Ideologies of Dominance and Crisis*, Berkeley (The University of California Press), 1999.

Woodhead, Linda, 'Spiritualising the Sacred', in: *Modern Theology*, 13 (1997), pp. 191–212.

Young, Frances M., *Sacrifice and the Death of Christ*, London (SPCK), 1975.

Zambrano, Maria, *De L'Aurore*, transl. Laffranque, Marie, Paris (Éditions de L' Éclat), 1989.

——, *Les Clairières Du Bois*, transl. Laffranque, Marie, Paris (Éditions de L' Éclat), 1989.

## Films, film scripts, film websites

*Armageddon*, dir. Bay, Michael, (Touchstone Pictures, 1998) [DVD].

*Dionysus in '69*, dir. Palma, Brian de/Schechner, Richard (Performance Group, 1970) [Film].

*Dr Strangelove*, dir. Kubrick, Stanley (Hawk Films, 1964) [DVD].

*Iphigenia*, dir. Cacoyannis, Michael (Greek Film Centre, 1977) [Film].

*Left Behind: The Movie*, dir. Sarin, Vic (Cloud Ten Pictures, 2001) [DVD].

*Left Behind II: Tribulation Force*, dir. Corcoran, Bill (Cloud Ten Pictures, 2002) [DVD].

*Left Behind: World at War*, dir. Baxley, Craig R. (Cloud Ten Pictures, 2005) [DVD].

*Left Behind* <http://www.leftbehind.com>, accessed 6 March 2012.

*Melancholia*, dir. Trier, Lars von (Zentropa, 2011) [DVD].

*Offret*, dir. Tarkovskiy, Andrei (Sandrew, 1986) [DVD].

*The Birth of a Nation,* dir. Griffith, D. W. (D. W. Griffith group, 1915) [DVD].

'The Birth of a Nation: Continuity Script', in: Lang, Robert (ed.) *The Birth of a Nation, D. W. Griffith, Director*, Rutgers Films in Print, Vol. 21, New Brunswick, NJ (Rutgers University Press), 1994.

*The Seventh Seal, The Script at IMSDb* (The Internet Movie Script Database), <http://www.imsdb.com/scripts/Seventh-Seal,-The.html> accessed 25 June 2012.

*The Seventh Seal*, dir. Bergman, Ingmar (AB Svensk Filmindustri, 1957) [DVD].

# Index